M000309313

A POLITICAL
HISTORY OF
THE TIGRAY PEOPLE'S
LIBERATION FRONT
(1975-1991)

A POLITICAL HISTORY OF THE TIGRAY PEOPLE'S LIBERATION FRONT (1975-1991)

REVOLT, IDEOLOGY AND MOBILISATION IN ETHIOPIA

Aregawi Berhe, Ph. D.

TSEHAI
Publishers & Distributors

LOS ANGELES | NEW YORK | PRETORIA

TSEHAI
Publishers & Distributors

A Political History of the Tigray People's Liberation Front (1975-1991)
Copyright © 2009 by Aregawi Berhe. All rights reserved.

Apart from any fair dealing for the purpose of private study, research, criticism or review, as permitted under the Copyright Act, no part of this publication may be reproduced in any form, stored in a retrieval system or transmitted in any form by any means—electronic, mechanical, photocopy, recording or otherwise—without the prior permission of the publisher. Enquiries should be sent to the undermentioned address.

Tsehai books may be purchased for educational, business, or sales promotional use. For more information, please contact our special sales department.

African Academic Press
a Tsehai Publishers imprint
Loyola Marymount University
1 LMU Drive, UH 3000, Los Angeles, CA 90045

www.tsehaipublishers.com
info@tsehaipublishers.com

ISBN: 978-1-59907-041-4

First Edition: July 2009

Publisher: Elias Wondimu
Series Editor: Maimire Mennasemay, Ph.D.
Typesetting: Yoseph Gezahegne
Cover Design: Lisa Fang and Yoseph Gezahegne

Library of Congress Catalog Card Number
A catalog record for this book is available from the Library of Congress.

British Library Cataloguing in Publication Data
A catalogue record for this book is available from the British Library.

10 9 8 7 6 5 4 3 2 1

Printed in the United States of America

To the memory of
Ato Gessesew Ayele (Sihul) and
all those who died struggling
for the cause of social justice, equality and
a brighter future for Ethiopia.

Contents

Acronyms and Abbreviations .... *xi*
Maps .... *xiii*
Preface 1

Chapter 1
Introduction

Background to the Study 3
Main Tenets of the Study 6
Structure of the Book 10

Chapter 2
Ethnicity, Mobilization and Revolt: Theoretical Considerations

The Power and Fluidity of Ethnicity 13
Ethno-Nationalism, Self-Determination and Secession 17
Ethnic Mobilization in a Multi-Ethnic Society 24
Peasant Revolt and Revolutionary Elite:
    Where Do They Conjoin? 27
Guerrilla Warfare and the State 31
The Linkage of Ethno-Nationalist Revolt and the
    TPLF: a Summary 34

Chapter 3
Prelude to the Struggle – the Emergence of the TPLF

Introduction 37
How It all Began 38
Historical Roots of the Problem 42
The Growth of Associations 47
A Political Movement 52
The Role of Sihul 54
The People on the Eve of the Armed Struggle 57
From TNO to TPLF 59

Chapter 4
Testing the Fire: Guerrilla Warfare Launched

Introduction 65
Journey to Dedebit 66
Training in Guerrilla Warfare 68
The Contingent's Return from Eritrea 70
Crisis Creeps in 73
Storming the Shire Police Station 76
The Aksum Operation 78
Encounter with the TLF 79
Deima – Eastern Base Area 84

Chapter 5
Mobilization and Armed Confrontation

Introduction 91
Self-determination as a Means of Mobilization 92
Uprooting the *Shifta*s (Bandits) 95
Organizational Development and Structure 98
The War with the EDU 103
The Second Internal Crisis (*Hinfishfish*) 113
Words and Bullets – Battles with EPRP 117

Chapter 6
The Military Government (*Dergue*) and the TPLF

Introduction 125
The *Dergue* on the National Question 126
The TPLF Military Build up 135
The Military Campaigns (*Zemecha*) of the *Dergue* 141
Debate over Military Strategy 151

Chapter 7
Ideological Controversies on Self-Determination

Introduction 155
The Early Phase of the Struggle 156
The 'Manifesto-68': Secession as an End 158
Organizational Policy and Plan of Action 162
'Narrow' nationalism Persists after the Second
    TPLF Congress 165

Chapter 8
Capture of a Movement: the Role of the *Marxist-Leninist League of Tigrai (MLLT)*

Introduction 169
Leftist Orientation of the TPLF 171
Forging a Leftist Party 174
The MLLT Founding Congress amid Famine 176
Organizational Restructuring and Take-Over of the TPLF 182
Extension of the MLLT to Puppet Organization 185
The Ideological Trajectory of the MLLT since 1985 and
    the Development of 'Revolutionary Democracy' 189

Chapter 9
TPLF and the Eritrean Fronts: Background of a Tense Relationship

Introduction 193
Historical Background 194
Launching the TPLF and the Eritrean Connection 203
TPLF and ELF Never Went Along Well 204
The TPLF and the EPLF: Cupboard-love relationship 210
Ethiopian and Eritrea under the TPLF and
    the EPLF respectively 221

Chapter 10
The Consolidation of the TPLF: Forging Power through Social Change

Introduction 225
Peasant Associations 226
Land Reform 230
Women's Organization: A New Phenomenon 236
The Youth: Cadres and Cultural Troupes 240
Neutralizing the Church and Mobilizing Muslims 244
The People's Council (*Baito*): Reconfiguration of
    Local Administration 248

Chapter 11
Turning Point: The Fall of the *Dergue* and the Triumph of the TPLF

Introduction 255
The *Dergue* Falters 256
The Descent of the *Dergue* and the Ascent of the TPLF 262

Futile Peace Talks 266
The TPLF/EPRDF's Initial Moments in Power 268
Wrangling over Power:
    Events Leading to the July 1991 Conference 269
The July Conference and the Transitional Charter 273
Whose Charter and Constitution? 277

Chapter 12
The TPLF and African Insurgencies: A Comparative Perspective

    Introduction 283
    Ideology 287
    Leadership 292
    Youth Mobilization 296
    Relations with the Civilian Population 299

Conclusion 303
Bibliography 317
Appendices
    1. Participants of the July 1-5, 1991 Conference 331
    2. Transitional Period Charter of Ethiopia 333
    3. Brief Profile of the Founders and Leaders of the TPLF 339
    4. List of Ethnic and National Parties in 2002 343

About the Author 346
Index 347

Acronyms and Abbreviations

AAPO	- All-Amhara People's Organization
ANDM	- Amhara National Democratic Movement
ARDUF	- Afar Revolutionary Democratic United Front
Baito	- People's Council (in Tigrai)
CDC	- Constitution Drafting Commission
COEDF	- Coalition of Ethiopian Democratic Forces
COR	- Council of Representatives
CUD	- Coalition for Unity and Democracy
Dergue	- Military Committee, ruling Ethiopia from 1974 to 1991
EDP	- Ethiopian Democratic Party
EDU	- Ethiopian Democratic Union
ELF	- Eritrean Liberation Front
EPDA	- Ethiopian People's Democratic Alliance
EPDM	- Ethiopian People's Democratic Movement
EPLF	- Eritrean People's Liberation Front
EPRDF	- Ethiopian People's Revolutionary Democratic Front
EPRP	- Ethiopian People's Revolutionary Party
IFLO	- Islamic Front for the Liberation of Oromia
Meison	- All-Ethiopia Socialist Movement
MLLT	- Marxist-Leninist League of Tigrai
OLF	- Oromo Liberation Front
ONC	- Oromo National Congress
ONLF	- Ogaden National Liberation Front
OPDO	- Oromo People's Democratic Organization
PDO	- People's Democratic Organization
PMAC	- Provisional Military Administrative Council
REST	- Relief Society of Tigrai
SEPDC	- Southern Ethiopian Peoples' Democratic Coalition
SLM	- Sidama Liberation Movement
TAND	- Tigraian Alliance for National Democracy
TDA	- Tigrai Development Association
TGE	- Transitional Government of Ethiopia
TLF	- Tigrai Liberation Front
TNO	- Tigraian National Organization (*Magebt)*
TPDM	- Tigray People's Democratic Movement
TPLF	- Tigrai People's Liberation Front
Teranafit	- Tigray Liberation Front-*Teranafit* Committee

UEDF   - United Ethiopian Democratic Forces
WPE   - Workers' Party of Ethiopia
WSLF   - Western Somalia Liberation Front

Maps

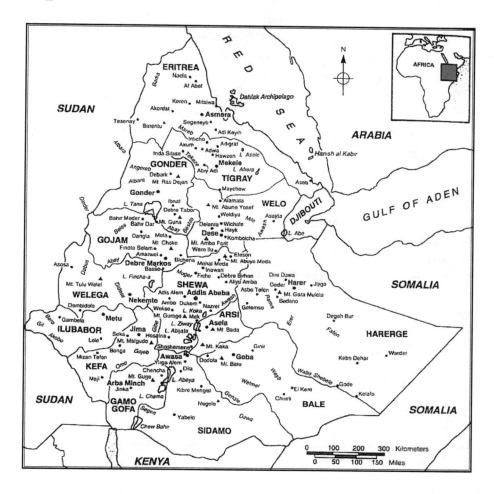

Map 1: Ethiopia (pre 1991) – Provinces and major towns

Source: Adapted from Harold G. Marcus, *A History of Ethiopia*, Berkeley – Los Angeles
           London, 1994, p. 222.

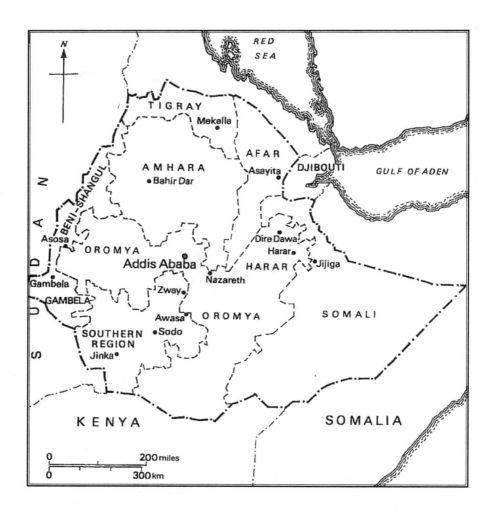

Map 2: Ethiopia since 1993 – Regions ('killil') and their capitals: Addis Ababa &
Harar – City states Dire-Dawa – Separate administrative region

Source: Information Section of the UNDP-Emergency Unit for Ethiopia, 1996.

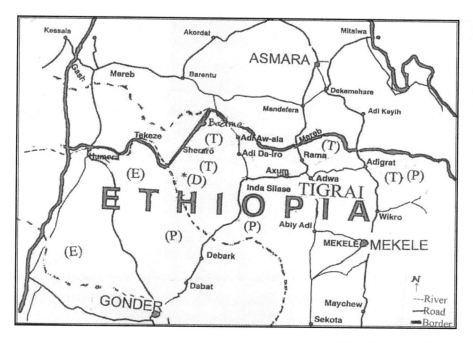

Map © Aregawi Berhe

Map 3: Fronts' Base Areas, Tigrai – Northern Ethiopia
     (D) – Dedebit, Initial TPLF base area
     (E) – EDU base areas.
     (P) – EPRP base area.
     (T) – TPLF base area.

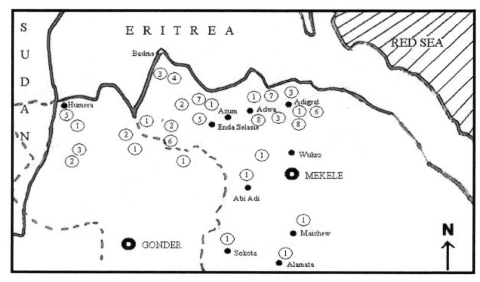

Map © Aregawi Berhe

Map 4: Major Battles (1975-1991) in Tigrai

Numbers in circles represent warring groups & approximate terrain of engagements:

Warring Groups	Battles	Year
TPLF vs *Dergue*	26	1975–1991
TPLF vs EDU + Teranafit	9	1976–1978
TPLF vs EPRP	5	1978–1979
TPLF vs ELF	2	1979
Dergue vs EDU	6	1975–1977
Dergue vs EPRP	5	1975–1978
Dergue vs ELF	2	1975
Dergue vs EPLF	3	1975–1976

Preface

It was in the mid-1990s that I decided to write my study of the political history of the Tigrai People's Liberation Front, but due to unforeseen circumstances, the actual writing began only in 2000 as a book-project. Before, my political activism and assignments to write articles (see the list of references) had made it hard to keep momentum with the writing of the book. Amidst this plodding time, an opportunity to write the book according to primarily academic standards arose and required me to restructure and rewrite the whole manuscript to meet the requirements of a PhD dissertation at the Vrije University Amsterdam. This rather arduous work has transformed the book from a lengthy narration of events to a concise analysis of the crucial events of the TPLF- led struggle, based on a multi-disciplinary theoretical framework. After still some additional work, what was a dissertation has now appeared as an accessible book to all those interested in the history and politics of contemporary Ethiopia.

In this laborious journey that brought the research to this level, many people and institutions have contributed a lot in so many ways. My sincere gratitude goes to all of them.

First, my sincere thanks and gratitude goes to Professors Jon Abbink and Christopher Clapham for stimulating me to write and for their profound comments, observations and suggestions they gave on various versions of the study. In addition, the constructive comments I received from external examiners have also contributed significantly in broadening the scope of my research. I thank them all.

I am also indebted to many friends who helped me in a number of ways (editing, translating, proofreading, giving comments, providing data, giving comfort, etc.) while toiling on the different chapters. Among them are Amanda Woolly, Melakou Tegegn, Girmay Gezahegn, Wondifraw Ambay, Mesele Seyoum, Emmanuel Tola, Kahsay Berhe, Tesfay Atsbaha, Giday Zeratsion, Wolde Selassie Asfaw, Atsede Kahsay, Rafael Tewolde, Meles Wolde Ammanuel, Berhane Gebretensai, Assefa Aynekulu, Asnake Kefale and Abiye Ashenafi. Heartfelt thanks also to the ample succor of Rita van de Looverbosch and to the constant encouragement of Paula and Krisno Nimpuno.

I am particularly grateful to the African Studies Centre, Leiden, for various facilities it provided me to engage in this research project. I extend my deeply-felt thanks to the professional and generous cooperation of Ella Verkaik en Sjaan van Marrewijk in the library, Maaike Westra, Gitty Petit and Hester Sandermans (who since left the ASC), Marieke van Winden, Joop Nijssen (who retired in May 2008) and Karl Dorrepaal in the administration. My thanks are also due to WOTRO and Stichting Werkbij (The Hague) for their financial assistance, and Rev. Auke Hofman whose assistance was a stepping stone to this project.

The love, care and endless support of my sisters, brother, nephews, cousins, uncles and aunts have kept me moving through this wearisome undertaking. My sister Elsa Berhe has been instrumental in keeping the family moving forward. I extend to her special gratitude although I am aware of the debts I owe to all of my family.

Vaguely understanding the intensity of my work, my lovely young children, Ezana and Sennay, who were often with me in spirit rather than in the flesh, and their mother Roman were very supportive throughout the duration of my research endeavors. Many passionate thanks!!!

Chapter 1

Introduction

Background to the study

This book is a study of the origins and evolution of an Ethiopian insurgent movement, the Tigray People's Liberation Front that emerged some 34 years ago and has determined much of contemporary Ethiopia's political development. The study is primarily a narrative political and military history but also intends to address general sociological issues of ethnic-based inequality, political conflict, social mobilization and revolutionary armed resistance in a developing country. In this Introduction I outline the main issues of the study and present arguments for the relevance of the extended case study for an understanding of conditions for armed rebellion in Africa and of recent Ethiopian political history in particular.

The evolution of the Ethiopian state, one of the oldest in the world, was historically marked by the interaction of ethnic, regional and religious factors that at times acted in harmony and at other times in conflict (Belai Giday 1983 E.C.[1]; Markakis 1990; Marcus 1994). Interwoven as they were, one of these aspects of interaction was prevalent at one time and the other at another time. Latent or openly, ethnicity or ethnic identification has played a major role in the contestation and conflict over who runs the state. In present-day multiethnic Ethiopia too, both 'ethnic politics' and ethnic mobilization in covert and manifest forms served as pathways to power

---

1 EC is 'Ethiopian Calendar', a Julian one that is seven years and four months 'behind' the Gregorian one.

and as the pillars that sustained it. The roots of this political process can be traced at least from the so-called 'Era of Princes' (or *Zemene Mesafint*, from 1769 to 1855), when Ethiopia was 'decentralized' or parcelled out in a disorderly fashion among local contending princes and lords who drew support from their ethno-regional, ethnic or sub-ethnic social bases.[2] Since then, ethnic referents have been important in forming the power base of Ethiopian political elites, and national integration has remained a highly contentious issue. Some historians (Bahru Zewde 1991; Teshale Tibebu 1995) argue that *regionalism* instead of ethnicity was the main feature upon which power was constructed in Ethiopia; however, it is the contention of this study that ethnicity in its latent or unveiled form was no less crucial, if not more important, as a factor in the power equation and the formation of state politics in Ethiopia, especially so when one observes the alignments of forces in the last four decades and the prevalence of 'ethnic politics' at present.

In the past century neither the 'national integration policy' of Emperor Haile Selassie (r. 1930–1974) nor the 'Ethiopia First' motto of the military *Dergue* regime (1974–1991), which hybridized Ethiopian nationalism with Marxism, helped stem the rising tide of ethno-nationalist rebellion. The regime of the Emperor was confronted by ethno-national and regional armed movements in Tigrai (1942–43), Bale (1963–68), Gojjam (1967) and Eritrea since early 1960s. While he managed to successfully suppress the first three, the Eritrean movement was intractable – mainly due to the external support that the others were not able to acquire. The *Dergue* too had to encounter another wave of ethno-national movements, some of them 'inherited' from the era of the previous regime and that ultimately brought its demise in 1991. Both these regimes collapsed in the face of the sustained onslaught of primarily ethnic-based national liberation movements and to a certain extent of forces of change at the centre. One of the ethno-nationalist movements which spearheaded the revolt against the military regime from 1975 to 1991 was the Tigrai People's Liberation Front (TPLF), the subject-matter of this study.[3]

2 Although ethno-regional alignments blended into the power politics of the Ethiopian state dating back at least to the *Zemene Mesafint*/Era of Princes (1769–1855), it was only under the EPRDF regime that the restructuring of the state on ethnic basis took a legally and officially recognized form for the first time.

3 Research studies on the TPLF especially by insiders are rare. Kahsay Berhe (whose second name coincides with that of the present author but is not related) is the only insider so far who published a book on the role of the TPLF in the political struggles in Ethiopia. Also several unpublished critical papers were produced by Tesfay Atsbaha & Kahsay Berhe, Giday Zeratsion, Asgede Gebreselassie, and the present author. There are also few studies by outsiders, like researcher John Young, who wrote the first academic

The TPLF started its struggle to ensure 'self-determination' for the region of Tigrai within the Ethiopian polity. It embarked on its armed struggle with a hybrid ideology[4] that mingled ethno-nationalism with Marxism. Its Marxism was of a different variant from that of the *Dergue*. Ethnicity was the prime mobilizing factor of the people of Tigrai, while Marxism served as an ideological tool of organizational and policy matters as well as to attract other 'oppressed social classes' outside of Tigrai. 'Self-determination' for every ethno-national group in Ethiopia was also upheld as a motto that in turn attracted various marginalized groups, some of which finally joined the TPLF to forge the Ethiopian People's Revolutionary Democratic Front (EPRDF) in its final march to power in 1991. The initial junior partners of the TPLF in forging the EPRDF were the Ethiopian People's Democratic Movement (EPDM), which later changed its name to Amhara National Democratic Movement (ANDM),[5] and the Oromo People's Democratic Organization (OPDO), ostensibly representing the Amhara and Oromo ethnic groups (peoples) respectively.

The TPLF thus could claim success, especially over the discredited military regime of Colonel Mengistu Haile-Mariam and a number of other opponents which were either ethnic or multi-ethnic political organizations. Although previously there had been a number of ethno-nationalist movements of one form or another that rose up to challenge the Ethiopian state, none of them were able to break the backbone of the central state. In 1991 after waging a sixteen years' protracted war, the ethno-nationalist TPLF finally managed to conquer Ethiopian state power, with a host of local and external factors contributing to its success.

With the seizure of power by an ethno-nationalist force, one might assume that in post-1991 Ethiopia ethnic-based conflicts would have a better chance of being resolved. Yet after almost two decades of controversies and experimentation, ethnic-based conflicts have not gone away but grown into new forms, and, according to some, to an unprecedented level. The realization of democratic governance and self-determination for Tigrai or the rest of the Ethiopian ethno-nationalities, for that matter, remains a moot

work on the TPLF (1997) and Jenny Hammond, a former literature teacher at Oxford Brookes University, with an account strongly sympathizing with the TPLF. Both will be touched upon in subsequent chapters.

4 See 'Manifesto-68' of the TPLF, February 1976, 'Program of the TPLF' (2nd edition), *Hidar* 1969 E.C. (in Tigrigna), 'Minimum Program of the Marxist-Leninist League of Tigray', *Hamle* 1977 E.C., 'Constitution of the MLLT', *Hamle* 1977 E.C. and *'May Day'*, MLLT Internal Organ, 1986, year 1, no. 3.

5 According to, among others, former EPDM members (e.g., Yared Tibebu 2003), it was the pressure of the TPLF that forced the former multi-national EPDM to change its name and program into an 'ethnic' organization, the ANDM.

point. As Solomon Gashaw (1993: 156) already put it as early as 1993, '…
the EPRDF is already encountering resistance by various groups – ethnic
groups such as the Oromo have openly challenged that the EPRDF is simply
a Tigraian front'. Even before 1993, as many as nineteen ethno-nationalist
organizations were created and legally registered to challenge the EPRDF
(see Appendix 1). The number of the unregistered ethnic organizations
probably even went beyond that. The new state policy did not take long
to have effects, both negative and positive. Abbink observed: 'The 'ethnic
policy' pursued – including the cantonization of the country into 'ethnic
zones' – has led to a new discourse of division and opposition, when
people are being classified in terms of their presumed ethnic group, or are
stimulated to follow the directives of an imagined primordial identity' (1995:
71). Clapham noted that: 'Any insurgency, dependent on mobilizing local-
level support, almost necessarily must articulate concepts of identity which
bind together its supporters and distinguish them from their adversaries. In
Ethiopia, the TPLF and subsequently the EPRDF explicitly articulated an
idea of 'nationality' which formed the basis for a state structure built on
the principles of ethnic federalism' (1998: 13). Yet, ethnic conflicts are still
looming even after the prevalence of the ethno-nationalist TPLF over the
Ethiopian state, suggesting the need for an in-depth historical study of the
TPLF, including its ideology, forms of struggle, means of mobilization and
political objectives that shaped its present standing in the Ethiopian power
politics.

Main Tenets of the Study

This study departs from a number of themes that can be summarized as
follows.

The historical question

Historically, the TPLF traced the origin of its struggle back to the
popular uprising of 1942 - 43, called the 'Woyyane', that was crushed by
the forces of the imperial state backed by the British air force, although
at that time the demand was 'legitimate regional autonomy', which may
be regarded as one form of self-determination or decentralization. As the
state, in subsequent years, pursued a heavy-handed administration in Tigrai
with the aim of quashing any potential rebellion rather than opting for a
peaceful and democratic handling of local demands, anger and frustration
of the population increased. Ted Gurr's words (1970: 354) asserted (omit
this word) that: 'Violence inspires counter-violence by those against whom
it is directed' were confirmed in Tigrai at the time. After 1943, the people

kept on invoking the history of Woyyane, reminiscent of their struggle against injustice. Munck (2000) was to the point when he noted that '... with a long-term view it is clear that regimes which refuse to recognize a legitimate interlocutor may only postpone the inevitable, with the ensuing years of accumulated bitterness and distrust making a democratic settlement that much more difficult and fragile' (2000: 11). Finally, calling it the *Kalai Woyyane*('second Woyyane'), the TPLF appeared to reinvigorate that struggle in the form of national self-determination against an oppressive state. As Abbink put it '[o]ften an ethnic revival is primarily a result of failing state policy...' (1997:160), and this clearly appeared to be the case in Ethiopia. The cause of the struggle for self-determination found adequate justification in the eyes of many disgruntled Ethiopians, including Tigraians.

Radical ideology

The main ideological source of inspiration for TPLF's ethno-nationalist drive was, however, none other than Stalin's theory on 'the national question', influential in the Leftist-Marxist thinking among the opposition movements of the time. One should not forget the origin of organizations like the TPLF in Leftist students' movements, which were charmed by these abstract ideas. The TPLF's departure point was Stalin's definition of a nation as 'a historically evolved, stable community of language, and territory, economic life and psychological makeup manifested in a community of culture' (1942: 12). Based on this definition, it was believed that Tigrai constituted a nation which had the right to self-determination. 'The right to self-determination means that only the nation itself has the right to determine its destiny, that no one has the right forcibly to interfere in the life of the nation, ... to violate its habits and customs, to repress its language, or curtail its rights' (ibid.: 22-23). Furthermore, if the rights of a given nation are curtailed, Stalin propounded 'a nation has the right to arrange its life on autonomous lines. It even has the right to secede' (1975: 61-62). So far, Stalin sounded a devout nationalist, and so was the TPLF, especially in bringing the issue to the people it claimed to liberate – the Tigraians. In contextualizing the right of self-determination up to secession, Lenin had asserted that 'the several demands of democracy, including self-determination, are not an absolute, but only a small part of the general democratic (now: general socialist) world movement. In individual concrete cases, the part may contradict the whole; if so it must be rejected' (1971: 132). And Stalin reasserted that: '[T]he Bolsheviks never separated the national question from the general question of revolution.... The main essence of the Bolshevik approach to the national question is that the Bolsheviks always examined the national question in inseparable connection with the revolutionary perspective' (op. cit.: 295). Hinging on both approaches of the national question for self-determination, the TPLF mobilized the Tigrai people, created a strong guerrilla army and cleared its way to eventually assume power in Ethiopia.

Although to mainstream Marxists ethnicity was thought to 'wither away' with the emergence of a class-conscious, worldwide industrial proletariat, the TPLF, nevertheless, since its inception attempted to homogenize both the ethnic and the class ideologies for the entire duration of its struggle. It was a daunting task or simply a loss of direction for the TPLF to combine these apparently mutually exclusive ideologies and wage a dual struggle. In recent years, after its rise to power in 1991, the TPLF seems to close the pages of its Marxist books and has bent towards ethnic politics; yet its declaration of 'Revolutionary Democracy' (EPRDF, 2000)[6] as a fresh policy guideline yields much uncertainty in determining where the TPLF exactly is heading. As for its ethno-nationalist stance, the TPLF demonstratively appears to be persistent and even proudly talking of the ethnic experiment it is conducting. This double-edged theory has been an important tool in enabling the TPLF to bridge the gap between the Marxist-Leninist ideology that necessarily emphasized class struggle encompassing the whole of Ethiopia, and the ethno-national demand of the struggle that focused on Tigrai, the harmonization of which is, however, problematic.

Problems of secession in a multi-ethnic state

With the commencement of the insurgent movement under the TPLF, the idea of national self-determination was understood to mean *autonomy* or self-rule for the region of Tigrai in a would-be democratic, poly-ethnic Ethiopia. Later, in the early days of the struggle, self-determination was stretched by an ultra-nationalist group within the emerging TPLF, to mean *secession* from the Ethiopian nation-state, with the aim of establishing an 'independent republic of Tigrai', as declared by the 1976 'TPLF Manifesto'.[7] The justification for this secessionist stance was drawn eclectically from the theoretical formulations of Stalin on self-determination. There were no other historical, legal or political provisions that substantiated the arguments for secession. This idea of secession was contemplated only by a section of the leadership that with Eriksen's term (1993) might be called 'ethnic entrepreneurs' and not by the rank and file or the people of Tigrai, who constituted one of the main historic cores of the Ethiopian

---

6 See EPRDF, 'The Development Lines of Revolutionary Democracy' Addis Ababa, 1992 E.C. [2000].

7 This was the first published program of the TPLF, also known as Manifesto-68. '68' indicates the year the Manifesto was published in the Ethiopian Calendar (E.C.). For further details, see also chapter 5.

polity. This extreme position was one source of subsequent divisions in the organization.

In 1978, the secession option was proclaimed to have been dropped, after pressure mounted from an internal opposition and also from other Ethiopians and friends of Ethiopia, who saw no merit in secession. Ironically, external pressure, particularly from the Eritrean People's Liberation Front (EPLF), had also a significant role in the denunciation of secession as a program of the TPLF. Given the fluidity of ethnicity and the divergent analytical approaches it developed, the TPLF as an ethno-nationalist force appears to have eclectically theorized and pragmatically acted as far as the 'national self-determination' of Tigrai was concerned. Especially, when one looks into how class analysis and the strategy of class struggle was blended into the ethno-nationalist movement of the TPLF until the early 1990s, the current political turmoil within the TPLF and the worsening insecurity and crisis of the Ethiopian state are perhaps no surprise. The TPLF embarking on self-determination for the people of Tigrai was, at the same time, engaged, or pretended to be engaged, in class struggle that encompassed all oppressed classes in Ethiopia. Yet, it fell short of creating the power base for the latter by focusing on the former objective, self-determination of Tigrai.

In the history of Ethiopia, no government other than that led by the TPLF since 1991 stretched ethno-nationalism to such a far-reaching point, although ethno-national challenges steadily trailed the evolution of the modern Ethiopian state. Constitutionally the post-1991 government granted the right to ethnic nationalities to secede and become independent states (ref. article 39.1 of the 1994 Constitution). Evidently, the relationship of the numerous ethnic groups in Ethiopia has entered a new but turbulent phase, which looks difficult to manage indeed. As far as the point of ethnicity and politics is concerned, as Abbink observes, '[T]here is no going back to a unitary state structure in Ethiopia which denies ethno-regional differences and rights, or which lets one group dominate the state' (1997: 174), although 'the history of Ethiopia ... is most obviously the history of a state, and the story that it tells recounts the ups and downs of what is assumed to be a broadly continuous political organization' (Clapham, 2002: 38). 'The implication is that', as Doornbos expounds, '... basic political identifications are generally not with the state but with sub-national units, such as linguistic, ethnic, religious, racial or regional collectivities' (1978: 170). Thus, the restructuring of the Ethiopian state in a way to create more stable and harmonious relationships among the multitude of ethnic groups becomes very difficult.

The practical application of ethnic identity in various fields of the struggle for national self-determination continued to manifest the diversity of interpretations, inherent in the elasticity of the concept itself and in the differing perceptions and inclinations of the TPLF leaders at all levels. In this regard, the issue of secession continues to challenge the stability of the Ethiopian state and the political elite at the top.

The link between elite ideology and mass movement

The explanations for the strength *and* weakness of the TPLF in mobilizing the people of Tigrai and building an army to wage a protracted war against the military regime of Colonel Mengistu Haile-Mariam and finally its success in conquering state power in 1991 are to be found in the specific and perhaps timely ideological blend of ethno-nationalism on the one hand and the Front's Stalinist rhetoric on the other. The systematic application of both ideologies in drawing the populace into the political battle seemed to have worked to the intended purpose. Colburn (1994: 16) noted that: 'The goals of this generation's revolutionaries have been elusive, but their scope and exhaustive pursuit drained their citizens materially and emotionally'. Despite this latter point, most of the local population was persuaded and/or coerced to focus on the project of the Front, i.e. to win the war and seize power.

Beginning in the late 1970s, an ultra-left ideological brand of Marxism–Leninism (Stalinism specifically) was gaining ground inside the Front and culminated in the formation of a party called the *Marxist-Leninist League of Tigrai* (MLLT) in 1985. This vanguard party, as was the fashion in authoritarian fronts and regimes, came to control every activity of the people under its sphere of action. Although the MLLT nowadays seems to be out of sight, the ideology it extolled served as a lens and compass to guide and control the movement. This feature will lead us to investigate the theoretical departure point(s) of the TPLF and also to give due consideration to key concepts and theories of ethnicity, nationalism, class struggle, and self-determination – concepts extensively utilized by the TPLF to create a broad-based mass movement both during the struggle and after the seizure of power. The intention, however, is not to discuss the concepts at length; rather, it is to emphasize their relevance to the retrospective analysis of the struggle and how they helped TPLF's ascent to power.

Structure of the book

As it is the objective of this study to look into how a tiny group of ethno-nationalist radical students developed into an organized mass-based movement that swept away one of the largest armies in Africa and became the government of Ethiopia, both solid empirical and historical description as well as theoretical reflection is needed.

In the next chapter, some theoretical arguments will be offered to give us a frame of reference for our discussion on the evolution of the TPLF as an ethno-nationalist group in contemporary Africa. This will help to explore the thinking of the radical or 'revolutionary' group that shaped and led the struggle of the Tigraians. Chapter 3 will discuss and fit together the objective conditions upon which the group evolved to become a cohesive organization to launch an armed insurrection. Chapter 4 shall explain the dramatic events of the initial year of the guerrilla movement that put the nascent front to a test. The unexpected early confrontations with the forces of the *Dergue* and also the encounter with a rival front, the 'Tigrai Liberation Front' (TLF), and their impact on future engagements will be assessed here. The measures taken to mobilize the population to support the war including the eradication of *shiftas* (bandits) and the armed confrontation with other rival organizations, the EDU and the EPRP will be treated in chapter 5. Chapter 6 takes up one of the main challenges confronting the military government (the *Dergue*) i.e. how it handled the ethno-national question, one of the most sensitive political issues in Ethiopia. The *Dergue*'s encounter with movements seeking self-determination, particularly with menacingly growing TPLF, will be the main focus of discussion. Chapter 7 looks into how the TPLF treated the central issue of self-determination at different moments of the struggle, the interpretation and application of which shall be discussed in light of the theoretical arguments advanced. Chapter 8 shall look into the ultra-left party, MLLT, which emerged from within the TPLF and took control of the whole Front. Its overt activities then and its covert activities later on and how that impacted political events in Ethiopia will be discussed at length. In chapter 9 the influence of the Eritrean movement on the Tigraian youth in general and the thorny relationships with the Eritrean Fronts (the ELF and the EPLF) in particular and how they evolved in to armed confrontations will be discussed. Chapter 10 is concerned with the socio-political and organizational activities of the TPLF to create a power base among the people on whose behalf the struggle was waged. Chapter 11 will discuss the final days of the *Dergue* and the military and diplomatic venture of the TPLF that paved its way to power. Chapter 12 will look into the ideological, political and military ventures of the TPLF rolled together by way of comparison with other four African fronts of the same era. Finally, there will be a concluding chapter that will elucidate the implications of the TPLF's rise to power with the emphasis on its ethnic politics vis-à-vis the inter-ethnic and intra-ethnic relationships and the stability of the nation.

Chapter 2

Ethnicity, Mobilization and Revolt: Theoretical Considerations

The Power and Fluidity of Ethnicity

If ethnicity happened to be an effective instrument of mobilizing people's power that could determine the realization of 'self-determination' or secession and even state re-making, its power and adaptability needs to be sufficiently understood. Indeed, well-established nations or even regions can be destabilized by ethnic conflicts. Despite their prevalence, though, so far there is no consensus among social scientists and policy makers on the nature and definition of ethnicity; yet as we see it at work it is essential to adequately grasp its scope and meaning.

Ethnicity is a very broad and complex concept that stretches in meaning at least between the domains of 'primordialists' who regard it as a 'collective identity, so deeply rooted in historical experience that it should properly be treated as a given in human relations and 'instrumentalists' who contend that 'ethnicity is not a historical given at all, but in fact a highly adaptive and malleable phenomenon' (Esman 1994: 10). Although there are wide-ranging interpretations of ethnicity, in general it is understood as the state of believing in and belonging to an ethno-cultural or ethno-linguistic group, which 'may be both an expression of primordialism and an interest group'

(Lal 1995: 431). 'It is manifested in all types of forms ranging from the desire to observe rites and customs of one's people to the demand of formation of a separate state. All depends on concrete historical conditions' (Ismagilova 1994: 9); in this case ethnicity '...describes both a set of relations and a mode of consciousness' (Comaroff and Comaroff 1992: 54). The set of relations are based on real or assumed primordial links of common origin, culture, language or physical resemblance, while the mode of consciousness can be constructed by a political, economic or even cultural group whose drive is to regain what was lost or safeguard what is at hand. In this respect, ethnicity has both an emotional and material basis, and could be manipulated in a flexible fashion. It is precisely from these elusive attributes that ethnicity draws out its power and fluid character. In both instances, ethnicity provides an effective uniting factor among those who feel relative deprivation, a real or imagined threat and the need for change as opposed to those who want to maintain the status quo. Therefore ethnicity remains a crucial phenomenon whether as a 'social construct' or 'as an artefact of human imagination and rooted in the darkest recesses of history – fluid and manipulable yet important enough to kill for' (Chua 2004: 15).

Owing to its power and fluidity, ethnicity can rise to the level of 'nationality' – an ethnic group that aspires peoplehood and political status - depending on the desire of the political actors that utilize it. When ethnicity is collectively expounded to the level of an organization that opts for political action or state formation in an existing state-society relationship, it becomes nationalism. At this point, the intrinsic relationship between ethnicity and nationalism becomes obvious. As Eriksen asserts, '...the distinction between nationalism and ethnicity as analytical concepts is a simple one ... A nationalist ideology is an ethnic ideology which demands a state on behalf of the ethnic group' (1993: 118). The demand of ethno-nationalists could be for a fair share or for full control of state power. Nonetheless, it is for this very analytical purpose that in this study the struggle waged by the TPLF is referred to as an ethno-nationalist movement. The politics of an ethnic group, in short, yield a nationalist demand that is widely claimed by such forces, including the TPLF, as the 'right to self-determination'.

The fluidity of ethnicity can depend not only on how an ethnic group identifies itself but also on how it may be identified by a certain ethno-political entrepreneurs at a particular point in time. As Chua (2004: 14-15) states:

> Ethnic identity is not static but shifting and highly malleable. In Rwanda, for example, 14 percent Tutsi minority dominated the

Hutu majority economically and politically for four centuries, as a kind of cattle-owning aristocracy. But for most of this period the lines between Hutus and Tutsi were permeable. The two groups spoke the same language, intermarriage occurred and successful Hutus could 'become Tutsi'. This was no longer true after the Belgians arrived and, steeped in specious theories of racial superiority, issued ethnic identity cards on the basis of nose length and cranial circumstances.

In this manner, ethnic awareness was raised to a different level that spurred ethnic bloodshed and that is 'what makes ethnic conflict so terrifyingly difficult to understand and contain' (Ibid: 15). Ironically, Belgium itself is at present (in 2008) facing a non-violent but serious ethno-linguistic divide of its own between the Flemish and Walloon communities – a situation that has paralyzed the government for a year now.

'Ethnicity' is not a scientifically determinable status, argue Horowitz (1985) and Chua (2004), . Indeed social scientists conceptualize ethnicity differently. Therefore we are confronted with a very broad domain for the definition of ethnicity that encompasses differences along racial lines (for example, blacks and whites in the United States), lines of geographic origin (for example, Malays, Chinese, and Indians in Malaysia), as well as linguistic, religious, tribal, or other cultural lines (for example, Kikuyu and Kalenjin tribes in Kenya or Jews and Muslims in the Middle East) (Chua 2004: 14), or the Afar, Agew, Tigrai, Amhara, Oromo, Sidama, Gambella, Gurage and other ethnic groups in Ethiopia.

In a more practical sense, Markakis asserts that '[e]thnicity has long been one of the factors determining political choice in Africa; as it has been in many parts of the globe. Given the nature of African societies, it would have been strange indeed, if this were not so' (1996: 300). Furthermore, Horowitz argues: 'Ethnic affiliation provides a sense of security in a divided society, as well as a source of trust, certainty, reciprocal help, and protection against neglect of one's interest by strangers' (1994: 49). Fitting in this line of thought, Mohamed Salih adds following the discussion on Anderson's imagined community (1983): '…unless ethnicity is taken seriously, Africa's struggle to democratize the state and development will suffer no better a fate than that of an imagined nation state' (2001: 25). Also Merera (2002: 25) seems to share this thinking when he writes: 'Mohamed Salih's position of fully condoning ethnicity as a positive social force in Africa, although rare in academic discourse, is relevant to our discussion on Ethiopia, where ethnicity has already become an 'official' state ideology and practice'. This line of discourse is well taken by the elites of the TPLF to justify the need for the restructuring of the Ethiopian state and the redefinition of the relationship of the multiple ethno-national groups which is not settled yet after almost two decades of rigorous experimentation. The problem of such approach, however, is that it is short of addressing the domino effect that could be generated by sub-ethnic groups within the ethnic entity that achieved the envisaged status. In Ethiopia many sub-ethnic groups are being mobilized to demand 'self-determination' the limits of which may reach secession and are also fighting among each other over scarce resources, territory and power (Dereje Feyissa 2006; Abbink 2006).

In all these cases, ethnicity seems to occupy centre stage in the stated quest for societal reform, stability, democracy and development. As the above-stated views may generate a lot of argument, just for the purpose of the comparison of the diverse positions and to demonstrate the problems compounding the comprehension of ethnicity, we consider some other social scientists' alternative views.

'The study of ethnic phenomena reveals', Roosens argues, 'how far ethnic ideology and historical reality can diverge from each other; how much people feel things that are not there and conveniently forget realities that have existed' (1989: 161). In its application for political organizations, Doornbos elaborates, 'if ethnicity is to be assigned any paramount constitutional role in this scheme of things, renewed disillusionments will be difficult to avoid: ethnicity can only provide an alternative basis for political organization at the cost of a whole new wave of misrepresentations, distortions and inequalities' (1998: 29). Such feelings, as observed in many places, could be expeditiously transformed into violent acts of responses to daily suffocating realities. Thus Gurr (1970: 36) noted: 'It is true, and the frustration-aggression relationship is significant for political violence, to the extent that actors in political violence manifest or admit to some degree of anger'. In these circumstances people are overtaken by group mentality even at the expense of rational thoughts, revealing that '[c]ollective human memories and attention spans tend to be quite ephemeral, and as news coverage flits from one crisis to another, processes of forgetting take place almost unconsciously' (de Silva 2000: 248). Furthermore, Alter contends that: 'Nationalism, to all intents and purposes, means undisguised political egoism. As an ideology it preaches solidarity with and willingness to make sacrifice to one particular social group' (1994: 118) and '[t]he other is seen as a knife in the throat of the nation', Keane adds (1995: 193).

Despite the conflicting views on ethnicity and its uses, the main issue, however, is that such divergent views do not remain analytical tools or theoretical postulates and positions confined to the social scientists or the politicians concerned. Those well-articulated views, divergent as they are in their interpretations and objectives, often find ground to influence millions of people to the one side or the other and guide them to some kind of action, more often to a political revolt. The consciousness and the sentiment created as a result of these views henceforth determine the type of action the people pursue to achieve real or imagined ends, like 'self determination' or secession, in many cases in violent ways. The role of aspiring spokesmen or elites is often vital here. Whether ethnicity - especially when politicized - has a positive or negative message, the debate looks far from reaching a conclusive end. In the meantime, it is out there at large, serving as a tool of mobilizing people on the one side or to meet certain perceived ends on the other, but always in relation to 'Others', who are seen as standing in the way. The power and fluidity of ethnicity is thus at the service of ethnic entrepreneurs and marginalized social classes that seek change for the better.

Ethno-Nationalism, Self-Determination and Secession

Although ethnicity and nationalism are intrinsically related concepts and the former, with its power and fluidity, may evolve to the latter to pursue some kind of political enterprise, they are not one and the same, and have essential features that distinguish one from the other. In brief, '[w]hat most clearly distinguishes nationalism from ethnicity is its political agenda' (Cornell and Hartman 1998: 37) and the political projection basically is the rise of ethnicity to nationalism, hence termed ethno-nationalism. The often tumultuous process through which ethno-nationalism evolves and the objectives it seeks to realize are vague and shrouded in subjectivity that often causes heated discourse and/or conflict.

It can be said that nationalism is politicized ethnicity, which means its entering into the realm of power politics. As McAdams, Tarrow and Tilly (2001) put it, '[e]thnicity is a constructed claim to common origin, shared culture, and linked fate but, unlike nationality, it affords adherents no necessary political standing and has a shifting and nonessential relation to nationality.... Like other identities, nationality and ethnicity refer to social relations rather than individual attributes, rest on socially organized categories, and involve claims to collective rights-cum-obligations' (2001: 231-232). Thus the linkage between ethnicity and nationality and the rise of ethno-nationalism is not without a political mission per se.

Considering the fluid nature of ethnicity, lending it the power to mobilize people in different circumstances using concomitant historical, cultural or political issues and symbols, similar things can be said of *ethno-nationalism*. Like ethnicity, there are also divergent views compounding ethno-nationalism. With regards to the complexity and vacillating features of ethno-nationalism, Bugajski observes that '[e]thnic nationalism may be a positive or negative phenomenon: it can be aggressive or defensive, rational or emotional, consistent or unpredictable; it has moments of intensity, period of passivity, and it is often contradictory' (1994: 102). On the positive side, Nabudere elaborates that 'it tries to cope with modernity whilst also at the same time defining one's identity for needs of stability and self-definition' (1999: 90), while on the negative side he goes on to show that the 'class manipulation and mobilization of the ethnic sentiments for purely narrow and self-serving interests of a small minority of elites who continuously struggle for positions in the state' (ibid.: 90). The positive and negative attributes of ethnic nationalism brought up by both Bugajski and Nabudere again highlights the potential power and fluidity of ethno-nationalism, but at the same time posses the danger of unpredictable outcome that is related to intensified conflicts and fragmentation of a multi-ethnic society like Ethiopia. The unpredictability of the ethno-nationalist drive was elaborated upon by McAdams, Tarrow and Tilly (2001: 232). They argue:

> 'In the case of ethnicity, claims to rights and obligations vary in degree and type, from passing recognition of kinship all the way to legal singling out for special treatment, negative or positive. Nationalist intellectuals, clerics, language teachers, bureaucrats, soldiers, and rent seekers have at one time or another hitched their wagon to an ethnic star, seeking to elevate it into a nationality by distinguishing it from others. Others have constructed ethnicity as the foundation for an existing state they hoped to erect in their own images. Still others have cordially ignored it, building national identity on criteria that emerge from common life together, on common suspicion of neighbours, or on state made boundaries' (2001: 232).

In general, however, it is widely understood that ethno-nationalist consciousness and movement aim at achieving a 'right to self-determination' of the people within the specific ethnic nationality that may or may not culminate in secession. But given the contradictory perceptions of ethno-nationalism, as noted above, one is inclined to ask what exactly is the 'right to self-determination', and why does it include 'secession' as one of its final aims? Does secession bring about the democratic right that triggered the demand for the right to self-determination in the first place? The internationally formulated but wide-ranging definitions of 'self-determination' may give some insight to tackle these questions. The idea of self-determination though, according to Nodia (1994: 9), '...emerged with movements for democracy and independence, both acting in the name of 'self-determination': 'we the people' (i.e., the nation) will decide our own fate; we will observe only those rules that we ourselves set up; and we will allow nobody ... to rule us without our consent'.

No matter how broadly used and how much people are inspired by the hopes it generate, self-determination is a vaguely defined political concept in both the political and academic realm. As Wolfgang Danspeckgruger[8] put it, '[n]o other concept is as powerful, visceral, emotional, unruly as steep in creating aspirations and hopes as self-determination'. In a more practical sense, Donald Watt defined self-determination as '[o]riginally the right of the subjects of a state to choose their own government or form of government ...encompass additionally the idea of national groups seceding from multinational states and empires in order to set up their own national state' (in Bullock *et al.* 1988: 766-767). The Unrepresented Nations and People's Organization (UNPO)[9] has a more broad definition which says that self-determination '[e]ssentially is the right of people to determine its own destiny; ... to choose its own political status and determine its own form of economic, cultural and social development'. Article 1.1 of the International Covenant on Civil and Political Rights of 1966 also states that: 'All people have the right of self-determination. By virtue of that right they freely determine their political status and freely pursue their economic, social and cultural development'. These three selected definitions understandably have a lot in common but they do not specify who the subjects (in the first case) or the people (in the second and third case) are. The assumption of who constitutes a people in these cases and in this study, however, is those members of an ethnic nationality who are opting for a political status.

Though embodied in various provisions of the UN Charter, one can easily observe the interpretation of self-determination as well as its objectives ranging from secession to regional autonomy and its application encompassing individual as well as group rights. Thus '[t]he right to self-determination remains one of the most intractable and difficult problem to be addressed by the international community.... The subject has been the basis for contention and war', (Rupesinghe and Tashkov 1996: 20). As to its objective, 'Self-determination can be achieved in various forms: unitary state, federation, confederation, autonomy' (Ismagilova 1994: 11). There lies the enduring appeal of self-determination, although the aspirations and hopes of the people in focus may or may not be realized.

This principle of self-determination has developed in many phases to include marginalized ethnic groups' quest for equal rights or self-rule.

8 At: http://www.unpo.org/content/view/4957/72, accessed 15-1-2008.
9 Ibid.

Bugajski puts it more specifically: 'Ethnic leaders may seek to recognize the administration of the state from a unitary to federal or confederate structure in which specific regions gain some degree of provincial autonomy or full republican status' (1994: 111). The pivotal political conviction of ethnic nationalism is then that each and every ethnic entity is entitled to self-determination. This seems impossible in a world where there are more than 2000 ethnic groups (Kly 2000). In Nigeria alone there are over 200 of them (Suberu 2006: 89). When we take Ethiopia, there are around 80 ethnic groups (Turton 2006: 18). Nonetheless, given the endless debate and controversy surrounding the subject, coupled with the powerful influence and the unruly nature of self-determination, differences on this point are likely to create more problems than solutions unless a consensus is reached on what people ought or should aim to achieve by their struggle for self-determination.

It appears there is a broadly acceptable understanding that self-determination can be achieved in one of the different forms discussed above, namely federation, confederation, autonomy or secession. While the first three possible outcomes are 'internal' political settlements of self-determination that fall within the realm of a democratic arrangement, the last one, secession, which involves partition of territory and is usually achieved with actual or under threat of force, entails the formation of a separate state which may or may not end up under democratic governance. Even if '[s]elf-determination is one of the most important principles of contemporary international law ... Equally important is respect for territorial integrity and political unity of states. A balance has to be struck between them'[10]. Looking for an acceptable balance for those who seek separation, on the one hand, and for those who want to maintain union on the other hand is not an easy task by any measure. 'Even when secession seems straightforward and the seceding areas appear reasonably homogeneous, new conflicts can emerge fairly rapidly' (McGarry and O'Leary 1996: 335). Perhaps, the balance could be struck in a thorough understanding of secession, which in turn leads us to investigate the merits and/or demerits of secession as a solution to the quest of self-determination.

Summarizing the complexities surrounding secession McGarry and O'Leary (ibid.: 334) write:

> The normative idea behind principled partitions and secessions is the principle of self determination. The key problem with the principle of self-determination as a means of eliminating ethnic conflict is that it begs four questions:

10 *Carnegie Project on Complex Power Sharing and Self Determination, 2002*, at http://www.unpo.org.

* Who are the people?

* What is the relevant territorial unit in which they should exercise self-determination?

* What constitutes a majority?

* Does secession produce a domino effect in which ethnic minorities within seceding territories seek self-determination (i.e. secession) for themselves?

Dwelling on all the above questions is beyond the scope of this study, but for the purpose of the argument and for what it entails in the multi-ethnic state of Ethiopia, we shall consider the fourth problem that seeks to inquire into the spiral effect that secession of one ethnic group induces on the other ethnic or even sub-ethnic groups. In this connection, in her article 'A critical analysis of the self-determination of peoples'. Danielle Achibugi (2002)[11] critically observes:

> The noble and necessary principle of self-determination of peoples is becoming the opening for a new form of tribalism and it is encouraging some of the most reactionary tendencies present in contemporary society. If we wish to prevent it, we need to include its demands in a legal framework shared both by the community claiming self-determination and by the community that is rejecting it...'

McGarry and O'Leary (in Hutchinson and Smith 1996: 336) also expound on this line: '[w]hen formation of a separate state (secession) becomes the aim of a struggle, more often there emerges a host of problems that lead to further crisis and conflicts and 'secession remains an option very likely to produce violence, and problems (initially) as bad as the ones it is intended to solve'.

Similarly so, N. Basic, D. Goetze and A. Smith (2004)[12] explain the problems associated with secession as follows:

> '..Many civil wars are provoked by secession crises in which minority groups seek to secede from an existing state, state governments object to secession plans, and violent confrontation is the result. We argue that the principles embodied in international

11 At: http://www.unpo.org. 2002.
12 See '*Non Exclusionary Criteria and Stability in International Policy Making about Secession Crisis*(2004), at: http://www.tamilnation.org/selfdetermination/04Basic%20 GoetzeSmith.pdf.

policy induce the actors in secession crises to engage in violent conflict to further their goals rather than seek peaceful resolution of their differences. Instead, we urge alteration of international policy to provide incentives for the adoption of peaceful behaviors and norms that can foster long-term cooperation and stability. We hold few illusions about the ease with which stability can be secured in many regions of the world...'

Gurr and Goldstone (1991: 332) argued that ' Ethnic self-determination in the twenty-first century is more likely to fuel civil wars – among the Karen and Kurds, the Tamils and Eritreans, nations fighting to establish their own state – than to motivate revolutionary movements'. The intention to break away is obviously opposed by unionists and more so by the state that has defended territorial integrity as acceptable international norm. McGarry and O'Leary (in Hutchinson and Smith 1996: 336) also added that '...the proposal of any community to secede from any state is likely to encourage key elites in the affected states to behave in chauvinistic and warlike ways. Normally secessionist movements provoke elites satisfied with the existing state into mobilizing 'Unionist' movements against traitors'.

Indeed, it is not arguable that all people have equal rights and more specifically the inalienable right of self-determination i.e. to freely determine their political status and freely pursue their economic, social and cultural development. When these inalienable rights are threatened or denied, there is a natural urge for people to struggle (peacefully, otherwise violently) to regain and protect these rights. Under a democratic system, such rights have grounds to be respected and the need for violent way of struggle would not arise, where as, 'Ethnic questions (leading to secession) raise relatively non-tradable issues. Nationality, language, territorial homeland and culture are not easily bargained over. They create zero-sum conflicts, and therefore provide ideal materials for political entrepreneurs interested in creating or dividing political constituencies' (ibid.: 337). Therefore it is fundamentally the absence of democratic means of settling social, economic and political matters that lead to the demand of self-determination in one form or the other. Once those popular demands are adequately addressed and resolved in the interest of the deprived people, which is the essence of the demand for self-determination, then the question of secession lacks validity because, on the one hand, two political equals have better chances of nurturing their rights to a greater satisfaction and on the other, there is no guarantee the rights constituting self-determination would be respected after secession is achieved. And more perplexing is the domino effect this trend would have in the seceding entity now forging a separate state. Sub-ethnic groups, as we see it in present-day Ethiopia, may come forward with perhaps legitimate claims which eventually may be politicized by ethnic entrepreneurs to call for secession. Once Eritrea seceded from Ethiopia officially in 1993, many other ethno-nationalist groups have emerged with similar claims. Although they have started their movement with rather vague program long before Eritrea got independence, the Oromo Liberation Front (OLF), the Ogaden National Liberation Front (ONLF) and the Sidama Liberation Front (SLF) groups, to mention but a few, are striving to achieve that goal, and unlike the general behaviour of states, the new Ethiopian Constitution (Article 39) acknowledges this provision, at least officially. Again, in separated Eritrea too, another wave of ethno-nationalist movements, like that of the Kunama or the Afar[13] for instance, is on the rise. It looks like a phenomenon without end.

If secession, as an outcome of the struggle for self-determination, does not lead to acquiring the democratic and human rights fought for, then what is its merit? What is it that, in the final analysis, people gain by seceding? As indicated earlier, there is no straightforward acknowledgeable answer, and the likely outcome is building a wall called 'national boundary' that curtails the free movement of neighbouring peoples, the significance of which is, however, diminishing in today's world. In other words, there is no more union of people that necessitates defining a palatable relationship, for secession simply happens to be an act of separation and not a process of formulating a system of living together in a mutually acceptable and advantageous setting. As for the political elite, it is a different matter; it has found a domain to rule over. In seceding states it is often, if not always, the political elite that is assured of power and prestige. This has been the general case with leaders of liberation movements in Africa (and elsewhere) which will be discussed in subsequent chapters particularly in the comparative analysis section.

With the fusion of exclusivist secession in the inclusive tenets of self-determination, it is more likely to lead to a clash of interests between those forces who see the merits in democratically settled union and those who opt for separation under any conditions. Evidently, such clashes have turned out to be violent and lethal. One of the problems of secession is that it intends to create a wall between 'we' and 'them' who hitherto have lived together under an undesirable system which has to be changed if people have to live in peace and harmony. Proposing secession as a solution, however, manifests the lack of understanding as to what secession entails among the parties involved, that is the emergence of new conflicts while seceding entities could face another wave of similar quest. Secession is not also necessarily followed

---

13 See the work of Abdallah A. Adou 1993.

by a democratic system. It has also been argued recently that the right to self-determination could be exercised 'internally', within an existing state. Internal self-determination would allow a people more control over their political, economic, social and cultural development, while stopping short of full secession. Unless the demerits of exclusionist secession are fully realized and separately treated from the inclusive attributes of self-determination, multi-national states like Ethiopia will continue to find themselves in endless crisis and conflicts.

Ethnic Mobilization in a Multi-Ethnic Society

Charles Tilly defined mobilization as a concept that '...conveniently identifies the process by which a group goes from being a passive collection of individuals to an active participant in public life' (1978: 69), and in this process the '...group acquires collective control over the resources needed for action' (ibid.: 7). If we may identify a host of effective tools of mobilization, definitely ethnicity is one, if not the most effective one. This is because ethnicity is portrayed as an embodiment of subjective and objective traits of human beings and through it any usable resource (human or material) can be provided to promote the actions deemed necessary for the fulfilment of shared interest. Thus in many parts of the world '[e]thnicity is the obvious basis for mobilizing opposition when an old regime has held power on behalf of a dominant ethnic group ...' (Gurr and Goldstone 1991: 336).

In relation to ethno-nationalist movements, ethnic mobilization can be defined as 'the process by which an ethnic community becomes politicized on behalf of its collective interest and aspirations' (Esman 1994: 28). The ethnic constituency of such a movement can be classified as and assume the role of 'leaders, activists, ordinary members, or sympathizers' (ibid.). While the leaders and a segment of the activists may fall into the category of often educated revolutionary elite, the ordinary members are by-and-large the peasantry and other rural or urban-based disgruntled social classes. Their interests and ultimate goals may also vary according to their position and the role they assume in the movement. To the revolutionary elite, the whole purpose of the movement could go as far as capturing state power, while members or sympathizers often aim at mitigating their unacceptable circumstances and induce the emergence of a state upon which they can impress their values to the satisfaction of the collectivity. Thus Esman generalizes:

> Mobilization may be prompted by a shift in the group's collective
> expectations or in the 'reference group,' the significant other,

with which they compare their own situation. Mobilization may be the result of events that seriously threaten the community or, alternatively, present opportunities too promising or attractive to resist (ibid., 30).

And ideology plays a role in systematizing the perception of the people's 'real' interest. 'One of the important ways ideology shaped choice was by inflating the perceived spectrum of possibilities' (Colburn 1994: 37) which allows different social groups to anticipate the demise of the old state and hope for the realization of their dreams in the state to come, thus mobilized to participate. This is why '[t]he spirit of the resistance thus lays the foundation for a new social order' (Selden, in Miller and Aya 1971: 215).

A wide and deep sense of grievance among ordinary people is a necessary condition for counter-elites who seek to mobilize a mass following. There was no shortage of grievances in the pre-revolutionary societies ... In virtually every instance threatened governments used force and violence in ways that increased popular resentment and active support for revolutionary movements (Gurr & Goldstone 1991: 334). As Tilly said: '[t]he poor and the powerless often find that the rich, the powerful, and the government oppose and punish their efforts at mobilization' (Tilly 1978: 75). The repressive action of the government in turn enhances the mobilization process already underway.

Mobilization can be performed in several ways depending on the situation in which the ethnic community intends to achieve certain objective or on the threat pointed at the community. Tilly (1978: 73-74) identifies three different ways mobilization is carried out: defensive, offensive, and preparatory.

Defensive mobilization is induced by a threat from outside. This is a collective action performed across the ethnic community challenging the assumption that mobilization is always is a top-down phenomenon, organized by leaders and agitators.

The offensive and preparatory mobilizations are necessarily carried out often top-down because they require an organization that can mobilize human and material resource to execute a defined set of action(s).

Once mobilization is under way, Esman (1994: 31-39) identifies seven critical factors that sustains and advances the ethnic movement:

Political opportunity structure: the context in which the movement shapes its strategies and tactics, and also its ideology and goals.

Leadership: this symbolizes the movement and bears major responsibilities for guiding it, articulating its values and collective interests etc.

Ideology: provides a coherent set of articulated beliefs which defines the collective identity, grievances, aspirations etc, explains and justifies the need of the movement and cost of participation in the collective action.

Organization: allows the aggregation and deployment of human and material resources to engage in sustained political combat, civil or violent and also facilitates the socialization of individuals into the movement.

Goals: set the intended outcome – self-determination in its variant forms - of the collective struggles that justify the cost and risk of mobilization.

Resources: that feeds the movement to advance which is available within the community or from external sources.

Strategy and tactics: this constitutes the long and short range methods employed to achieve goals, the range of which may include from legal, civil disobedience and non-violent disruptions to terrorism and insurrectionary violence.

In ethnic politics, an intensive agitation is underway to mobilize human and material resources, the agitation of which is based on real or perceived content but often stretched to the extreme and even dramatized with the obvious intention to marshal greater people's power into the political arena. For the purpose of ethno-nationalist mobilization, ethnic symbols, memories and traditions are introduced often in a dramatic fashion. 'Once deep ethnic divisions are mobilized into electoral and party politics (and more pointedly into the struggle of self-determination); however, they tend to produce suspicion rather than trust, acrimony rather than civility, polarization rather than accommodation, and victimization rather than toleration (Diamond and Plattner 1994: xix). It is this character of ethnicity that fosters the collectivity and mobilization of people to commit violent action. In this process,

> 'If, on the other hand, we hold mobilization constant and consider collective action itself, common sense is vindicated. Relatively poor and powerless groups which have already mobilized are more likely to act collectively by claiming new rights, privileges, and advantages. At the same level of mobilization the rich and powerful are more likely to act collectively in defence of what they already have' (ibid.: 75-76).

Likewise, '[T]he hegemonic order reflects and thus reproduces the interest of the dominant 'ethnie', by representing the 'order of things' in a distorted manner as legitimate, democratic and moral, and by concealing its oppressive or more questionable aspects' (Yiftachel and Ghanem in Kaufmann 2004: 191).

Offering an ethnically charged alternative program in time of a general crisis and presenting themselves as being the custodian of the Tigraian 'national virtue', the revolutionary elite of the TPLF found the numerous Tigraian peasant and other small social groups responding positively to their calls. They were thus able to mobilize support against their opponents who were portrayed as outsiders, and it was not difficult for the TPLF to organize and create a power base in rural areas where the state had no effective means of control or access to the people.

Peasant Revolt and Revolutionary Elite: Where Do They Conjoin?

Revolution does not occur without well-grounded reasons and there is always a group of leaders or an elite that theorize and give it the ideological flesh to walk it through to the goals set in advance, no matter how general or incoherent they may be. The revolutionary elite usually aim at capturing state power while the populace may only fight for a better life under a new state where its voices could be heard and have an impact.

Ted Robert Gurr advances a broader perspective of revolution by tracing theories from ancient history:

> For Aristotle the principal cause of revolution is the aspiration for economic or political equality on the part of the common people who lack it, and the aspiration of the oligarchy for greater inequality than they have, i.e. a discrepancy in both instances between what people have of political and economic goods relative to what they think is justly theirs (1970: 37).

From this definition, one can observe that revolution is a dynamic process which would occur whenever people feel denied of the rights that affect the well-being of their lives and when the urge to restore them is heightened. This revolutionary dynamism is a sine qua non of modernization and beyond. As Huntington (1968: 265) has it, 'Revolution is ... an aspect of modernization. ...It is most likely to occur in societies which have experienced some social and economic development and where the processes of political modernization and political development have lagged behind the processes of social and economic change'. In most developing countries like Ethiopia where overwhelming majority of people are subjected to low level agrarian economy and where social and economic development is sluggish, peasants are prone to revolt. In this circumstance Skocpol writes:

> Peasants are potentially rebellious at all times, and a political crisis gives them the opportunity to revolt.... important at this juncture are the specific agrarian structures. Revolution is likely when peasant communities (a) have high degree of communal solidarity, (b) are quite autonomous as local communities, yet (c) are supervised by a centralized bureaucracy (1979: 116-117).

Moshiri also emphasizes that '[i]t is the combination of the state's political crisis and the peasant revolt that produces the social revolution' (in Goldstone, *et al.* 1991: 28). With this line of analysis McLane elaborates:

> Three general conditions seem necessary for revolution to occur in peasant societies. The first is the failure of rural social structure to meet the material and other functional needs of the peasantry. The second is the decay or removal of traditional agencies of social control, including the village landed elite and the territorial administration. The final condition is the involvement of the peasantry in a new or revolutionary social and administrative order (in Miller and Aya 1971: 69).

The above noted factors for a revolution to occur are complementary if not the same with those of Skocpol, argued earlier in different words.

Discontent can be caused by a variety of intervening factors but often is articulated in relation to the state that claims to possess the moral and legal authority to manage the affairs of the populace. Once discontent has been created, it can be easily politicized by the elite who seek change and civil disorder may follow. In this circumstance '[l]oss of government legitimacy is an important *if not critical* factor in explaining civil strife events. The legitimacy of the political regime is one of the most important of these normative factors', (Brinton 1965; Johnson 1966; Gurr 1970). And 'If discontent is intense and widespread in a society, revolutionary tasks are simplified; if not, there are means by which it can be increased. Ideological appeals offer the best means, to the extent that their content is designed to justify new aspirations and specify means towards their attainment' (Gurr 1970: 353).

But since '[p]easants are especially handicapped in passing from passive recognition of wrongs to political participation as a means of setting them right (Wolf in Miller and Aya 1971: 49), the role of revolutionary elite that mobilizes and organizes forces of change becomes compelling. This is to say 'Revolutions depend not only on structural preconditions but also on actors committed to radical change' (Colburn 1994: 17). In a society which has been heavily suppressed by reactionary political and religious forces and where the peasant has been reduced to destitution for much longer period of time, revolutionary zeal does not come easily. It requires organized revolutionary elite that can galvanize a peasantry left destitute to the level of active participant in a revolution through which it hopes to be liberated. It is true, '[i]n societies long stagnant, corrupt, and repressed, revolutionary change has come to mean the possibility of formerly wretched, impoverished masses seizing control of their own destinies and forging the dynamic institutional foundations of liberation' (Miller & Aya 1971: xiii-xiv).

Without the revolutionary elite that has acquired the knowledge to see beyond existing conditions of life and paint the picture of the future, and draw the peasantry from its preoccupation of earning daily bread, peasant revolution is less likely to occur, although spontaneous peasant revolts may come and fade away. Therefore, revolutionary elite is an indispensable ingredient of peasant revolution. McLane elaborates: '[e]ven when revolutionary preconditions develop, a revolution requires mobilization of the masses by leaders with organizational skills and ideology relevant to those particular preconditions. Rebellion may be spontaneous; revolution needs leadership, planning, ultimate purposes, and their own institutions' (in Miller and Aya 1971: 70). 'The values, expectations, phraseology, iconography, and implicit rules that expressed and shaped collective intentions and behaviour can be called the intellectual culture of the revolution. And it has been this intellectual culture, I will argue, much more than the imperatives of social structure, that has provided the logic of contemporary revolutions' Colburn (1994: 14). As revolutionary ideas are more than a kind of intervening variables that mediate interests and outcomes, the intellectual skill of the revolutionary elite is crucial in the formulation and guidance of the revolution. 'They shape actors' perceptions of possibilities, as well as their understanding of their interests' (ibid.: 104). Finally, '[r]evolution derives its significance from its contribution to long-term social and political outcomes' (ibid.: 10) and '[t]hus when the peasant protagonists lights the torch of rebellion, the edifice of society is already smouldering and ready to lake fire' (Wolf in Miller and Aya 1971: 67).

Another important factor that influences peasant revolution is the involvement of external forces which have the technological skill and the material power that could tilt the balance of forces in favour of those who are on their side. In the study of peasant-based revolutions, Skocpol (1994: 235) persuasively argues that 'peasants are only part of the story. A holistic frame of reference is indispensable, one that includes states, class structures, and transnational economic and military relations'. Furthermore, '[w] hen domestic elites sought change and superpower support depended on limiting repression and international cooperation, the states faced a dilemma' (Moshiri, in Goldstone *et al.* 1991: 34). To corroborate with this view, Colburn (1994: 13) has this to say:

> .... Skocpol's suggestion of the importance of interstate relations is especially persuasive. The machinations of foreign states have played a decisive part in the history of the world's poor countries, most of which are small and weak....Yet, it is important to acknowledge that the participants make the crucial difference between a potentially revolutionary situation and an actual revolution. Once the revolution is under way, their thinking and behaviour influence the revolutionary process. In turn, the course of the revolution, its ebbs and turns, inescapably shapes the outcome.

Although Skocpol's point has a strong bearing, it is the participants in the revolution, as Colburn argued that make the ultimate difference. The success of the initially weak but mass-based movements in Algeria, Cuba, Vietnam, China, Mozambique and Ethiopia demonstrate the point made by Colburn.

Finally, revolutionary leaders create and deepen mechanisms of control in the society they claim to liberate, 'but this building and extension of control must involve a complex dialogue with the villagers in whom the outsider learns as much, if not more, about local organization and criteria of relevance than the local inhabitants.' (Wolf, in Miller and Aya 1971: 45-46). Through the different mechanisms created by the revolutionary elite, the old system is replaced in any way possible including the use of violence and 'what is done with the power seized is consequential. An attempt at social transformation entails a massive, and inescapably violent, restructuring of social stratification. ...Thus, the designation of what is and what is not a revolution is, in the end, somewhat arbitrary' (Colburn 1994: 7).

Whether we call the TPLF-led struggle for the right to self-determination 'a peasant revolution' (as Young 1997 and Hammond 1999 put it) or not may require further investigation. In any case, '[t]he linkage between intellectual trends and revolutions is more apparent in the numerous revolutions that took place in the 1960s and 1970s (Colburn 1994: 28) and this has been also the case in Tigrai in particular and Ethiopia in general.

Surely, revolutions occur not only because forces leading toward them are strong, but also because forces tending to inhibit, or obstruct, them are weak or absent (Colburn 1994: 40). In traditional rural Ethiopia, the Marxist military *Dergue* was weak and absent in many parts. This situation definitely gave ample opportunity for the revolutionary force of the TPLF to manoeuvre freely in the rural areas and build a formidable peasant force that finally enabled it to prevail over the state's forces in Ethiopia.

Guerrilla Warfare and the State

When people find it impossible to peacefully engage a government that fails to bring about political freedom and social justice, and their reasonable demands are met with harsh measures, they react individually or collectively in defiance of the status quo, often with the intent of bringing about the desired change. In this process, when conditions are conducive, an organized movement is formed. In many cases, the movements resort to unconventional ways and means struggle to achieve what they believe is legitimate, socially just and politically right. The fact that revolutionary social movements are reactions to social dislocation, perceived or real exploitation and disorder explains the salience of their search for social redress and cultural authenticity and their moral rigor (Walzer 1965; Arjomand 1986; Goldstone 1991). Committed revolutionary groups set the stage of the struggle but such groups do not necessarily have the organizational capacity and strength to confront head on an established state at least at the initial stage. Therefore, such revolutionary groups resort to unconventional method of struggle, one of them known as guerrilla warfare. Guerrilla war or as sometimes called insurgency movement is carried out by irregular forces to win over the mass of the population from the control of a government with the aim of finally overthrowing it. Guerrilla warfare is indeed an age-old tactic '[b]ut only in modern times has it become the acknowledged weapon of the weak, a symbol of our age, registering successes no less than setbacks from China to Cuba, Malaya to Mozambique' (Ahmad in Miller and Aya 1971: 137) and considered a component of the doctrine of 'peoples' war' as articulated by modern revolutionaries like Mao Tse-tung, Amilcar Cabral or Che Guevara. 'Once a revolutionary movement enters the guerrilla phase', Ahmad goes on, 'its central objective is not simply to achieve the moral isolation of the enemy but also to confirm, perpetuate, and institutionalize it by providing an alternative to the discredited regime through the creation of 'parallel hierarchies'' (ibid.: 157). This will be an ongoing process as the guerrilla forces gain strength and the warfare progresses from simple hit and run tactics to more regular engagements, like 'mobile' warfare or even pitched-battles.

The emergence and development of the guerrilla warfare as a means of engaging a repressive state assumes above all an uneasy relationship between the state and the peasant society. It is within this crucial relationship of the state and the peasant society that revolutionary groups find space to act. Some of the main features of peasants that create the ground for revolutionary movements are best explained by Harrison (2002: 48):

- Peasants are neither passive nor traditional, but are part of modern social system, acting and reacting from a position of relative weakness.
- Peasant society is defined by its resilience and flexibility in the face of external forces.
- A key feature of postcolonial agricultural 'development' has been the extraction of resources from the peasantry by state institutions.
- State elites have been antagonistic towards the plurality and 'tradition' of their peasant societies

The state, thus, faces not only ideologically motivated and elusive armed revolutionary elite but also a disgruntled mass of peasantry which is prepared to liberate itself from a repressive regime and consenting to embrace the challengers of the state. Various social classes that were repressed or marginalized by the regime are also agitated to join or support the armed revolutionary movement. It is quite evident that the form of the regime and its link to society is a crucial factor, for it in turn influences both the dynamics of the domestic political conflicts and coalitions (Skocpol 1994; Goodwin and Wickham-Crowley 1994). Furthermore, as Goodwin and Wickham-Crowley (1994) argue: '[a]rmed revolutionaries become truly mass-based challengers, only when they mobilized sustained support from more than peasants alone; they had to build nationalist support coalition that include rural people, urban workers, middle-class people, and even (in some cases) upper-class acquiescers'. The essence of the revolutionary struggle is therefore to completely isolate the state from the populace and push it to its grave. This is why '[g]uerrilla warfare is dependent on a high level of popular involvement to provide the demographic 'sea' for the insurgent 'fish' in Mao Tse-tung's oft-quoted metaphor' as Ahmad (1971) and Selden (1971) demonstrated.

As we discussed above, Skocpol (1994) looks into another dimension of the dynamics of the political conflict outside the domestic factors i.e. the external factor that heavily influence the balance of forces between the peasant-based armed revolutionaries and the state in third world countries. The involvement of foreign forces both materially and diplomatically at international level, evidently, influence outcomes of the armed confrontation between the state and insurgent movements as demonstrated empirically in the struggle of the TPLF against the Soviet-backed military government of Ethiopia.

If organizational and administrative coherence are maintained or disrupted by the intervention of external force which often is the case than not because of the prevalence of transnational forces globally, the balance will tilt accordingly depending on who harnesses the external reinforcement best. Therefore, welding together a broad coalition of different social groups – large segments of the middle class, the peasantry and urban workers - and foreign interests has been the key to successful insurrections (Dix 1984; Colburn 1994). Because armed revolutionary movements can have one or the other external support on their side either for ideological reasons or tactical interest, they understandably would have a better chance of winning the war against a repressive and isolated state. But even if we assume, more or less, similar level of external involvement, it is the internal dynamics, considering the coalition of revolutionary social classes and the peasants as actors, that dictates events at the end of the day.

Following the on-set of the revolutionary struggle, the behaviour of the state also plays a significant role in influencing the bondage between the elite segment of the revolution and the peasant masses. Skocpol (1994: 311) argues

> ...although all kinds of repressive and exclusive authoritarian regimes are potentially vulnerable to the growth (even sudden growth) of broad-based, cross-class organizations or alliances of revolutionary challengers, the fact is that such regimes can crush or fight off such challengers as long as their state organizations remain administratively and coercively coherent.

In their comparative analysis Skocpol (1994: 305-6) and Goodwin (1994) seem to agree that, 'neither sheer poverty nor peasant discontent, not merely modernization or class oppression, and certainly not the simple appearance of guerrillas or foreign aid to them, can explain the relative successes and failures of guerrilla revolutionary movements ..., apart from domestic governmental conditions'. Also Gurr in his introductory remarks emphasizes, '[t]here is a wealth of evidence and principle that repressive policies defeat their purpose, in the long run if not necessarily in the short run. ...But exclusive reliance on force eventually rises up the forces that destroy it (1970: x), and often a self-defeating fallacy is the perception of well established states, that dissidents will give up their resistance by the threat or application of great force. This analysis helps us understand to what extent a repressive regime (the militaristic *Dergue* of Ethiopia is a case in point) by employing sheer force and terror creates favourable conditions for revolutionary guerrilla movements (like the TPLF) to grow and be crowned as upholding a just and legitimate cause on behalf of the oppressed people. Indeed, '[i]f a regime responds to the threat or use of force with grater force, the effect is likely to be an intensification of resistance: dissidents will resort to greater force (Gurr 1970: 232) as they did so as to overthrow the *Dergue*'s regime.

The Linkage of Ethno-Nationalist Revolt and the TPLF: a Summary

From the theoretical discussions advanced this far, we can put in perspective the emergence and prevalence of the TPLF in the Ethiopian power politics and what the struggle guided by ethno-nationalist ideology has brought for the people of Tigrai and the various ethnic nationalities of Ethiopia. We can also look into whether such line of struggle has resolved or reduced, or on the contrary aggravated ethnic conflicts and tensions that have contributed to political instability and lack of development for a long time in the historical evolution of the country.

For people to revolt in the first place, there has to be repressive causes. These causes are often skilfully articulated by a group or coalition of contenders for power who advance an alternative organizational setup that removes the constraints hitherto imposed. The idea of self-determination, as encompassing 'all' rights including secession, seemed an attractive project of revolutionary movements in the 1960s and 1970s although its limits and application remain full of controversies. The secession option in particular tends to cement the 'we' vs. 'them' dichotomy and may end up in the disintegration of multi-ethnic societies like Ethiopia. In poor societies where resources are scarce and power is seen as a means to appropriate resources, ethnic groups and even emerging civil society can find it difficult to live in harmony.

As a mobilizing tool, ethno-nationalism has been effectively utilized by the revolutionary elite that led the TPLF. Evidently, the effective utilization of ethno-nationalism has created a formidable power of organized social classes that could have the strength to shake the government and change the status quo. Guided by the elite, the struggle of the mobilized people might have shaken a government and helped its elite to rise to power but whether that mobilized people could in turn effectively influence its leaders (the revolutionary political elite) remains questionable. Therefore, using the instrumentalist approach to ethno-nationalism, the TPLF evidently appears effective in swaying the masses of peasants and other social groups that conquered the well established Ethiopian state under the Dergue. It is within this theoretical framework that we venture to retrospectively and empirically assess the history of the TPLF.

Chapter 3

Prelude to Struggle: the Emergence of the TPLF

Introduction[14]

The movement for the 'right to self-determination' led by the TPLF began in the hills of western Tigrai. The origin of this movement was neither spontaneous nor an act of a few disgruntled elite members. There were well-grounded objective and subjective factors that gave rise to it. These could be explained both in historical as well as recent processes of state formation and the attendant power politics that marginalized the people of Tigrai and specifically its political elite. This chapter discusses, first the underlying causes of the widespread resentment in Tigrai that became the fertile ground for the emergence of a militant Tigraian elite that effectively utilized ethnic mobilization to create a force that would eventually capture state power. This refers to the political history of Tigrai. Tigrai was the centre of power and influence in the evolution of the Ethiopian state. The subsequent shift of the centrality of power and influence away from the Tigraian to the Amhara elite more often through force and manipulation but also because of external interventions put Tigraians at a disadvantage. The second aspect of the discussion focuses on the rivalry of the competing elites for hegemonic

14 Most of this chapter has appeared in *African Affairs* 103 (413), 2004, pp. 569-592 under the title *'The Origins of the Tigray People's Liberation Front'* and is used with kind permission of the publisher.

status, which obviously required a force to maintain dominance – a force that was generated by mobilizing an ethnic and/or regional constituency. This competition evidently depleted human and material resources of every region and ethnic group where such rivalry took place. Due to historical circumstances, Tigrai was one arena of elite contention and its people had to pay the consequences. The dismal situation in Tigrai in turn gave rise to the unrest in the form of armed uprising, associational activities and political movements.

Aware of this historical interaction, the Tigrai National Organization (TNO), an urban-based precursor of the TPLF, took the initiative to mobilize the people of Tigrai so that they would struggle to assert their rights in the form of self-determination. They articulated the theory and form of struggle that would help the people to come out of their prevailing despair. Their capacity of articulation and skill of organization gave them the vantage-point to lead the struggle on behalf of the people. Ethnic-based rhetoric accompanied by class interest theories were the main tactics of mobilization. Influential elderly people were also involved in the struggle as it was transformed from an urban-based movement to rural-based guerrilla warfare.

How It All Began

'Nothing can stop one who rebelled at heart' (*Bilebu zishefete memlesi yebilun*) is an Ethiopian-Tigraian saying, meaning 'Enough is enough'. When one is said to have 'rebelled at heart', one is poised to go even to war to achieve a certain goal. It is like saying 'War begins in the minds of people'. So was the war that was started by the Tigrai People's Liberation Front (TPLF) as a result of cumulative resentments felt by Tigraians against successive Ethiopian governments. With the certain expectation that thousands would embrace it, the TPLF's armed struggle against the Ethiopian government of the time, the military dictatorship of the *Dergue* (military committee) started on 18 February 1975 in an uninhabited remote region of Tigrai. A handful of Tigraians with four outdated rifles launched the armed struggle from Dedebit in the remote hills of Western Tigrai. In a subsequent protracted struggle that lasted for sixteen years, they mobilized Tigraians behind the front and created a large disciplined army that defeated not only rival fronts but also the military government itself. They finally seized power in Addis Ababa in May 1991 by toppling the military regime, one of the strongest in Sub-Saharan Africa. Prior to this historic event, a tenacious struggle in Tigrai had, however, been going on for many years in various forms against Emperor Haile Selassie's monarchic rule, creating the conditions for the

TPLF to emerge and grow rapidly. Beginning with the peasant uprising known as *Woyyane*[15] in 1942-43, legal and illegal political activities, strikes, underground activity, sporadic rebellions and even appeals for divine intervention were methods used to challenge repressive rule and to mitigate the difficult life of Tigraians.

Although such anti-government activities had also been taking place since 1961 in the other parts of Ethiopia, including armed uprisings[16] in Bale (1963-1968), Gojjam (1967) and Eritrea, none had been successful. Finally, in February 1974, a spontaneous revolution broke out at the centre that galvanized the entire Ethiopian population and brought a dramatic change of government. Almost without resistance, the once mighty Emperor was overthrown, and the whole monarchic structure and feudal system collapsed, but only to be replaced by a military dictator of the worst order. The military regime, which picked Marxism as its ideology *en route* to power, came to be more brutal in its dealings with the Ethiopian people than the imperial regime, notably vis-à- vis those who aspired for democracy and justice, and even more so with Tigraians and other marginalized nationalities whose demand was self-determination.

By July 1974 political power was fully in the hands of the military, a force better organized than any other socio-political group in the country because of its long-standing militarist tradition and organizational structures. On 12 September 1974, the *Dergue* had put the Emperor under house arrest and officially declared it had seized power. The young officers who constituted the majority of the *Dergue* elected the experienced and charismatic General Aman Michael Andom, an Eritrean and Tigrayan from Diramba-Tembien raised in Sudan, as a leader, only to execute him a few months later in November 1974 because of disagreements over a host of issues, among them the question of Eritrea. Aman M. Andom was replaced by General Teferi Banti, an Oromo, who was also killed shortly after being elected. Neither general was a *Dergue* member but they were chosen ostensibly to calm the swirling ideological and power controversies within the hastily formed *Dergue*. Colonel Mengistu Haile Mariam, a younger officer from the 3rd Army Division based in Harar and radicalized by the heat of the revolution, was at the centre of all these measures. Mengistu Haile Mariam emerged as a domineering leader of the *Dergue* and 'Ethiopia *Tikdem*' (Ethiopia First)

---

15 The Tigrigna term *Woyyane* means to rebel, or rebellion against an authority, as in *Abeye* or *Abeyot* in Ge'ez (an old Semitic language now used by the Ethiopian and Eritrean Orthodox Churches) and Amharic. The peasant uprising of 1942-43 in Tigrai was named *Woyyane*. The TPLF also called its movement *Kalai* (= 2nd) *Woyyane*.

16 For more understanding on the uprisings, including the '*Woyyane*' in Tigrai, see Gebru Tareke (1991), John Markakis (1990), Patrick Gilkes (1975).

which started as a common army slogan became the leading motto of the revolution. In fact, Ethiopia *Tikdem* turned out to be an ideology which had both a nationalist and a modernizing stance, thus '...directed against the weakening of the state by 'secessionist' movements' (Halliday and Molyneux 1981: 29). 'Mengistu's regime in no time revealed itself as essentially no different from the previous regime towards the assertive ethnic-nationalities, only this time accompanied by the harshness of military dictatorship' (Aregawi 2000: 99). The *Dergue*'s motto defined Ethiopia as a monolithic society, thereby declaring any ethno-nationalist grievance or demand for self-determination as being contrary to Ethiopian unity and interests. This rigid stand of centralization coupled with Marxian rhetoric of the military officers was warmly embraced by the former superpower, the Soviet Union, and supported both ideologically and politically. As Ismagilova (1994: 28) observed, 'advisors from the Soviet Union upheld dogmatic positions and advocated for the suppression of nationalist movements by force'. Although the *Dergue* pronounced a peaceful transition to socialism – 'garrison socialism' in the words of Markakis (1990: 237) – and enacted a series of populist declarations that seemed to benefit the working class and the peasantry, the moves of the *Dergue* were in themselves far from peaceful.

Nationalists, who opted for some sort of autonomous rule or self-determination but by no means amounting to demands for secession, were the prime targets of the *Dergue*, as were other democratic Ethiopian elements. With the emergence of a military regime in the midst of the political upheaval that had no organized leadership or well-thought-out guiding objectives, many people already anticipated what was to follow. The Tigraian University Students' Association (TUSA) was one such group that had foreseen the predicament that would come with the *Dergue*. It was during this period of political uncertainty, accompanied by the drums of terror, that many socio-political groups emerged as national and multinational political organizations to challenge military dominance. One such organization was the Tigraian National Organization (TNO) which evolved into the Tigrai People's Liberation Front (TPLF) and after sixteen years of guerrilla war became the government of Ethiopia.

This is how it all began. On 14 September 1974, seven university students, Zeru Gessese (Agazi),[17] Fantahun Zeratsion (Giday), Mulugeta Hagos (Asfaha), Ambay Mesfin (Seyoum), Alemseged Mengesha (Hailu), Amaha Tsehaye (Abbay) and Aregawi Berhe (Berihu) met in an inconspicuous café located in Piazza in the centre of Addis Ababa. *Ato* Gessesew Ayele (Sihul),

---

17 The names in bracket are 'field-names' (pseudonyms) given to the respective individual members of the Front to disguise their identity for fear of an enemy pursuit. In the early days of the guerrilla movement, most fighters had such field names.

twice an MP and still a popular representative of the Tigraians at the time, belonged to this group but could not attend the meeting for security reasons. All of them, including Sihul of course, had known each other for years in the struggle against the repression of Tigraians in particular and Ethiopians in general.

The aim of the meeting was to: (a) wrap up their findings about the nature and disposition of the *Dergue*'s regime with regard to the self-determination of Tigrai and the future of democracy in Ethiopia, (b) discuss what form of struggle to pursue and how to tackle the main challenges that would emerge, (c) outline how to work and coordinate activities with the Ethiopian left, which had until then operated according to much broader revolutionary ideals. These grand issues, quite general in scope, were not new as they had been digesting them informally for a while and by the end of the day became the basis of a two-page general guideline. The guideline[18] declared that:

- The strategy is the formation of a democratic Ethiopia in which equality of all nationalities is respected;

- A national armed struggle should be waged and advance from the rural area of Tigrai to the urban area; and

- The movement should be led by an urban-based organization known as the Tigraian National Organization (TNO) until the start of the armed struggle.

It was unanimously agreed that the TNO was a preparatory phase in the armed struggle and its founders collectively assumed tasks including propaganda and political work to prepare for the ensuing armed struggle, recruiting individuals as TNO members from whom combatants in the armed struggle would later be recruited, collecting materials and information necessary for the struggle, etc. To accomplish these and other tasks, TNO's founders had to reach and then organize the active elements in the Tigraian association and political movements, on whom they would rely in the painstaking fight ahead. It is therefore necessary to give a short account of the activities in the association and political movement from which the TNO sprung and on which it would depend so much in the following sixteen years of armed struggle in its attempt to bring down the military government. But first it would be pertinent to start with a brief historical overview that explains Tigrai's standing and the perception of Tigraians in the making of the Ethiopian polity.

---

18 The two-page guideline, handwritten in Tigrigna, was filed as a classified document in the TPLF archives and kept in Meqele, Tigrai. But after the split of the TPLF leadership in 2001 such documents are under the direct control of PM Meles Zenawi and stored in Addis Ababa.

Historical Roots of the Problem

It was not only the associational and political activities of the young elite that led to the ethno-nationalist mobilization of Tigraians in pursuit of change. Ethno-nationalism, after all, is not a phenomenon that should be characterized exclusively as an elite agenda, as some analysts perceive it. Esman (1994: 14) rightly pointed out that '...ethnicity cannot be politicised unless an underlying core of memories, experience, or meaning moves people to collective action'. Historical symbolism and accumulated grievances transmitted from generation to generation thus had their pivotal contribution in the Tigraian uprising. For many years, as will be seen later, Tigraians had been agitating for self-rule or self-administration in place of the remote autocratic control that prevailed. It is still the belief of many Tigraians that Tigrai, being the site of the ancient Ethiopian state, deserved much more than what the modern Ethiopian state could offer.

The recorded history of Ethiopia as a state has its foundation in the present Tigrai region in the 3rd century AD, then known as the kingdom of Aksum. The historian Kobishchanov (1979: 59) quotes the Persian prophet Mani (216-276 AD) who wrote: 'There are four great kingdoms on earth: the first is the kingdom of Babylon and Persia; the second is the kingdom of Rome; the third is the kingdom of the Axumites; the fourth is the kingdom of the Chinese'. Dating back to that time, the Aksumites had developed their own civilization that could be illustrated in their script *Ge'ez*, the number system *Kutir* and the calendar *Awde-Awarih* which are still in use today. Trade took them as far as Persia and India in the East and Greece and Rome in the West through the Red Sea ports of Adulis and Zeila. Their impressive architecture is reflected in the obelisks, buildings and tunnels that are still standing in Yeha and Aksum. At the end of the 3rd century AD, they had also started minting their own coins. In 340, the Aksumite King Abraha (Ezana) adopted Orthodox Christianity, which quickly became the religion of the inhabitants and provided the symbolism and substance of the royal ideology. With Aksum as a pivot, the Empire expanded over the Ethiopian highlands. The Aksumite civilization, according to Teshale Tibebu (1995: 3), who refers to it as Ge'ez civilization, had 'its core concentrated in the region from Debra Bizan in Eritrea to Debra Libanos in Showa'.

The flourishing of the Aksumite civilization however did not last beyond the 7th century. The expansion of Islam at the end of the 7th century, followed by the emergence of a pagan Agew Queen called Yodit at the beginning of the 10th century, led to the demise of the Aksumite Empire. Thus the political centre of the Ethiopian state began to shift southwards where it revived in the 13th century as a restyled Aksumite kingship under the dynasty of Zagwe, which succumbed to Yekuno Amlak in 1268. But a few centuries later another debacle occurred. The re-emergence of Islam from the east under Harari imam Ahmed ibn Ibrahim, nicknamed Ahmed 'Gragn' (= the left-handed) (1527-1543), with the support of the Ottoman rulers, followed by the Oromo (then termed 'Galla', a now pejorative term) migration from the south was a devastating blow to the remaining religious culture and declining civilization.

The gradual loss of dynamism of the centralized state in turn gave rise to the emergence of local kings and princes who were often entangled in endless wars for supremacy, ushering to a period of total anarchy. For instance, 'Northern Ethiopia (Tigre and present-day Eritrea) was divided into no less than twenty-four independent units' (Zewde Gabre-Selassie 1975: 2-3) and had by far the highest number of firearms compared to any other region in the country. During the period 1830-1850, Zewde Gabre-Selassie noted, there were 28,000 matchlocks in Tigrai while Begemidir, Showa, and Wollo had 4,000, 1,000 and 1,000 respectively (ibid.: 19). With the incursion of foreign invaders through the gateway of Tigrai, firearms became abundant in the region. This period of anarchy, which totally undermined the state, was known as the *Zemene Mesafint* (Era of Princes) and lasted from 1760-1855. War became a common occurrence, particularly in Tigrai, and the gun a highly revered asset of settling differences, replacing the tradition of peaceful conflict resolution by religious leaders and *shimagiles*[19] that had persisted for centuries.

Amid this anarchy, Kassa Hailu, a rebel from Gondar, became Emperor Tewodros (1855-1868) after defeating all the local kings and *rases*,[20] and managed at last to resurrect a semblance of centralism and stability in Ethiopia based on the same Aksumite religious ideology. Kahsay Mircha, a rebel from Tigrai, succeeded Tewodros as Emperor Yohannes (1872-1889) and was crowned in Aksum. Despite their success in re-establishing the Ethiopian state, the reigns of these two emperors were neither stable nor peaceful due to internal conflicts and external invasions. Locally, lords who aspired to power had been rebelling whenever conditions favoured them (see Wylde 1970; Zewde Gabre-Selassie 1975; Gilkes 1975; Erlich 1981; and Markakis 1990). Also, external forces, including Britain in 1868, Egypt in 1875-76, Sudanese Mahdists in 1889 and Italy in 1887-96 and

---

19 A *shimagile* literally is an elderly person but in a broader sense of the word it connotes one who has the wisdom and legitimacy to help resolve conflicts. While religious leaders use their power to restrain conflicts, *shimagiles* use their wisdom and influence to resolve and settle conflicts.

20 *Ras*, literally 'head' and equivalent to a duke, was a title next to the king in power and could be given to a provincial governor, a prince or a minister.

1935, carried out a series of incursions that made defence of the country the main preoccupation of the rulers and the people, thereby disrupting stability. The greatest war burden, as mentioned above, was inflicted on the gateway to Ethiopia, Tigrai, and on the Tigraians. Noting the recurrence of wars against foreign invaders, Haggai Erlich (1981: 195) wrote that 'some 20 major battles were fought on Tigraian soil between the Battle of Adwa (1896) to the Italian invasion of 1935. Even before the Battle of Adwa, a series of similar battles took place in Tigrai. For instance, *Ras* Alula encountered foreigner invaders at least sixteen times, 'winning some ten decisive battles – from the clash with the Egyptians in Gurae in 1876 to the Battle of Adwa against the Italians twenty years ago' (Erlich 1996: ix). When such battles against foreign forces declined, local wars that were equally and sometimes even more devastating took place. The battles against foreign invaders were fought to protect Ethiopia from aggression and some took place outside Tigrai. Ethiopians of different ethnic nationalities, religion and gender have shed their blood on fronts far from home. Yet, the fact that many of them and the major ones took place in Tigrai – the gateway of the invaders – had long-lasting and devastating effects on the region that were felt deeply by succeeding generations.

Local wars among regional chiefs and to resist the emergence of Kassa Hailu and later Kahsay Mircha as Emperors Tewodros and Yohannes were countless. The peasant population was constantly forced to side with one or other warlord in the battles and to feed their predatory armies. Not only was a family's food supply for a year or more consumed instantly but food production was also hampered as the population was forced to engage in war too.

On top of these wars, famine was taking its toll, dislodging the working population and dismantling the fabric of society that had been built up for centuries based on Aksumite civilization. As Young observed (1997: 49), '... in the period between the death of Yohannes in 1889 and the present day an estimated seventeen famines have struck Tigrai, the biggest being in 1958-9, 1965-6, 1972-4, and 1983-4'. During these periods of famine, millions died and still more were displaced from their homes. The spiralling combination of foreign assaults, local wars and famines left Tigrai destitute.

Subsequent Ethiopian leaders – Emperors Menelik II (r. 1889-1913) and Haile Selassie I (r. 1930-1974) did not bother to address or attempt to mitigate the state of Tigrai, which was left to find its own course. The interest of the dominant elite during the imperial period had been to defend the interest of the landed class and Orthodox Christianity in general and the Amhara elite in particular (Addis Hiwot 1975; Gebru 1977, 1996; Teshale 1995, Merera 2002). In addition, the extensive wars in this Ethiopian gateway, notably at Adwa (1896) and Maichew (1935) sapped the energy of the productive forces and the region was devastated. During Menelik's reign, Gebrehiwet Baykedagne (1912: 12), a political economist at the time wrote, 'there are hardly any Tigraian youth left in their birth place, Tigrai. Like a swarm of bees without their queen, they are aimlessly scattered in four corners of the earth. Some people ridiculed their widespread poverty. Unfortunately, whilst other people live in tranquillity, Tigrai has never been free from wars, leave alone outlaws and bandits'. Although the Italian occupation of Ethiopia in 1936-41 roused resistance throughout Ethiopia (see Aregawi 2003), the intensity of the guerrilla movement was more pronounced in Tigrai, as it was the aggressors' launching pad. This situation seemed to have no end. While regions adjacent to Tigrai were also markedly affected by these calamities, the southern part of Ethiopia was relatively stable and gave sanctuary – but also derogatory names – to fleeing Tigraians. Their mobility was sarcastically linked with a Land Rover to highlight how they roamed over large rugged areas of the country and that their region was condemned to 'growing rocks' instead of grain.

Years later, when in 1942-43 central and southern Tigrai peasants began to rebel not only out of desperation but also as *Blata* Haile Mariam, one of the rebel leaders put it, '...to liberate Tigray from Showan Amhara hegemony if the central government failed to respond to the call of the rebels and reform itself' (in Gebru Tareke 1991: 186), their plight was met with a harsh response. Haile Selassie's government in collaboration with the British Royal Air Force (RAF) after first dropping threatening leaflets addressed to 'The Chiefs, *Balabats* – People of Tigre Province' on 6 October, devastated the region including Meqele, the capital of Tigrai, also in October 1943.. The peasant uprising known as Woyyane (meaning 'revolt') was quelled. Thousands of civilians lost their lives as a result of aerial bombardments. 'On 14th October 54 bombs dropped in Meqele, 6th October 14 bombs followed by (unknown number) bombs on 9th October in Hintalo, 7th/9th October 32 bombs in Corbetta' (Gilkes 1975: 180). But it did not stop there. The people in that region were also forced to pay large sums of money and their land was confiscated and distributed to loyal gentry as a punishment and deterrent against future revolt. A new taxation system was imposed that 'cost the peasants five times more than they had paid under the Italians' (Erlich 1981: 219). In the name of centralization, Haile Selassie took away regional power from hereditary leaders and gave it to loyal administrators, most of whom were from Showa[21]. This predicament

21 Showa is a region from which the Amharic-speaking ruling elite of Ethiopia, who largely monopolized political power, originated. This class of Showan elites governed the rest of Ethiopia from the beginning of the nineteenth century, the period of consolidation of modern Ethiopia. See also the Gerry Salole, 'Who Are the Showans', in *Horn*

again raised the level of collective resentment, taking the form of ethno-nationalist sentiment against the Showan ruling class. As Gilkes (1975: 187) observed, 'Independence from Showan rule was raised as a rallying cry and proved popular'. The British administrators in Eritrea at the time – for their own strategic interests – keenly supported the popular cry of Tigraians that their hereditary leaders should rule Tigrai, thereby concurring with the growing awareness of Tigraian nationalism. 'Before the British, the Italians had already advanced this policy in what they named *politica tigrina*', (Erlich 1981: 195). Indeed there were many factors that nurtured the simmering Tigraian ethno-nationalism.

Not only grievances but also collective resentment towards power holders at the centre were gradually building up and were passed on to future generations. As a result, nobody seemed to recognize the authority of the central government, and sporadic rebellion, locally known as *shiftinnet* (banditry),[22] became a common occurrence. The idiom in which it was expressed was ethno-regional identity. As Esman stated, 'Ethnicity is, thus, shaped by environment, by the threats and opportunities it affords' (1994: 14).

In the 1950s and 1960s some of the rebels, however, were attempting to set up a movement with a broader perspective. Like Haile-Mariam Reda who led the Woyyane, the 1942-43 Tigraian peasant revolt, Gessesew Ayele was striving hard to create a broad-based rebellion against the government. When the forerunner of the Eritrean Liberation Front (ELF), Hamed Idris Awate, who had started as an individual *shifta*, set out to wage armed struggle in Eritrea in 1961, many Tigraians, including Gessesew Ayele (Sihul) made contact with him. Many politicized Tigraians showed sympathy and admiration for the insurgents in Eritrea not in support of the secessionist agenda that was gradually taking shape but out of their resentment for the government that had left the people of Tigrai in misery and despair. Emulating the Eritrean movement as a courageous challenge, many radical elements had, since 1970, been forming groups that were contemplating an armed struggle to assert the rights of Tigraians. Besides Sihul, many other individuals, among them Amare Tesfu, Tekeste Wubneh, Mussie Kidane, Gebre-Meskel Hailu, Raswork Ketsela, Aregawi Berhe, Mulu Tesfay, and Atsbaha Hastire, were involved in such challenges. In 1973, for instance, Amare Tesfu's group would have started an armed rebellion in Tigrai had it not been for the split that occurred at the last minute on the nature of the

---

of Africa 2(3), 1979, pp. 20-29.

22 For a broader understanding of *shiftinnet*, see Timothy Fernyhough, 'Social Mobility and Dissident Elites in Northern Ethiopia: the Role of Banditry, 1900-1969', in D. Crummey (ed.), *Banditry, Rebellion and Social Protest in Africa*, 1986, pp. 151-172.

Eritrean fronts with whom a working relationship was to be established. Amare and Tekeste preferred cooperation with the ELF, while others favoured the EPLF. These groups retained their differences until later years, when they found themselves in one or other front but actually fighting the regime they all wanted to get rid of.

Although it was hoped that the Ethiopian revolution that overthrew the Showan-Amhara-dominated regime of Emperor Haile Selassie would address the plight of the Tigraians, such expectations soon proved unrealistic as the military fully intervened towards the end of 1974. The military regime of Colonel Mengistu Haile Mariam that emerged did not waste any time in proving to be an enemy of Tigraian aspirations. Thus, many Tigraian ethno-nationalist groups were formed who would not mediate with such a regime but geared up to assert their rights through the 'barrel of the gun'[23]. One such group was the TNO, which eventually evolved into the TPLF.

The Growth of Associations

With its ancient and medieval historic monuments and churches across the land, Tigrai still looked like a ruined village ravaged by wars and neglected by successive governments. Local conflicts and major Ethiopian wars against foreign invaders fought in Tigrai severely damaged its agricultural system, the livelihood on which 98% of its population depended, and stifled the initiative of the peasantry to produce and lead a more prosperous life. The series of battles that ravaged Tigrai were mentioned earlier. Recurring drought and famine also caused general decline. At the close of the 20th century, agricultural practices were still ancient and backward. No single industry existed to mitigate the stagnation of agriculture. Under *Ras* Mengesha Seyoum, the last hereditary governor of Tigrai, an incense-processing factory was opened in Meqele in late 1960 but soon collapsed. The machinery was bought from India but was outdated, was probably second or third hand, and there was no money to revitalize it. Tigraians had to migrate to the former Italian colony of Eritrea, or to Addis Ababa and other southern Ethiopia cities in search of work, as conditions were relatively better there. But at the same time it earned them derogatory names that wounded their pride. This dismal picture of Tigrai persisted for decades and its young generation grew up with feelings of desperation, which contributed to revolt. The neglect of Tigrai in the 1900s until the 1974 revolution was perceived by many Tigraians as a deliberate and systematic

---

23 'Political power grows out of the barrel of a gun' was a dictum of Mao Tse-tung, frequently reiterated by the revolutionary generation of the time, ethno-nationalists and/ or multi-nationalists alike.

policy of the Showa-Amhara ruling class to weaken and demoralize them. This view was a reflection of the historical rivalry between the two ruling houses and the Tigraian and Amhara aristocratic classes. Once again it should be emphasized that, as Hizkias Assefa (1996: 35) rightly puts it, 'this situation does not mean that the great majority of the Amhara people have been 'dominators' or beneficiaries of the political, economic or social system that bore their name'.

The educational situation in Tigrai was also dismal. There was no university or college until the mid-1990s and there were only four high schools, but these offered inadequate teachers and facilities for a population of about 3 million people and had only been built in the late 1960s. High school students had been engaged in sporadic movements to protest the dismal conditions of their schools and the misery reigning in the region in general, but had no associational structure through which they could pursue their demands. A few educated Tigraians began to raise their voice against the social injustices that had befallen Tigrai. Among the initial activists according to Mitiku Asheber,[24] an activist himself, were Desta Bezabih, Abebe Tesema, Tesfay Teklu, Rezene Kidane and Gebremeskel Abbay, while elders like *Ato* Gessesew Ayele and Bahta Gebrehiwet were giving them official backings. With the collaboration of *Ras* Mengesha Seyoum, a semi-legal cultural association called *Bahli*-Tigrai was formed, thanks to the efforts of people like *Ato* Gessesew Ayele, *Ato* Hagos Alemayehu, *Ato* Desta Bezabih, and others. Hundreds of students and teachers participated actively in this association to promote their culture and assert their Tigraian identity. But so many hurdles were imposed by the central government that the association fizzled away in the space of two to three years. A weekly newspaper called *Semyenawi Kokeb* (Northern Star) was also set up but that closed as well.

At the Haile Selassie I University (H.S.I.U., now renamed Addis Ababa University), however, the political atmosphere was to a certain extent conducive for students to articulate their grievances and get together to form associations of one kind or another, but not without cost. At home and at school, students were persistently uneasy about the difficult life and oppressive system that the majority, from which they came, had to endure and the luxurious lifestyle the ruling classes were enjoying in this poor country. Thus most students from Tigrai, when they joined the university, took it as part of their student life to participate actively in protests calling for change either at a national or regional level. This was why many university students from Tigrai had been playing a prominent role in the struggle against Haile Selassie's feudal regime. They were not aiming to

---

24 Interview: Mitiku Asheber, Silver Spring, MD, USA, 24 July 2003.

restore Tigraian hegemony, as some naïve politicians have presented it. In actual fact, they were comrades in struggle with revolutionary students like Wallelign Mekonnen (a Wollo Amhara) who had been writing persuasive articles, including 'On the Question of Nationalities in Ethiopia'.[25]

Teachers and students from all districts of Tigrai also converged at H.S.I. University in Addis Ababa and raised issues concerning their region. Land degradation, recurring famine, mass unemployment, political marginalization, cultural domination and different social problems were some of the issues raised by students. They compared the level of these problems with those in other regions of Ethiopia and believed the conditions in Tigrai to be by far the worst. This assessment was more often expressed sentimentally in relation to the past glory of Tigrai and its standing in the history of Ethiopian nation building. This movement began in the late 1960s when the pan-Ethiopian student movement was growing in scope. Earlier prominent activists in the Tigraian students' movement included people like Sibhatu Wibneh (killed by Haile Selassie's security agents in 1970), Giday Gebrewahid (killed in mid-1975 by the *Dergue* soon after it came to power), Amare Tesfu (killed in early 1975 by a group called the TLF, of which he was a member), Tesfay Teklu, Mitiku Asheber, Abebe Tesema, Desta Bezabih, Atsbaha Hailemariam, Gebrekidan Desta, Rezene Kidane and others. The Tigraian University Students Association (TUSA) was formed in the early 1970s. The TUSA had pledged to function not only in Addis Ababa but also in Tigrai when the university closed for vacation. Many Tigraian university students, including all the founding members of the TNO (precursor of the TPLF) were involved in the association's activities both during and after the school year. As members of the university community, they were also actively participating at all levels of the Ethiopian student movement and, in most cases, taking a leading role. Oqbazgi Beyene was writing revolutionary articles. Meles Tekele, later killed by the *Dergue*, and Abbay Tsehaye, who still survives in the EPRDF leadership today, were TUSA members who led the editorial branch of the university students' union. Aregawi Berhe headed the university's political science students' association for a year (1972-73) and Berhane Eyasu, a leading member of the leftist Ethiopian People's Revolutionary Party (EPRP) who was killed fighting the *Dergue* was also a TUSA activist before he joined the EPRP.

In Addis Ababa, TUSA's function was limited to discussions of a political nature and to contacting influential people such as parliamentary

---

25 Wallelign Mekonnen had unmasked the plight of oppressed nationalities of Ethiopia with his influential article *'On the Question of Nationalities in Ethiopia'* in the publication of the University Student's Union of Addis Ababa, *Struggle,* vol. V, no. 2 (17 November 1969).

members, businessmen and professional people from Tigrai to encourage them to contribute something tangible to mitigate the dismal situation in Tigrai. To broaden ethno-nationalist awareness and reflect on necessary measures, occasional informative papers like *Etek* (Get Armed) and *Dimtsi Bihere Tigrai* (Voice of the Tigrai Nation) were produced and distributed freely to the people. Such activities were inflammatory in nature nevertheless attracted many Tigraians who were engaged in various walks of life to the political arena where the authority of Emperor[26] was beginning to face open challenges from different section of the society other than students. The contribution of Tigraian Members of Parliament like *Ato* Gessesew Ayele (Sihul), *Ato* Asfaw Wolde-Aregay, *Ato* Alemseged Gebre-Egziabiher, Weyzero Tsehaytu Gebresellassie, *qegnazmach* Teklit Mekonnen and *Ato* Zenawi Tekola was immense, both in terms of financial input and advice. Also intellectuals and professionals, among them *Ato* Bekele Berhane, Dr Assefa Abraha, Dr Itbarek Gebre-Egziabiher, *Ato* Tsegaye Hailu, *Ato* Hagos Atsbaha, *Ato* Kidane Asayehgn, *Ato* Aynalem Aregehegn and Dr Tesfay Berhe gave initial support to the movement. Such people and many others saw themselves as victims of ethnic repression and political persecution. *Ato* Alemseged G. Egziabiher, for instance, was tortured in prison for months under the Haile Selassie regime for his progressive views as a parliamentarian.[27] The major activities of the association, however, were carried out in the eight *awrajas* (districts) of Tigrai, particularly during the rainy season Ethiopian winter when the university closed for vacation. Supplementary education for high school students, developmental work like reforestation and political awareness-raising were the focus of the association's activities. The educational and developmental activities were discharged with legal permits and the cooperation of the then governor of Tigrai, *Ras* Mengesha Seyoum. On one occasion, when leading TUSA members approached the *Ras* in Addis Ababa, he went so far as to openly criticize various ministers, particularly the minister of education at the time, for standing in the way of his developmental policies in Tigrai. This was an unexpected remark from a governor who belonged to the ruling class. Unlike his traditionalist father *Ras* Seyoum, who belonged to Emperor Haile Selassie's generation, *Ras* Mengesha was well-educated and styled himself as a modernizer. By setting himself as an example, he made several attempts to reform the negative attitude towards manual labour that was prevalent

26 Under Emperor Haile Selassie, the 1955 Constitution stated in no uncertain terms that the king was above censure: 'By virtue of His Imperial Blood, as well as by the anointing which He received, the person of the Emperor is sacred, his dignity inviolable and his powers indisputable ... Anyone so bold as to seek to injure the Emperor will be punished' (Article 4).

27 Interview: Alemseged Gebre-Egziabiher, Los Angeles, CA, USA, 18 August 2003.

among the well-to-do class in Tigrai. He in person participated in several development activities that required hard labour: he opened new roads, built a number of bridges and encouraged entrepreneurs in the field of agriculture, particularly in cash crop plantations. His reformist endeavours earned him a degree of popularity among a section of the urban elite. Later when he formed the EDU to counter the *Dergue*, it was part of this group that joined his movement or became clandestine supporters for his movement from the towns. In the eyes of many, *Ras* Mengesha was a benevolent governor in Ethiopian royalty who opened up, among other things, a limited space for TUSA members to conduct their activities.

The political awareness activities of the TUSA, however, were carried out without the knowledge of the *Ras* or other government authorities, which would have thwarted every activity of the association were they to learn that they themselves were blamed for collaborating with the oppressors in the central government. Essentially, *Ras* Mengesha himself was seen as an accomplice of the ruling stratum both by marriage and class-interest, and hence an element to be removed by the winds of change.

While advancing the associational programme, clandestine groups were organized to study Marxist dialectics, the class struggle, the national question and other revolutionary issues at the time. These study groups would use every legal opportunity to disseminate their revolutionary ideas with the aim of raising the level of consciousness of the people as a whole. The dissemination of revolutionary ideas was carried out through leaflets, songs and informal discussions. Everybody seemed motivated at the time either to give or receive revolutionary ideas that advocated change, and the call for armed struggle to get rid of the oppressive feudal regime was entertained without actually ever being mentioned.

Within the association, a politically conscious group that aimed at creating a higher form of organization by the name of *Mahber Gesgesti Bihere Tigrai* (MAGEBT) evolved at the beginning of 1974. Literally translated it read as the Association of Progressives from the Tigrai Nation, but for convenience it was named the Tigraian National Organization (TNO). TNO was later to become the mother organization of the TPLF. While these TNO-led activities were underway, another group called the Political Association of Tigraians (PAT or *Mahber Politica*), led by Yohannes Teklehaimanot and Gebre-Kidan Asfaha was involved underground in a purely political mobilization of Tigraians against the Ethiopian regime. This association advocated outright independence of Tigrai and later emerged as an armed organization known as the Tigrai Liberation Front (TLF), which will be discussed in later chapters.

A Political Movement

The Ethiopian student movement of the 1960s and 1970s was marked by a political radicalism the country had never before experienced. It was full of eventful struggles against 'imperialism' and 'feudalism' – systems that were believed to have kept Ethiopia in a backward stage of development. Most of the younger generation who had been through high school and university were revolutionary enthusiasts along this ideological and political wave. Their dream was to change Ethiopia's backwardness in a revolutionary manner by paying whatever sacrifices were required – sacrifices that sometimes surpassed their limits. At times, they played the role of a political party in opposition. The experiences of Bolshevik Russia, Maoist China, Ho Chi Min's Viet Nam and Che Guevara's internationalism were espoused as guiding precedents to redeem Ethiopia from its predicament. The revolutionary student generation of the time was, as it proved later on, poised to render any service in uprooting the grips of 'imperialism' and 'feudalism' in the country. This revolutionary fervour was part of the international wave of the 1960s. Marxist revolutionary ideals were thought to be the only appropriate guiding tenets through which the country could be transformed.

Although a class-based ideological orientation was prevalent among the student body, ethno-national mobilization was an additional and concomitant ideological stance in the students' movement. Marx's position on the Irish national question, i.e., that it had to be resolved for the British proletariat to advance to socialism, was recalled to justify the question of nationalities in Ethiopia. Also Leninist and Stalinist theories on the national question were utilized as tools in combating national oppression in Ethiopia. Revolutionary students referred to Ethiopia as the 'prison house of nationalities'.

Ethno-nationalist sentiment among the young educated class was expedited by several factors. On the one hand, the monopoly of power in the grip of the Showan-Amhara 'feudal class' that fostered its ethnic hegemony and was held as keeping Ethiopia in the dark was the prime cause for ethnic resistance. On the other hand, the influence of the previous rebellions in Tigrai (1942-43 Woyyane), in Gojjam (1967 revolt), in Bale (1963-68 rebellion) and in Eritrea (the 1960s and 1970s armed struggle) served as historical precedents to challenge the existing state of affairs. Those who came from marginalized ethnic nationalities wanted to assert their denied identity and equality by all means. Revolutionary students from the dominant nationality, the Amhara, also upheld the principle of the 'right of nations to self-determination'. Wallelign Mekonnen (see above) in his influential article on the national question in Ethiopia in November 1969 had stated that '…Ethiopia was not a nation, but a collection of nationalities ruled by the Amharas. To be an Ethiopian, you will have to wear an Amhara mask' (cited in Kiflu Tadesse 1993: 54). Moreover, the negative and repressive reaction of the state towards such sentiments and the dreadful conditions in respective ethnic localities were other important factors that solidified ethno-nationalist sentiment among the various ethnic groups.

Members of the TNO, who saw no contradiction or ignored any idea of incompatibility in the class and ethno-national forms of struggle, actively participated in both forms of the struggle. If and when guided by a Marxist ideology, the ethno-nationalist movement was presumed to be a sub-set of the class struggle, the former levelling the way for the latter. For them the struggle for a democratic Ethiopia was tantamount to bestowing the right to self-determination to its components, where all people could live harmoniously in a fairly defined political and economic relationship. However, those who saw ethno-national struggle as a tactic for achieving equality within a united Ethiopia and not as a strategy for secession were not aware of the turns and zigzags that ethno-nationalist mobilization could take. They were not able to see that 'the more politicised ethnicity becomes, the more it dominates other expressions of identity, eclipsing class, occupational, and ideological solidarities' (Esman 1994: 15) and would turn ominous. The young revolutionaries focused only on the positive contribution of ethno-nationalist mobilization as the most effective and shortest way to uproot the oppressive system. They appeared to agree with Horowitz (1994: 49) who put emphasis on the positive aspect of ethnicity and ethnic affiliations as providing a sense of security. The turns and zigzags inherent in ethno-nationalism were later to surface with the growth of the TPLF. They failed to see in advance elements that managed to obscure class, occupational and ideological solidarities and, even more so, common historical realities.

In Tigrai, the Woyyane uprising of 1943 in it alone might not have invoked the ethno-nationalist sentiment exhibited in the young revolutionaries of the 1970s. There was more to it. The subsequent punitive measures of the central government and especially the bombardment of Meqele, the capital of Tigrai, by the British Royal Air Force (RAF) on behalf of Haile Selassie's government, was one popular grievance. The neglect of the region even when it was experiencing its worst famine on record, in 1972-74, that left more than half the population destitute, plus the cultural domination, as reflected in the linguistic disparities, were some of the other factors that led to ethno-nationalist-based resentment. These grievances were well articulated by Tigraian students. The persistent failure of the state to resolve the simmering resentments in their respective localities became clear and spurred ethno-nationalist mobilization.

In this political atmosphere, progressive Tigraian students formed the TNO and continued participating actively in the Pan-Ethiopian student movement. They played an active role in all the major political activities that brought about the downfall of Haile Selassie's monarchy. When the Provisional Military Administrative Council (PMAC) or *Dergue* took over, they still persisted in forming a Pan-Ethiopian front to get rid of the military administration and institute a civilian participatory democratic system. TNO members played an outstanding role in exposing the cynicism behind the *Dergue*'s 'Campaign of Development and Co-operation' in 1975-76 – a scheme intended to disperse the critical student body and control or eliminate its radical elements. In the course of these revolutionary days it was discovered that eight prominent members of the TNO because of their high profile in the revolutionary activities were on the hit list of the *Dergue*'s security office. This revelation forced not only those on the list but also other radical Tigraians to go underground or leave the *Dergue*-controlled areas and find shelter in rural Tigrai or abroad. Some of these who stayed behind in the *Dergue*-controlled area – revolutionaries like Meles Tekle, Giday Gebrewahid, Abraha Hagos and many others were soon killed by the *Dergue*. Those who left for rural Tigrai were not just going in search of mere shelter but also to find the ways and means to launch resistance against the government. The TNO had contacts with many of these radical Tigraians and later it was not difficult to assemble them in the TPLF. The TNO's political goals seemed to have been achieved ahead of time when it transformed itself into an armed organization, the TPLF, later in February 1975. Some critics argue that the TNO should have joined either the 'revolutionary *Dergue*' or other multi-national organizations[28] before rushing to forge the ethno-nationalist TPLF. However, under the circumstances of that period which was already discussed above, both options turned out to be unacceptable.

The Role of Sihul[29]

In the traditional society of Tigrai, hardly anybody took the students' movement seriously, and when it came to waging an armed struggle, elders scorned it immediately and said mockingly: 'they must be joking'; 'they

---

28 The nearest any organization the TNO could have worked with was the *Democracia-Abeyot* group which later formed the EPRP, but differences on the question of self-determination and more so on the nature of the struggle that had to be waged against the military *Dergue* kept them apart. TNO stressed rural-based armed struggle while the EPRP opted for urban-based insurrection.

29 Sihul was a 'field name' (pseudonym), given to Gessesew Ayele during the armed struggle.

will return to their mothers tomorrow'. People probably remembered the harsh experiences of past suppression, like in the 1943 Woyyane revolt. But for one elder Tigraian politician, *Ato* Gessesew Ayele (Sihul), though of a different generation than the revolutionary students he joined, to wage an armed struggle in the 1970s was not an impossible notion. Sihul was in his late fifties when he left his family and his well-paid public post to indeed start armed struggle with a few young university students in their early twenties. It was not the first time for Sihul to rebel against a repressive system. As a young boy of 14, he had resisted the Fascist Italians who occupied Ethiopia from 1935 to 1941 and went with his uncle as far as the Southern Front to fight the invaders. In 1962, he rebelled against Haile Selassie's monarchic rule and once met Idris Awate, a prominent fighter in the Eritrean Liberation Front (ELF), to create a 'unity of struggle'. It did not materialize because of the Eritrean secessionist stance. Gessesew was a committed Ethiopian nationalist who never embraced the secession of Tigrai as an option, unlike some of his young revolutionary comrades. He was a man who rebelled against higher authorities whenever he observed that they were failing to respect or render justice to ordinary people.

His rebellious character in imperial Ethiopia, where absolute loyalty to higher authorities was expected and could not be questioned, gained him popularity not only in his own district of Shire but also in the whole province of Tigrai. Whether he held a government post or not, his house at Enda-Selassie, Shire, was full of peasants with problems seeking his advice and influence. He held many government posts but soon when he found himself at loggerheads with senior authorities, including *Ras* Mengesha Seyoum, the last hereditary governor of Tigrai, he went back to his locality to pursue his rebellious life. In the early 1970s, the people of Shire had overwhelmingly voted for him to represent them in the Ethiopian parliament. Time and again, he stood not only for the cause of his constituency but also for general Ethiopian causes. At last, he felt he had to rise up in arms against the military dictators who had toppled Haile Selassie's regime, although the new rulers had promised to elevate him to higher posts considering his background and popularity.

Gessesew Ayele was not only just one of the founders of the TPLF but also a person whose background and personality made an immense contribution to the smooth development of the TPLF, especially in the initial stage of the struggle. Dedebit, a remote terrain in Shire, was selected as the place to start the armed struggle because Sihul had prior knowledge of this area and, more importantly, he had the respect of the people living in the villages adjacent to this land. The people in these villages would definitely have been hostile to the unknown students whose activities were centred only in the towns. When representatives of the people in Shimelba, Tselimoye and Adi-Mohamedai, three villages surrounding Dedebit, were approached by the front to render their support, they did not hesitate. This compliance was granted not because they understood the objectives of the emerging front or because of the young revolutionary students, but simply because Sihul, whose views they knew well and whom they respected deeply, was in it. Thus, it was not surprising that for some months to follow the front had been referred to not by its proper name, the TPLF, but as a group that belonged to Gessesew Ayele.

When the armed struggle started on 18 February 1975, Gessesew got his nickname 'Sihul' after the 18th century powerful Tigraian warrior and king-maker *Ras* Mikael Sihul whose strength was felt as far as Gondar and Wollo (cf. Abbink 2007). *Ras* Mikael Sihul was known for his decisive action and for getting rid of, in his opinion, inept or 'illegitimate' emperors and replacing them with those of his own choice. He removed King Iyoas in 1769 and '... was responsible for placing the next two Emperors on the throne' (Gilkes 1975: 7). But Gessesew Ayele was a man of higher political persuasion in a different era. He grew up in the heat of the Ethiopian Patriotic struggle against the Italian invasion (1935-41) and was politically shaped in the era of Ethiopia's struggle for modernization and democratic revolution of the 1960s and early 1970s. His passion for justice for ordinary people explains why, at an elderly age, he joined young radical students to wage an armed struggle for political change and more self-determination for Tigrai.

Sihul belonged to an extended family, was married to *Woizero* Zimam Gebre-Hiwet, who supported him throughout his rebellious life, and had seven children. Although he was kind and caring to his family, domestic responsibility did not stop him from once again engaging in the armed struggle against the new military dictators that later would cost him his life in 1976. This commitment earned him a lot of respect, even from his rivals. Asked about the death of her husband, *Woizero* Zimam often said '*Nebir bitemot lij teketta*'[30] (i.e., 'If a panther dies, it leaves behind offspring').

Sihul's role in the struggle was irreplaceable. As said above, without him the unknown TPLF would have found it difficult to survive and expand in the *shifta* (bandit)-infested district of Shire. Some of the *shiftas* of the criminal type, like Alem Eshet, considered themselves kings of their domain. They owned automatic rifles and commanded large groups of bandits. They knew the rocky terrain like their backyard and how to negotiate it. They could sweep from their territory any unfamiliar group like a TNO if not for the respect and popularity commanded by Sihul. The name Sihul and that of his

30 *Woizero* Zimam also said this in an interview with the daily *Addis Zemen*, Meskerem 9, 1991 (Ethiopian Calendar).

younger brother Berhane Ayele appeared more than a match to any group of *shiftas* in the district. At that early stage of the struggle, even fellow peasant fighters used to treat the student fighters as 'kids who only know how to play with paper' and believed that they should be led by the peasants who could manage a gun. Unless the university students proved that they were worthy to fight and lead an armed struggle, the path for the front would have been rocky and costly, had it not been for the presence of Sihul. Mainly because of what he stood for in the previous years the TPLF had no problem in building up legitimacy and popularity right from the beginning. Thus, from the start the respect he earned to this day and the determination he exhibited in fighting for the cause of Tigraians gave the Front this legitimacy and popularity, that none of its other members could procure. Indeed, Sihul's role in the struggle was immense and requires special emphasis. Further details of Sihul's role in the TPLF will come up in coming chapters.

The People on the Eve of the Armed Insurrection

The population of Tigrai in the 1960s was estimated to be about two million (Markakis 1990: 250) and in the 1970s was estimated to be about five million (by the TPLF party magazine *Woyeen*, August 1978: 4). But the 1994 Population and Housing Census of Ethiopia recorded it as 3.1 million.[31] More than 75% of the population speak *Tigrigna*, an old spoken and written language but since the 1940s forbidden in schools and courts by the central government. It could therefore not develop. The other spoken languages were Afar, Saho, Agew and Kunama. More than 90% of the people lived in the rural areas, engaged in agriculture with a small percentage of pastoralists living in the lowlands. In the densely populated highlands, because land had been privately owned for generations in a system known as *rist,* in which every lineal family member could claim a plot, land fragmentation increased the fragile base of agricultural production, forcing the bulk of the peasantry to live below subsistence. Still worse, recurring famines (like that of 1972, 1973 and 1974) as a result of drought and locusts claimed the lives of tens of thousands of peasants. The government authorities not only neglected the plight of the people but also kept on levying numerous taxes that were practically impossible for the peasants to pay. As a result, thousands of peasants abandoned their villages with or without their families and roamed elsewhere in search of food and work. It was a common scene to observe desperate families seeking shelter in churches and mosques and begging for food on the streets. Life was literally intolerable and desperation reigned.

---

31 See: Report of the Population and Housing Census Commission, Government of Ethiopia, Addis Ababa, 1996, p. 10.

The people of Tigrai in general and the educated section in particular were in a continuous state of suspense following the radical student movement of the early 1970s, which called for radical changes, and the spontaneous revolution of 1974 which uprooted the imperial system. All seemed anxious to see a reliable organization to lead them through this state of uncertainty and harsh life. People voiced their readiness through songs, writings and other available means to pay any price for the struggle that could bring them the anticipated better future. A series of events like the dramatic fall of the Emperor, the flight of the hereditary provincial governor of Tigrai, *Ras* Mengesha Seyoum, and the seizure of power by an unknown group of military officers with an unfamiliar agenda, increased their expectations. However, a legitimate organization to guide them through this erratic period was lacking. Someone had to fill this vacuum.

Except for the weak feudal class and the clergy that wanted to retain the existing land tenure relationships, members of the other social classes were entangled in endless heated debates as to what should follow and how to go about it. In the absence of any kind of political organization or union to coordinate the opinions of the people, the level of confusion that reigned during this period in the early 1970s is not hard to imagine.

Underlying this general apprehension were the dire conditions of the peasantry with their accumulated grievances. The persistent call of the young educated class – basically students and teachers – for radical change and the 'self-determination of Tigrai' as a rallying slogan fuelled their aspirations. With this, the imposition of central control, the domination of the Showan-Amhara ruling class, heavy taxation and the neglect of the leaders in mitigating the difficult life of the people were reiterated in every forum. 'The state's most painful act of all was the banning of the Tigrai language in a region where, as late as the mid-1970s, only 12.3 per cent of the males claimed to speak Amharigna and only 7.7 per cent could read it' (Stavenhagen 1996: 8). All this unrest in Tigrai could be seen as a reaction to a number of oppressive factors for which the ruling class, the Showan *Mek^wanent* (nobles), based at the centre of political power, was responsible. 'Showans have, of course, continued to run Ethiopia, to monopolize the top administrative and political positions, to govern the provinces and to reap the economic benefits of the concentration of industry and urbanization in Showa. Yet they are now identified as 'Amhara', not as 'Showan'' (Salole 1979: 27). And indeed, 'Amhara domination' does not include the Amhara peasantry as dominators but only refers to the ruling elite of Showa (Clapham 1975). These circumstances placed the call for self-determination as the central rallying slogan, even during and after the outbreak of the Ethiopian Revolution in 1974, when issues like land reform and the formation of a government accountable to the people were the rallying hue and cry all over Ethiopia. The slogan 'Land to the tiller', for instance, was a powerful one in many parts of Ethiopia and galvanized millions to embrace the revolution - but not in Tigrai, where anybody could claim a piece of land under the *rist* system, which in a way was communal. There was also widespread scepticism of changes that came from the centre and Tigraians wanted to initiate changes by themselves and be masters of their own destiny. Because of historical factors that lingered in Tigrai, the 1974 revolution did not arouse Tigraians as much as it did other Ethiopians. So, revolution in Tigrai took its own, autonomous course, focusing on achieving self-determination for the region.

In the rural areas of Tigrai, in farming and at celebrations of religious holidays or wedding ceremonies, men and women alike made it routine to sing 'blues' or lamentation songs that either expressed the dismal conditions they had to endure, or called for the moment to rebel against the repressive system. In a predominantly peasant and illiterate society like Tigrai, ideas are usually communicated orally and expressed through songs and poems. Two of the old but popular songs that reflected the feelings of anger were:

> *Tigrai kinday malti kitsebeyeki*, (Tigrai, how long should I linger)
> *Ab maegerey geyre kimalaalki* (Let me get 'it' [the gun] for you)

> *Gobez Tigrai! Gobez Tigrai!* (Brave of Tigrai! Brave of Tigrai!)
> *Zebenka iu tsemede bieray!* (Now it is your season to mount the ox/ weapon)

Students on the other hand used to write, demonstrate, organize in study groups, and sing songs of a revolutionary nature that were more straightforward and programmatic. It was university students who took the lead in these revolutionary activities. Almost every Tigraian, even the feudal lords and the clergy, who might have had to lose some of their privileges after the revolutionary struggle, seemed to admire the call for self-determination, the vision of the educated younger generation and their efforts to realize it. It was in these circumstances that the TPLF emerged.

From TNO to TPLF

The core task set by the TNO was to prepare the groundwork for the armed struggle. All TNO's other activities revolved around this objective. University and high school students, teachers and civil servants were all recruited as members of the TNO with the aim of initiating armed struggle. Although all the members understood that the direction of the TNO was to enter an armed movement, only the younger and more able ones were advised to engage in mental and physical preparation for the protracted war ahead. They were encouraged to read experiences of guerrilla movements in Algeria, China, Cuba, Eritrea, Guinea-Bissau and Vietnam, and the endurance and revolutionary discipline exhibited in these revolutions was emphasized. The older ones, on the other hand, were advised to remain unnoticed and to work underground in government-held towns to back up the front. Recruiting and organizing the urban dwellers in cells and supplying them with revolutionary equipment, collecting money and other necessary materials like medicine, and stealing relevant information from the enemy camp were some of the tasks assigned to them.

The other important task the TNO undertook was establishing a working relationship with the Eritrean fronts, the EPLF and ELF, for practical reasons. Although the EPLF claimed to be 'more progressive' than the ELF and the ELF likewise claimed to be 'more truly nationalist' than the EPLF, the TNO considered both fronts as nationalist organizations fighting for the independence of Eritrea. No research or formal discussion was conducted to reach a position on the nature of the fronts and the future of Eritrea and this view was adopted purely for pragmatic reasons, without serious consideration of the consequences. TNO leaders focused only on the support they could gain from the Eritrean fronts to facilitate their own struggle against the military regime in Ethiopia.

With its geographic proximity and similar language patterns, it was not difficult for Tigraians to trace and contact ELF or EPLF fighters. Above all, Tigraians were sympathetic towards Eritrean fighters, especially at the university where some of the Eritrean students were trying to break the exclusionist nationalist stance and forge a people's movement all over Ethiopia. When the ELF was contacted, the response was not completely positive because another Tigraian group, the TLF, lead by Yohannes Tekle-Haimanot and Gebre-Kidan Asfaha had already established a working relationship with the ELF and the TNO was a remote option at that time. Perhaps the ELF might also have considered the TLF as truly nationalist for they had upheld the independence of Tigrai, like the Eritreans. The response from the EPLF, on the other hand, was prompt and positive. Two factors might have expedited this swift reply. Firstly, the EPLF must have been aware that their arch rival, the ELF, had already established working relations with a Tigraian front, the TLF, which could help expand its area of operation. And secondly, a group of the founders of the EPRP were already in the field with the EPLF but their relationship was not very smooth because the former could not adopt a clear-cut position on the question of Eritrean independence.

Communication by letter lasted for more than five months until Mehari Tekle (Mussie), an EPLF fighter but a Tigraian by birth, finally appeared to facilitate matters, meeting with two TNO representatives, Seyoum and Aregawi, on the outskirts of Asmara. Initially, the TNO leaders thought Mussie was the contact person representing the EPLF but in their first formal meeting they discovered that, with the consent of the EPLF leadership, Mussie was coming to join the TNO and fight for the self-determination of Tigrai. He also disclosed to the TNO leaders that many other Tigraians who had been fighting on the side of the EPLF were keenly talking about an armed struggle soon to commence in Tigrai and that they were eager to come to their region to fight the enemy. It was usual for Tigraians who went to Eritrea in search of work to join the Eritrean fronts to fight the government, which was seen as the cause of their misery. Girmay Jabir, Iyassu Baga, Marta (Kahsa) Tesfai, Haile Portsudan and Kokeb Wodi-Aala were just some of these fighters. As it later turned out, Mussie became a very important link in many aspects, especially between the EPLF and the TNO at a critical time (the end of 1974) when the ELF and EPLF were fighting against each other to gain ground from the demoralized and retreating government forces. The situation was otherwise very difficult to handle for inexperienced TNO leaders in a territory they were not familiar with.

In the initial discussions with Mussie, the first issue of concern was military training, as all the founders of the TNO, except for Sihul, had no military experience whatsoever. TNO members, most of whom were university and high school students plus a few teachers, were available at any time to engage in training. Mussie spoke with certainty about how the EPLF was willing to train as many Tigraians as the TNO could produce. He also made it clear that the EPLF leadership would like to see fewer student trainees and more peasant trainees, the rationale being that peasants who were already accustomed to hardship would be better able to endure the tough rural circumstances they would find themselves in... TNO leaders were not convinced of this argument but as they had no reason to oppose it, proceeded to find peasant trainees as well. The EPLF's request to increase the recruitment of peasants for the future TPLF army was to neutralize the educated element, which otherwise would keep on critically scrutinizing and challenging the manner of leadership, as had been experienced in the 1973 *Menkae*[32] incident.

It was not difficult to raise recruits for military training. Many were prepared to take on challenges under the leadership of the TNO. In a matter of days a group was set up to take the initial challenge. The first

---

32 This was a crackdown on pro-democracy activists, who were labelled as *Menkae* (or 'bats'), in the EPLF.

group selected for military training in the EPLF-liberated area arrived in Asmara in January 1975. Among these future *tegadelti* (fighters) were Abbay Tsehay, Hailu Mengesha, Sahle Abraha (Seye), Atsbaha Dagnew (Shewit), Yohannes Gebre-Medhin (Walta), Tikue Woldu (Awealom) and Legesse (Meles) Zenawi, Ethiopia's current prime minister. They had to stay in hotels in Asmara for a few days as the route to the EPLF field of operation, including Asmara itself, had suddenly become a war zone and was unsafe to travel through unarmed. During this somewhat tense situation, only Meles[33] slipped away unnoticed from the group that was due to move to the field whenever the situation normalized. Within a few days however, the situation was calm and under the guidance of the veteran fighter Mussie, the group got away from Asmara at night and two days later arrived at the nearest EPLF training camp, Riesi Adi where they immediately started rigorous military training. In their books on the TPLF, both John Young (1997) and Jenny Hammond (1999) vaguely indicate that Meles Zenawi and Sibhat Nega were founders of the TPLF, but that is incorrect. Both Meles and Sibhat joined the Front months after it had been established.

Back in Tigrai, Sihul and his brother Berhane Ayele (Fitewi) had taken on the task of assembling peasant trainees in their district of Shire. Their recruitment campaign was focused towards active and motivated peasants who could cope with the rigorous military training required. Within three days, some thirty individuals from both peasant and urban backgrounds, including a few students like Niguse Taye (Kelebet), had volunteered to join those who had already started training in Eritrea. Agazi and Seyoum led this group all the way from Tigrai to Eritrea across enemy-held territory. They joined the first group and in less than three months all had done well in their training and were ready for combat.

In the town of Enda-Selassie in Shire, with Sihul as their indispensable host, the rest of the TNO members were organizing in order to declare the actual beginning of their armed struggle in the countryside of Tigrai. For more than a week, most of the TNO leadership (among them Sihul, Giday, Asfaha, Seyoum, Agazi, and Berihu) had been discussing when, how and where to start the long-awaited war. On Sihul's recommendation, it was decided to start it from Dedebit as soon as possible. Other colleagues who joined this group at this preparatory stage were Asgede (a former soldier in the Ethiopian army), Kahsay Berhe (Misgina), Michael, Melay and Abraha.

---

33 According to Hailu Mengesha (a member of the group), a month later on their way with a mission to Tigrai, Hailu and Abbay found Legese (Meles) Zenawi in an Italian billiards café in Adi Quala, 75 km from Asmara, where his mother comes from. They demanded an explanation for his retreat from his comrades in Asmara but Meles has had nothing to say about this matter to this day.

It was believed the armed struggle should start before the ultra-nationalist TLF, the Ethiopian 'Bolshevik' EPRP, and the 'monarchist' EDU,[34] who also were poised to fight the *Dergue* from Tigrai, gained ground with the people.

The final preparations for the guerrilla campaign were concluded at Sihul's home. He made available three rifles and a fourth came from Giday who pilfered it from his father in his absence. Field equipment and other logistics were either bought or collected from members and supporters and assembled at Sihul's house. Sihul's family prepared a few days' rations for the contingent that would march to Dedebit. The day before the group's departure, Sihul's house looked like the military base of a small contingent. The future guerrilla fighters dressed in khaki clothes suitable for the heat and the rough terrain they would face. All wore shorts and *temalatet* (locally made sandals); most of them for the first time, and everyone were provided with vital supplies weighing about 20 kg. A mule was bought to help carry extra but vital materials. At midnight on 18 February 1975 (11 Yekatit 1967 E.C.), Fitewi led the way out of the town, which was guarded by police and government militia. The hours of darkness had been chosen for the contingent to leave, to avoid an unwanted confrontation with government forces. The group headed towards Dedebit, declaring the beginning of the armed struggle and the birth of the TPLF. The journey to Dedebit, which is about 80 km from Shire and 900 km from Addis Ababa, took two nights. Dedebit thus became the starting point and the initial base of the TPLF.

---

34 The three fronts (TLF, EPRP and EDU) including the TPLF were working hard to gain ground in Tigrai one before the other, so that they would secure easy access to the neighboring Eritrean fronts which had well-established base areas not far from the border lines with Tigrai and gain military backing.

Chapter 4

Testing the Fire: the Launch of Guerrilla Warfare

Introduction

For an armed mass insurrection to take place requires a dedicated political elite that can plan and lead the insurgent war against much stronger and well-established state armed forces. The ups and downs of waging guerrilla warfare are not just a series of physical and psychological confrontations with a stronger enemy, but also complex endeavours of welding together elements of a socially stratified society to stand up in unison in support of the movement that just started the war and without which the survival and growth of the movement would be unthinkable. In this chapter we look into how and why the 'revolutionary elite' shifted its movement from the usual urban areas to the remotest parts of the rural areas and also how, based on this revolutionary approach, it handled the various internal as well as external difficulties that it encountered.

While in general the TPLF from its inception was armed with the Marxist revolutionary thought, its theory of guerrilla warfare was by-and-large based on Maoist principles. These were put to the test in the struggles in China, Cuba, Algeria, Vietnam, Guinea-Bissau and elsewhere. Aware of these precedents, the TPLF tried to effectively put revolutionary guerrilla warfare theory into practice in the rather different circumstances of Tigrai. The 'authoritative' nature of the theory coupled with the iron discipline required in military undertakings also led the TPLF to try and exert very strict control over internal developments and confront external pressures head-on.

Journey to Dedebit[35]

This chapter narrates the events during the first year of the TPLF's struggle to create the physical and social bases that would embrace it in the coming years. It was a year in which its *raison d'être* was defined and explained and its influence was spreading.

The first year of the armed struggle was full of challenges, with numerous ups and downs. Few moments were as exiting as the first day of the journey to Dedebit, with its unfamiliar jungle for all the founding members of the TPLF except Sihul. Armed for the first time, the group left Sihul's house in Enda-Selassie in Shire at midnight when the town was asleep. Police or militia guards on duty could have confronted the young students, who did not even know how to carry a gun let alone aim one and shoot. At this point, their only infallible tool was their unbridled confidence, but this would have been ineffective in actual combat. Thanks to Berhane Ayele, who knew every corner of the town and the guards' patrol patterns, the group slipped through Enda-Selassie without incident, which would have been disastrous both in terms of likely casualties and the future of the front. Once the group reached the outskirts of the town, it met pre-arranged peasant guides in strategic villages all the way to Dedebit. The peasant guides, like Meley, were all relatives of Sihul.

They kept moving all night to avoid government forces that might have been seen it assembling in Enda Selassie, but also because the temperature rose as they descended from the highlands of Shire towards the lowlands of Dedebit. Walking during the day would have been difficult for the young fighters. At daybreak, the group retired to the jungle to rest, find water and avoid meeting passing peasants. Although they were exhausted after walking all night and carrying field materials no less than 20 kg each, there was joy and relief on their faces. There was the excitement of opening a new page of armed struggle in order to turn the aspirations of Tigraians into a reality, and their readiness to pay any cost in its realization meant that they could bear the physical discomfort of their harsh surroundings. The second night of the journey to Dedebit was more debilitating, as temperatures were even

35 Dedebit is the initial base area of the TPLF where the armed struggle was launched for the first time. It is located in one of the remote areas of the sub-district of Asgede, Shire-Enda Selassie, Western Tigrai along the gorge of River Tekeze. The author of this study was part of the scene.

higher and drinking water became scarce. As they approached the southern side of Dedebit, they continued their journey during daylight but found it hard to keep up the same pace in the unfamiliar circumstances. More than once they had to chase a colony of monkeys from small pools of muddy water where they wanted to drink. As the drained group of fighters was forcing itself to keep moving, a sudden gunshot was heard close behind. Everybody was nervous but regained their composure and kept up their normal pace. This first shot turned out to be nothing but a trick planned by the experienced Sihul to test the group's nerve. In the evening, they reached the centre of Dedebit and then moved on into the hills where Sihul selected the highest one as a temporary settlement area until the whole region had been surveyed. Having cleared a part of the bush, they lay down to sleep on the hill with the sky and bright stars above them.

Dedebit is a rugged hilly area stretching along the Tekeze River gorge and close to the Tselimoye forest. With three months of rain during the Ethiopian 'winter' (June-August), the area grows thick tropical bush that looks impenetrable. In some isolated spots where the land is cultivable, a few seasonal farmers used to clear the bush to grow cash crops like sesame to supplement their earnings. The other nine months of the year, it is dry and extremely hot, with temperatures rising to 40+ degrees Celsius and water becoming scarce. Its rough and irregular bush makes the area the ideal sanctuary for guerrilla fighters and in such terrain it is easy to get lost. To these beginners of the guerrilla campaign though, it did not take long to get to know the terrain and get used to guerrilla life. The will and readiness to overpower any hardship that guerrilla warfare would entail was already there. Sleeping in the open and on the ground in this season with falling rains was worse than the heat of the summer. Without shelter from the rain, not only was sleep difficult, but also the group's guns got wet and would be unusable until they were greased again the next day. One other problem was maintaining the food supply, that was usually, if not always, rations like parched corn and peas or ground wheat and sesame, which came from supporters in Shire-Enda Selassie, Sheraro and Mai-Kuhli. Food was prepared in the most rudimentary way, such as putting instantly prepared dough on a hot flat stone and which in a few minutes was ready for consumption. When flat stones were not available, small hard balls of rocks were picked, heated until they glowed and then each hot rock would be covered with dough and placed near the fire. After the dough had received enough heat from the hot rocks inside and glowing fire outside, it would be ready for consumption and could also be kept for several days. This kind of food is called *birkuta* and is common among pastoralists. Wild fruits and roots also served as food when the dry rations were finished. Hunting was discouraged to preserve the wildlife but also to avoid traces of the guerrilla group's existence in the area.

In a matter of days most of these fresh fighters seemed to get used to the rough life in the jungle and were prepared to take up serious engagements, of the kind they heard from Algeria, Angola, Vietnam, Cuba, etc. Thus, guerrilla life started and was embraced with passion by almost every one. Yet, this did not mean everybody was adjusting to the guerrilla life at the same pace - one or two complained about the food or the night walks and the physical endurance required in this self-imposed rough venture.

Training in Guerrilla Warfare

Military training was the top priority for these young fighters who knew little or nothing about guns or how to set an ambush. Most of them had read about the Vietnam war and about the Cuban and Algerian revolutions and, above all, about Mao's guerrilla warfare. Theories of revolutionary war had partly been acquired during their university years, when there were even attempts of secret training in guerrilla tactics in the university campus. In theory they knew about hit-and-run attacks, advance and retreat, ambush and surprise, but not about the complexities of their practical application. In military engagement the gap between mock fighting and real fighting is wide, but still wider is the theory and practice of this venture. In practical warfare everything counts, including the objectives of war, armaments, moral and physical composure of the combatants, intelligence, leadership qualities, terrain and the weather, and even the direction of the wind.

These young fighters were however poised in every sense of the word to translate their theory into practice. They put their theory together with the practical experience of Sihul and Asgede Gebre-Selassie, a former corporal in the Ethiopian army, who joined the group at the last minute as they headed for Dedebit. Asgede and Sihul organized and led the training exercises. Every evening, the day's training was evaluated collectively to improve performance the next day. Although there was no formal organizational structure, the modest Sihul was regarded as the leader of the group and had the final say in the whole process. For two weeks they went through rigorous military training that was typical of guerrilla warfare, combining informal, traditional and conventional aspects of war. Most of them were suffering from bruises and cuts which were left to heal by themselves, as medical aid was not available at that early stage of the struggle.

The next stage of training was long-distance walks during the day and at night in the excruciating conditions of Dedebit. This arrangement was coupled with mastering the terrain not only of Dedebit but also the sub-districts of Asgede and Adiabo where the Tekeze River gorge runs through the western edge.[36] The group would split in two and at times into three groups for a few days to survey a specific area and regrouped to exchange their findings and plan the next phase. These activities lasted for more than three months and towards the end an additional scheme of visiting remote villages was included. Among these were Adi Mohamedai, Tselimoy, Misgar Tekez, Shimelba and Mai Kuhli. The heads of these villages were well-armed, strong figures and some of them were renowned *shiftas*, like Alem Eshet, who could have inflicted grave damage on the small TPLF band. But thanks to Sihul's influence, they would not contemplate this. Alem Eshet of Tselimoy and Osman of Misgar Tekeze had gone as far as providing feasts for the whole TPLF group by slaughtering an ox and a goat as a sign of respect in the traditional way. Later on, as the contacts with these villages became well-established and peasants were organized in line with the TPLF's political agenda and parallel to the village heads' network, they became the source of vital information and logistical help. Whenever government agents approached them for information about the front, it was customary for the peasants to disorient the agents by exaggerating the number of rebels as 'countless like the hair'. In Misgar Tekeze, women like *Woizero* Tsehaytu Fekadu, later better known as 'Mother' by TPLF fighters, were ardent supporters of the TPLF from the beginning. The double mobilization process of the TPLF – Tigraian nationalism to mobilize all the people and the class ideology to organize the poor – had already started manifesting itself even at this initial stage of the struggle.

The mobility of the TPLF to Wolkait, across the River Tekeze in the west and to the larger villages of Sheraro, Bademe, Adi Awala and Adi Nebried in the northeast continued without serious impediment. Indeed, there were no meaningful government forces in these areas and the few scattered ones seemed to prefer co-existence with the front.

At this early stage of the struggle, news of the tiny front was spreading like wildfire not only in the villages but also in the big towns and cities, including Meqele, the capital of Tigrai, and even Addis Ababa. Several young people began to flow to the front, although it was not simple to trace the location of the constantly mobile guerrilla fighters. Formerly associated members, among them Wolde-Selassie Nega (Sibhat) and Legese Zenawi (Meles)[37] who were later to play a controversial role both in the Front and later in the government they controlled, also joined the TPLF at this time.[38]

36 These areas were the haven of all kinds of *shiftas* (criminal or social bandits).

37 For brief profiles of both Meles and Sibhat, see Appendix 3.

38 For details, see Aregawi Berhe 2004.

They all had to pass the military training, which was not yet fully developed but enough to give confidence and provide the basic know-how of fighting.

While the number of the fighters increased, there were no arms available except for the initial four outdated rifles that everybody was anxious to get hold of. The expectation that the contingent under training in the EPLF in Eritrea would come with enough weapons to arm the Dedebit group was still high. The scarcity of weapons did not however deter this group from carrying on with training and executing necessary missions in the whole district of Shire. Meanwhile it was decided that a delegation should be sent to the ELF, which was operating in nearby Bademe, not just to look for arms but also to establish lasting contact with them. Asfaha, a founding member of the TPLF, and Meles were assigned to accomplish this mission but it was aborted when they reached Bademe because of trivial disagreements that erupted between them for which they blamed each other. Another delegation had to take up the mission and it managed to establish contact but never was the contact as cordial as that with the EPLF, since the ELF was committed to another Tigraian group, the TLF.

Without adequate arms and with self-improvised training schemes, the first group in Dedebit completed the basic military exercises that would enable it to wage guerrilla warfare. The whole group became confident about defending itself or even attacking an advancing enemy detachment with the meagre arms it possessed. More military training was expected when the contingent from Eritrea returned.

The Contingent's[39] *Return from Eritrea*

In the EPLF, military training conditions were no less harsh than in Dedebit, but the experience and quality of the training was far more advanced. It was well-established and structured, supported by ample reading materials and the necessary weapons for practice. There were also qualified instructors trained in the Ethiopian military academy, or in Syria and China. The experience gained in fourteen years of guerrilla warfare against the Ethiopian government was the equivalent of that in a military college. In early 1975, when the Tigraian contingent arrived in Eritrea for training, the EPLF was already engaged in pitched battles with Ethiopian government forces in the vicinity of Asmara and at times inside the city itself. The city was besieged for months. The bulk of the EPLF forces and their logistical supply were placed to serve this frontline. The training for this group had to take place

39 As mentioned earlier, the contingent was sent to the EPLF-held territory in Eritrea for military training a month before the TPLF was launched in Dedebit in February 1975.

not far from the war zone where continuous air raids and heavy artillery bombardment made their days miserable. Equally miserable were the chilly weather and the lack of water, which had to be fetched from deep gorges that were not easily accessible even when not carrying jerrycans full of water.

In addition to the TPLF group, an EPRP group led by Berhanemeskel Redda that made its way from abroad and the Assefa-Hailu Habtu group who joined them from Addis Ababa were in the same area to undergo military training. The stay of the Habtu group in the EPLF area was short-lived as they had a serious dispute with the Berhanemeskel group - which later became the core of EPRP - over the strategy of their struggle and later with the EPLF over their attitude towards the nature of the Ethiopian revolution and went into exile abroad. The EPRP group however persisted with their training although they too had differences with the EPLF on the issue of the Eritrean quest for independence.

In the course of their training, the TPLF group took the initiative of contacting the EPRP group, so that a working relationship could be established. This initiative was communicated though the EPLF to the EPRP but they rejected the offer, claiming that a party such as the EPRP should not lower its status by talking to a nationalist front. This negative response was the beginning of a rocky relationship between the two organizations that ultimately ended in armed conflict. The differences that led to the conflict were basically related to the treatment of the ethno-national question in multi-ethnic Ethiopia.

When the training course came to an end, it was time to approach the EPLF leadership for arms so that every TPLF member could carry a weapon. The reality however did not meet everyone's expectations. The request for arms was made before the training came to a close, but nothing was forthcoming. Then, a second and a third requests were forwarded after the training was completed, but still no arms were made available. The young Tigraian fighters who had completed training began counting the days and later weeks in idleness. Fighters like Ahferom started to complain loudly, insisting that if only they had joined their comrades in Dedebit, with whatever was available there, they could have snatched more arms from the enemy than the EPLF could offer. Finally, Mussie was sent to Isayas Afeworki, then vice general-secretary, to make a direct complaint. Isayas gave orders to his aide-de-camp that a few rifles collected from a nearby camp be given to the Tigraians. With Mussie's efforts, some ten rifles (2 Kalashnikovs, 8 various semi- and non-automatic rifles) and 3 hand grenades were collected and handed to the Tigraian contingent - useful, but still a pittance. Although they were expecting enough automatic rifles to arm their comrades in Dedebit as well, the contingent did not want to waste any more time looking for arms. Immediately after they secured these few rifles, they began their long-awaited journey back to Tigrai. A few other Tigraians, former EPLF fighters like Yemane Kidane (Jamaica), Girmay Jabir, Dirfo, Wodi Ala and Kokeb joined this group to fight in Tigrai. At the time of departure, the contingent's numbers rose to 21 fighters but only half of them were armed with the few rifles they had managed to acquire.

In mid-May, this contingent of 21 fighters arrived in the district of Shire in Tigrai, but they did not know the exact location of Dedebit where those who launched the armed struggle could be found. On the advice of Alemayehu Gessesew (Dirar), Sihul's youngest brother, who was part of the peasant group that had undertaken training in Eritrea, the contingent headed to Hirmi, an extended gorge near the village of Kelakil, where most of Sihul's close relatives lived. From Kelakil, it was not difficult to trace the Dedebit group through Sihul's family network. As the message reached the Dedebit group, it wasted no time in making the three-day journey to Hirmi to join the contingent that came back from military training in Eritrea.

With a lot of excitement on both sides, the two groups met at Hirmi and formed a company of 43 combatants. There was great jubilation and for the next four to five days almost everybody was given time to relax and share their experiences of the first four months of the TPLF and the EPLF. Since Hirmi was not too far from the village of Kelakil, the fighters would go to the village in groups to mingle and socialize and also to get homemade food (*injera*) and drinks (*siwa* or *tella*, local beer). It was on one such occasion, while a group that included Asfaha, Yemane, Sibhat and Aregawi were ascending through the cliffs of Hirmi to go to Kelakil, that the aim of the Tigrai struggle was raised by Sibhat, in a joking manner. Known for his jokes, he propounded that it could be regarded as a 'colonial question', like that of the Eritreans. Some of them ridiculed Sibhat's overture, asking '… where on earth are you going to cook up the history and politics to justify it'. All laughed but not Sibhat, who felt insulted. Nobody took what seemed to have come up in informal jest as a serious position. This was a mistake, for the same position would appear in different forms later during the struggle, and was to have a disruptive impact not only in the Tigraian movement for self-determination but also later in Ethiopian power politics in general.

After the launch of the TPLF in February 1975, the whole leadership (eight founders of the organization, namely Sihul, Agazi, Giday, Hailu, Abbay, Seyoum, Asfaha, and Aregawi) met in June at Hirmi for the first time. With all the developments in the previous five months, they had to work out short- and long-term plans for the struggle ahead. Settling Mussie's status was top of their agenda. Considering his long experience in struggles and his crucial role in the relationship with the EPLF, they decided to incorporate

Mussie in the leadership. At first, Mussie looked surprised when he heard the arrangement of including him, but he could only accept it. So with the consensus of the entire leadership, Mussie became the ninth member of the TPLF leadership until the first congress of all fighters that was held in Deima, Agame a year after the founding of the TPLF.

The main issues of concern at this point were restructuring the organization, assigning new tasks and obtaining additional military training that would enable every fighter to cope with the realities of guerrilla warfare and work towards bringing down the oppressive system for the benefit of Tigrai. Initially, the whole organization's structure was a simple military formation with the idea of waging the guerrilla warfare for the years to come. The company of 43 combatants formed three squads of 14 to 15 men. At a brief meeting that did not last even half an hour, the leadership elected Sihul as the chairman, Mussie as military commander and Aregawi as commissar, with the other leadership members heading a squad as commander and commissar. With this formation, it was decided to undertake intensive military and political training that would bring the Dedebit and EPLF-trained group to the same level. For this purpose and to lay out a comprehensive plan for the next phase of the struggle, Dedebit was again selected as the ideal place to accomplish these tasks. So everybody had to march to Dedebit once again.

However, unforeseen circumstances began to emerge in Dedebit. The peasant fighters, most of who had prior knowledge of managing rifles and were better acquainted with life in the bush were dissatisfied with the reorganization and appointments that followed. They began to regroup secretly, which eventually led to the first crisis within the TPLF.

Crisis Creeps In

The reorganization, which was accompanied by intensive military and political training, had not brought anything dramatic. Everybody seemed to be focused on training to launch attacks on the enemy. By taking the initiative and the leading role, the founders of the TPLF were just doing what was regarded as a normal process of setting up a politico-military front to fight an aggressive state regime. The Front was in the process of shaping itself and taking the form a political organization should possess. Interestingly enough, all the members of the front warmly welcomed the inclusion of Mussie into the leadership, perhaps because everybody realized the role he had played so far and his potential in the future. Evidently, there had been opportune moments to observe the experienced Mussie, while the inexperienced 'student leaders' were yet to be tested. In the eyes of the peasant fighters however, the issue of the student leaders turned out to be a rallying point for their grievances and subsequent actions.

Major decisions were made by the leadership at this period. One was to move the base area from Dedebit to the central Tigrai area where other Ethiopian fronts, namely the EPRP and the TLF were operating. It would then be easier to hold political discourse with the fronts on issues of common interest and coordinate forces to fight the common enemy. The other significance of this area was its accessibility and proximity to the Eritrean fronts, in particular to the EPLF from whom considerable military assistance and weapons were expected to come. A second decision was to assign two groups composed of members of the leadership to survey the next transitory base area to central Tigrai and to travel to the EPLF base area to request the leadership for arms. When the plan to move the base from Dedebit to central Tigrai was disclosed to the fighters, the peasants from this area were against it. They thought that if they left the territory they were familiar with, their role and hence the weight of their influence would decrease. From this point on, they became engaged in clandestine activities.

Even before this divergence of views occurred, the peasant fighters were not content with the student leaders. In their first encounter with them, they felt they were a group of clumsy schoolboys who 'could only play with paper' and not shoulder the heavy burden of armed struggle. The peasants thought the struggle was just a military campaign and that they were in a better position than the students to handle it. For them, a leader meant someone who could lead them in battle. They believed themselves to be battle-tested heroes considering the number of shots they fired in their villages or in the bush. They seriously thought battles tested (battle-tested) and determined who one was and that the political or propaganda work was just a waste of time or the work of a weak person. They also did not like the idea of collective leadership which placed the students on the same level as them and more so with Sihul, who they considered was the sole leader and should remain to be seen as such. The notion of equality, which was brought up by the young students and began to be entertained in the front, was unacceptable to them. They did not want the traditional relationship, which they considered a better one, to be eroded. With these feelings, they started creating a separate circle that undermined the organizational structure that had not yet had time to mature. Alemayehu Gessesew (Dirar) was at the centre of this disgruntled group. Perhaps, his dream was to make sure his eldest brother Sihul remain as a dominant leader and he himself became the second or third in command. Dirar's dream was definitely contrary to Sihul's revolutionary convictions.

Dirar was no ordinary peasant, nor were his closest associates. They were people who made their living in both urban and rural areas. During the rainy season they went to their farms and then they came to town to look for work or to engage in petty trade. Some of them could also have been involved in criminal *shiftinnet,* which was common in those days in that region. This pariah group was engaged in secret talks for days and nobody seemed to understand what it was all about. Gradually it became clear that the group was dissatisfied with the leadership most of which happened to be young students, but at that early stage of the struggle it was hard to imagine that they were plotting to eliminate the leaders of the organization still in its infancy.

As Kahsay Berhe[40] explained the events, it was at lunchtime one day that they were to execute their plan. Tsegay Tesfay (Kokab) who happened to be the cook that day detected an unfamiliar regrouping and movement among the peasants. He then found that Sihul, who normally sat with the student group for lunch, was away on a mission. Again he noticed the peasants were not converging on the lunch site but instead were moving around to positions favourable to aiming and shooting. He altered the customary way of sitting for lunch and dispersed the likely targets of the peasants' plot. Now that their intended targets had been dispersed, the peasant plotters for their part were confused by their own strange rearrangement. Their plan was messed up and they were unable to execute their assault. Thanks to Kokab, the plot was aborted. Their plan, as was revealed later on, was to kill the student leaders, except for Sihul and Mussie. That same day, about ten of the arch plotters, including Dirar, Meftuh and Hiluf, fled the scene never to return. To the embarrassment of all the committed fighters, they took with them some of the rifles the organization depended on for its defence, training and future activities. A state of confusion and uncertainty reigned. Everybody seemed to suspect the other of plotting to kill or run away with the guns. A night passed with everyone watching each other, and the next day an emergency general meeting of all the fighters was called to resolve the first crisis in the organization, which was then termed as *Hinfishfish* (chaos). At the meeting, the plotters' conspiracy was revealed by some of the peasant fighters who had been trailing them. Some cried bitterly while relating what had happened. At the end of the day a decision was made to give all the peasant fighters a second chance. They were allowed to remain in the organization as long as they abided by its principles or they had to leave peacefully. A few who could not cope with the stiff revolutionary discipline left, but also left all the front's belongings behind.

---

40 Interview: Kahsay Berhe, Münster, Germany, 27 March 2004.

With the first *Hinfishfish* as a backdrop, the leadership met to assess the situation and to rekindle the mood of enthusiasm about fighting the *Dergue* that had originally been prevalent among most members. It did not take much time or effort to regenerate the fighting spirit. The two crucial missions mentioned earlier were immediately launched. But again, in just two weeks time, both missions – the movement to the centre and the trip to Eritrea – were foiled by tragic incidents that befell Sihul and Mussie.

Government militia in Adi Daero caught Mussie, who belonged to the delegation to Eritrea, as he entered the small town to buy food and cigarettes. As soon as the other members of the delegation, Seyoum and Yemane, learned about the incident, they fled to the base area to report back and seek help. But before a rescue attempt could be made, Mussie was transported to Enda-Selassie in Shire where there was a police garrison. There he was chained and locked in a cell awaiting orders to be transported to Meqele or Addis Ababa. The other group on mission, which was being led by Sihul and was not far away from the Mussie group, learned from peasants that Mussie had fallen into the hands of the enemy and been taken to Enda-Selassie prison. Sihul, together with the other members of the group, Gebremichael and Awalom decided to rescue Mussie by storming the prison in Enda-Selassie. A very daring resolution! The three of them hurried off to Enda-Selassie but were compelled to stop at the River Chiameskebet due to flooding. Worse still, Sihul was swept away by the river flooded by heavy rainstorms as he attempted to cross it. Fortunately, he was thrown out of the river alive but he had serious injuries and was taken to a supporter's house to recuperate. Their intended mission was aborted. The front appeared to have entered a difficult, testing period; nevertheless, the other determined fighters were there to propel the fight forward, as exhibited days later in the raid on Shire Police Station.

Storming Shire Police Station

News of the tragic incidents struck the base area when Yemane and Seyoum returned after they lost their comrade Mussie to the *Dergue* agents in Adi Daero. Everybody was shocked and became restless; proposing a contingent be hurriedly dispatched to Enda-Selassie to rescue him. Everyone showed readiness to be part of the first risky mission since the TPLF's formation. In no time, a squad of eleven combatants[41] was formed and hurried to rescue Mussie before he was taken to a bigger garrison where it would be impossible even to attempt a rescue operation. It was early August

---

41 The author of the present study was one of the combatants in the Enda-Selassie operation.

and the rain was falling incessantly day and night hindering mobility and disabling the few rifles picked for the operation. Rain coupled with darkness made the squad's journey of what should have been a day take almost two days. One could hardly see through the dark and yet night time was preferred for the operation, because the inadequate number of combatants and their limited arms were no match for the force in Enda Selassie. Darkness could help camouflage them.

At 02:00 h. on 5 August 1975 (29 Hamle 1967 E.C.) the squad stormed the prison and in an operation that took about 20 minutes, Mussie and about sixty other prisoners were freed from their cells without being injured. Caught completely by surprise, the police guards fled their posts, leaving one of their colleague wounded. Right away, the TPLF squad with Mussie in its midst swiftly headed for Hirmi, the nearest gorge and now familiar territory for all the members of the squad. After resting in Hirmi for a couple of days, the squad made the long journey to Widak close to the Mereb River. In Widak, the bigger contingent that had started moving to the central region from Dedebit was awaiting to regroup with hit squad.

This highly risky first operation by the TPLF came at a precarious time for the front. The front was not prepared either in assault skills or in arms to undertake incidental combat. The success of this imposed operation therefore turned out to be a memorable event that influenced the future course of the TPLF. It was the first successful operation since the founding of the Front, and as a result, an important figure in the organization was rescued from the hands of the enemy. The misgivings lingering in the organization seemed to have been removed, or at best the feeling that no mishap would deter the Front from ever growing was implanted in every member's mind. What was feared to be a negative if not a humiliating precedence turned out to be a glorious victory and boosted the morale of the fighters and their sympathizers. All of a sudden, the TPLF became known all over Tigrai, and in the enemy quarters, it was seen as a force to be reckoned with. The implication of this first victory both inside and outside the organization was way beyond what could be comprehended at this stage of the struggle.

The emergence of a Tigraian front that could defeat a government force opened up new horizons in the hitherto repressed mentality of Tigraians. To many people the future seemed promising and led them to embrace and pursue the path the TPLF had initiated. It was precisely because of this reinvigorated feeling in the front that the aborted mission to the EPLF field in search of arms was ignored and instead an operation that could enable the Front to procure arms and money from the enemy became the priority. This resolve led to the Aksum operation a month later.

The Aksum Operation

Unlike the storming of Enda-Selassie police garrison, there was no urgency or compulsion that led to the operation in Aksum. It was carefully thought out and meticulously planned and conducted in broad daylight at 16:00 h. on the afternoon of 4 September 1975. The Aksum operation had multiple purposes that included the procurement of money and arms – so badly needed to keep the growing front on the move – and publicity, which that was no less important at the time in terms of generating public awareness and support.

The ancient historical town of Aksum[42] (see also Chapter 1) is one of Ethiopia's most famous tourist attractions, and had a bank and a police garrison much larger than that in Enda Selassie. Although it would not be easy, it was thought that the success of this operation would have a big impact on the future development of the front. Besides the relatively big force in the town, the 10th ground battalion of the government army was stationed at Adwa, 20 km east of Aksum. A swift advance by this battalion to Aksum would have definitely foiled the planned operation had the radio and telephone communications not been cut beforehand. A clandestine member of the TPLF, Abadi Mesfin, a health officer and head of the Aksum Hospital at the time, was at the centre of the operation's technical arrangements from within this government-held town. Hailu Mengesha served as liaison person between the field and the clandestine units in the town.

Unnoticed because of their camouflage, fourteen guerrilla fighters pretending to be local peasants from the eastern part of the town regrouped and dashed through Aksum in a Land Rover that had been requested just minutes earlier from the health centre, ostensibly to provide emergency assistance. The squad split into two groups: one to go to the police garrison led by Mussie, the other to the bank led by Aregawi. With negligible resistance and in a matter of minutes, both the police garrison and the bank fell into the hands of TPLF fighters. Three police officers in the garrison and one at the bank were killed in the shoot-out while one TPLF fighter was slightly wounded. Substantial amounts of arms and ammunition and Birr 175,000 (US$ 84,000) were collected in the raid.

As the sound of gunshots subsided and the squad began withdrawing from the town, the people of Aksum, especially the youth cheered the TPLF fighters, from their windows and balconies. It was a clear indication that the TPLF had already found a space in the minds and hearts of the people and the message of the Enda-Selassie operation was well received. With their booty loaded into the Land Rover, the squad immediately retired to a nearby

42 For further details, refer to Yuri M. Kobishchanov, *Axum*, 1966.

village that was accessible by car. From there, the men had to carry most of the things by themselves and some on the backs of donkeys purchased from peasants and taken to Medebai near the River Mereb.

Since Aksum was – and still is – a well-known historical and religious town in Ethiopia, news of the raid reached not only every corner of the country but also the European press. TPLF fighters rejoiced as they heard the news of their operation over the BBC and German Radio (Deutsche Welle - Amharic service). This made them believe their cause was gathering recognition outside their country and reinforced their determination to pursue it. The fact that the European news media showed interest in the Aksum operation by the still-unknown TPLF, even in Ethiopia, has to be seen in the context of the Cold War. At this time, the government in power was a self-proclaimed Marxist junta, called *Dergue,* that was establishing ties with Communist China and the Soviet Union – ties that the West did not espouse for years to come.

The government, on the other hand, chose to downplay the resounding impact of the Aksum operation as an act of isolated *shiftas.* Yet, it proceeded to organize military campaigns aimed at sweeping away what it termed the 'bush mouse', i.e. the TPLF, with the further intent of destroying the 'bandits' in Eritrea. The *Dergue*'s dream was too ambitious for it had only been in government for a year and had begun to implement unpopular policies among a population where sympathy lies with locally born rebel forces. The *Dergue* was unable to observe its subjective and objective limitations, especially in the northern part of Ethiopia where rebellion against the central government was raging openly in Eritrea and under the surface in Tigrai. From then on, TPLF guerrilla units continued their surprise attacks and ambushes on isolated stationary or mobile government forces and at the same time created an area under their sphere of control. Once the movement entered the guerrilla phase, its central objective was not simply to isolate the enemy but also, as Ahmad put it, '...to confirm, perpetuate, and institutionalize it by providing an alternative to the discredited regime through the creation of 'parallel hierarchies'' (in Miller and Aya 1971: 157). In such a manner and with the all-round support of the poor peasants their area of operation in central and eastern Tigrai broadened.

Encounter with the TLF

The TLF initially started as a clandestine urban-based movement under the name of *Mahber Politica Tegaru* (Political Association of Tigraians) in the early 1970s. Its leaders were two university graduates, historian Yohannes Tekle-Haimanot and Gebre-Kidan Asfaha, who was a chemist. Some sources indicate that Yohannes Tekle-Haimanot, Amare Tesfu and Giday Gebre-Wahid formed the TLF in late 1972 but whether this is true or not, the fact remains that before the organization declared its existence, Amare was eliminated by the organization he was creating and Giday was executed by the ruling *Dergue*, leaving the responsibility of leadership to Yohannes and Gebre-Kidan. Unlike most politicized university youth, these two *Mahber Politica* leaders were not seen as real participants in the revolutionary Ethiopian students' movement of the day. The reason for their withdrawal from the Ethiopian students' movement became clearer later, when they issued their position paper on the question of Tigrai, known as *Kiya Tigrai (History of Tigrai)*. In *Kiya Tigrai*, they stated that Tigrai had never been an independent entity from the rest of Ethiopia and implied that their struggle was meant to realize this position. Apart from this locally disseminated paper, very little was known of the organization's activities at that time.

The TLF's contact with the Eritrean Liberation Front (ELF) on the other hand appears to have started in the early 1970s, long before it emerged as a front. It was during this time that some revolutionary nationalist individuals like Tekeste Wubneh, Mussie Kidane and Amare Tesfu from the ranks of the Ethiopian students' movement joined them. This group, however, was soon to find itself at odds with Yohannes's group which had a long-standing relationship with TLF leaders like Melake Tekle. While the TLF as an organization had strong and cordial relations with the ELF, it had no relationship with the EPLF, which at the time had already established some sort of working relationship with the Ethiopian Left. The TLF appeared determined to demonstrate their Tigraian ultra-nationalist stance by keeping a distance from the EPLF, which was showing some efforts to accommodate the Ethiopian Left. In fact, at times it rallied with the ELF in condemning the EPLF of harbouring Ethiopian revolutionaries who they thought would forge a multinational leftist party that might unite the Eritrean and Ethiopian revolutionaries under one banner.

Knowing the advantage of maintaining working relations with both the Eritrean fronts and that the ELF was harbouring the TLF, the TPLF still kept on knocking on the ELF's doors. For obvious reasons, the ELF was never enthusiastic about its relations with the TPLF. Association with the EPLF was also not dependable, for the EPLF continued to adore the general Ethiopian Left of which the EPRP was their most favourite. There was a remote hope, however, that by forging unity with the TLF and by extension, a good relationship with the ELF would develop.

For practical reasons, even before the TPLF moved to the central Tigrai region, it had established contacts with the TLF while the latter was making occasional appearances in Tigrai from its initial base in the ELF-held territory. In October 1975, the TPLF took the initiative to establish formal contact with the TLF and invited the organization to send its delegates to the TPLF area of operation for an introductory meeting. Yemene Gebre-Meskel and Gebru Bezabih were entrusted by the TLF with that task and came to the TPLF area for a couple of days to get acquainted and conduct a series of discussions with the leadership and all TPLF members. The discussions covered a range of topics, among which three remained unsettled. These three main differences with the TLF were:[43]

- The nature and scope of the Tigraian national movement, which the TLF put as a struggle for independence, while the TPLF considered itself to be a movement for self-determination. This contentious issue brought into the picture individuals within the TPLF, like Sibhat Nega, who held similar positions to those of the TLF but were unable to articulate or substantiate them and hence were forced to keep a low profile.

- The setting up of the leadership, which for the TPLF had to be elected by the front's members, while TLF leaders were simply replaced by the top leaders when the need arose.

- The conditions of prominent fighters, like Amare Tesfu, Mussie Kidane and Tekeste Wubneh, whose whereabouts had become mysterious since they joined the TLF.

Although an atmosphere of cordiality and the wish to become one stronger organization existed, these unresolved issues pending higher level meetings definitely left some unfinished business between them. However, both sides emphasized the need to forge unity between the two fronts and to fight the common repressive system represented by the *Dergue*. The two visitors from the TLF returned with positive feelings. A higher-level meeting was agreed upon for the following month, once the TPLF had established a permanent base in the eastern part of Tigrai.

The TPLF continued its march to the east and in early November 1975 it established a temporary base area at Zegebla in the district of Agame to where the TLF was invited by the TPLF to conclude the unity agreement. By the time the TLF and its top leaders had reached Zegebla where the TPLF was stationed, an unexpected development had arisen: the TLF had been split into three factions, one led by Yohannes Tekle-Haimanot, the second by *gerazmach* Kahsay Dori and his brother Subagadis Dori, and the third by

---

43 For a broader understanding of the differences and the subsequent clash between the two organizations that led to the elimination of the TLF, see TPLF, *'Fitsametat-Woyyanena'* (in Tigrigna, 1978 E.C.), pp. 99-104. Also in a leaflet that was distributed throughout Tigrai immediately after the incident, the TPLF had informed the public about the inside story of the TLF and the measures taken by the TPLF.

Dejen Tessema. While the whereabouts of the second and third groups were shrouded in secrecy at that time, only the group led by Yohannes came to Zegebla to deliberate and conclude the agreement of unity.

The news of their split spread among TPLF fighters as it reached them from fleeing fighters, among them Haile Sobia and Abraha Wodi Sebaa, who were disgusted by the causes that triggered the division in the TLF. It was reported that the main cause of the split was the criminality of Yohannes's group, which dominated the organization. They were alleged to have had about seventeen fighters killed who were thought to be standing in the way or were seen as potential opponents. No comprehensible or sound reason for the alleged killings transpired. Among the victims were prominent nationalist revolutionaries, like Amare Tesfu, Mussie Kidane, Sied Mohammed Tiam and Tekeste Wubneh. The executions of these nationalist revolutionaries were secretly carried out. This tragic story infuriated all TPLF fighters who demanded that the process of unity with the TLF be halted and measures taken to clarify the situation. In the TPLF, Sibhat Nega, Yemane Kidane and Meles Zenawi, without the consent of the leadership, took the lead in encouraging the fighters to take immediate measures against the TLF. They also accused the TPLF leadership of engaging the organization in a process of unity with bandits of the criminal type. They even coined a slogan that ran: 'It is better to unite with *Hawelti* Aksum (i.e. the Aksum stelae, an inanimate object) than with such reactionaries'.

The TPLF leadership had no option but to call an emergency meeting and discuss how to handle this delicate matter that had the potential of bringing serious disruption in both camps or even of triggering a bloody conflict between the two fronts. After a lengthy debate, the TPLF leadership unanimously decided to take the less risky measure of physically overpowering and disarming the TLF fighters, who numbered less than a third in number of TPLF fighters. This was the safest way to tackle the crisis that divided the TLF and had left the TPLF in shock. It was arranged in such a way that three or four TPLF fighters and one TLF fighter would constitute a unit within a squad and leave for the trenches where they would sleep at night in the normal guerrilla formation during rest hours. Then early in the morning of 11 November 1975, a secret signal, which was only given to the TPLF fighters, would alert them to pin down the TLF fighters and snatch their weapons. As the ratio of TLF-TPLF fighters was one to three or four, it was believed this tactic was the most efficient and likely to cause the least or no bloodshed. It was carried out as planned, but two of the TLF fighters were killed in a skirmish that got out of hand in two of the units, as the two attempted to escape violent arrest and were confronted by panic-stricken fighters.[44] Sadly, one of the fighters who lost his life in the unexpected skirmish was Yemane Gebre-Meskel who had led the TLF delegation to the TPLF a few months earlier. The others were all arrested without further casualties.

The same morning, a meeting of all the TPLF fighters and the arrested TLF members was called and the whole purpose of the operation was discussed. In the afternoon, each TLF member was asked two key questions: Why did the split arise? And where are the other seventeen prominent fighters? All fingers pointed to Yohannes Tekle-Haimanot and his close associates Gebre-Kidan Asfaha, Tefera Kassa, Taddesse Tilahun, and Yemane Gebre-Meskel, including the absentees Desta Tesfay and Hailekiros Aseged as 'people with sinister motives' who had caused the fighters' disappearance. When the leaders were asked about these missing fighters, they did not hesitate to admit their misdeeds but claimed that it was for 'political reasons'. What this meant, however, was not clear except that Yohannes's group, which had the upper hand in the organization, was uncomfortable with their general attitude. They all testified without exception that Amare Tesfu in Meqele, Mussie Kidane in Addis Ababa, Tekeste Wubneh in Eritrea (ELF territory), Sied Mohammed Tiam in Gundagunde, Tigrai, had been killed. So, except for the few leaders who admitted responsibility for the crimes, there was no reason to hold the other fighters as prisoners. The same day, the majority of the TLF fighters were set free and given the chance either to reorganize the TLF or start afresh the unity process, or join the TPLF on an individual basis or go to any place of their choice. A lot of them joined the TPLF and some left to go home but the idea of reorganizing the TLF was buried with Yohannes and Taddesse, who were later executed by the TPLF for their acts. Tefera Kassa escaped from prison, thus avoiding any kind of punishment.

Before a final decision on the fate of the two imprisoned TLF leaders was reached, the TPLF leadership invited the ELF and the EPLF to send delegates to look into the delicate criminal case of the TLF and share their views as to how it should be handled. Delegates of both Eritrean fronts came up to Deima, the TPLF territory, and conducted their own independent investigation by discussing the matter with the two TLF leaders. Finally, they arrived at the same conclusion as the TPLF leaders had earlier. Both delegates concluded that Yohannes's group had committed crimes against their own colleagues for reasons that were not acceptable by any measure.[45]

---

44 Berhe Hagos, who was present during the incident and who later abandoned the TPLF, remarked that the inexperienced and nervous fighters who fired at the two victims were partly to blame. Interview: Berhe Hagos, Ottawa, 27 August 2008.

45 According to Yohannes Tekle-Haimanot, the Amare group was suspected of abandoning the ethno-nationalist TLF to joining a multi-national organization like the EPRP,

No one could figure out why at the earliest stage of their struggle they should first turn on their comrades while there was a common enemy out there. The ELF delegates were also annoyed by the revelation of their colleagues' collaboration in some of the killings. The fact that some of the TLF fighters were killed in their own territory and that the execution of two TLF members had been carried out by ELF fighters with the consent of their commanders, on behalf of the TLF, was indeed a stain on the group.

Some people, especially TLF sympathizers, accused the TPLF leadership simply of annihilating an organization which had its own rights. From the outset, one can logically argue that way without considering the whole context of the matter. It was true that the TPLF had taken severe measures that amounted to the liquidation of its counterpart. From a legalistic point of view, the conduct looks unacceptable but there was no legal framework to which the two organizations could be bound. At such a time, it was left to one's conscience to assess under what circumstances the measure was taken and arrive at a balanced conclusion, in the light of the unjustifiable elimination of seventeen young Tigraians who had just started to fight for the sake of their people, and without providing sound justification but only suspicion. On the other hand, if one has to charge TPLF leaders with measures they committed against fellow fighters later in the struggle, then one has the obligation to use the same yardstick to pass judgment on the extreme measures committed by the TLF leaders as well. Finally, it can be said that initially the TPLF had no reason or interest in destroying the TLF. In fact, as its previous activities and relations with the TLF indicated, it was committed to forge a broader union and to evolve as a stronger front capable of challenging the government in power. Basically, this was why the TPLF had to make the long march to the east (unfamiliar territory at the time) and conduct a series of meetings not only with the TLF but also with other organizations like the EPRP, as we will discuss in the next chapter. This was why the TPLF offered the innocent TLF fighters the chance to reinstate their organization, and made efforts to contact the latter's urban members in order to cooperate on this track.

Deima – The Eastern Base

The meandering march of the TPLF group from the western to the eastern part of Tigrai seemed to have ended at Deima, one of the elevated plateaus in the chain of escarpments facing the Danakil lowlands. Deima is located in the district of Agame, northeast Tigrai. This place was selected as a base because of its rugged terrain which made it less accessible for

---

an allegation that was not corroborated by the facts.

enemy infiltration. It was also strategically situated at the centre of the future deployment of forces to the south and west of Tigrai. A base area was necessary in order to function as an organization that waged politico-military war, although the tactic had to be guerrilla warfare until a substantial force was created to match the government forces. Without a base area, it was difficult to cope with the almost daily arrival of newcomers to the Front (varying from 5 to 20 at the time) and to carry on with military training. There was a need to establish departments that could support the guerrilla forces. After the controversial measure that decided the fate of the TLF, the mountainous Aaiga area had served as a base area for about a month but was not suitable in many aspects: it was too cold to live in and too rugged for the transportation of supplies. Deima, however, was better situated to the group's requirements, so it was established there.

In Deima, a few departments – like the political, economic and medical sections – were established for the first time to act as back-up for the guerrilla army, which constituted the major force in the TPLF with well over a hundred combatants at the time. Here the movement quickly grew. Squads of 25 to 30 fighters in each were deployed from Deima in all directions to mobilize the people and attack the enemy whenever the opportunity arose. Enemy-held towns were penetrated at night to reach clandestine members and give them assignments or receive reports, to punish or warn enemy collaborators, especially those who inflicted serious damage on the organization and its members, and to attack enemy posts that hindered the front's mobility. In March 1976, a TPLF squad entered Adigrat, the capital of Agame, where a heavy government artillery unit was stationed and took printing equipment from the high school situated next to the unit.

Armed *agitprop* groups were created to stir up public feeling in the struggle for self-determination and organize the peasantry at various levels, including forming clandestine groups that could carry out secret missions. Such secret peasant cells played a crucial role in infiltrating and destabilizing rival organizations and reaching members in *Dergue*-held territories. The political fight against the EDU and the EPRP started in such a subtle manner until the rival organizations were finally isolated from the people and the people would join the TPLF side.

While the TPLF's activities seemed to be moving smoothly from Deima, another shock suddenly beset the young organization. This time it was the work of a spy sent by the government military forces based in Deki-Amhare, Eritrea. He was a young boy of about fourteen. There was no place in the organization at that time for boys of his age, but he claimed that he had no parents to help him and was forced to work for military officers who mistreated him. He was therefore allowed to stay in the base area. He was charming and became popular in a very short period. He started his mission by being involved and reporting minor mistakes made by ordinary members. From there on, he began reporting more serious matters, including the fact that certain fighters were spreading feelings of apathy and some had even gone as far as devising plans to kill other fighters by putting poison in the food and water they consumed. He strengthened his allegations by adding that there were peasant collaborators who were supplying the poison for this purpose. He gave a list of more than fifteen fighters and two peasants living nearby and implicated them in the alleged spy network.

Disturbed by this news and not having experience in how to handle such espionage charges, the leadership hastily ordered the arrest of the named fighters and peasants, which was followed by interrogation under torture. One innocent fighter, Bahta, died during this amateurish investigation. Chaos and fear among the rank and file began to reign and many doubted the informant when they began to realize that the investigation was leading nowhere. At that point, the leadership understood that it was following the wrong course and the investigation of members was halted and turned on the boy who had caused the havoc.

After a long investigation and interrogation, the boy admitted that he was a spy sent by military intelligence at Deki-Amhare to gradually create mistrust among the fighters and anarchy in the front. He admitted that he had been sent for that specific purpose, and was sent to prison where he was finally executed. Although this incident was solved in a relatively short span of time, it nevertheless created bad feelings and lingering elements of mistrust among the fellow fighters.

Another undertaking in Deima was the preparation for the fighters' congress and celebration of the first anniversary of the TPLF's formation, due to take place on 18 February 1976 (11 Lekatit 1968 E.C.). Until this time, the organization's founders had assumed the leadership role without any special mandate. Now that the organization was growing in size and poised to embark upon much broader tasks and responsibilities, the authority to lead had to be mandated in a congress, as tradition in democratic organizations dictates. From experience in university student politics, the leading elements of the TPLF knew how elections were organized and they had, at least in theory, read about Western and Eastern examples. An organization like the TPLF that claimed to be Marxist needed to develop a flawless character that some such organizations had demonstrated elsewhere. The leadership formulated a set of criteria to elect a leader. These were: someone who had struggled for at least two-thirds of the front's existence; was above the age of 21; was determined to preserve the culture and language of Tigrai;

had a strong stand against feudalism, imperialism, fascism and national oppression; and was courageous, disciplined and loyal to the organization.

Weeks earlier, all the units had begun to converge on Deima. About 120 *tegadelti* (revolutionary fighting members) from the front assembled and began discussing the future programme, constitution and bylaws. Until this time, the organization's guidelines had been those inscribed in a two-page TNO document, drafted a year earlier in Addis Ababa. The document stated, in a nutshell, that the struggle was for the realization of the self-determination of Tigrai within the bounds of a democratic Ethiopia and that it would be waged in the form of an armed insurrection that would start in the rural areas of Tigrai. The general discussions and understanding reached in Deima reflected the basic tenets of this document. The details of the programme were to be written and published in the months ahead, as the materials required for publication purposes were not yet available. The interpretation of self-determination, however, was altered by a group of more parochial nationalists to mean the 'secession' of Tigrai from Ethiopia later in 1976, as was stipulated in the so-called TPLF manifesto then issued.

The congress also elected a seven-man *Marrihentte* (leadership) as an executive body to lead the TPLF for the coming three years. Every fighting member had the right to vote but, to be elected as a leader one had to pass the criteria set in advance. Accordingly, six former leaders (Agazi, Mussie, Abbay, Seyoum, Giday and Aregawi) got the highest votes. Sibhat, a latecomer, also obtained enough votes to secure him a seat in the leadership. Of the former leaders, Sihul voluntarily withdrew from the running for a *Marrihentte* position with the intention of playing a reconciliatory and public relations role, while Asfaha and Hailu failed to secure enough votes. Only Hailu complained of not being elected, accusing his former colleagues in the leadership of spreading negative information about him. Despite individual misgivings, the congress carried on with high enthusiasm and a sense of commitment to sacrifice whatever the struggle required. For the first time, a cultural troupe was assembled by Girmay Lemma to mark the founding of the TPLF. They invoked, among other things, the spirit of the original 1943 Woyyane revolt while referring to the current uprising as the Second Woyyane, and played folk music with a revolutionary content to adorn the occasion of the first anniversary, to boost the fighting spirit of the *tegadelti*. This cultural troupe later played a crucial role not only in raising the spirits of the fighting forces but also in the mobilization of the entire Tigraian society.

Under the executive body, three main committees (one political, one military and one socio-economic) plus the chairmanship and the foreign section, each run by a member of the *Marrihentte*, were set up. The

Marrihentte was collective, with Aregawi elected as chairman to coordinate the committees, while Mussie, Abbay, Agazi and Seyoum headed the military, political, socio-economic and foreign committees respectively. The nature of the guerrilla warfare that had stretched through western, central and eastern Tigrai forced *Marrihentte* members to expand their interests and be involved in all the committees' activities. Each committee had several departments. The departments of culture (coded 01); political work (04), security (06), public relations (07) and administration (08) fell under the political committee. Departments of military intelligence (00), training (02), ordnance/arms (09) and the whole fighting forces (regular, militia and special units) were under the military committee. Health (03), the logistical supply (05), education (001), and agriculture (011) were departments that were centralized by the socio-economic committee. With military engagement being the front's main preoccupation in those early days, departments that had no immediate contribution to the guerrilla war were left to function with a bare minimum of personnel.

Two platoons, whose collective name were *Haili* (force) and with no fewer than 45 combat troops in each, were formed. A *Haili* could have been the equivalent of an English company, but number-wise the *Haili* was about the size of a platoon. One was called *Haili Woyyane* and was deployed to the east and the south, where the First Woyyane was started, while the other, called *Haili Dedebit,* was to cover the central and western regions. These *Hailis* had serious tasks to accomplish, ranging from fighting government forces to challenging rival fronts and local *shiftas* (bandits) who were still rampant in Tigrai.

To sum up, the first year of the TPLF's struggle was for setting up the organization, defining the many aspects of the struggle and testing them on the ground. Establishing the right relationship within the front and with other Ethiopian organizations and the Eritrean fronts was a complicated task that, at times, resulted in armed confrontation. When politics falls into the hands of young revolutionaries, the tendency to resolve the crisis too hastily and violently seems often to be there. This tendency lingered throughout the struggle, and continued to be the source of conflict and often despair within and outside the TPLF.

Internally, the crisis that was instigated by the peasant group and was seemingly aimed at the annihilation of the educated leadership was foiled thanks to the sharp observations and reaction of Tsegay Tesfay (Kokab) and persistent advice from Sihul. Although the initial relationship with the TLF was for a constructive journey, it was destined by the internal circumstances of violence in the TLF itself to end violently. Although one could not deny the presence of a radical youth mentality in the TPLF which could led to countervailing violent measures in such circumstance, whether there was an alternative way of managing the TLF case remains a question even today.

The hardships of guerrilla life especially in the early days of the struggle in the rugged terrain of Tigrai, the elevation of which ranges from five metres below see level in the Afar region to over 4000 metres above sea level in the Mount Alajie range and to even 4620 meters in the operational zone in the Semien mountains across the Tekeze River, were immense. Often the legs of half of the squad members were burnt as they slept around a fire to keep warm in the cold climate in Semien. Yet neither such hardships nor the frequent battles against adversaries had a restraining influence on the spirit of the TPLF fighters. Their determination to finish the war and defeat the enemy remained intact throughout. Although the systematically planned and structured approach of mobilizing the people had not yet begun at this stage, the ideologically motivated guerrilla activities by themselves as well as the revolutionary objectives proclaimed were effective mobilizing means, and the people began to give their total support to the front. The extent of the Tigrai people's support was encouraging and the guerrilla units did not have to worry about food and other basic supplies when they passed through villages. And some parents even went as far as urging their children to join the front.

Chapter 5

Mobilization and Armed Confrontation

Introduction

Before the armed struggle was launched and as discussed in chapter one, the disgruntled elite of Tigrai was focused on mobilizing the different social groups in and outside Tigrai on one core objective: the 'right to self-determination'. This was basically an ethno-nationalist call for the attainment of political space within the Ethiopian state structure. This movement was peaceful but the idea grew that could get the TNO nowhere and that a higher form of struggle was called for. Chapter 3 treats the continuation of the same political struggle with a different *modus operandi*, i.e. revolutionary armed struggle. This entailed not only the ultimate destruction of government structures and means of control in the rural areas by isolating the enemy from the population, but also the winning of hearts and minds of the peasantry by painting a better future for them. This comprised the introduction of reforms, uprooting bandits and eliminating rival forces that were considered as obstacles to the realization of the self-determination and social improvement of Tigrai. With this approach to tackling opposing forces, the organization would also deal with internal dissenters.

With the prevalence of the TPLF through armed confrontation, it was also creating the necessary organizational structures to administer and effectively engage the people in the struggle. Through its administrative structures, the Front was eventually able to direct the affairs of the people and saw itself capable to respond to the needs of the people in ways that would embolden the general struggle outlined by the Front, ostensibly to liberate the people from all sorts of oppression and domination.

Self-determination as a Means of Mobilization

'How did the TPLF manage to mobilize the people of Tigrai and seize power in Ethiopia after defeating one of the strongest armies in Africa?' was, and still is, a question often asked by academics, historians and others[46]. Indeed, it seemed unthinkable that a small ethno-nationalist organization claiming to represent about 3.5 million people could ultimately defeat the state army of Ethiopia, which had a population of 55 million with a well-established, strong army. There seems to be no short and simple answer to this multi-faceted question. Nevertheless, we can see that the answer lies in the interplay of many factors, among them the active participation of ordinary people (the 'masses'), the will of the fighting force, well-thought-out strategy and tactics, competent leadership focused on the cause, and, to a certain extent, external support, as is the case in almost every war waged by an inferior force against a superior government army.

Considering the mobilization process and the fast growth of the TPLF, a combination of many old and contemporary factors, grounded on ethno-nationalist sentiments, drew the people of Tigrai to rally behind the TPLF. Some of the long-standing factors were the evocation of the glorious past coupled with the history of the Tigraian struggle for justice such as the uprising of the first *Woyyane* in 1942-43 and the sacrifices the forefathers made. The increasingly dismal situation and deep dissatisfaction of Tigraians at the time was the most immediate factor that drew the people to embrace the insurgent movement. On the other hand, one should always bear in mind that the *Dergue*, a ruthless military dictatorship since its inception, created a host of opponents and enemies throughout Ethiopia because of its authoritarian and coercive policies. First of all, it rejected every call for self-determination, genuine or not, by imposing the motto of '*Ethiopia Tikdem*',[47] the interpretation of which was obscure even to the members

---

46 Social scientists, including Prof. Christopher Clapham and Dr. Stephen Ellis, have raised this very question repeatedly with the author. This study, among other things, attempts to provide an answer via an insider's analytical observations.

47 According to some *Dergue* members '*Ethiopia Tikdem*' meant securing the territorial integrity of the country and to others it meant transforming Ethiopia to a socialist state and still to others it meant creating a vibrant capitalist nation. This was a reflection of the ideological variants within the spontaneously formed military ruling group, the

of the *Dergue* themselves. Second, it espoused and imposed Marxism-Leninism in a predominantly traditional society of Ethiopia where a dictatorship, be it 'proletarian' or military, would not have been tolerated in any measure. In addition, the harsh policies of agricultural collectivization and the regimentation of society in *qebele* associations, followed by a lack of economic success, infuriated vast sectors of the population. Also, unpopular and mistaken government policies in reaction to legitimate, collective demands of the people, accompanied by repressive measures the severity of which was new in the history of the country, pushed the people towards accepting the TPLF as a saviour from the policies of the *Dergue*. The heightened use of violence by government forces, as Gurr and Goldstone (1991: 334) demonstrate, '…increased popular sentiment and active support for revolutionary movements' such as the TPLF. Confrontations that tied up government forces on various fronts throughout the country (e.g., Eritrea, Somalia in 1977-78) certainly facilitated TPLF mobilization efforts and its subsequent progressive and rapid growth.[48] And last but not least, the TPLF's organizational structure down to the village level as well as its tactics of mobilization and the pragmatic style of its leadership and the determination of the rebel army were crucial factors that continued to attract people to the Front. Finally, with its tactics, the TPLF began the war by engaging the enemy in isolated battles where they could be fairly sure of victory. Success in these battles, in turn, were used to demonstrate the 'invincibility of the people's war' led by the Front. Once the TPLF had created the conditions for mass mobilization and a 'people's war' to feed on one another in the struggle for self-determination, its outdoing the rival fronts and triumphing over its main enemy, the *Dergue*, became imminent.

War by its nature has the tendency of urging people to take sides and participate at various levels. The war waged by the TPLF, likewise, urged the Tigraians to participate and pay sacrifices by declaring that the war was waged 'on behalf of the oppressed Tigraian masses'. Many people were attracted by the courageous challenge taken up by 'their sons and daughters', the change the Front promised, and the hopes they put forward of achieving victory. As the war intensified, becoming increasingly a war of survival and necessity with social and economic aspects, more and more people saw no alternative but to support the TPLF, in the hope of winning as soon as possible and get back to normal life. This momentum in itself was a mobilizing factor that drew the common people to the struggle and

Dergue. Understandably, the people in general had no clear thought of what '*Ethiopia Tikdem*' meant.

48 In the vast rural areas of Tigrai, there was no meaningful government hold or influence to deter the mobility of the TPLF. In rural Tigrai, all *Dergue* activity generated resistance and was nipped in the bud.

kept them tied to the Front, the organization of their sons and daughters. Still, however intrinsic the relationship between the Front and the people might now appear, elements of coercion, at times disguised and proclaimed as 'necessary' for the success of the struggle, could not be ruled out in such circumstances.

The entire mobilization drive of the TPLF was geared to winning the war against the *Dergue*. For many rural Tigraians, the *Dergue* was an unfamiliar force that had emerged in the centre of the country, far from Tigrai. This intensive mobilization was accompanied by promises of progress in all aspects of life under a system of 'true socialist democracy' after the defeat of the *Dergue*. Although the *Dergue*, like the TPLF, had come up with similar revolutionary slogans to mobilize the Ethiopian people, it could not impress Tigraians, whose grievances against governments from the centre had gone too far to mend. Trust in the central government had been gradually eroded since the early 1940s and in Emperor Haile Selassie's last years it had got worse, with famine, poverty, repression and hopelessness more pronounced than ever. As mentioned above, this situation had already created responses of covert ethno-nationalist mobilization, growing to full intensity among the young generation. The *Dergue*, which since 1974 started its reign hitting the drums of war and terror, had neither the legitimacy nor the wisdom to reverse this trend and improve the gloomy conditions or ease tensions. By the mid-1970s, the great majority of Tigraians were already anticipating locally grown resistance to lead them out of the quagmire and found the TPLF filling the gap. With a well-articulated ethno-nationalist ideology and eclectically crafted class rhetoric, the TPLF answered the clamour of Tigraians. Had the TPLF failed to fill this gap, it was likely that another local force, for example the TLF or *Teranafit*/EDU, would have become the leading organization in Tigrai given the readiness of the people to take matters into their own hands. However, with the determination of its fighting forces and excellent mobilization tactics, the TPLF was in a position to prevail.

Since the hardship and neglect caused by central governments were obvious to the people, there was no need for the TPLF to convince people of the dismal conditions existing in Tigrai. Instead by making several practical and daring socio-economic moves to mitigate the situation, such as opening clinics and schools in remote villages, it demonstrated that it was there to pose a real challenge and enable the people to stand up and do something. The decades-long neglect of the region by the central government, the lawlessness and the rampant banditry (*shiftinnet*) of the criminal type and other social miseries could perhaps be stopped and corrected only by a home-grown force. The argument that the TPLF should have given the *Dergue* the chance to put its revolutionary promises into practice and redress hardship and fulfil the aspirations of the people is not convincing – there were no indications that this was occurring.

In the late 1970s, TPLF guerrilla units, first in a number of platoons and later growing fast into companies, could easily penetrate any part of rural Tigrai, as far as the suburbs of the towns held by government forces, to carry out political or military missions. Attacking isolated military posts, ambushing enemy troops, kidnapping or killing enemy collaborators and sneaking into enemy-held towns to take in or out necessary materials for the Front had become routine activities for the units. Most such operations were accomplished as planned because they were conducted in circumstances and at the time of choice and with the devotion of highly motivated young fighters. Such activities boosted the morale of the fighting forces and of the people, whose trust in the TPLF was growing steadily. Government troops appeared to have no effective defence, let alone show meaningful counter-offensives, except for rear attacks organized in a huge campaign form and in most cases ending in failure.

Uprooting the *Shiftas* (Bandits)[49]

In the first and second year of the struggle, if there was resistance of any significance at all in rural Tigrai, it came from the criminal *shiftas* (bandits) who under previous regimes had been able to swarm all over the region. Now, not only the territory the various *shiftas* controlled was vital to the growth of the TPLF but also their very existence had to be terminated to allow the TPLF to develop a social base. Clearing away the scourge of the *shiftas* was thus one of the top priorities of the TPLF, its execution proving to be an effective catalyst of mobilization.

The criminal *shiftas* in Tigrai were numerous and lived off robbery and subjecting people to torment. They slaughtered peasants' animals for a day's meal, raped women, robbed and burned down houses whenever their demands were not met. They also killed anybody who dared to stand in their way, living in the bush outside and above the law. Some of the *shiftas* were well established in the remote rural areas, with the sizeable wealth they had amassed from the peasantry, and they even had a quasi-autonomous territory that they ruled at will. They levied tax, fines or ransom as they wished. They used family connections as their intelligence network; and in return, family members were protected from intrusion by other *shiftas*. Alemshet Tewolde, who gave himself the title of *dejazmach*, which was changed to *major* when

---

49 The broad meaning of banditry (Tigrigna: *shiftinet*), ranging from social protest to criminal practices, should be considered in reading this section. Here we are dealing with the *shifta* of the criminal type.

he joined the EDU later on, was just one well-known example. Along the river gorges in Tekeze and Mereb and deep in the rural areas, there were hundreds of such *shiftas* who lived off exploiting and humiliating peasants and merchants.

In the few months after the start of the armed struggle, the TPLF began to adopt strict measures on the *shiftas* by identifying those who were fighting back and at times inflicting serious damage on TPLF units. By dealing with the important *shiftas*, the numerous small ones became demoralized and gave up without resistance. Many notorious *shiftas* were apprehended and paraded before the community they had disgraced. At public gatherings, their misdemeanours were exposed and they were punished for the crimes they committed. Some who had committed only minor crimes were set free after pleading guilty and those who were convinced of the causes of the national struggle were allowed to join the Front. Many of the *shiftas* who resisted arrest were killed in shootouts. A number joined other fronts like the EDU, where they were welcomed without question. Later, in the confrontation with the EDU, they were the ones who fought fiercely to avenge their grudges against the TPLF.

The TPLF army was highly disciplined. Its behaviour exceeded the expectations of the people because it used to be common practice in Tigrai for an armed individual to exhibit coercion whenever s/he wanted something. If there was any one thing that earned praise for the TPLF, it was the way it maintained discipline in its army all the way through the struggle. Initially, all the leading elements of the TPLF were familiar with the manual entitled 'Who is a Revolutionary' – a text that contained a list of 'do's' and 'don'ts' for those engaged in a revolutionary and/or liberation movement. They strictly maintained the discipline of the army according to this manual. There was also a set of internal rules that told fighters what they could and could not do, accompanied by disciplinary measures to be taken if someone was found to be breaking the rules. For instance, rape was punishable by death. The rigorous political education which was given to the army almost every day was partly political and partly a rehearsal of 'Who is a Revolutionary'. There were *political cadres* in every unit, small or big, who ensured adherence to the code of conduct and who took care of the weekly (sometimes even daily) 'criticism and self-criticism sessions' (*gimgema*) where 'undesirable behaviour' was scrutinized. A fighter's every single movement was under surveillance and he could not leave his unit even for water without the commander's permission and if s/he had secured permission to leave, there would be someone accompanying him/her. When the fighters showed such (unprecedented) discipline, the people began to relax and participate more freely in the activities initiated by the Front.

Women could mix with the TPLF army without the fear of being raped. Children would sit around TPLF fighters to discuss relevant issues on an equal basis. They also played, learned and listened or told stories related to the struggles of the past and present. The peasants began to enjoy their rights over their property. Nobody could touch their property. When a TPLF platoon or company arrived in a village and needed food, it would present its request through the village public relations officer called *kuadere* who would collect whatever kind of food the villagers had to offer. Those who could not afford to provide their share were exempted, thereby observing the principle of equality in the TPLF's administration. However, if a well-to-do peasant refused to provide the expected supply, the *kuadere* would bring the case before the community for scrutiny and punishment, which could be carried out by the TPLF. Such administrative enforcement was applied with every other service the Front required, and refusal was unacceptable.

When in late 1976-77 the TPLF had prevailed and *shiftas* had no more place to hide and the consequences for them were too obvious if they dared to show up, people began to feel free to move from place to place to trade, to farm or visit relatives without the fear of harassment and robbery. The barriers of freedom of mobility seemed to have been removed, and also the flow of young recruits from the community increased with every passing day. To the peasants, it was a time of relief, demonstrated by their new-found mobility and their prompt response to calls from the Front. Organized to handle matters in their respective villages, the peasants began to feel powerful with or without the presence of the TPLF in the vicinity. Locally elected peasant leaders ran the defence and administrative functions of their respective localities. Trust and confidence were thus growing both ways. Thus the TPLF in less than a year since the launch of its mobilization of the people was taking lasting shape. Peasants were organized at different levels to support themselves and the Front. They had to defend and administer the territory and elect capable men and women from their ranks to lead them. Militia forces were created not only to keep peace and order in their territory but also to back the regular guerrilla forces in major engagements with the enemy, sometimes far from their villages. Peasants, women and the youth formed separate associations and became involved in the different activities outlined by the Front or their association. Participating in the literacy campaign and political education, supplying the fighting forces with food and water, carrying the wounded to safe places for treatment, burying the dead and passing information on *shiftas* who were still on the loose, were some of the routine activities of the village people and executed by their respective associations. Other activities were undertaken directly by the organization, which had several departments for the purpose (see Fig. 3.1).

Organizational Development and Structure

The diagram in Figure 3.1 was adopted by the TPLF Fighters' Congress held in 1976 and it developed into the diagram in Figure 3.2 in subsequent years leading up to the First Organizational Congress, convened in 1979. Mass (civic) associations were represented at the latter congress.

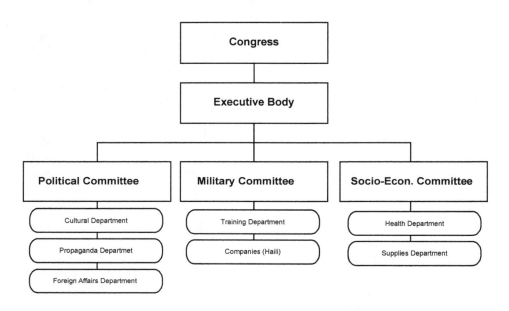

Figure 3.1 TPLF Organizational Chart, 1976

The organizational structure of the TPLF started to take shape during the Fighters' Congress held in Diema, in the district of Agame. The Fighters' Congress elected a seven-man executive body commonly called the *merihnet* (leadership). Once the executive body was formed, the task of creating and developing the remaining structure with the need and size of the Front fell to it. As the leaders were Marxist revolutionary by persuasion, it was obvious both the initial and the latter structures resembled that of a Marxist-Leninist vanguard party. The rest of the fighters had to accept what the few top leaders decided. All departments in the Front fell under three large committees: political, military and socio-economic, with each composed of members of the central committee (CC) led by a member of the politburo. Only the foreign affairs department, which fell under the political committee, was also led by a politburo member. Each committee got its directives from the CC through the politburo that was coordinated by the organization's chairman and vice chairman. The three committees executed CC directives through the various departments assigned to them. In this section we will look at the departments that were directly involved in the mobilization and organization of the people although in practical terms every TPLF section and individual member was somehow involved in self-imposed mobilization tasks.

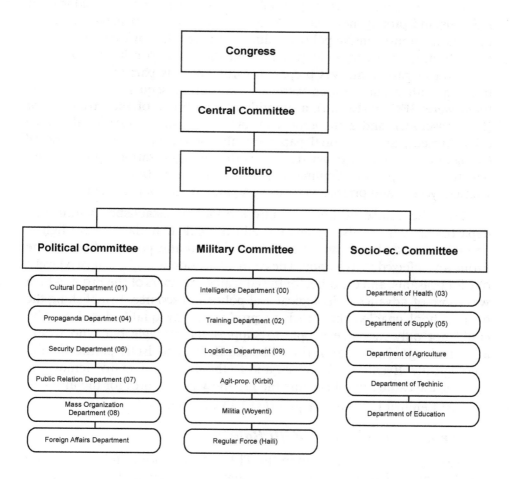

Figure 3.2 TPLF Organizational Chart, 1979

Department of Propaganda (Kifli Politica)

Unlike the other departments, the propaganda department was the seat of the political committee headed by Abbay Tsehaye, and the political directives of the CC and politburo were put into effect under his direct supervision. Meles Zenawi was assigned as deputy head of the department, on the recommendation of Abbay Tsehaye.

The department was responsible for preparing political education manuals and propaganda materials at different levels. For newly recruited fighters, a comprehensive political education manual, providing the essence of revolutionary struggle in general and the right to self-determination of Tigrai in particular, was prepared, to be given as part of the standard training. Other publications were also appearing sequentially. Some of them were: *Woyeen* (Revolt), a monthly official organ of the Front, *Nikah* (Be Conscious), and a theoretical magazine appearing occasionally, *Ittek* (Get Armed), an occasional paper mainly for the peasants, and *Tegadel* (Struggle), an internal paper dealing with the organization's positive and negative developments. Seminar papers for various sections of society, like women, youth, and priests, were also prepared in this department.

Over the course of time, a cadre school was established within this department which also prepared educational materials. Any fighter committed to and well versed in the ideological and political lines of the Front was referred to as a *cadre*. The cadre education was given at two levels: one for peasants, and the other for the educated members of the Front, which was more of advanced ideological and political discourse. Establishing the cadre school enabled the TPLF to produce many qualified cadres who could not only mobilize people to support the struggle but who would also challenge rival organizations like the EPRP and EDU politically and ideologically. Eventually however, and to the dismay of many democratic fighters, the cadre school became the ground where cadres for the ultra-left Marxist Leninist League of Tigrai (MLLT) were hatched.

Department of Culture (Kifli Bahli)

A major agent of mobilization in the TPLF struggle for self-determination was the cultural department. It had been established in 1976 just a few weeks before the first anniversary of the TPLF and was to play a crucial role in the mobilization the mass of Tigraians in the years to come. It was established with Girmay Lemma – then better known as Girmay *Bahli* – as its head, a young dedicated fighter who before he joined the TPLF had been a member of the *Bahli* Tigrai, a cultural band during the last years of Haile Selassie's era. The general directives for the *Kifli Bahli* came from the political committee of the Front, which also had departments of mass organization (*kifli hizbi*), security (*halewa Woyyane*) and public relations (*rikib*) in its administrative structure.

The task given to this department was to undertake the mobilization process through cultural activities that would create social awareness to act collectively in the liberation movement. In other words, the mobilization mandate was aimed at enabling the people of Tigrai to participate in various types of political and military activities involving the promotion of self-determination and the defence of concomitant ideas, values and history that would have to prevail in the future, following the defeat of the repressive *Dergue* government. Girmay was responsible for organizing a cultural troupe and implementing the mobilization directives. After completing the political and military training of the Front, experienced musicians and actors were assigned to the *kifli bahli* to promote the fighting spirit of the entire Tigraian community. It composed poems that reflected the existing condition of the people vis-à-vis its past glories, music that was based on the popular songs of resistance and heroism and short plays that depicted the essence of the struggle. The titles of some of the early songs were: *Zeytishifen hakegn Kiya* (Inextinguishable True History), *Kiltsim hafash* (Forearm of the Masses), *Meny'u bedelegna* (Who is the Culprit), *Aawot n'witsue* (Victory to the Oppressed), *Ka'a jemere!* (Here They Rise Up!), *Walta hizbi* (Shield of the People), *Zeyhilel kalsi* (Irresistible Struggle). The verses of the popular 'Irresistible Struggle', for instance, ran as follows:

> Our sea is the mass of the people,
> Our logistics is the revolutionary courage,
> Our trenches are the mountains around us,
> Our trust is in the correct principles we uphold.

It was the duty of the cultural troupes to visit the villages, playing revolutionary and nationalist songs and perform short plays to educate, entertain and mobilize the people. All cultural activities were performed at night because of the fear of air raids. When a cultural troupe arrived in a village, everybody expected an eventful night. The area designated for assembly and the cultural show would be packed with people long before the show began. When it was time for the show, the cultural troupe would be introduced to the people by a mass organization cadre (*kifli hizbi*) assigned to that area, who in almost every case would narrate the current achievements of the Front and the debacle of the enemy to date. The cadre would then appeal to the people to intensify their participation in the struggle and conclude with the ceaselessly reiterated slogan, 'Our struggle is long and bitter; our victory is definite!' and the crowd had to repeat it raising its fists high in the air. This slogan, which was popularized in various ways, served as therapy whenever government troops had inflicted damage from the air or on the ground. Most of the time, such occasions served as a recruiting ground for new fighters.

One or two songs were dedicated to each section of the society. Children, youth, women, peasants, workers and the militia all had at least one song dedicated to them. The songs often evoked the struggle and sufferings of the working people and recited the responsibilities and expectations of each group. The group got up to dance when its respective song was played and everybody seemed moved by the messages in the lyrics. The lyrics of almost every song ended with messages arousing all the social groups to participate in the war of liberation. Emulating the works of the *Kifli Bahli*, many cultural groups were created in the *woreda* (district) and the small villages. In some *woreda*s, the youth, women, children and older people had formed their own respective cultural troupes and performed at intervals. As events unfolded, the work of the *Kifli Bahli* definitely pulled in millions of people to hear the politics of the day and by so doing proved to be an effective mobilization tool. The department's impact was such that many people were aroused to fight the enemy and also to talk emphatically about it to others.

Department of Mass (civic) Organization (Kifli Hizbi)

It was the *Kifli Hizbi* on the ground that connected the people with the Front in almost all aspects of the struggle, and through it, the Front was able to make its presence felt. Better-educated cadres of the Front were assigned to this department, which dealt directly with the people on matters concerning their administration, organization and fighting spirit or morale. Every liberated district under control of the TPLF had one *kifli hizbi* cadre as an executive administrator, educator and, at times, leader of its fighting militia. In the absence of the *hailitat* (regular fighting forces) in the area, often the cadre was engaged in coordinating the militia to fend off enemy units that attempted to infiltrate their villages.

During the day, the cadres gave political education at public meetings, heard cases that had not been resolved by the local authorities and organized the people to carry out tasks that were required either by the community or the Front. At night, they worked with village cells to learn about enemy activities inside or outside the community and exchange views on how to deal with the situation. They had to foil enemy propaganda or infiltration and, in later years, the activities of rival organizations like the EDU or the EPRP, believed to be obstructing the Tigraian struggle for self-determination and thus falling into the enemy category. If a person was thought to be standing against the TPLF, the *kifli hizbi* cadre would report them to the Security of the Revolution Department (*Halewa Woyyane*) for further investigation. This department would carry out an investigation, usually by putting the suspect in prison. After the investigation was completed, the *halewa Woyyane* would include its recommendation and submit the case to an area CC member for a verdict. Any CC member had the power to review an investigation and pass a verdict. In this short and simple process, the fate of an individual believed to be an enemy or to be against the Front in one form or another could be decided. The idea of defence lawyers or appeals was considered an unnecessary bureaucratic and a counter-revolutionary practice. Many fighters and civilians fell victim to this simplistic and harsh system of handling cases of wrongdoers.

The War with the EDU[50]

When the *Dergue* had seized power in 1974, it began arresting former high-ranking government officials and members of the monarchy. Though it was gloating over its sweeping away all the senior members of the old system, there was one exception. It did not dare to arrest the last hereditary Governor of Tigrai, *Ras* Mengesha Seyoum, mainly for fear of a rebellion by the Tigraians against such an act, which would have been reminiscent of the 1942-43 uprising in Tigrai. During these uncertain days, the *Ras* slipped away to the ELF-controlled area in Eritrea. With the help of the ELF, he made his way to Sudan where he joined other members of the old regime, like General Nega Tegegn who earlier managed to escape arrest by the *Dergue* marshals. In Sudan, members of the old regime and well-known feudal lords prepared the formation of a nationwide organization and later created the Ethiopian Democratic Union (EDU) in London in 1976. Their aim was to overthrow the *Dergue* and reinstate the former pro-western system of governance, but perhaps in a reformed set-up (democratic, as they claimed). The governments of Sudan, Saudi Arabia and many western countries including the US were on their side. This alliance fitted into the Cold War alignment, for the *Dergue* appeared to embrace a Soviet-Union style socialist path.

Before the EDU declared its existence, supporters of *Ras* Mengesha Seyoum all over Tigrai were regrouping and awaiting their leader's call. In Shire in western Tigrai, several of such groups were emerging. Initially, in 1975, an independent group known as the Tigrai People's Liberation Movement *Teranafit* Committee (here after referred to by its acronym

---

50 For further details see TPLF, *'Fitsametat-Woyyanena'* (in Tigrigna, 1978 E.C.), pp. 104-110.

Teranafit) was formed in Gulgula in western Shire. The founders of this movement included Tigraian nationalists like Lieutenant Berhane Girmay and *haleke* Tesfay Gebre-Hiwet. According to Lt. Berhane, Tamene Gebru (Lingo), Teklai Mehari (who later defected to the TPLF), Tesfay Asgedom, Giday Bahrishum, Berhane Desta, Hagos Desta and captain Kahsay Abraha (who also defected to the TPLF), contributed to the formation of this organization.[51] The word *Teranafit* means an authoritative co-coordinator and, as the name suggests, this group was assuming for itself the responsibility of organizing the scattered anti-*Dergue* groups of ethno-nationalists and possibly those waiting for *Ras* Mengesha too. Lt. Berhane elaborates:[52]

> 'The aim of the *Teranafit* Committee was to fight national oppression and bring social justice and equality for all nationalities and citizens. But the struggle was not unified. We saw the need of bringing together all the anti-*Dergue* elements, which were fighting in groups separately under one centralized command. This was the reason why they added the name *Teranafit* Committee to the organization. We were engaged in an unnecessary war with the TPLF. After the EDU was formed in London and began its activities in Sudan, we were contacted to work together, to which we concurred. Subsequently, we were supplied with a few arms and jointly we attacked the *Dergue* forces in Humera and Metema. Although there was no formal merger, the *Teranafit* Committee eventual became part of the EDU in the struggle against the *Dergue*'.

Although this movement had mobilized a few hundred combatants, mainly of a peasant background but also a good number of feudal lords, it was a loose organization awaiting political or military guidance from *Ras* Mengesha's EDU, whose return was thought to be the key solution to all of their problems. Until a structural link was established, however, the *Teranafit* acted on its own whims, without a clearly defined organizational structure and political programme. It vehemently rejected the idea of socialism or 'land to the tiller' – ideas emanating from the revolutionary sector, the *Dergue* and the TPLF. At the same time, preserving tradition was their main concern and the central theme of their political agitation. This situation left many of its members in confusion, and some with an educational

51 Giday Bahrishum (1985 E.C.: 130) in his memoir '*Amora*' (in Tigrigna) puts Berhane Girmay, Tesfay Gebrehiwet, himself, and Tesfay Asgedom in order of their importance as founders of Teranafit.

52 Interview: Lt. Berhane Girmay, Atlanta, GA, 28 July 2003.

background defected to join the TPLF, as confirmed above by Lt. Berhane. The *Teranafit* Committee did not like the TPLF's growing popularity, and even less the defection of members from its ranks to the TPLF. As a result of its internal flaws, the apprehension of this organization became a source of confrontation with the TPLF.

At the beginning, the TPLF was looking for a political solution to the confrontation with the *Teranafit* Committee. The TPLF held the view that the *Teranafit* Committee was a collection of 'feudal elements and bandits' who rallied poor peasants with false and opportunistic promises. So by working together against the *Dergue* or simply co-existing with the *Teranafit* Committee, the TPLF believed that over the course of time, it could attract the peasant army whose class as well as national aspirations was best addressed in its own programme. For the *Teranafit* Committee, on the other hand, the TPLF was just a collection of radical elements and anarchists who were part of the tide that had wrecked an orderly system for which their future leader *Ras* Mengesha was an icon. So, knowing the return of *Ras* Mengesha would lead them to the final state of defining their relationship with the TPLF, they also tended to prefer reconciliation based on peaceful co-existence. Despite the duplicity on both sides for reconciliation to buy time, neither side was in any position to tolerate the other, even on trivial matters.

Meanwhile, elders (*shimageles*) of the Shire district, in the traditional manner, were involved in creating the conditions necessary for the two groups to reach a negotiated settlement towards working together against the common enemy, the *Dergue*. In fact at one point, after long difficult negotiations that took several days, a general agreement was reached and it was accompanied by an elaborate festive ceremony. The agreement, however, did not last long, mainly because neither side was genuinely committed to reconciliation and because the 'devil was in the details' which were not worked out. Loose as it was, the *Teranafit* could not control its army, which was fragmented under sectarian chiefs often engaged in looting and other banditry activities. On 13 June 1976, a detachment of the *Teranafit* group seized control of a civilian bus in the town of Enda Selassie that belonged to a private businessman, *Haji* Abdu. On the way to a different mission, a small TPLF unit led by Gessesew Ayele (Sihul) stopped the detachment of the *Teranafit* Committee with the bus they appropriated at Adi Nebriid and demanded its return to its rightful owner. The response was an unexpected fury of bullets, which killed Sihul and Senay on the spot and wounded a third fighter. The sudden death of Sihul shocked the entire TPLF membership and many people who knew about him in- and outside Shire. The TPLF regarded this incident as a declaration of war, which indeed defined the remaining relationship between the *Teranafit* Committee and the TPLF. To make matters worse, the forces of the *Teranafit* began flexing their muscles with an aggressive attitude towards the TPLF or anybody who did not support them. This attitude was aggravated by the news that fresh EDU forces were appearing in the Wolkait region, as fellow armed groups from the Humera farm area and also from across Eastern Sudan were joining them.

Following Sihul's death, the TPLF leadership unanimously decided to take abrupt retaliatory action with the aim of sweeping away the *Teranafit* Committee forces from Western Tigrai. Sihul's death was the immediate cause of the political vendetta to eliminate the *Teranafit* Committee, but it was not the fundamental cause, as some critics of the TPLF would like to believe. From here on, the *Teranafit* became a target of TPLF attack. The EDU, however, was not easy to discount, as its forces gradually would take over from the *Teranafit* and became armed with modern arms supplied by Sudan. For the TPLF, the EDU was constituted of 'feudal class remnants' of the old regime who mobilized the numerous bandits and jobless peasants with a go-ahead to loot from the people. Worst of all, in the eyes of the TPLF, was EDU's apparent aim to reinstate the old monarchic order.

The plan to deal with the relatively stronger EDU was already in preparation and required a force with superior war tactics. This necessitated changes in the deployment of TPLF forces, which were at the time in *haili* (company) formation. Two companies (*haili* 11 and 12) were on their way to the southern front for a series of operations, beginning with an attack on the *Dergue* force at Abiy Adi-Tembien. On 12 June 1976, they annihilated a counter-insurgency force of the *Dergue* called *Nebelbal* (Flame) at Serro, between Adwa and Adigrat. Now, they had to cancel their mission to the south and head west to where the EDU/*Teranafit* army was based and inflicting severe damage on prominent TPLF fighter units. Led by Mussie, the experienced military commander, and with company commanders, Haile Portsudan and Awalom for *haili* 11th and Ahferom and Shewit for *haili* 21st, they came close to Adi Nebriid and began planning where and when to attack the *Teranafit*. *Haili* 41st, led by Seye and Walta, was in the lowlands of the west in a defensive position as threats of assault from the *Teranafit* were looming over it, but relaying vital information about the rapidly changing *Teranafit's* strength and mobility to the advancing forces under Mussie.

In mid-July 1976, a strong EDU/*Teranafit* force of well over 500 troops marched to Adi Nebriid, not knowing that an infuriated TPLF force under Mussie had arrived in a nearby village the night before. In the morning, *Teranafit* forces were completely encircled and after a fierce battle that lasted no less than four hours, its forces were defeated. One hundred and twenty-five of them were taken as POWs and the rest were either dead or wounded. With high morale and better equipped now with captured semi-automatic guns, TPLF forces advanced towards the western lowlands of Adiabo to mop up. With Sheraro, a small town in the lowlands where the TPLF always enjoyed popular support, as a centre, both the mop-up operations and wider mobilization began. In the following three months, intensive mobilization was carried out throughout western Tigrai, highlighting to the local population the 'revolutionary mass-based' programme of the TPLF vis-à-vis the 'reactionary nature' of *Teranafit's* pursuit and the character of its undisciplined army. Such mobilization was also deemed necessary to deny any ground to the anticipated comeback of such a force, whose leaders were now congregating in neighbouring Sudan.

Many EDU/*Teranafit* fighters who survived the Adi Nebriid offensive fled to Sudan to consult their leader *Ras* Mengesha. This time the *Ras* had acquired the support of both the Sudanese government and the ELF, and thus was in a position to reorganize, arm and finance his cohorts. The defeated *Teranafit* troops were retrained and became part of the new organization, the Ethiopian Democratic Union (EDU), formed by generals, governors and diplomats of Haile Selassie's defunct regime. Although they were regimented under the EDU, the *Teranafit* force remained as an autonomous contingent, poised to grab Tigrai while still paying allegiance to *Ras* Mengesha. It also mobilized thousands of demobilized farm labourers from the districts of Wolkait and Armacheho, particularly from the Humera agricultural belt, and supplied them with modern arms, like Russian-made Simonov and RPGs (rocket launchers). With renewed morale and a revengeful intent to punish the TPLF, a large EDU contingent was dispatched to western Tigrai in the middle of September 1976. A detachment of about 250 (led by Giday Bahrishum, Mebrahitu Aradom, Alemshet Tewolde, Gebremeskel Kahsay and Blata Admasu) arrived in a village called Chiameskebet (not far from Sheraro) on 26 September 1976. It was the eve of *Meskel* (the 'Finding of the True Cross'), a Christian holiday celebrated by burning a large pile of long woods that releases dense smoke and whose direction was held to signify the community's future. On *Meskel* day, a pitched battle erupted in the village between a TPLF company led by Haile Portsudan and Awalom and the main EDU force. The TPLF Company was soon reinforced by a larger force under Mussie, which was lulled by the presence of an ELF unit to a nearby strategic place called Mentebteb through which EDU forces were expected to come. For hours, both sides fought hard and the air filled with thick smoke. The battle was so fierce that local people related it to the 'anger of God' who, as tradition on the battle has it, ordered the burning of people instead of wood on this *Meskel* day. What should have been a scene of celebration turned out to be a scene of carnage. Both sides suffered heavy losses that they had not seen before. The TPLF lost many of its militant commanders like Ahferom, Abraha Manjus, and Bahabelom. Mussie, the TPLF's general commander, was seriously wounded and died soon afterwards. On the EDU side, two of their commanders, Gebremeskel Kahsay and Blata Admasu were captured, while the others escaped into the wilderness. Although the EDU detachment lost the battle of Chiameskebet, the war was clearly just beginning, as EDU leaders in Khartoum were earnestly mobilizing people for a major comeback. The defeated detachment of the EDU, however, retired to remote villages and across the River Tekeze expecting strong reinforcements from Sudan that would pave their way back to the battlefield in Tigrai. This was to happen in five months' time.

From the day the EDU was defeated and forced out of Tigrai, a situation was created for the TPLF to actively mobilize people by establishing mass organizations, armed militias and administrative units in every village, and to try hard to satisfy the expectations of the people, as promised in its programme. They thought the nature and intentions of the EDU were aggressively exposed and it was believed that the EDU would not set foot any more in Tigrai.

TPLF units were thus engaged in a wide range of activities in the central area. They had to thwart the anti-TPLF campaigns of both the EPRP in eastern and central Tigrai and of the ELF along the borders with Eritrea. They were also engaged in frustrating the *Dergue*'s mobility by disrupting its communication system, conducting spectacular ambushes, and foiling military campaigns like the *Raza Zemecha* (see Chapter Four). They also took hostage some foreigners who had come to work in government-held areas and through such media-sensitive measures made it known to the world that the TPLF was in control of the greater part of Tigrai. To the dismay of the British government and its journalists, in May 1976 a British veterinarian Dr. Lindsey Tyler and his family, and later in June, John Swain, a British journalist working for *The Sunday Times*, were taken hostage in Tembien and Serro in central Tigrai respectively. Swain had come to cover the *Dergue*'s Raza Campaign, launched in May 1976. All the hostages were taken to the EPLF base area in Sahil for that was more secure than that of the TPLF at the time. The EPLF was willing to have them not only to comply with a TPLF request but also because of the diplomatic advantage in dealing with the British. After months of captivity when the propaganda objectives were met, all the Britons were released through Sudan with the mediation of the Sudanese government. Although the Sudanese government at this time favoured the EDU and gave it diplomatic and material support, it could not ignore the fast-growing TPLF that was operating across its eastern border.

After its first debacle in Tigrai at the hands of TPLF forces, it took some five months for the EDU to reorganize, train and arm its troops, who were recruited not only from Tigrai but also from Gondar, Gojjam, Wollo and other regions of Ethiopia. Due to the political alignments during the Cold War, they had acquired the support of Sudan, Britain, the US (see Markakis 1990: 243) and some other Western governments, like Germany. They declared they would remove the *Dergue* in a couple of weeks and smash the TPLF on their way. They were able to provide the thousands of Ethiopian refugees in Sudan and the farm labourers in Western Ethiopia with modern light arms, including rocket-propelled guns. Their declaration and provision of modern arms attracted many peasants, especially those outside TPLF-held territories. When they set forth on their march from eastern Sudan to Ethiopia, they numbered well over ten thousand but as they passed through village after village more and more peasants joined them. To attract more people to their ranks, EDU commanders confidently bragged about their ability to crush any force on earth and that their troops would own the arms handed to them, including whatever they looted.

In early March 1977, EDU forces began their major offensive by attacking government forces at Humera and Metema, towns bordering Sudan. The fall of these towns was a humiliating setback to the Ethiopian government. Apart from the military defeat, the *Dergue* lost substantial income from farm revenue. Also a huge agricultural labour force that could potentially be easily mobilized as a fighting force was now falling into the hands of the EDU. By demolishing the military garrisons at Metema and Humera, the EDU opened up a strategic corridor that linked it with Sudan. The morale and material gains achieved as a result of this victory meant that the EDU had the upper hand, and this tilted the balance of power in northwest Ethiopia in its favour. At the end of March, with over ten thousand militia, the EDU crossed the River Tekeze and overran the entire district of Adiabo, where the TPLF had cultivated popular support during the previous two years.

Although the well-armed and numerically superior EDU was advancing aggressively, the TPLF, which had only about a thousand fighters at the time, opted to confront the EDU. The reasons for confronting the much stronger EDU at the time were many and are thought to be valid to this day. For the TPLF, and indeed for all the revolutionary forces in Ethiopia, the emergence of the EDU from the crumbling monarchic system was to 'reverse the wheel of history' and resurrect the old political order. The revolutionaries considered the EDU venture to be futile. Secondly, the TPLF passionately believed the people should be protected from all sorts of pillage by the undisciplined and loosely commanded ravaging army of the EDU, thereby proving to the people that popular, 'anti-feudal' principles mattered a great deal. Thirdly, the need to defend its main base area, Bumbet, and other establishments in this region that were sources of income to the Front, was also a serious matter that could not be compromised.

In mid-March 1977, EDU forces made a swift move to Sheraro, where just one TPLF company confronted them. A fierce battle raged near Sheraro and in a matter of two to three hours, the TPLF Company was overwhelmed by swarms of EDU units whose sheer number was alarming. Most of them were armed with modern machine guns, automatic rifles and rocket-propelled guns, far excelling the meagre rifles of the TPLF. With manageable casualties, the company retreated to its base area in Bumbet, north of Bademe, where the ELF, now a close ally of the EDU, was creating havoc for TPLF units and Tigraians living there. This swift re-emergence of the EDU in such huge numbers and well-armed shocked the TPLF. In the meantime though, the TPLF was pulling its forces from the eastern and central regions to the west for a major encounter.

At Adi Nebriid, east of Sheraro, seven out of nine TPLF companies had dug trenches for a defensive battle. The terrain had been selected for its strategic advantage over an enemy coming from the northwest. Taking advantage of the terrain and to avoid encirclement by the numerically superior force, all seven companies were stretched on a long line of defence without any reserve. Giday Zeratsion and Aregawi Berhe, both CC members of the TPLF, commanded them. The 'motivated' forces of the EDU who thought the TPLF was no longer in a position to pose a meaningful threat, continued their march to Enda Selassie, the capital of the district of Shire, where the *Dergue*'s brigade was stationed. They were over-confident about overrunning any TPLF force. On their way to Shire, they had to pass through Adi Nebriid, where TPLF companies were positioned to stop them and, if the circumstances allowed it, to push them back to where they had come from. But would it work out the way the TPLF planned it? EDU forces flocked in three directions towards Adi Nebriid at midday on *12 March 1977*. The battle raged in all three directions, both sides fighting with passion. In many instances, the EDU force attempted to break the TPLF defence lines at various spots but they were repulsed leaving behind their dead and wounded every time they attempted to make a charge. After a whole day of fighting, darkness fell and the barrage of gunfire came to a halt, at least for a while. Unable to make any headway, the EDU force camped in nearby villages not far from the TPLF defence lines, only to resume the fight at dawn. At night, TPLF forces, whose human losses were minimal, regrouped and made arrangements because they were short of ammunition and guns. The next morning, EDU forces, reinforced with fresh battalions, resumed their offensive moving back and forth close to the TPLF trenches which at the time made calculated charges on their assailants. The battle again raged the whole day with no one claiming victory or conceding defeat but with casualties rising on both sides. Towards the end of the day, TPLF units completely ran out of ammunition and most of their guns were useless, several of them had their barrels twisted from the excessive firing of bullets. They reached a stage where they could not continue fighting a static battle with an enemy whose human and material resources appeared not to be dwindling. After removing their casualties to safer areas at the end of the second day, TPLF forces retreated in an orderly fashion to nearby terrain where they would not be attacked without the enemy also paying a high price. The TPLF force was reduced by a third and three-quarters of their guns were gone. In the evening, EDU forces entered Adi Nebriid with hundreds of casualties. They found a deserted town, which was much easier to loot. For the moment the battle between the EDU and the TPLF seemed to have come to an end, but not in a conventional way. However, for the EDU, which could wage war in no other way than the conventional, a deadly confrontation continued with the government army in Enda Selassie in Shire days later.

In the two-day battle at Adi Nebriid, TPLF forces were forced to retreat after inflicting substantial loses on the EDU army that made it think twice about confronting the TPLF again. From then on, the EDU could not proceed through TPLF-held territory without paying a heavy cost to mobilize the feudal and *shifta* elements in the central region and beyond. The significance of this battle was that it deterred the EDU from growing fast. Had the EDU remained unchecked, it could have mobilized all feudal elements and *shiftas* in the region thus becoming a formidable force in Ethiopia that could bring back the defunct old system and reverse the tide of history.

A few months later, after reviewing its tactics and strategy on how to deal with the EDU, the TPLF came back to strike but this time adopting the tactics of guerrilla warfare, which required high discipline and perseverance. EDU forces, particularly its privileged and absentee leadership, (residing overseas) were not prepared for such a painstaking venture. They were continuously ambushed and attacked by surprise in Shire district, where they remained contained until their final defeat. In a war that took almost three years (April 1977 - November 1979), the TPLF managed to weaken and at last drive EDU forces out of the whole of Tigrai. The battle of *Quinat-Arbaete* (the Four-Day Battle) in November 1979 over a long stretch of land and during which time EDU forces were chased out of Adiabo, was the final and decisive one.

After this blow, the EDU never returned as a fighting force. On the diplomatic and political front too, the EDU did not match the rigorous strides of the TPLF. The Nimeiri government in Sudan allowed the TPLF through its humanitarian wing, the Relief Society of Tigrai (REST), to open offices in Khartoum, Port Sudan and several border towns. The 'land to the tiller' issue, the behaviour of its undisciplined army and the lack of leadership to give strategic guidance on the ground contributed to the EDU's isolation and, finally, its defeat. In Sudan, where the EDU's top leaders were based, the political and diplomatic offensive was intense, with the TPLF gradually gaining the upper hand. The TPLF was able to mobilize significant numbers of refugees there and at the same time began to enjoy success on the battle field not only against the EDU but also against the *Dergue*, and thus outstripped them in the political and diplomatic battles. The endurance exhibited by TPLF fighters followed by success on the battlefield was expounded by the Front as an illustration of the 'correct and popular principles' it was upholding. This played a big part in the TPLF's further mobilization process among the population not only in Tigrai but also further afield.

In these years, parallel to the formation of regular fighting forces, a militia army, as a rearguard, was established throughout rural Tigrai. Only 5-10 % of the militia were women, as most of them were occupied at home with family matters and there were cultural and religious restrictions too. Young girls and single women however were joining the Front in such large numbers that the Front had to introduce and enforce a quota system to limit the flow. Women were attracted to the Front because they said they wanted to run away from the repressive culture at home and also to fight alongside their male compatriots, both for the self-determination of Tigrai and their own liberation.

The formation of the militia (*Woyenti*) was organized at *woreda* (sub-district level) but when necessary, especially during engagements with the enemy, there were contingency formations of the *Woyenti* at district or regional level. Another army structure that operated between the regular and the militia forces was the formation of frontline troops called *Kirbit*, which were mainly engaged in guerrilla activities. The *Kirbits* were small units comprising 10-15 combatants that monitored enemy mobility at district level and, together with the area's militia, defended the 'liberated' territory. When serious engagements took place with the enemy, a task force of the regular *Woyenti* and *Kirbits* was formed to defend territory or attack the enemy when the opportunity arose. The militia, which was essentially a civilian force engaged in farming, was the best link between the Front and the local people in every district. When there was the need to involve the general public in fighting or peace activities related to the struggle, the militia played a crucial role in mobilizing the required support. Such support ranged from supplying food and water during battles, burying the dead, carrying the wounded to safety and transporting war materials across rough terrain.

The Second Internal Crisis (*Hinfishfish*)[53]

In the two trying years of 1977 and 1978, the TPLF had to endure the onslaughts by the larger EDU force on the one hand and by the *Dergue* on the other. Furthermore, internal dissent was hatched by some of the Front's educated members (high school and university students). The struggle against the EDU in particular was tiring, because it was a movement armed with modern weapons and numerically superior – over ten times larger in number than the TPLF army and operating in the same territory. In addition, the EDU was getting military advice and intelligence from the ELF, a veteran front which knew the local territory very well. As this situation appeared to become unbearable, many fighters began raising questions, among them about the calibre of the TPLF leadership to guide the struggle. This clandestine movement of dissent emerging from within eventually caused a breakdown in morale and led to the defection of several fighters, which in turn drove the organization to near collapse. Since the dissent did not emerge in open forums and was simmering as gossip, it was labelled *Hinfishfish* ('disruption' or 'anarchy').

Parallel to the emergence of the EDU as an imposing force, a few members of the educated section of the TPLF started to form a network and began advancing, among themselves, issues directed against the leadership of the TPLF. To air their discontent they used informal, person-to-person contact, thereby rallying dissenters. The cadre school sessions, seminars and congresses could have been used to air this discontent, but since these forums were run by either members of the leadership or their deputies, who themselves were the targets of the denunciation, the dissenters chose not to use them. At the base area of Bumbet, issues related to sectarianism, authoritarian practices and undemocratic culture within the Front were raised in a general meeting but they were answered authoritatively by TPLF leaders on the spot and the discord seemed to be resolved. Most of the charges were brought by veteran members, like Hailu Mengesha and his uncle Abebe Tessema, but only a few of the charges had grounds to argue on. Hailu Mengesha was one of the founders of the TPLF but he was well-known for his maverick character and never abided by the rules and norms that governed the leadership. He was consequently removed from his leadership post at the first Fighters' Congress in Deima in February 1976. It is true that when the dissent, instigated by a leading member, arose behind the leadership's back, it was natural for it to emerge as a power struggle, to which the TPLF leadership responded harshly.

---

53 For the TPLF version of the story which puts the blame squarely on the activists of the *Hinfishfish*, see TPLF, *'Fitsametat-Woyyanena'*, (Tigrigna, 1978 E.C.), pp. 123-126

The points of discontent that were spreading amongst the rank-and-file fighters varied in content and impact, depending in part on the attitudes and regional origin of the individual or group. Although the dissenters came from all the different districts in Tigrai and targeted a leadership that was also composed of members from most of the same districts, the charges were constructed on a regional or district basis. Some accused the leadership of coming only from three western districts, namely Adwa, Shire and Aksum, for which they coined a derogatory word 'ASHA'. They also said that the politico-military activities of the Front focused only on these three districts, implying that the eastern and southern regions, which the detractors claimed to represent, were ignored. The controversial measures taken against the TLF were brought out in this context, i.e. ASHA vs. the other districts of Tigrai, although leaders of this organization also came from all over Tigrai. Yohannes Tekle-Haimanot, chairman of the TLF, for instance was from Feresmai, Adwa. Others blamed the leadership for inaptitude and for leading them into wars they could not win with outdated weapons they named *erfe-meskel*, a wooden handle of a big cross. The war with the seemingly mighty EDU, which caused so much havoc for the TPLF, was their case in point. Still others denounced the leadership because of the unequal treatment of members; they spoke of loyalty as a criterion over merit to promote individual fighters to a higher position in the Front. They also criticized the application of the Front's rules and regulations over those who violated them as unfair and discriminatory, especially in reference to Meles Zenawi, for the lenient punishment he received as a result of his behaviour in the battles of Adwa and Adi-Daero. With regard to these last cases, they had valid points, although it was presented in the usual covert way. In a village called Kotsalo, Shire, for instance, initiated by a member of the leadership, Zenawi was summoned before company no. 11 to answer accusations about his failure in coordinating the operation at Adwa police station. But no one was putting the allegation in strong enough terms to influence the verdict that would follow. Apparently, the decision of the leadership at the time helped him to walk away with a light punishment. Acquiescent of Wolde-Selassie Asfaw (1992: 33), who wrote: 'It would be wrong to assume that there was no reason for the opposition (the dissenters) to complain about the leadership's dictatorship', one should add that prevalence of the Stalinist ideological stance in the thinking of the leadership had created a situation where any divergence of views was not tolerated.[54] Yet, there were also

---

54 The intolerance to opposition ideas was later clearly reflected in the constitution of the MLLT, chapter I; section B (*Le*), no. 3. Accordingly, one should first get the permission of the CC to express his/her ideas in public or pass through a chain of units beginning at basic (local) organization, then going higher to *woreda*, zoba and region, and at each stage securing more than 50% support votes.

unfounded and sensational allegations from the dissenters that shocked the organization to the verge of collapse. The allegations by and large were far from ideological or political challenges.

Before the leadership realized the seriousness of the matter, many fighters deserted to Sudan and even back to government-held territories. The harshness of guerrilla life coupled with gruelling battles acted as a catalyst in aggravating the crisis. As to the allegations, one could closely examine their validity and would be forced to discard most of them as mere concoctions. Let us have a look at some of the allegations and see if they have anything to do with the conduct of the leadership. One was that members of the leadership belonged to the three western districts and were paying attention only to these three districts. This was incorrect. In the first place, the leaders at that time were young revolutionaries who upheld Marxism and the class struggle as ultimate guides to the solution of the Ethiopian people's problems and considered the struggle of national self-determination as a timely tactic for achieving the former goal. In this case the leaders would not reduce themselves to district politicians, as this would be both theoretically wrong and undermine their wider ideological appeal. As Wolde-Selassie (1992: 32) put it, 'They were radicals who transcended this issue comfortably'. Secondly, certainly many of the leaders were born or grew up in one or the other of the three western districts. However, this by no means indicated that they only 'belonged' to this area, and in fact some of them had their roots in the southern districts. Regarding the third point, the struggle had to start somewhere in the western part of Tigrai for reasons discussed in Chapter 1, and had to grow gradually as it did, eventually to cover every part of Tigrai. Naturally, people in these districts were prone to the influence and accessibility of the Front. This situation created the condition for many young students and peasants from the region to join the Front in large numbers. Contrary to accusations, the Front was forced to return some of them while letting recruits from the rest of the districts join, in a process of positive discrimination. So, the blame surrounding this point was unrealistic. The allegation of going to war with outdated rifles should not have arisen at all, for it was obviously clear from the beginning that the war was going to be protracted and starting from scratch against a well-established and much stronger government army. Everybody knew in advance or during the training period about this uphill struggle and the tenacity it required. Guerrilla warfare of the type Mao Tse-Tung applied in his war of liberation was adopted as the best tactic to compensate for the weakness of the Front. Such tactics as hit and run, ambush and surprise attack were conducted mostly at night and with high mobility but this required great endurance, which some of the critics did not like.

It was difficult for the leaders to respond to covert allegations, for no one was forthcoming with concrete charges. Even when some of the leaders attempted to bring a case into the open for scrutiny, no one was there to argue or take on the leaders, understandably for fear of reprisal. This fear must have been created as a result of the lack of democratic practices in a Front that was preoccupied with military matters in facing war on two fronts and where strict military discipline had to be observed.

One could continue to discuss the multiple allegations put forward by the critics. While most of these allegations were unfounded, the detractors who kindled them, for often personal reasons, made them appear true. The appeal was so sensational that many fighters found it hard to avoid or rationally assess its credibility. Yet one cannot escape the fact that there were certain legitimate issues that swayed many innocent fighters to the side of the main detractors. Of course, as said, the complaints could have been resolved through open discussion had the culture of democratic debate been in place, and many fighters would not have then deserted. It was unfortunate that fighters fled to areas under the *Dergue*, the very enemy these young folk set out to fight. Still more tragic was the fact that many of these combatants became the source of information and weapons for the *Dergue*, and eventually organized and were forced to fight the Front they once wanted to be a democratic and successful organization.

In early 1978, the leadership decided to investigate the *Hinfishfish* at a big meeting of leading fighters, called *Wetaderawi Baito* (Military Council). It was a prelude to a campaign of cleansing before holding an organizational congress. 'Tewold W. Mariam' and 'Abbay Tsehaye', the head of the TPLF's political committee, chaired the council.

The hardest and most sensitive part of the *Hinfishfish* was the manner in which it was resolved. Although the entire membership of the leadership had a similar stand on the *Hinfishfish*, it was Sibhat Nega who was in charge of the investigation and the verdicts that followed. Those who were exposed in their units to be the main detractors were sent to prison. After months of interrogation, some recanted and were set free to resume their struggle, while many others who did not wish to do so had a sad ending; regrettably they were killed for their dissent by people who claimed to fight the *Dergue*, an enemy of dissent. Only a handful of CC members who were stationed in the base areas knew about the details these harsh, irreversible measures.

Words and Bullets – Battles with the EPRP[55]

Leading elements in both the Ethiopian People's Revolutionary Party (EPRP) and the TPLF were off-shoots of the Ethiopian student movement. Their political language was more or less the same Marxist rhetoric, both advocating 'the right of nations to self-determination including and up to secession', at the same time crying for socialist transformation (for details see Kiflu Tadesse 1993: 117). To both groups, Ethiopia was a prison of numerous nationalities whose freedom could be attained in a democratic Ethiopia. To achieve this objective, the EPRP sought first a unity of struggle under its party, while the TPLF gave primacy to the components of the whole. In the events leading to the armed struggle, a series of consultations among the radicals in both groups was taking place in the cities, particularly in Addis Ababa, as to how the Ethiopian Left should be organized to play a leading role in the revolutionary transformation of Ethiopia. Cordial dialogue with the intent of exploring the right form of struggle and organization had been on going (ibid.: 140-41) for a while, for instance, between Giday Zeratsion (TPLF) and Getachew Maru (EPRP), between Aregawi Berhe (TPLF) and Haile Abbay and Birhane Eyassu (both EPRP). But there was one sensitive area where the two sides had different views: the form of the struggle. While the TPLF believed in waging a protracted armed struggle from the rural area, the EPRP side was focused on insurrection from the urban areas. This difference was again a reflection of the divergent analysis of the nature and effectiveness of the military establishment of the *Dergue*. How the national movements should be organized and led was another sticky issue, where the EPRP showed the tendency to control such movements under their multinational organization while the TPLF was adamant about its independent existence. Without reaching a conclusive agreement, both sides went their own ways to launch the struggle.

The next time the groups came face to face was in early 1975, in one of the EPLF's military training camps, Riesi Adi, in Eritrea. The TPLF group led by Mussie took the initiative to contact the EPRP group led by Berhane-Meskel Reda, a Tigraian who considered self-determination to be a side issue. The EPLF facilitated the meeting and a host of issues, including the nature of the *Dergue* and the question of democracy, were raised and discussed amicably. At last the need for a national struggle, which the TPLF had gone so far towards, was raised but to the dismay of Mussie and his

---

55 For details of the differences between the EPRP and the TPLF, see also *Ye-Tigil Tiri*, a bi-monthly journal of the TPLF foreign committee, vol. 1, no. 2 (March 1977 E.C.), vol. 1, no. 1 (September 1977 E.C.), vol. 1, no. 3 (May 1977 E.C.), and *Ehapana Ye-Ethiopia Abyot*, TPLF, April 1972 E.C.

group, Berhane-Meskel held the position that the national struggle was an 'obstruction of the proletarian revolution' on which his party was to embark. The implication of this position, which was revealed in the following months of struggle, was that the national movement had to be either held by the EPRP or relinquished altogether. The meeting ended not only without bearing any fruit but also leaving sour feelings and with premonitions of a bleak future for their relationship. A few days later, both groups headed for Tigrai – the EPRP to Assimba in Agame (northeast Tigrai) and the TPLF group to Dedebit in Shire (northwest Tigrai), where the main group had established a base area.

In August 1975, the EPRP declared its political programme, which appeared to be democratic and accommodative. Taking account of the EPRP's programme, many members of the TPLF seriously believed some kind of working agreement could be reached in the fight against the *Dergue*. Undeterred by the hostile reaction of Berhane-Meskel and keen to establish a working relationship with the EPRP against the common enemy, the TPLF leadership sent a delegation led by Agazi and Seyoum from Dedebit to Assimba, where EPRP leaders could be found. It was a one-sided initiative where the other side had no prior notification, so the response of the EPRP was therefore reluctant. Later, in October 1975, the TPLF invited the EPRP to Marwa in Agame, a base area of the former. The delegation from the EPRP was composed of Tsegay Gebremedhin (Debteraw), Abdisa Ayana (Roba), Berhane Iyasu and Getahune Sisay. On the TPLF side, Zeru Gesesse, Giday Zeratsion, Abbay Tsehaye and Aregawi Berhe were present. The discussion started with exploratory queries, both sides desperate to know the position of the other on various strategic and tactical matters of the struggle. Towards the end of the discussion, the TPLF side suggested that the wider region of Ethiopia south of Tigrai become the area of operation for the EPRP and Tigrai left for the TPLF. This suggestion was meant to avoid any type of competitiveness that might lead to unnecessary confrontation or even armed clash. Since it transgressed upon their rights to operate in Tigrai, the EPRP group was infuriated by the suggestion. The atmosphere in the meeting dramatically changed. The TPLF group tried hard to explain the intent of the suggestion but the EPRP seemed never to want to listen, as if they were looking for an excuse to blame the TPLF. In fact, later on the EPRP used this very point to accuse the TPLF of 'narrow nationalism'. Thus the meeting ended in disaster.

Although not much was said about the contentious political positions in the leaders' meeting at Marwa, the cadres of both organizations engaged in heated debate wherever and whenever they met. In general, each side claimed it had correctly analysed the Ethiopian political situation and had adopted the corresponding form of struggle, implying that the other side had the wrong line. This trend of self-centred superiority was rampant among all revolutionary or Marxist groups of the time in general, and among those two Fronts in particular. As a 'revolutionary party of the proletariat', the EPRP believed it was waging a class struggle that would liberate every oppressed class or nationality in the country. Therefore a national movement for self-determination, like that of the TPLF, unless guided by their party (EPRP) 'would play a counter-revolutionary role' and they thus considered the TPLF as a 'reactionary, feudal party'. If we extend the revolutionary logic, the TPLF was characterized as the enemy of the revolution and had to be dealt with. The TPLF, on the other hand, believed that its formation was a direct reflection of the existing contradictions within Ethiopian society and any party that did not recognize this objective reality was not on track to resolve one of the fundamental problems of Ethiopia. It therefore referred to the EPRP as a 'petty bourgeois chauvinist party' no better than the ruling class that oppressed Tigrai, hence an enemy to fight. These notions were deeply engrained in the thinking of most senior members of both organizations. And finally it was this notion that would lead to the unnecessary war that took the lives of many young Ethiopians and not because of one or the other provocation that later surfaced as a result of the ideologically charged premise. Explaining the position of his party, Fassika Bellete, an EPRP CC member, said[56]:

> The fundamental cause of the conflict between the EPRP and the TPLF in 1978 was ideological incompatibility. The EPRP was formed as a left-wing, radical organization committed to establish a socialist political system over the whole of Ethiopia. For the EPRP, the primary contradiction within Ethiopian society at the time was class contradictions and the resolution of the class contradictions was the main objective of the organization. EPRP has also tried to address the problem of nationalities by recognizing the principle of rights of nationalities and espousing the doctrine of unity through equality. TPLF was formed as a narrow nationalist organization. Although modified later, its programme of 1976 clearly stated that the organization's main objective was the liberation of Tigray from the rest of Ethiopia and the formation of an independent state. It has also aspired to be the sole representative of the Tigray people. This ideological rift between the two organizations was the fundamental reason for the armed conflicts that led to the major war between the two in the late 1970s.

56 Interview, 10 August 2003, Washington, DC.

Amid these allegations and counter-allegations, some emotion-driven fighters were exceeding the limits of the debate and threatened armed confrontation. Yet, some of the leaders of both organizations came forward to calm this risky game and conducted meetings to create a better understanding. These meetings, however, never changed the confrontational atmosphere that persisted at this time.

In January 1976 such a meeting was convened on the advice of and under pressure from the EPLF, who obviously understood the benefit for their own struggle against the *Dergue*. Both the EPRP and the TPLF agreed at least to peacefully coexist and eventually explore areas of cooperation. Despite these agreements, the actual relationship was drifting from bad to worse. Enraptured by their organizational dreams, cadres and combatants of both fronts were increasingly becoming involved in heated debates capitalizing on their differences rather than putting the emphasis on points of common interest. In some cases, the debates became so emotionally charged that they led to armed confrontation. Leaders on both sides did not make enough serious efforts to mitigate the gradually deteriorating relationship. Some of the leaders, including Sibhat Nega, were said even to have given their tacit go-ahead for confrontations rather than endeavouring to put an end to them or calm the volatile situation.[57]

The people of the surrounding areas, especially those of Agame and Adwa, were the main targets of mobilization. Day and night, cadres were out organizing and creating underground cell structures to perform organizational missions that aimed at denying support for the other fronts. Occasionally, the people were not only agitated but also pressurized to shift their loyalty from organization to organization. Permits to travel from region to region or to enemy-held (*Dergue*) towns and access to medical treatment in the field were some of the soft tools used to keep people on the side of one or the other organization. If a peasant was thought to be working aggressively or diligently for one of the fronts, he/she might even end up being imprisoned or killed by the other. Freedom of expression and the right to be a member of the party of one's choice were tampered with by the very organizations which were waging armed resistance ostensibly to defend these democratic rights.

Again, in April 1977 formal negotiations started between the two organizations. At their first meeting, both sides agreed to set up a conciliation committee that would look into disputes whenever they arose, and settle them peacefully. This agreement led to a second meeting where more substantive issues like the formation of a united democratic front were

57 Interview: Berhe Hagos, Ottawa, 27 August 2003 and Tesfay Atsbaha, Köln, 25 March 2004.

raised and discussed. Both organizations even reached an understanding of the nature and the process as to how the united front should be formed. They also outlined details of creating the conditions for its realization. This apparently cordial relationship and the subsequent negotiations continued from April to August 1977, but then collapsed. This was partly because the EPRP had maintained the vanguard attitude that all member organizations of the united front should acknowledge the party (EPRP) as their leader (see Declarations of the Party's CC 4th Plenum) – a position the TPLF vehemently opposed.

The abruptly elevated enthusiasm of the EPRP at this point were interpreted by the TPLF as motivated by other, dishonest factors. The TPLF by then believed that the EPRP had lost all its support and was isolated from the people of Tigrai and so by forming an alliance in a united front it might enjoy the acceptance the TPLF had acquired. In a twist of events, it had now become the turn of the TPLF to show reluctance to create a working relationship with the EPRP against the common enemy. Both fronts continued to play political games without seriously engaging in meaningful discussion that could enable them to achieve unity for the collective good, although Fassika Bellete insisted that 'EPRP leaders took the process of the negotiations as a genuine effort to mitigate the conflict between the two parties' and that 'they considered the TPLF as a democratic organization and proposed merger, broad alliance or peaceful co-existence' (ibid.).

Members of both fronts were harassing and also killing active supporters and fighters of the other – measures that could not be executed by and large without the prior knowledge of the leaders. For instance in the town of Enticho, an EPRP contingent killed a civilian and wounded a TPLF fighter while working in their clinic. On the other hand, a TPLF fighter nicknamed Gadafi killed an EPRP fighter in a village near Sobiya and fled to Adigrat, a *Dergue*-occupied town at the time. Similar attacks and acts of sabotage were also carried out now and then in *Dergue*-occupied towns. When the *Dergue* planned the Campaign of 'Red Terror' on its alleged opponents in the town of Adwa, clandestine members of both fronts in the *Dergue* were aware of whose supporters were singled out. As it came clear that TPLF supporters were the targets of the Red Terror, the secret members of the TPLF, led by Wolde-Selassie Girmay, organized the killing of the leading group of the campaign of which EPRP members were a part. It was no longer a secret that the *Dergue* was infiltrated by EPRP members from top to bottom with the intention of overthrowing the incumbent regime from within.

Finally, in February 1978, while a meeting of the conciliatory committee was in progress, an EPRP contingent carried out a raid on the TPLF clinic in Aaiga, Agame, killing one fighter and wounding two others. The next day, EPRP forces began encircling a TPLF company based in Sobiya. After a hasty mobilization of its militia and active supporters, the TPLF platoon retreated to the nearby district of Adwa, where it was better established at the time. The withdrawal of the TPLF units and its militia from the region of Agame was a military as well as a political blow to the TPLF. Its supporters now began feeling abandoned and defenceless. To take advantage of the imbalance of forces in that region, the EPRP began pursuing the retreating forces of the TPLF. The EPRP went on attacking other isolated TPLF units outside Agame, leaving them with no option but to engage in a defensive war. In Mye Merieto and Bizet, TPLF forces defended their positions inflicting heavy losses on the attacking forces of the EPRP. The TPLF remained defensive, for its main forces were still engaged in war with the EDU in western Tigrai, but the EPRP, aware of this imbalance, was keen to push the war to its extreme limit. What the EPRP failed to realize was that, in December 1977, the TPLF had inflicted a decisive blow on the EDU and was engaged in mop-up operations. Although exhausted by a year-long war against the EDU, TPLF forces had emerged from the war with high morale and great fighting spirit and extensive experience.

Two TPLF companies were pulled from the west to the central region and, in April 1978, the EPRP forces encountered them at Azeba. Now that the fighting skills of the TPLF forces were much superior to those of their adversary, the EPRP forces lost not only the battle but also the initiative and were forced to retreat to their base area in Assimba. At this juncture, the real war between the EPRP and the TPLF began. It was the turn of the TPLF to chase away the EPRP forces not only from their area of operation but also from their base areas of Assimba and Alitena. There was no stiff resistance as the TPLF forces rolled on through the rough terrain of northern Agame, the EPRP-held territory and base areas. In a series of battles that took less than one week, the whole EPRP force in the central region was defeated. About fifty were taken prisoner of war and the rest were forced to retreat to the ELF-held territory inside Eritrea and sought ELF protection. No wonder then that the ELF, which was aiding the EDU in western Tigrai against the TPLF, now grabbed the opportunity of supporting the EPRP in its perilous days, with the strategic aim of weakening, if not destroying, the TPLF.

The defeated EPRP army retreated from the eastern part of Tigrai through ELF-held territory to Awgaro in Eritrea across western Tigrai. The ELF supplied them with the necessary materials to recuperate and reorganize the available forces. During this period, many of the fighters who lost faith in their leadership abandoned the EPRP and ended up in Sudan as refugees. The ELF, which always grabbed any opportunity to weaken the TPLF, this time began encouraging and helping the EPRP to launch an attack on the western front of the TPLF through Bademe. They even deployed some of their contingents with EPRP forces. At Gemahlo, a strategic point between Bademe and Sheraro, a fierce battle raged between the TPLF and the combined forces of the EPRP and the ELF. After a day of fierce fighting, the combined forces of ELF/EPRP were defeated and were forced to retreat to where they had come from across the Mereb River, way beyond Bademe. Their plan was to crush the TPLF forces in western Tigrai and enable the EPRP to establish a base area in Wolkait across the Tekeze River, from which it could launch successive attacks on the TPLF. The plan collapsed and from there on they had to stay away from TPLF forces. Consequently, they had to travel further west on Eritrean territory and crossed to the highlands of Wolkait. In the meantime, many EPRP fighters stopped fighting and left the organization, the bulk of whom went to Sudan to seek asylum.

The TPLF, knowing in advance of the EPRP's plans to cross to Wolkait to reorganize and launch attacks from there, began preparations to pursue the demoralized EPRP army before it recovered from the shocks and injuries inflicted in earlier defeats. The TPLF was well acquainted with the people of Wolkait and had ample knowledge of the rough terrain from their days of fighting the EDU. TPLF fighters like Mekonnen Zelelow, who came from that area, and civilian members, like Hagos Atsbaha, had already created an adequate network in support of the TPLF. So Wolkait would not be an unfamiliar area of operation as the EPRP would have liked it to be. After all the defeats, desertions and long marches of retreat, it was only the most determined EPRP fighters who remained in Wolkait to continue the struggle. Understandably, fighting against such a committed group would not be an easy encounter. Nevertheless, the TPLF too was determined to take the war with the EPRP to its final conclusion.

In November 1979 TPLF fighting forces crossed the River Tekeze and began chasing EPRP units. Although they were posing as a restraining resistance, the EPRP units were no match for the highly motivated and better-experienced TPLF fighting companies. After a series of short battles that culminated with the retreat of EPRP units, in December 1979, the main forces of both antagonistic fronts in the region finally met at Shirela. This time, it was the EPRP units who took the initiative to attack and inflicted heavy losses on the TPLF. Martha (Kahsu), a woman commander of a TPLF unit, and some others were killed in this battle. After almost a day of fierce fighting, however, the resilience and fighting skills of the TPLF units exceeded those of the EPRP forces and the battle came to an end with the crushing defeat of the EPRP. The remaining EPRP units could not sustain their positions as the TPLF kept on striking with superior force. Eventually all their units withdrew from the Wolkait region and began to assemble in Armacheho, a remote area further south. Thereafter, the EPRP ceased to function as a military threat to the TPLF, while the TPLF continued to grow and challenge bigger enemies like the *Dergue*. But had both organizations, who had a similar ideological posture, been endowed with the wisdom and farsightedness of settling disputes amicably, a lot of young and dynamic lives would have been spared to fight a more meaningful war against the common enemy, the tyranny of the *Dergue* that was responsible for the death of tens of thousands of Ethiopians during the Red Terror, the shocks of which are still felt by many Ethiopians today.

Besides the uninterrupted and successive offensive of the TPLF, another main reason for the defeat of the EPRP on the military front was stated in the declaration of its own CC 4th plenum:

> Because the focus of the party leadership was on urban organizational work, the army could not get a necessary guidance and leadership structure; the leadership was unable to closely monitor the army's mobility and progress. This had a big impact on the development of the army and was a serious weakness in the leadership at the highest level (translation from Amharic by the author).

The defeat of the EPRP on the military front gave the TPLF the opportunity to focus on the main enemy, the military government of the *Dergue*, and broaden its area of operation further to the south to Wollo and Gondar.

Chapter 6

The Military Government (*Dergue*) and the TPLF

Introduction

Keeping in mind the historical factors that shaped ethnic polarization and conflict in Ethiopia as a background, this chapter backs the contention that the national movement in Tigrai under the TPLF surfaced, developed and toppled the military regime partly as a consequence of the overbearing policies the latter pursued towards ethno-regional groups / nationalities in Ethiopia that sought autonomy as opposed to rigid centralism. To secure a 'revolutionary democratic' image in the initial process of its consolidation, the military government brought forth the issue of 'self-determination to nationalities' as a legitimate demand and a right of oppressed ethnic groups. However, bent on its authoritarian ultra-nationalist ideology, the regime was opposed to all types of nationalist movements, popular or not.

In the theoretical discussion advanced in Chapter 2, it was argued that a regime that responds to the demands of people with repression will likely intensify the hostility and thus speed up its own destruction (Gurr 1970; Goldstone 1991; Clapham 1998). The conduct of the Ethiopian *Dergue*, demonstrated the validity of this postulate. This will be discussed in light of the politico-military confrontation between the *Dergue* on the one hand and the various national fronts, with the emphasis on the TPLF, on the other.

Owing to the fluidity of ethnic nationalism, there were deeply felt controversies among the policy makers of the TPLF over the theory and practice of ethnicity and the quest for ethno-national self-determination, starting from the very beginning of the armed struggle. The consequences of these controversies were dire, not only on narrowing the scope of the struggle but also on retarding the speed of victory. The ideological and political controversies will be discussed in detail in the next chapter 7. In this chapter though, these differences will be treated in a way to show that they had direct bearings on the military as well as political strategies and tactics to be pursued in the struggle against the Ethiopian government. The last section of this chapter focuses on the controversies surrounding the struggle for the 'right to national self-determination' as it played out in formulating the Front's military strategies and their application, and indicate how it impacted on the out come of the struggle.

The *Dergue* on the National Question

First, a look at some aspects of the historical background to the national question in Ethiopia, touching upon the origins of ethnic conflicts, the related movements, and cases with the potential for conflict when the military government, officially called Provisional Military Administrative Council (PMAC), took power. Later, the evolution of the TPLF is considered as it encountered the military regime. It should be borne in mind that the PMAC, commonly known as the *Dergue* (an old Amharic word for *'Committee'*), was a collection of middle and low-ranking military officers who spontaneously joined together during the 1974 February revolution when a political vacuum was created as a result of the demise of the Haile Selassie regime. As Clapham (1988: 39) rightly observed: 'The armed forces were initially no more united or prepared than any section of the civilian population', but the hierarchical structure that connected them and perhaps the inspiration they inherited from the generals who attempted a coup in 1960, all coupled with their movement for salary increase, helped them to be in the forefront of the revolution. Instantaneously, the *Dergue* was mobilized by Atnafu Abate and Taffera Taclaeb from the Fourth Division (Halliday and Molyneux 1981: 86), with the headquarters of the army based in the centre of Addis Ababa. Both held the rank of major and were bringing in officers of the same rank and below from all over the country. In a dramatic development, lt.-col. Mengistu Haile-Mariam from the 3rd Division in Harrar, 'who distinguished himself by a fiery speech at the first *Dergue* conclave' (ibid.), on 28 June 1974 joined them and later on became their leader. Four days later on 2 July, the *Dergue*, consisting of 109[58] members, announced its hastily prepared programme and took power, ruling the country with long periods of mayhem and bloodshed for the next seventeen years.

The fundamental historical drive for ethnic identification in Ethiopia resulted from the general processes of state and nation formation in the region as a whole and that of the modern state in Ethiopia in particular. The conflicts along the ethnic divide emerged and developed not so much from the sheer expansion of the central Ethiopian state as from the radical changes in social and economic organization that followed in its wake. Those in power obviously exercised political, social and economic hegemony, while others (the ethnic nationalities, including the ordinary populace of the dominant nationality) in most cases lived in conditions of oppression, subjection and humiliation. The modern state continued to build upon this foundation while Haile Selassie intensified the process of modernization since the late 1930s. By that time, the country had already joined the world capitalist market and a bureaucratic ruling elite dependent on the West had evolved, intensifying the process of centralization to meet the new interests of the ruling class. As Goulborne (1991: 233) observed for Africa in general,

> A unitary political system has been seen as the cornerstone of national unity, which in turn, was necessary for development. Typically, this political system has been characterized by the single political party, a strong executive presidency, with the national army, police force, and administration each owing allegiance to the party and president. Political pluralism was therefore perceived to be anathema to African traditions; pluralism was divisible where African village democracy was unitary. To one degree or another, political pluralism was, and remains, suspect throughout most of the continent.

This state of affairs caused ethnic rebellions. Eritrea posed a different problem to the Ethiopian state, for it had since 1941 been under the jurisdiction of the United Nations and the British after the defeat of the Italians there.

By the time the military government took power in 1974, the Eritrean liberation struggle had entered its 13th year, two border wars were fought between Ethiopia and Somalia on the question of the Ogaden, where ethnic Somalis demanded self-determination, and revolts had occurred in Tigrai (1942-1943), Sidamo (1960s), Gojjam (1963), Bale (1965-1967) and some

---

58 The names of the 109 *Dergue* members can be found in '*Neber*' (Amharic) by Zenebe Feleke, 1996 E.C. and in '*YeLetena Colonel Mengistu Hailemariam Tizitawoch*, (Amharic) by Genet Ayele Anbesie, 1994 E.C.

other places (see Gebru Tareke 1991; Markakis 1990; Clapham 1988; Gilkes 1975). Such was the state and nature of the ethnic problem that the military government inherited: conflicts that were both current and potentially possible. The policies pursued by the new government to 'resolve' the ethnically based and other rural questions would become repressive as the years went by.

From the first days of its constitution in June 1974 until the proclamation of the 'National Democratic Revolution' (NDR) programme in April 1976, and despite its rhetoric about a radical revolution and class conflict, the *Dergue* had neither renounced nor criticized the positions of the old regime on the national question. Nor had its members had a clear position on the issue other than that of maintaining the country's unity and territorial integrity in the old way. In a nutshell, on the question of the right to self-determination or self-rule by ethnic nationalities, the *Dergue*'s position was in substance no different from its predecessor. Fred Halliday and Maxine Molyneux (1981: 262) wrote that '...the continuation of chauvinism at the centre was concealed behind an apparently faultless rhetoric of class conflict'. There is support for this contention: there was its slogan *Itioppia Tikdem* ('Ethiopia First'); it turned a deaf ear to ethno-national plights; its first chairman, General Aman M. Andom (of Eritrean origin), was most likely assassinated for 'leniency' on the Eritrean question; there was a terror and assassination campaign against Eritreans in the urban areas; military offensives were resumed in February 1975 in Eritrea against rebel positions while they were demanding a peaceful settlement of their question[59]; and prominent Oromo nationalist leaders such as General Tadesse Biru and Kebede Bizuneh (March 1975) were executed, as were Tigraian radicals like Meles Tekle, Rezene Kidane, Abraha Hagos and Gidey Gebre-Wahid (March 1975). All this happened before the declaration of the NDR programme. Markakis and Ayele (1978: 119) summed up the character of the military regime in its first year in power as follows: 'The wanton manner of the executions and the inclusion of military radicals in the massacre shocked many Ethiopians.... The revolution is no longer bloodless, and ruthlessness increasingly marks its course from now on.' No matter how loudly the *Dergue*'s slogan 'Ethiopia Tikdem' resonated, as early as 1976 opposition to the military regime was already gathering momentum in the urban and the rural areas, leading to armed struggle by different fronts.

Although the April 1976 NDR programme proclaimed self-determination for the various nationalities, the *Dergue* was organizing its infamous '*Razza* project', a peasant-army march, mainly on Eritrea but also including

---

59 See EPLF's November 13, 1973 declaration of 7 points on a peaceful resolution (in EPLF, January 1980).

Tigrai. that would be launched the following month. The *Razza* project, which is discussed at length later on, turned into a massacre of ill-armed peasants sent to the well-armed rebels as cannon fodder, The campaign, as Halliday put it, '... was not only intrinsically inconsistent with any prospect of conciliation that might have been raised by the NDR and Nine Point proclamations; it was also marked by the revival of themes redolent of the chauvinist campaigns of the imperial past, with the Christian peasants being rallied to fight off Muslim invaders' (ibid.: 163). While this latter remark may be simplifying things, despite the article on self-determination in the NDR programme, the above-mentioned incidents indicate that the *Dergue* had not moved an inch from the positions held by the *ancien régime* on the national question, but even aggravated them.

Eritrea

Neither the *Dergue* as a body nor its leaders individually, with the exception of Captain Moges Wolde-Michael, had a prudent viewpoint on the national question in general and on the Eritrean problem in particular different from and/or critical of that of the imperial regime. Captain Moges was later killed by Mengistu's assassins for his position on the question of nationalities. The same day, 3 February 1977, the PMAC Chairman General Teferi Banti and Captain Alemayehu Haile were also killed; 'all of whom in December 1976 had attempted to restrict the power of Mengistu and Atnafu Abate' (Schwab 1985: 37). The *Dergue* was devoted to the old policies but with a difference, namely in language and ideological discourse that it used to legitimize its claims and the 'solutions' it put forward. It argued that the Eritrean people had the same enemies as their Ethiopian counterparts: 'feudalism, bureaucratic capitalism and imperialism' and the fact that they did not need to fight for self-determination. This was an approach that negated the essence of the movement in Eritrea. In this respect, the fact that the new Ethiopian regime's first chairman, but not a an original member of the *Dergue*, General Aman Andom, was Eritrean by origin was the leverage that was used. Detesting the Italian occupation of Eritrea, Aman's parents had lived in Sudan where he was born and educated. Upon the return of Emperor Haile Selassie from exile through Sudan, Aman as a young military officer accompanied the Emperor and came back to Ethiopia where he built his career and became a renowned general. He led the Ethiopian army to victory in the 1964 Ogaden War against Somalia. He was one of the commanding officers in the Korean War and was well-known in the West. As a skilled general and a patriot, he was respected not only in the army but also among ordinary Ethiopians. Because of his origins and negotiating skills, Aman did a remarkable job in coming close to acquiring a peace settlement with Eritrean rebels. 'He never accepted independence but sought to negotiate with the two guerrilla groups' (Halliday 1981: 88). He warned 'Those who advocate separation are enemies of the nation and must therefore be dealt in a stern manner'.[60] The peace settlement would have been useful to the *Dergue* and disadvantageous to the liberation movements, but Mengistu, with his own personal ambitions, twisted the logic of the peace settlement Aman was nurturing and had him killed in his home on 23 November 1974 by a hit squad. By killing such an experienced Ethiopian general, who sought peaceful resolution to the conflicts in the country, Mengistu, whose lust for power and personal fame was unbridled, pushed Ethiopia on the road to break-up.

Mengistu's wing prevailed within the *Dergue* and reaffirmed a dogmatically nationalist and authoritarian stance. In addition to a policy of terror against Eritreans in the urban areas, the *Dergue* in February 1975 resumed a military offensive against rebel positions. These two developments antagonized the Eritrean population and led thousands of youngsters – including some from Addis Ababa University – to join the two liberation movements, the ELF and the EPLF. As early as 1976, Anthony D. Smith (1976: 140) observed '...where Eritrean nationalism is receiving immense impetus from the circumstances of its repression by the Ethiopian army warns us that the creation of such new nationalism results more often from testing in the crucible of suppression by a superior government than from the mobilization of the population from below'. Even the leader of the EPLF, Issayas Afeworki remarked that the *Dergue* swelled the ranks of the Eritrean movements. The Eritrean-nationalist and the ethno-nationalist movements thus grew in leaps and bounds, and ethnic mobilization and (violent) resistance became the dominant means of confronting the *Dergue*. Below, we briefly discuss some of these movements.

The Ogaden

The organization that was active in the Ethiopian Ogaden, the Western Somalia Liberation Front (WSLF), was in fact run by the government of Somalia. Ostensibly a nationalist movement, the WSLF had substantively mobilized the people of the Ogaden at the beginning of 1963, and its military activities had intensified by early 1977, when Mengistu launched his coup and became the unchallenged head of the *Dergue*. In the summer, the Somali Republic invaded the Ogaden, clearing the ground for the third stage of the border war between the two states. Mobilizing the people under the 'call of the motherland' and supported by Cuban troops and a huge Soviet arsenal, the *Dergue* defeated the Somali army and won back the Ogaden. Militarily, the Ogaden issue was settled in a relatively short period of time but politically

60 *Ethiopian Herald,* October 17, 1974

with the issue of self-determination embedded in it, an uncertain long way ahead was awaiting. Since then, the ethno-nationalist movement for self-determination, although dented, has never been away.

Oromo

The Oromo nationalist movement has a long and complex history which is beyond the scope of this study. It dates back to the early 1960s and was based on 'a common history of central domination and exploitation. ... From the mid 1960s onwards, attempts were made by educated Oromos to articulate this awareness of domination into an Oromo ethnic nationalism' (Clapham 1988: 216). The activities of *Mecha Tulama,* an Oromo cultural and development association, and later the insurgency in Bale (1963-70) led by Waku Guto (see ibid.) were some of the movements that inspired and gave shape to the Oromo ethno-nationalist upsurge. In the early 1970s an Oromo group that believed in the formation of 'a coalition and alliance of anti-feudal and anti-imperialist forces whose immediate task was to overthrow the imperial autocratic regime' (Yohannes Petros 1993: 6-7) formed the Ethiopian National Liberation Front (ENLF). After 1972, *Shaikh* Hussen Sorra, Chairman of ENLF, had close contacts with leaders of the Ethiopian Student Union in Europe who later formed MEISON, the party that adopted the position of giving critical support to the *Dergue* in the early years of the revolution. When the *Dergue* enacted its radical land reform proclamation on 4 March 1975, the Oromo people, more than any other ethnic group in the country, applauded it and MEISON, which had advocated less radical land reform – confiscating the land of big land owners and dividing it among the landless peasants (see Andargatchew Assegid 2000: 235) – nevertheless went on mobilizing the Oromo peasants to support the reform and thus create their own social base. This was followed by the establishment of peasant associations to organize collective farms and control the peasants, and to run a command economy. The Oromo people found this collectivism repugnant but they wanted a political space to exercise their right to self-determination which had been denied by the previous regime. Slowly but certainly the elation and hope raised by the land reform were overtaken by the ethno-nationalists' quest for self-determination. The *Dergue,* however, did not budge on this issue and armed struggle was looming. The *Dergue*'s attitude towards any ethno-nationalist group opting for the right to self-determination was hostile and aggressive, as was its reaction towards the Oromo who raised this issue. It did everything to crush nationalist assertiveness among the Oromos, whether in the form of an independent mass organization or a liberation front. It eliminated Oromo personalities whom it suspected of being engaged in a nationalist activity. Prominent Oromo activists like General Taddesse Biru, Mekonnen Wossenu and many others were murdered in 1975 after serving long prison sentences. Such acts tended to strengthen the adherence of many Oromo nationalists to the Oromo Liberation Front (OLF), which had emerged early in 1974 amid the political turmoil. Many Oromo intellectuals and university students who were part of the Ethiopian Left felt forced to join the OLF or flee the country and become diaspora sympathizers.

The Afar and Sidama

Elsewhere in the country, some other ethno-nationalist fronts were formed to assert the right of self-determination. The Afar in the northeast and the Sidama in the south were also engaged in resistance that eventually evolved into ethno-nationalist movements with a demand for autonomy or self-determination. The Afar nationalist movement has a long history stretching back to the colonial era. The longevity of the movement is well-documented by historians and Afar writers. As Abdallah Adou (1993: 44) put it: 'The Afar nation has never been subject to any external rule at any time prior to the Scramble for Africa...[it] had a long political history of self-rule and in fact, at times, powerful and influential states/sultanates in the Horn of Africa'.[61]

The Sidama movement goes back to the early 1960s, when local peasants demonstrated for land reform. In 1978 Wolde-Emmanuel Dubale, Betena Holesha and Matias Meshona led a nationalist movement known as *Kaie,* which means 'revolt', and which was later called the Sidama Liberation Movement (SLM).[62]

Tigrai

Let us now look at the case of Tigrai, the focus of this study, in its evolving relationship with the *Dergue*.

The *Dergue* soon revealed repressive policies towards Tigraians and their national movement. This movement, tracing its historical roots to the Woyyane uprising of 1942-43, had been simmering among educated and radical Tigraians since the 1960s. Later, in early 1974 the Tigraian National Organization (TNO) was formed, the mother organization of the TPLF, that was born on 18 February 1975 (see Chapter 3).

---

61 Also see the interview of Mahamooda Ahmed Gaas, then Deputy Secretary for Foreign Relations of the Afar Revolutionary Democratic Unity Front (ARDUF), by Fikre Tolossa, in *Ethiopian Review*, September 1993.

62 Interview with Meles Wolde-Emmanuel, The Hague, 10 July 2004. Also see John Markakis 1990.

The people of Tigrai had hoped the downfall of Haile Selassie's regime would open a new era of progress, mutual respect and equality, to resolve, among other things, ethnic-based regional contradictions and allow the exercise the principle of self-determination or achieve regional autonomy. The military regime, however, foiled these hopes. Rigid centralism of the Stalinist kind, militarism and socio-political repression came to characterize the *Dergue* and guided its policies to counter the ethno-nationalist movement.

Before even consolidating power in early 1975, the regime began imprisoning hundreds of radical Tigraians who were participating in various social activities and organizations, such as the teachers' unions, the student movement and other social and professional associations. In March 1975, scores of radicals including Giday Gebre-Wahid, Meles Tekle, Rezene Kidane and Abraha Hagos, were summarily killed without due process of law, and some of the dead bodies were thrown into the main streets of the city on display. The objective of such measures was to terrorize Tigraians and other rebels so that they would be scared to raise their political demands for change.

On 20 December 1974, the *Dergue* declared 'Ethiopia *Tikdem*', the definition of which was very elastic, comprising Ethiopian socialism, self-reliance, and the idea of the indivisibility of Ethiopia, accompanied by the slogan 'Ethiopia or Death'. 'Ethiopia *Tikdem*' meant, in effect, the rejection of a pluralistic parliamentary system in which various interest groups were represented in a struggle to determine national policy (Ottaway 1978: 63). To the Tigraians, whose belief in a historical Ethiopia was deep-rooted, the motto of Ethiopia *Tikdem* bore the message that their plight as an oppressed nationality was seen as trivial if not reactionary and divisive. By this time, Tigraian students in the H.S.I. University had decided to boycott the 'Development through Co-operation Campaign', launched by the military government in 1975 and to prepare for organized resistance. They soon turned their association, TNO, into a front, the TPLF.

In Tigrai, the existence of the TPLF was heralded by the first successful military operation on 5 August 1975 in the town of End-Selassie (Shire), that secured the freedom of a leading member of the movement, Mehari Tekle (Mussie) and of 21 other prisoners, five months after the birth of the TPLF (see chapter 3). A month later another military operation was conducted in the town of Aksum, where all government establishments and in fact the whole town were put under the control of the TPLF for hours. Crowds cheered as TPLF fighters marched through the streets..

Such acts of resistance hastened the Ethiopian regime to take aggressive measures and pursue a military policy against the Tigraian population. The same year, Tigrai was declared a military zone. Ground and air forces were sent in to combat the insurgents, in the process devastating towns, villages, market areas, farmland, churches and mosques. E.g., the villages of Abi Adi, Chila, Hawzien, Sheraro and Yechla were bombed on market days with the aim being to destroy and intimidate. The *Sunday Times* journalist Jon Swain (1996: 224-25) in May 1976 observed: 'From the village above Zerona (Tsorona), I watched government jets wheel in the sky, hit the town and rake a goatherd on the hill with cannon fire.... The frequent air attacks did have one important effect. They forced the peasants to change the pattern of their lives. Now they slept during the day and worked in the fields at night, when they were assured of empty skies.' With such massive force, however, the *Dergue* believed it could bring the people to submission.

In the course of the conflict, famine conditions emerged, not only because of policy ineptness but also because of the *Dergue*'s logic of war: if the people were hungry they could not supply food for the insurgents and would also turn to the government for hand-outs, in which case it might be possible to control them. The organization Africa Watch, which was closely monitoring the situation in Tigrai during this time, had this to report: 'The nature of the rebellion in Tigrai led to a new variation on the army's counter-insurgency strategies. These strategies were instrumental in setting the famine in train. There were three main aspects:

- Large scale military offensives, aimed at the surplus-producing Shire district...

- Aerial bombardment of markets...

- Tight controls on movement of migrants and traders, enforced in all garrison towns, in eastern Tigrai and northern Wollo...

The logic behind the government's strategy was 'draining the sea to catch the fish'. This amounted to counter-population warfare' (De Waal 1991: 140-41).

To make matters worse, in the late 1970s the regime came up with a resettlement plan for regions of ethnic conflict such as Tigrai, where farmers were to be permanently relocated against their will to new places. This was designed to destabilize ethnic and social relations and impede the physical and psychological support the resistance movement had gained. These policies, accompanied by propaganda, further aroused bitterness among Tigraians against the government, and the nationalist movement gained impetus. The policies of the *Dergue* thus came to serve as ammunition for the TPLF, and in the eyes of the population justified the latter's characterization of the *Dergue* as a dictatorial force. More young peasants and students began to flock to the front, nurturing the growth of the TPLF from a small guerrilla band to a formidable mobile army supported by a solid social base. In three to four years, TPLF forces grew so strong that the military government, equipped with Soviet weapons, was forced to challenge the TPLF in huge military campaigns.

From May 1976 onwards, the *Dergue* began launching these military campaigns once or twice a year, attempting to destroy the TPLF and punish the people that it blamed for supporting the Front. Between 1976 and 1980, there were six major campaigns involving several ground force divisions, airborne troops, mechanized brigades, battery units and air-force squadrons.. The devastation inflicted by the armed forces was intense. Indeed these military campaigns changed the pattern of life of every inhabitant of the region. However, by keeping its wits about the *Dergue*'s intentions, the TPLF was able to adopt a different, plausible tactic that helped it not only overcome the military onslaughts but also to 'benefit' from the campaigns and grow. By repeatedly attacking isolated enemy contingents, TPLF guerrilla forces snatched new weapons and armed its militia and new recruits. The rapid growth of the TPLF force from a band of no more than 20 guerrilla fighters to an army with a deep-rooted social base and later organized in regular divisions with heavy artillery and tanks, in addition to thousands of militia, can to a considerable extent be attributed to the indiscriminate and brutal repression of the *Dergue*-led Ethiopian army of the Tigraians. The assertion of many analysts, like Gurr (1970), Skocpol (1970), Goodwin (1994), Wickham-Crowley (1994), Clapham (1998), and others that in certain conditions of social inequality and political oppression violence invigorates counter-violence by those against whom it is intended, finds adequate illustration in the case of *Dergue* violence and the response of the people in Tigrai.

The TPLF Military Build-up

Initially nobody in the government or among the population seemed to take the TPLF seriously. As we saw, the movement was initially a tiny guerrilla band of 10 men who were armed with 4 old-fashioned rifles and a pistol. They appeared to be an unknown, adventurous group of radical university students tackling the impossible. The group was able, however, to combine the theoretical understandings of various armed struggles throughout the world and the practical wisdom of their forefathers, who fought the battles of Gundet, Gurae, Dogali, Metema, Adwa and Maichew against foreign invaders. The group had also the guidance and the stamina of fighters like the elderly Sihul as they embarked upon bringing down a repressive system and aiming to progress and transform Ethiopian society.

These young students had read passionately about the revolutionary armed struggles in Algeria, China, Cuba, Guinea-Bissau and Vietnam, with the intention of applying principles learnt there to removing the reactionary regime at home. In their search for military knowledge, they became familiar with the war theories and tactics of Sun Tzu, Carl von Clausewitz and Mao Tse-tung, to mention but a few. Closer to home as well, there were lessons to learn from. Emperor Yohannes's victories over invading Egyptians at Gundet in 1875 and at Gurae in 1876, *ras* Alula's victory over the Italian colonial troops at Dogali in 1887, the defeat of the huge modern Italian army at the hands of Emperor Menelik II at Adwa in 1896, the anti-fascist guerrilla movements (1936-41) led by patriots like *Dejazmach* Gebre-Hiwet Meshesha, and the Woyyane of 1942-43, an uprising of Tigraians for an autonomous administration led by reformers like *Blata* Hailemariam Redda, were some of the experiences ingrained in their minds. This added up to the perception of a glorious history of their region that invoked the spirit of resistance against a regime that they believed was the source of their misery, and helped mobilize the people to fight for a better future.

The rugged topography of Tigrai presented an immeasurable advantage to the TPLF. Tigrai and the entire northern part of Ethiopia offer an ideal terrain for guerrilla warfare. Egyptian warriors, Italian superior military organization with fighter planes, tanks and heavy artillery had already been proven indecisive on several occasions against ill-equipped and scattered Ethiopian patriots (rebels or *shiftas*) in this mountainous terrain. In fact, this was why, on a number of occasions, *shiftas* (social bandits) had found it expedient to rise up against the state as rebels and had even managed to seize power – as in the cases of Emperors Tewodros and Yohannes. This in a way also explains why the TPLF were confidently able to engage in an armed struggle against the state, despite their modest start with only a few rifles.

The TPLF pioneers had been closely following developments of the armed struggle in neighbouring Eritrea. 'If the Eritreans could rebel, why not we who are neglected the most!' was a repeatedly reiterated rationale of Tigraian youth at the time the Eritreans were intensifying their struggle. They established connections with their Eritrean counterparts when possible. Some Tigraian students and farm labourers in Eritrea even joined the Eritrean fronts just to fight the common oppressor. Many of the Eritrean fighters had been at school and at the university with the TPLF pioneers, and had maintained contact even when the former became engaged in the armed struggle. These relationships definitely paved the way towards initial cooperation. With friendly fronts fighting the same government forces at their side, the TPLF fighters had no fear of enemy encirclement and military debacle, as was the case with many young rebel movements elsewhere.

Let us now look specifically at the growth of the TPLF fighting force in its confrontations with the *Dergue*. The TPLF forces were made up of regular fighters (*hailitat*), guerrilla units *(kirbit)*, and people's militia (*woyenti*). Even though the small contingent that sparked off the emergence of the TPLF on 18 February 1975 in Dedebit was composed of only ten men with scant weaponry, news of their existence and the inflated size of their strength spread all over Tigrai in no time. As it did so, young boys and girls, but mainly students, started to come to the rural areas in search of this newly founded front. A lucky few would find someone to guide them to Dedebit, but many came into contact with one of the other fronts and had to stay there until they could find a safe exit strategy. Once you joined a front, it was often difficult – and in some cases impossible – to defect or run away, because you would be suspected of returning to the enemy.

In a matter of three to four months, the small band more than tripled in size and everyone was engaged in rigorous military training in the jungle of Dedebit. Asgede Gebreselassie, a retired corporal in the previous government army, was the group's first trainer. He was supported by Sihul on practical issues and by the students concerning theoretical matters. Everybody contributed something, depending on past experience, and this made the training lively and productive. By the end of May 1975, the group that had been sent to the EPLF base area for training had returned, armed with two AK47s, one Simonov, one Uzi, three hand grenades and eight old rifles, supplied by the EPLF. As we saw in Chapter 3, this arms supply was nominal and frustrated the group, whose expectations had been very high. It sent out a message that the EPLF was not serious in the progress of the Tigraian struggle, and almost everybody in the TPLF was offended by the token arms offered by the EPLF. The idea of obtaining arms from the enemy began to take root about this time. The EPLF-trained group joined the Dedebit contingent at Hirmi, a few hours' walk from Shire-Enda Selassie. It was one of the first positive moments for both groups who were often far apart at critical times in the struggle. They had the support of the nearby villages for food and drink as well as security. As Sihul had popular support in this area, fear of enemy intrusion could be checked by the community, keen to report any possible threat. Soon afterwards, four squads with about 10 fighters[63] in each were created. While Sihul assumed overall leadership, Mussie and Aregawi were made the squads' commander and commissar respectively. The other leaders, Zeru, Giday, Asfaha, Seyoum, Abbay and Hailu assumed squad leadership or departmental posts. The whole contingent had to move again to Dedebit for comprehensive training and consolidation of the new

63 The number of fighters in each squad often varied, as some were dropping out because of fatigue, sickness, or being wounded or killed in a battle and/or with new fighters joining.

squad formations. With the flow of new recruits to the Front, the number of fighters in each squad was growing steadily and new recruits were forced to pass through military training while assigned to one of the squads. With the rainy season beginning to make the ground muddy and everything becoming wet, life for the whole new fighting force – whose roof was only the sky – was not easy.

In early August the same year, as we discussed in Chapter 2, two incidents occurring inside the young organization – the capture of its military commander, Mussie by the enemy, and another leader, Sihul, being swept away in a flash flood, although he survived it – shocked every member. But for a front that was just starting out their rescue was seen as an ominous success story and a blessing in disguise. Not only was the novice army of the TPLF elated but everyone in the district was talking about them and their actions. The news of their operations reached the whole of Tigrai, and from then on, TPLF squads began to enter villages and hold public meetings. As the squads passed villages, people cheered them and provided food and drink, while the younger boys begged to join the Front. The fact that they had committed twelve fighters to rescue just one comrade demonstrated the extent to which the Front was concerned about its members and how strong comradeship amongst the fighters was. Thus, a heroic precedence that was to reverberate for years to come was set just six months after the TPLF's inception. The leadership gained the confidence to initiate another strike and planned an operation that would satisfy its need for arms and financial resources.

With the successful operation at Aksum a month later, the TPLF gained not only badly needed arms and money but also wider publicity. All anti-*Dergue* elements and particularly Tigraians were filled with hope. The older ones wanted to be connected with the TPLF so that they could offer material help or advice and the younger ones wanted to join the Front and fight.. Initiated by the two military victories a month apart, thousands of the young generation were waiting to take up the challenge. It was this pressure of youngsters wanting to join the Front at that early stage of the struggle that prompted the TPLF to establish public-relations units that could control the flow of new recruits, and instead organize and advise them to stay and work for the Front where they lived, until such time that the Front was able to accommodate them. Yet many of them were pushing to get to the Front by presenting reasons such as if they were to return to their homes they would fall into the hands of government cadres and might be executed. Almost all these young Tigraians were facing this dilemma. But because the Front was simply not able to accommodate them, many were forced to stay in villages as daily labourers rather than return to their towns that were under the control of the *Dergue*.

Within a few months of the TPLF's formation, the number of combatants in each squad (*mesree*) had grown so rapidly that the squads had to take up the formation of platoons (*ganta*), with three squads under each platoon. By October 1975, there were three platoons each comprising 30-35 combatants. In February 1976, on its first anniversary, all TPLF combatants gathered at Deima for the celebrations and participated in the regular fighters' (*tegadelti*) congress that elected a leadership for the first time. The total number had risen to 126 combatants in the first year of the guerrilla movement. It was at this time the platoon changed to company *(haili)* formation and from then on, the company formation multiplied. Initially two companies called *Haili* Dedebit and *Haili* Woyyane were created. Within three months, additional new *hailis* were being formed by mixing the experienced combatants with the new arrivals. This system of putting older and fresh combatants into new companies called *Mitehnifats* became regular practice as new recruits were arriving regularly. By July 1976, the number of companies had risen to nine and each company was made up of no fewer than 100 combatants. Each company was identified by a numbered code-name as follows: 11, 21, 31, 41, 51, 61, 71, 81 and 91. A different series of numbers was given to departments that were primarily supporting units of the fighting forces at the time. 00 was radio intelligence, 01 the cultural unit, 02 training, 03 the health department, 04 propaganda, 05 economy, 06 security, 07 public relations, 08 administration and 09 army logistics. Later on, when departments like general logistics, education and agriculture were created, they were given the new codes 011, 012 and 013 respectively.

The companies were engaged purely in guerrilla activities like hit-and-run, ambushes and surprise attacks on small isolated enemy posts where they were sure of victory. They were scattered throughout almost every district in Tigrai, with high mobility that made them appear greater in number than they actually were. They moved at night to gain maximum surprise. Such engagement helped the TPLF to minimize casualties and embolden the fighting sprit of its combatants. But it did not mean all engagements were free of setbacks. The incident at Amentila, a few hours' walk to the southeast of Meqele, was one setback when, on 18 November 1976, a platoon of company 71 was forced by enemy surprise attack to retreat at night over unfamiliar rugged terrain and most of its members plunged into the rocky ground from a cliff of over ten meters high. In this disorderly retreat, a few died, many were injured and the whole company had to leave the region until it could reorganize and make a comeback. This was a minor incident compared to what was going to happen in March 1977 in western Tigrai, the TPLF's main base, when the major battles with the EDU emerged (See Chapter 4). However, the real war with the *Dergue* army still had not occurred in this period of TPLF organizational build-up.

In order to prepare for the long war with the *Dergue* army, the TPLF took to seriously organize its own training, stimulated by the continuous swelling of the number of recruits. Once base areas were established in the late 1970s, all TPLF forces passed through rigorous three-month military training programmes, although crash courses had to be given at times when the military campaigns (*zemechas*) by the *Dergue* were in full swing. Basic military training was compulsory for all TPLF recruits and was given at the department of training (*taelim*) code-name 02. Refresher courses called *Mitnekar* were also arranged to fill gaps that transpired, especially after 1980 when the flow of peasant recruits began to outnumber those of the urbanized students. Peasants needed more time to grasp the skills and tactics required in war than the students whose numbers were dwarfed by increasingly large groups of peasant recruits. With the growth of the army and the formation of larger units such as brigades, support detachments and able military commanders were needed at all levels. Immediately after the first organizational congress in 1979, the Hakfen Military School was opened at a place called Bakla in Tembien to give advanced training for middle and higher-level commanders. Although a few of the instructors, like Halefom and Hadgu, had formal military training in Harar military academy and other government military schools most of the instructors were self-proclaimed tutors. The Hakfen School developed manuals for different aspects of command by incorporating local experience with manuals from the Vietnamese, Chinese and other liberation movements who were engaged in armed struggle. Government army manuals, which were found in garrisons the TPLF had overrun or were brought with defecting officers, were extremely valuable in understanding the nature of the army and developing comprehensive tactical manuals to counter it.

At this time, the TPLF seemed to have all the basic essentials that were necessary to engage in the war against the *Dergue*. It had popular support in every aspect, the size of the fighting force was growing steadily, and there was determined and capable leadership at all levels. Perhaps the Front's only visible limitation at this point was the quality of its arms and the quantity of ammunition it had at its disposal, but every fighter was instructed from the start that the main source of arms was the enemy and they had to collect what they could from them. In one of the popular TPLF songs, *Bahhrina* (Our Sea), the idea of arming from the enemy is engrained as a venerable verse.

Bahhrina ti hafash hizbina
Eerdina gobotat Aadina
Et'kina kabtom tselaetena ...

Our sea is our people
Our trench is every mountain of our land
Our source of arms is the enemy ...

With preparation for the final war accomplished and the *Dergue*'s violent actions towards the people via air raids and ground attacks becoming more alarming, the TPLF was preparing to take on the *Dergue* on any front, even in a conventional manner. The TPLF's prevalence over its former adversaries (the EDU, EPRP and ELF, see the previous chapter) emboldened its determination to mete out a similar fate to the *Dergue*. Let us now turn to how the confrontation with the *Dergue* on the battleground evolved over the years.

The Military Campaigns (*Zemecha*)[64] of the *Dergue*

When the *Dergue* assumed power in 1974, it promised it would tackle Ethiopia's problems in a strictly peaceful way and coined the song *Yale minim dem, Ethiopia Tikdem* (Without Bloodshed, Ethiopia Shall Move Forward), which was exceptionally popular in the first few months. Initially, 'Ethiopia Tikdem' as a motto was acceptable to the general public and seemed to address the latent but daunting problems of the suppressed and ignored nationalities. Among the problematic social issues were the longstanding economic question, evoking the slogan 'land to the tiller', and the question of self-determination. The 'Ethiopia *Tikdem*' slogan was so general that nobody except the *Dergue* perhaps, knew what the motto meant in practical terms. Nobody understood how it would be applied to mitigate the deeply rooted and sensitive problems in the multi-ethnic polity of Ethiopia. The land-reform proclamation had solely generated support for the *Dergue* in the south, but that support soon evaporated with the introduction of collectivization and forced recruitment to the army. Whatever the overall intentions of the *Dergue* might have been, it took no time to resort to heavy-handed force to silence any kind of dissent, independent thinking or legitimate demands such as freedom of expression and regional autonomy or self-determination. Emerging national movements for self-determination were the prime targets of their assault. All were equated with the Eritrean secessionist movement, even though the latter had offered '...a peaceful

---

64 For additional assessment of the *Dergue*'s military campaigns, see TPLF, 'Te*mekiro Zemechatatna*' (in Tigrigna), Tiri 1974 E.C.

political resolution that could result in independence, federation or regional autonomy through internationally supervised referendum' (EPLF 1981: 109). Such movements in the eyes of the *Dergue* were a thorn in the flesh of the 'Ethiopia *Tikdem*' dictum, and with the same tone such opponents or even those with much less strident demands – like the TPLF – were warned that they should submit or would perish. As Halliday and Molyneux (1981: 160) noted: '... the way in which Aman Andom, the first *Dergue* Chairman, was accused in November 1974 of having shown weakness in his negotiation with the Eritrean guerrillas' was to be seen in the light of the *Dergue*'s dogmatic approach to the 'Ethiopia *Tikdem*' slogan.

Just a year after it seized power, the *Dergue* started preparation for a military campaign, commonly known as *zemecha*. Part of the preparation was beating the drum of war accompanied by terrorizing slogans like 'Ethiopia will move forward, its oppressor shall perish' (*Ethiopia tikdem aqourquazhwa yewdem*), 'If you do not surrender, you shall be destroyed', and 'Shower bullets on the renegade'. On the other hand, the TPLF was posturing 'never to budge', regardless of what might happen. This was reflected in its own slogans: '*kalsina newihin merirn, awetna nai-giden iyu*' (our struggle is long and bitter but our victory is certain). A major war was inevitable.

Subsequently, the TPLF had to face eight major military campaigns (*zemecha*) in the ten years between 1975 and 1985. Below, the nature and execution of these *zemecha* are discussed, as are the responses of and impact on the growth of the TPLF.

Raza Zemecha, May-June 1976

The *Dergue*'s first military offensive was known as *Raza Zemecha*. The name *Raza* came from the big bird of the same name that could fly through swarms of locust and ingest them. *Raza Zemecha* was hastily organized and purely adventurous. The *Dergue* forced thousands of peasants from southern Tigrai, Wollo, Gojjam, Gondar and northern Showa to march through northern Tigrai (the TPLF's initial mainstay) and end up in *Eritrea*, where the main rebel forces (*wombedé* - bandits - as the *Dergue* called them) were found. The majority of the peasants were rounded up in their own homes or farms or at market places, and had no idea where they were going.

This massive peasant army, which stretched out for over 100 km in a mountainous area from Adwa to Adigrat, had neither adequate training nor sufficient arms to engage in battles with the guerrilla fighters, who had mastered the terrain and had the training and motivation to fight. They had no rations but were allowed to appropriate any war bounty they could find. Swayed by *Dergue* agitators, many of the peasants had in fact joined the *Raza* march with only spears and whips to beat the bandits and force them to submit. According to Dawit Wolde-Giorgis (1989: 88-89) who was a major and in the *Dergue* leadership at the time,

> It was Mengistu's idea, supported by Atnafu. They were dreaming of the past when emperors such as Menelik had called on the Ethiopian warriors to attack in semi-organized hordes, relying on their courage to win the day. Unfortunately this was 1976, and the enemy was not armed with spears. More than 100,000 peasants were given ancient Portuguese and Czech rifles, some of them 50 years old. They were given no logistical support: virtually no ammunition, no rations …. The march was doomed from the start. First, because it was a march against our own people.

The aim of the *Raza Zemecha*, according to the *Dergue*, was to nip the TPLF in the bud, advance to Eritrea and annihilate the ELF and EPLF. The TPLF was a young organization at the time but its fighting force, though small in number, was motivated and experienced enough to counter any attacking force by using guerrilla tactics. Looking to the hastily planned and clumsy organization of the *Raza Zemecha*, however, it appeared that the *Dergue* was ignorant of the rebels' resolution and tenacity.

Realizing the poor quality of the army and the organizational weaknesses of the *Raza Zemecha*, the TPLF took swift measures to disrupt the campaign before it began in earnest in a planned setting. Agitation units were deployed in towns and villages on the route of the ill-informed peasant soldiers to make them aware of the dangers awaiting them and inform them of the *Dergue*'s duplicity. The aim was to disperse this hastily mobilized peasant army before it engaged in pitched battles with the small but well-trained guerrilla fighters. By sending out skirmishers to disorient the two vanguard units heading from Adwa to Mereb and from Adigrat to Zalambesa (both bordering Eritrea), the TPLF accomplished the bigger task in foiling the *zemecha*. There were some ELF surveillance units following the advance of the march. Soon, the whole campaign began to fall apart, even before the main body of the peasant army had taken up its intended strategic position to strike, let alone having reach Eritrea. The peasant troops ran away from the battlefront in droves, and people in nearby villages cooperated by assisting them in their withdrawal. By the end of May 1976, the bulk of the peasant troops were dispersed and heading back to their respective villages in a disorderly manner. 'The operation, code-named '*Raza*', ended in total humiliation…. Over 25,000 peasants perished in this fiasco …' (ibid.). The *Raza Zemecha* had a hugely demoralizing effect in the *Dergue* camp, while it boosted the morale of the Fronts and the people who supported them. For the TPLF, in particular, it was the first victorious counter-offensive that injected a lot of spirit into its fighting forces.

The Jibo Zemecha – June 1976

A month after its failed Raza *Zemecha*, the *Dergue* organized its *Jibo Zemecha*, which means 'to devour like a hyena'. The *Zemecha* was spearheaded by a regiment of well-trained counter-guerrilla forces known as *Nebelbal* but, like the *Raza*, the accompanying body of the *Nebelbal* was the untrained mobilized peasant army. The *Jibo* was also doomed to failure when its vanguard, *Nebelbal*, was wiped out at a place called Siero, between Adwa and Adigrat, by the joint forces of the TPLF and EPLF.

The Semien Zemecha – June 1978

This *Zemecha*, which directly followed the Ethiopian-Somali war of 1977-78, was quite different from the previous two campaigns in terms of both quality and quantity. It was massive in human and material resources and it had taken two years to mobilize, organize and train over a quarter of a million peasants. 'The limit was 300,000 both for eastern and northern war fronts' (Dawit Shifaw 2005: 101). The Soviet Union not only supplied all the necessary weapons, ranging from MiG fighter planes to tanks and heavy artillery but also assisted in training and planning the war strategy. 'The Soviet Army general V.I. Petrov went to Ethiopia in November 1977 to work on the plan for the counter offensive against Somalia (…) later visited Northern Ethiopia, now Eritrea' (ibid.: 108). 'Overall, the USSR ferried over $1 billion worth of armaments…; dispatched about 12,000 Cuban combat troops, 1,500 Soviet military advisors, 750 soldiers from South Yemen and 'several hundred' East German technicians; and sent four Soviet generals' (Patman 1990: 223). By all accounts, the largest army in Africa was created in famine-stricken Ethiopia. By then, the *Dergue* had joined the Communist bloc and managed to secure the full support of their military resources and expertise.

With a section of this huge army deployed to the Eastern Front earlier in March 1978, the *Dergue* had decisively defeated the invading Somali forces in the Ogaden. This victory in the eastern part of Ethiopia helped to galvanize its army to try and attain a similar victory in the north. In fact, the slogan of the day was 'The triumph won in the East shall be repeated in the North' (*be Misraq yetegegnew dil be Semien yedegemal*) followed by: 'Mop up Tigrai and annihilate Eritrea' (*Tigraien massees, Eritrean medemssees*). As Dawit put it (1989: 109), 200,000 heavily armed troops were deployed to the north. The morale of the army at its peak, it looked as if the end was approaching for the Tigraian and Eritrean fronts in the north. But conditions there were not as they appeared in the east. The war strategy of the fronts in the north was unconventional, which gave them ample flexibility to deal with their militarily stronger opponent. In the east, it was an invasion of Ethiopian territory by the Somali regular army supported by local rebels, while in the north it was a liberation movement supported by larger segment of the masses.

Assessing the magnitude of the military campaign, the northern fronts were prepared to avoid frontal confrontation and adopt classical guerrilla warfare to foil the third massive *Zemecha*, but not without putting their strength and morale to the test. The *Dergue* deployed its forces on several fronts, including Serro Adigrat, Enticho, Adwa, and Shire as the main attack fronts. The TPLF made attempts to stop the *Dergue*'s advancing forces on the Enticho front in collaboration with EPLF units at Gerhu-Sernay and on the Shire front with ELF units at Zagir, but to no avail. Facing little resistance, the forces of the *Dergue*, in large task-force formation, swiftly rolled on deep into Eritrea. The ELF dispersed its forces into the lowlands of Barka while the EPLF retreated to its base area in the hills of Sahil, in the northern tip of Eritrea and dug trenches around the strategic town of Nakfa. The TPLF, on the other hand, deployed its units to the rear of the advancing enemy and began disrupting its supply lines and at the same time avoided frontal confrontation with an army whose infliction of loss would have been severely damaging.

The TPLF, for the first time, faced a large conventional army and experienced how to confront it. Without any meaningful losses in a frontal confrontation, the TPLF resumed its guerrilla activities at will behind enemy lines. The heavy burden rested on the EPLF, which was preparing to confront the enemy in static warfare in the trenches of Nakfa. This strategy would later become one of the sources of difference with the TPLF that led to the break-up of their cooperation. At this time, there were nearly 3,000 TPLF recruits finishing their military training with the EPLF in Sahil. The EPLF requested these fresh fighters be deployed as support troops in their defence line at Sahil. The TPLF conceded this for a short period, until the dust of the *zemecha* settled. The concession of the TPLF was not without valid reason. At that time, the TPLF wanted all the 13 plus divisions of the *Dergue* to be engaged in that corner of Sahil until such time as it had reorganized and trained its forces to meet the challenge of the day. Deployment of just two or three of the *Dergue*'s divisions to Tigrai from Sahil could cause great havoc for the TPLF, whose total force was then still not more than 1,000 fighters, i.e. 8 companies (*haili*). This deployment was purely based on the military logic of the day in the interest of the TPLF, and obviously it helped the

EPLF to foil the *Dergue*'s *zemecha*. It was not the pressure of the EPLF that forced the TPLF to involve its fighters in the Sahil encounter, as some critics of the TPLF love to portray it. Nonetheless, the TPLF made it clear to the EPLF that static warfare against an opponent with far greater human and material resources was strategically ill-fated and that it would withdraw its forces any time soon.

However successful it appeared, the third *Zemecha* never led to mopping up the TPLF in Tigrai, and it remained stuck beneath the hills of Sahil facing the EPLF's well-dug defence lines. 'The greatest of all achievements in the campaign against Eritrea was the opening of the Addis Ababa-Asmara highway... but the attempt to recapture the main stronghold of the EPLF, Nakfa, failed' (Dawit Shifaw 2005: 120-121). The TPLF, however, emerged from this *zemecha* with its forces intact and more experienced, and having acquired new arms from retreating soldiers. The growing morale of its people in general, and the youth in particular, emboldened it and drew more recruits to its army. A few months later its forces had increased in size, and a new formation of battalions was created. It subsequently extended its mobility to eastern and southern Tigrai by attacking isolated enemy posts and lying ambush for military convoys on the highways. As TPLF forces were gradually increasing in size and the formation of its army growing steadily, the nature of warfare was also transforming from guerrilla to mobile warfare, involving frontal and positional confrontation.

The Fourth Zemecha – March 1979

The failure of the Red Star campaign was a big blow to the entire military establishment. In the wake of the campaign, Bealu Girma, the Deputy Minister of Information under the *Dergue* regime, published a book, called *Oromai* (= Lost Case), which detailed the collapse of the Red Star campaign and the ineptness of Lt.-Col. Mengistu as commander-in-chief of the Ethiopian armed forces. Bealu Girma was later mysteriously killed for this revealing work and Ethiopia lost one of its most famous novelists. From here onwards, the *Dergue* was engaged in frantic military ventures to contain and crush a rapidly growing TPLF. For this reason it organized a fourth *zemecha,* exclusively to deal with the TPLF.

With the TPLF's military exertions escalating in Tigrai to the extent that its highly guarded supply lines were continuously disrupted and its garrisons threatened, the *Dergue* swiftly pulled back one of its mechanized brigades from Eritrea and with its forces in Tigrai launched the Fourth *Zemecha*. The *Dergue* took this move while it was still trying to penetrate the EPLF's trenches in the rough hills of Sahil. This *zemecha*, which did not have a coded-name like its predecessors, was launched in mid-March 1979. The campaign focused on the western lowlands of Tigrai, where the TPLF had established strong base areas and in which it kept its materials including eight transport vehicles that it had recently captured from the *Dergue*. The mechanized brigade and its Tigrai-based auxiliary forces were lured deep into the Adiabo lowlands where it was possible to launch flank attacks. Unable to sustain the TPLF's swift and unconventional assault, *Dergue* forces retreated to the highlands and joined the militia brigades under Major Tefera Woldetensai. His campaign was more of a show of force than combat, although it inflicted vindictive measures on the people of central Tigrai. The troops under the command of Major Teferra were well known for their indiscriminate killing of civilians purporting to be disguised members of the 'bandits' (TPLF) and setting villages on fire. Without waiting to face an organized counterattack from the TPLF, *Dergue* forces hurriedly retreated to their garrison towns, Meqele and Adigrat, and the fourth *zemecha* came to an end.

The Fifth Zemecha – February 1980

As the TPLF appeared to become invincible in the campaigns conducted by the regular army and seeing its menacingly swelling forces, the *Dergue* started to forcefully involve local Tigraian elements. This scheme was a sign of frustration rather than of any military logic. First, it organized all defectors from various fronts, including the TPLF, the EDU and the EPRP, and formed a contingent that was given the code-name *Zendo* (python). The defectors were by no means supporters of the *Dergue* and most had abandoned the fronts simply because they could not endure the hardships of guerrilla life. So basically, they were inimical to the idea of returning to a situation that induced their defection in the first place. In addition to this, all physically fit Tigraian civil servants were ordered to participate in the *Zemecha* without even a day's military training. The *Dergue*'s rationale behind this was to create a rift between the TPLF and its would-be Tigraian supporters. The whole scheme was counterproductive for the *Dergue* because both the people and the TPLF were aware of its duplicity, and the Front avoided direct confrontations with the *Dergue* forces in the entire *Zemecha*.

The *Dergue*'s plan with this campaign was to clear southern and central Tigrai of insurgents. Yet unable to sustain the unconventional attacks of the TPLF, the regular army, the *Zendo* and the reluctant civil servants were mixed up as the battle started in an effort to avoid direct confrontation with TPLF fighters. Failing to coordinate the offence and eventually their defensive tactics too, they ran in disarray to the garrison town of Enticho, where the Fifth *Zemecha* came to an end in a matter of three days. Its abrupt failure sent out a loud message that the TPLF, now organized in battalion formation, was growing stronger and could not be defeated with such hastily mobilized forces and faulty tactics.

The Sixth Zemecha – August 1980

The *Dergue* seemed to have realized its weakness from its failed campaigns. For the next campaign, it trained a counterinsurgency force code-named *Terara* (Mountain), which could penetrate any mountainous region where guerrillas could be found. It was armed with modern light machine-guns, had long-range snipers and was ready to attack at any time and at any place. It was also supported by MiGs and MI-24 helicopter gunships to fight the insurgents at close range. Its accompanying political campaign was also quite different from before. With recently trained cadres embedded in the army, it heralded the approach of a people's army and was quite different from its predecessors. Cadres of the recently established Commission to Organize Party of the Workers of Ethiopia (COPWE) were preaching 'lasting peace', 'good governance' and 'all-round development' for the people. They told the population that mistakes had been committed by blaming innocent people for the criminality of the *wonbedé* (bandits) and from here on that they were only after the bandits of the TPLF.

Indeed, *Terara* began advancing across the rough terrains of Tembien in central Tigrai and along the Worie River. Initially, it looked militarily superior in tactics and penetrated as far as the Worie gorges, one of the TPLF base areas. The TPLF, however, adopted mobile war tactics with small units on the terrain where the enemy could not get effective air support, and launched several attacks. It also began attacking the enemy's rear, blocking its supply line as well as destroying isolated posts in the adjacent provinces of Wollo and Gondar. In this way, the TPLF's theatre of operation was broadening as the *Dergue* attempted the campaign. This strategy forced the *Dergue* to retract its counter-insurgency *Terara* to the big towns, which had become increasingly vulnerable to TPLF raids.

The Sixth *Zemecha* came to an end with yet another debacle of the *Dergue* forces and meant a morale boost for the TPLF. Getting used to *zemecha*, all the departments of the TPLF were now capable of operating as planned, and the training section was producing new fighters that increased the size of the battalions, which in turn gave way to the formation of brigades. Socio-economic activities among the people were also moving in the intended direction, despite short-lived disruptions caused by the campaigns. 'From this campaign, the TPLF not only confirmed that its forces could not be wiped out as the *Dergue* planned it but also gained the experience to carry on its program of tackling socio-economic problems of its people uninterrupted even while *Dergue*'s *zemecha* was in full swing' (TPLF 1981: 55).

The Seventh and Eighth Zemecha – 1983 and 1984

These two *zemecha* were carried out at a time when the morale of the *Dergue* was on the decline and the fighting spirit of its army was plummeting while the TPLF was emboldened by its successive victories.

The Seventh *Zemecha* was launched in mid-1983 and the Eighth *Zemecha* a year later, but neither could withstand the counter-offensive of the TPLF army. In the summer of 1983, a whole brigade under the Tigrai command, part of the Seventh *Zemecha*, was annihilated on the Kafta terrains, a rugged place between Gondar and Humera, and all its armaments were either captured or destroyed. The Eighth *Zemecha* was also a desperate attempt by the *Dergue* to penetrate the 'liberated' central and western areas, only to face a humiliating defeat by a combined attack by the TPLF's regular and militia forces. The Eighth *Zemecha* was the last of its kind although there were desperate attempts by the *Dergue* to reverse the growth and onslaught of the TPLF.

All the *Dergue*'s *zemechas* ended in military failure. But it also suffered politically, which discredited its legitimacy and political hold on the country. Conversely, the TPLF came out stronger, and from then onwards the balance of forces steadily tilted in its favour as the *Dergue* forces had to retreat more and more.

Towards the end of 1984 and at the beginning of 1985, the TPLF was by-and-large engaged in advanced mobile warfare and working on conventional warfare. Air raids were the attacks its people suffered from most, but now it began training anti-aircraft gunners with the heavy weapons captured from the *Dergue*. As it intensified its mobile warfare, *Dergue* forces began taking defensive positions in garrison towns like Meqele, Adigrat, Adwa, Shire and Maichew. The area between the towns was in the hands of the TPLF and the *Dergue*'s contingents could only travel with caution with a part of the force giving cover to the other. Rural Tigrai by-and-large was now under the control of the TPLF, and many villages were administered by 'elected people's councils' called *baito* (for a detailed analysis see Chapter 10) The *baitos* operated under strict supervision of the TPLF cadres.

Meqele, the capital of Tigrai, also felt the heat of the expanding movements of the TPLF. At midnight on 7 February 1986, the main prison in the capital was attacked and all the 1,300 political prisoners were freed. They were taken to the TPLF base area and most joined the Front. It was a shock to the command regiment of the *Dergue* forces, which the same day had dispatched a contingent to attack TPLF diversionary units in a nearby village. Out of sheer frustration, the *Dergue* intensified its retaliatory measures and continued its air bombardment of villages, towns and market places to terrorize the people in the hope that they would withdraw their support for the TPLF. On 22 June 1988, when it was a market day in Hawzien, a town in central Tigrai, MiGs and a squadron of helicopter gunships carried out a massive bombing raid in which over 1,800 civilians were killed. Abi-Adi, Yechela, Sheraro and Chila towns and more villages were attacked in a similar way, also on market days and/or when other large-scale gatherings were taking place. The Hawzien massacre was conducted under the leadership of Legesse Asfaw, the commander of the armed forces in Tigrai at the time. As Dawit Wolde-Giorgis (1989: 300) put it, 'He [Legesse] never tried to hide his dislike of the Eritreans and Tigraians'. Such acts swelled people's anger and hate of the regime, and by the same token tightened their support of the TPLF, the only alternative. Many elderly parents who had been reluctant to let their children join the Front were now not only encouraging them but also themselves requesting to be armed and join the militia forces. While the numbers of TPLF brigades grew to more than 20,000 fighters, the *Dergue*'s forces were dwindling. An August 1988 report by the TPLF's military intelligence showed this, pointing out how between 1979 and 1980 the *Dergue* had had 300,000 troops but by 1988 the number had dropped considerably (see Table 4.1).

According to the August 1988 TPLF report, the *Dergue* had lost a little over half its army. At the end of 1988 an additional 108,000 recruits were trained that replenished the army, increasing the number of its troops to 247,500 and the divisions to 25. This process of filling the gaps created by previous losses would continue, but at the same time the Ethiopian people were increasingly against it. Augmenting its troop numbers did not save the *Dergue* from successive defeats at the hands of the still-growing TPLF.

Command centre	Divisions	No. of Troops
Eritrea (SRA)	11	71,500
Tigrai (TRA)	4	37,000
East	3	12,000
Centre	2	10,000
South	2	9,000
Total	**22**	**139,500**

Table 4.1 Distribution of *Dergue* Divisions in 1988

Debate over Military Strategy

Bringing down the *Dergue* by any means was the TPLF's unanimous objective, even though there was serious difference as to how to go about achieving this goal. So far, the military strategy of the TPLF had reflected the political objective highlighted in its programme, namely the self-determination of Tigrai, and thus the war against the *Dergue* had to be waged essentially by mobilizing the Tigraian population in Tigrai. Based on this strategy, the war against the Ethiopian regime was confined to Tigrai, and the cost was too heavy for Tigraians, with up to 10 small and large-scale military engagements every month.[65] However, considering the overall engagement with the Ethiopian military forces, fighting and winning battles only in Tigrai could not bring the war to an end as long as the *Dergue* prevailed in the greater part of Ethiopia – a very large rearguard compared to that of the TPLF (see Figure 4.1 below). The *Dergue* had the advantage of massive human and material resources under its control and continued to draw on these vast resources of Ethiopia as a whole to feed and prolong the war. Consequently there was a real need for the TPLF to carry on the struggle throughout Ethiopia to stop the flow from the rearguard that was prolonging the war.

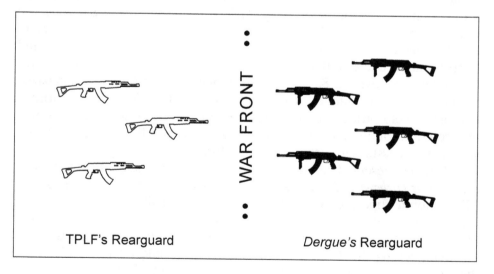

Figure 4.1 The *Dergue*'s rearguard in relation to the TPLF's rearguard

---

65 For instance, according to the official organ of the TPLF, *Woyeen*, August 1978, pp. 40-41, there were 3 military engagements in the month of May 1978, 9 in June 1978 and 4 in July 1978.

This strategy required not only military vision but also the political will to work with other Ethiopian organizations that could fight for collective interests, i.e. the removal of the *Dergue* and the establishment of a democratic state. The TPLF was tied up in Tigrai with its own political strategy of liberating Tigrai. This became an obstacle to its military strategy of defeating the *Dergue* outright, which still had control of the greater part of Ethiopia. This was a long-term dilemma that confronted policy makers in the TPLF's politburo. If its struggle was to achieve self-determination for Tigrai, then this could only happen by replacing the *Dergue* with a democratic system that respected such a right. The *Dergue* therefore had to be removed from the whole of the country, and a democratic force had to take its place.

The TPLF's politburo could not reach a consensus on this strategic matter that had such widespread ramifications. Those who leant towards the separation of Tigrai (Sibhat, Abbay, Seyoum and Meles) advocated an intensification of the struggle in Tigrai under the pretext of strengthening the rear. Others, like Aregawi, Giday, Teklu and Atsbaha, pushed for broadening the struggle with participation of other Ethiopian forces. Some of these fighters gave repeated recommendations to this effect in writing. In February 1983 (Lekatit 1975 E.C.), Aregawi Berhe, politburo member and head of the military committee at the time, presented a paper to the politburo entitled 'Concerning our Military Strategy' (*Wetaderawi Stratejina Bezemelket*). He showed the build-up of the *Dergue*'s brigades from 36 brigades in 1977 to 135 brigades in 1982, of which 92 were deployed in the north (Tigrai and Eritrea) and he declared that this trend would continue as long as the *Dergue* had full control over 75-80% of the Ethiopian population. He emphasized the need to create a united front among all democratic Ethiopian forces, not just to help oust the military regime but also to build a better system that could accommodate all the stakeholders. The politburo was reluctant to discuss the issue seriously let alone to formulate a strategy to this effect. In 1984, he presented another paper entitled 'Protracted People's War' (*Zetenawihe Hizbawi Kuinat*) in which he discussed the nature of the war the TPLF should wage and the need for alignment with all democratic forces in Ethiopia focusing upon the rear and the front of its war *vis-à-vis* that of the *Dergue*. This time a challenge emerged in a politburo meeting on the idea of strengthening the TPLF's rearguard, which would also mean limiting the mobility of the Front and confining the struggle to Tigrai. But the point was that a strong rear feeds its front and this could only be achieved by denying the rear at the disposal of the enemy. Aregawi (1984: 52-53) argued, 'The rear of the *Woyyane* (revolution) could be safe only by disabling the rear of the enemy which is the source of energy for the front of the latter'. The debate continued into the following year. For the third time, in April

1985 (Miyazia 1977 E.C.) and just a few months before the formation of the Marxist-Leninist League of Tigray, see Chapter 7 below), another paper entitled 'Integrated War in Tigrai' (*Kule-Medayawi Kuinat ab Tigrai*) was presented to the politburo. This paper elaborated on and summarized what had been proposed in the first two papers.

The Sibhat camp came up with a dubious response, arguing that they were forging an all- Ethiopia struggle with such organizations as the EPDM (now ANDM), which in actual fact was a satellite organization. This response, although it looked like a solution, was more of an escape mechanism and was concocted to avoid discussing the issue at the upcoming TPLF/MLLT congress. By bringing the EPDM into the picture, they were trying to suggest that cooperation with other Ethiopian organizations was in progress. Yet the EPDM was a tiny satellite group of EPRP dissenters, organized and financed by the TPLF to systematically project such an image and help keep at bay challenging organizations elsewhere in Ethiopia. Two months later, after the third paper was presented and in the wake of the MLLT formation in July 1985, Aregawi Berhe and Giday Zeratsion, who challenged the politburo in the congress on ideological issues, were removed from their positions as politburo members of the TPLF/MLLT. Charged with concocted allegations, both were discharged from the Central Committee by the politburo, even though they had been elected by the congress only a few days earlier. It later transpired that this was a plan designed long before by Meles Zenawi and Sibhat Nega, who managed to sway the rest of the politburo.[66] The TPLF's military strategy was to remain in Tigrai, registering tactical gains until the entire force of the *Dergue* was racked from within, opening the way for the TPLF to advance into the rest of Ethiopia.

---

66 Those politburo members were to become victims themselves of the same plotters years later. In 2001, after disgreements over the 1998-2000 war with Eritrea, TPLF politburo members like Gebru Asrat, Aregash Adane, Tewolde Woldemariam and Seye Abraha were removed from their party positions and their parliamentary seats revoked, in breach of the constitutional rights of the people which elected them.

Chapter 7

Ideological Controversies on Self-Determination

Introduction

There was and still is no international consensus on the scholarly and legal definition of 'self-determination', as discussed in the theoretical Chapter 2. This was true throughout the struggle of the TPLF, even though self-determination itself was allegedly the cardinal motivating issue of the struggle in the first place. Initially, as self-professed Marxists whose theoretical models emphasised class analysis, self-determination was understood by the TPLF leaders as the right to express and determine the 'collective political will of an ethnically/linguistically defined group within the multi-ethnic society of Ethiopia. What concrete political from this had to take was initially not clearly defined, although it was expressed with vague references to democracy and people's rights. In the course of the struggle, however, the initial understanding of self-determination was narrowed down, if not derailed, by a group within the leadership, which equated self-determination for the various 'nationalities' of Ethiopia with *secession*. This group reformulated the objectives of the TPLF into achieving a separate statehood. This was, however, always controversial within the Front. Thus, after an internal theoretical and political disagreement, the idea of secession was withdrawn in 1976, but not decisively, as the nature of the issue itself – self-determination – was malleable. The fluidity of ethnicity associated with the right to self-determination continued to be the tool of the political elite to manoeuvre and reshape the perceptions of the people of Tigrai. This chapter discusses the malleable nature of self-determination as the goal but also as a tool of mobilization of 'ethnic entrepreneurs'.

The Early Phase of the Struggle

Almost all leaders of the TPLF thought of themselves as Marxist revolutionaries. Among them, an informal group which later named itself the 'communist core' within the TPLF was constituted by Abbay Tsehaye, Meles Zenawi and Sibhat Nega. It was this core group that engineered the formation of the Marxist Leninist League of Tigrai (MLLT) in July 1985, and became the leading ideologues on pertinent issues such as self-determination.[67] Yet the nature and intentions of this group were not fully known to many until it seized power in Ethiopia in May 1991. It is, however, possible to explain its salient political features and its organization from different perspectives. None of its ideological characteristics are as revealing of its nature as its stance on the question of self-determination for the people of Tigrai.

This matter is highlighted here for the following reasons: 1) since its articulation by the Ethiopian students' opposition political platform, the national question was construed opportunistically and even distorted in many ways and yet has remained one of the popular demands that has not found a proper resolution to date;[68] 2) in a more political vein, unless clarity is achieved on this issue and its uses by political actors, the prevailing confusion may unnecessarily drag the effort to find solutions to the question, both in the particular Tigraian and the general Ethiopian context; 3) a proper analysis of the problem will also cast some light on the behaviour of political groups such as the MLLT/TPLF who seem to be bent on redefining popular demand and exploiting grievances to promote a desire for power. It is likely that the entire ideological frame of reference concerning 'revolution',

---

67 The secession guise of self-determination brought this group together more than the principles of communism and the party MLLT served as a pretext to get grip of the TPLF and work for the implementation of their version of self-determination.

68 The powerful campaign and subsequently constitutional recognition of ethnic nationalities to self-determination including and up to secession created the centrifugal tendency of even sub-ethnic groups to claim this right, without giving due consideration to the adverse effect on the centuries-old social fabric and the connected economies of the Ethiopian people which seem very difficult to set apart. For a comprehensive understanding of this dilemma and the conflicts it has generated, see Abbink (1998), 'New configurations of Ethiopian ethnicity: the challenge of the South'.

'vanguard party', 'self-determination', etc., inherited from Marxist thinking, has to be fundamentally rethought and politically brought up-to-date.

To understand the national question in Tigrai, ideologically appropriated by the MLLT, it is necessary to start with the political programme of the movement that coherently articulated it for the first time. This historic programme was drafted by the Tigraian National Organization (TNO), better known as *MAGEBT* in Tigrigna, a clandestine organization formed by progressive Tigraians in Addis Ababa in early 1974.[69] It was stated in this document that 'the people of Tigrai have suffered national oppression' and that 'it is essential to create a nationalist organization in order to attain freedom from national oppression and exploitation'.[70] The programme, written in Tigrigna, clearly maintained that the form of the struggle would be nationalist while its content would remain class-based. The creation of a 'united and democratic Ethiopia' where the rights of all the 'nations and nationalities' to self-determination are respected was the programme's main goal.

The proclamation of a struggle for justice and equality for Tigrai within the context of a united Ethiopia attracted many members of this region to the organization, both from abroad and from within the country. This in turn led to the rapid growth of the organization. *MAGEBT* issued and distributed propaganda material designed to elaborate on its main themes at the end of 1974 and the beginning of 1975, when the programme itself was not yet made public. Even though the right to secede as a democratic right was entertained by the Left in general, it was not incorporated in these publications, but this is not to say that there were no individuals reflecting what came to be called 'narrow nationalist sentiments' within *MAGEBT* at the time. There were such members but owing to the popular support that the aims of the movement outlined by the organization had attained, they were not in a position to rewrite it according to their own wishes. As a result, the original programme, on the basis of which early political activity in the urban areas was undertaken, continued to provide the guidelines for the armed struggle until it was eventually replaced in 1976 by the so-called *Manifesto 68* that advocated the secession of Tigrai. In fact, the original programme not only attracted Tigraian nationalists to the struggle but also laid the foundations upon which a class alliance with multinational organizations could be built. The call extended to the EPRP to create a united front is a case in point.

On the whole, there was a concerted effort at the time to coordinate the struggle with other nationalist and multinational political forces in the

69 See *Woyeen*, August 1978, p. 11.

70 TNO (MAGEBT), 1974, unpublished document.

country. The decision to resolve the differences with the TLF and create a joint leadership was additional testimony that the movement's original aim was to establish a united country based on the equality of all its nationalities. In other words, the decision that the organization made to move its forces from Dedebit to Agame in the early phase of the struggle was aimed at facilitating close collaboration with other political organizations such as the EPRP and the TLF that were active in the area at that time. The aim was to create conducive atmosphere for the formation of a united front to strengthen the common struggle.

Despite the TPLF's initial attempts to win legitimate rights for Tigraians in a democratic, united Ethiopia, the direction the movement took was subsequently altered to accommodate the strategic inducements of the MLLT core. Why the changes that took place later in the movement happened, what the internal and external factors were that led to this, as well as the intricacies of the conflict related to this event, are issues that are dealt with in the following section. The issues at hand illustrate the intricacies of *ideology* within an emergent rebel movement that tried to fight for collective rights of a constituency, but also to redefine a new social and political order in the process. This phase of 'ideological struggle' on visions of the national future was closely tied up with power struggles inside the movement and reflected the felt need for a strong political-military ideology that could buttress the leadership of the movement. But it was remarkable how these and subsequent discussions were conducted in the rather abstract idiom and parameters of the Leftist student movement rather than being informed by a solid grass-roots appraisal of the needs, aims and expectations of the local (largely peasant and non -literate) population.

The Manifesto 68: Secession as an End

The most conspicuous feature of the Manifesto 68 is its reformulation of the people of Tigrai's fight as a struggle to establish an 'independent republic'. This objective of creating a separate Tigraian state was in marked contrast to the movement's original aim. It is therefore necessary to ask why and how this new change took place.

As mentioned earlier, and as the elasticity of ethnic nationalism dictates, not all members of the movement had been happy or fully convinced about the value of creating a united country on the basis of equality, as was envisaged in the original programme. Some members remained sceptical and were biding time to reverse this aim to replace it with their own ideas. In fact, the authors[71] of the new direction set out in the Manifesto 68 were

71 It was not clear at the time who was organizing these like-minded ethno-nationalists,

none other than the individuals within the leadership who had been waiting for an opportune moment to impose their wishes on the other members of the movement. Rewriting the original programme in detail (but not altering it) was a previous decision taken by the entire leadership, but which now became a pretext for derailing it.

The future leaders of the MLLT exploited the vanguard and paternalistic attitude of the EPRP towards nationalist organizations as an excuse for pursuing a separatist agenda. They wrote: 'The chauvinist attitude of the EPRP is not only on the oppressed nations in Ethiopia but it is also manifested by its policy on the Eritrean question' (in *Woyeen*, 1978: 23). Indeed, there were elements within the EPRP that showed contempt for those who were not included in or led by their organization. Yet this was not in itself sufficient to reverse the direction that the movement had originally approved as the right path to attain the goal of unity with diversity and equality.

Before the actual reversal of the programme took place, intense discussions on the 'hegemonic attitudes' reflected by multinational organizations were held. On the basis of these discussions, a consensus was reached that stated that it was difficult to create a common front with organizations like the EPRP and still promote the common cause. Despite this assertion, there was an understanding as to the need to create a united front with other organizations deemed to be free of chauvinistic attitudes. Thus, even if the perceived differences were stretched to mean that it was impossible to create a common front with the EPRP, it could not have warranted the subsequent reversal of the original programme undertaken by the MLLT leaders.

As we saw, Abbay Tsehaye, Meles Zenawi and Sibhat Nega were among the main protagonists of the group that instigated the idea of secession. In June 1975 already, Sibhat had gone as far as characterizing the Tigraian demand for self-determination in the context of a 'colonial question', similar to that of the Eritreans.[72] Together, they then proceeded to draft the Manifesto 68, and gave it to Seyoum to print in the Sudan. Seyoum,[73] as a facilitator,

---

but later it became obvious that Sibhat (Woldeselassie) Nega was the mentor behind inexperienced younger members who pursued the secessionist line.

72 Sibhat brought up the idea of 'colonized' Tigrai in an informal discussion with Asfaha, Aregawi and few others at Hirmi on their way to Kelakil in May 1975. Aregawi in particular showed scepticism on the subjective proposal of Sibhat, and henceforth their relation remained strained.

73 Seyoum retained a similar secessionist position, like the rest of the group. The present regional map of Tigrai, with its new, clearly marked boundaries (see for instance the one at: www.dppc.gov.et/downloadable/map/administrative/Atlas_Tigray.pdf), was also his making.

printed a number of copies and sent them to Tigrai for distribution. Some copies were also dispatched to prominent members like Hagos Seyoum in the USA. Before this however, there had been no one in the movement who called for a revision of the original stand on the national question that opted for a realization of self-determination within a democratic Ethiopia. The revision was not predicated on a comprehensive study or a broad-based discussion within the organization itself. Neither was it preceded by a collective decision by the members of the organization. So despite its strategic importance, the idea of secession in the new manifesto and the changes accompanying this position were made without being deliberated upon in a CC meeting or conference or presented to the general assembly for ratification.

It took a few months before the Manifesto reached the other members of the TPLF leadership. On the other hand, its very distribution prompted criticism from various organizations that accused the TPLF of issuing a 'narrow nationalist' and 'separatist' Manifesto. For their part, the other members of the TPLF leadership, who were not yet aware of the publication of the Manifesto, construed the criticism as baseless charges by adversaries.

When copies of the Manifesto 68 arrived from Sudan in July 1976, some of the leadership (Mussie, Sibhat, Abbay and Aregawi) and a few other fighters were at Tsorona. Anxiously, they all started to read it. Since its contents were clearly not in line with the organization's previous position, a heated discussion developed among the leadership members present. For their part, however, the three individuals who wrote the Manifesto argued that their proposal to establish an independent Tigrai was based on earlier consensus within the movement regarding the impossibility of creating a united front with the 'chauvinist' political organizations active at the time. The new position was, in the end, seen as a mistake by the TPLF leading members, and agreement was reached about maintaining the organization's original point of view on the matter. In other words, since the new formulation was thought to be wrong and was expected to lead to political misunderstandings, historical contradictions and even internal conflict, an immediate decision was reached to abandon it and resort to the movement's original position.

Faced with this scepticism, the authors of Manifesto 68 did not argue for their new position strongly. In fact, they seemed to drop the secession standpoint without debating the concomitant points thoroughly. In hindsight it would appear that the authors did not believe in earlier class-based approaches to the national question. Since they could not provide credible historical and theoretical arguments to back what they actually believed in, they formally retracted their secessionist stand. Yet, they resorted to searching for an excuse for having advanced it by pointing to the 'chauvinistic attitude' of the other Ethiopian insurgent organizations towards the TPLF, thereby informally justifying own their call for secession. All this created a false impression within the organization that the issue was resolved.

Despite its exclusivist or 'narrow nationalist' leanings, the communist core group did not want to be singled out for criticism and be labelled as an anti-unity force thwarting the collective and democratic aspirations of the Ethiopian people. Ironically, the group went to great lengths to pose as a champion of the latter cause by advocating measures to neutralize or liquidate organizations that had the same political stand on the national question. A good case in point in this regard is the Tigray Liberation Front (TLF), which like the originators of the Manifesto 68 maintained that the national question of the Tigraian people was to yield a demand for independence. While these two groups had the same goal of creating an independent state for Tigraians, the TPLF Manifesto core (later to become MLLT) accused the TLF of 'narrow nationalism'[74], and subsequently congratulated itself for following 'the correct line' on the national question at the MLLT congress in 1985.[75]

As a matter of fact, the group retreated from publicly stating its secessionist position because of EPLF's pressure[76] and EPRP's repeated accusation in the form of a campaign against the TPLF's separatist project. Even though the criticisms of these two organizations against the secessionist stance were made for different reasons, their impact and the internal opposition to the revision of the programme forced the communist group to withdraw it and desist from propagating it in public. But had it not been for the internal and external factors, the communist group could have pushed the secessionist agenda to its limits. There is indirect acknowledgement of this fact in the group's own evaluation of its ten-year activities:

> The main reason for the emergence of this narrow nationalist tendency was the lack of clarity in the outlook of the communist force even though a similar trend among the population and the chauvinistic attitude reflected both by the government and multinational organizations had also contributed towards its expression (MLLT 1985: 24-25).

---

74 An accusation heard until this day levelled by TPLF or government members at groups advancing an ethnic autonomy or ethno-nationalist agenda.

75 See: 'Evaluation of the Ten Years Journey of the Communist Core within the TPLF/ Adopted in the Founding Congress of the MLLT', July 1977 E.C.: 17

76 EPLF's pressure was not induced out of a principle to see a united Ethiopia, but to avoid an international censure that they were separatists fostering the breakup of Ethiopia.

This self-evaluation of the communist core was self-contradictory. On the one hand it maintained that the political line it had followed was correct and that it had exposed the narrow nationalism of the TLF (ibid.: 17, 27), while on the other hand, it suggested that this same outlook lacked clarity and, as a result, the TPLF had made a mistake on the national question. This apparent contradiction makes sense only if we disregard the self-justification of the group and we stick to what actually happened during the early phase of the struggle. The communist core attempted to replace the movement's original programme with its own secessionist stance and was forced to abandon it as a result of internal and external pressures. Not only was the narrow nationalist standpoint unacceptable to most of the militants and many Tigraians aware of the region's history, it also deprived the group itself of the progressive mask it wanted to wear in public. Incidentally, the inclusion in the current, 1995 Ethiopian Constitution of the right to secede for all the 89 ethnic groups of Ethiopia (Article 39.1) is a result of their approach and proves the position they pursued for so long. But their progressive mask seems to have confused a lot of people, including the researcher John Young, the author of *Peasant Revolution in Ethiopia: the TPLF, 1975-1991* (1997: 99). He emphatically wrote: 'Opponents of the TPLF charge that such statements demonstrate its goal is to dismantle Ethiopia along ethnic lines. This is not the case', and goes on: 'Although the Manifesto was produced by elements within the leadership, no names accompany the document'. Firstly, it is unacceptable to expect or think of individual names when the Manifesto came up bearing the name of the organization, the TPLF; besides, it was partly the authors' strategy to make it as broadly accepted document as possible. Secondly, a researcher who spent more than a year interviewing cadres and leaders of the TPLF, including Sibhat, Meles and Abbay, could have asked just one question to the top members of the Front: 'Who wrote the Manifesto?' and discover the authors. By not tackling this issue and not giving the attention it deserves, Young[77] by implication makes it clear that the men in power were responsible for the controversial stand in the Manifesto that they perhaps had been trying to cover it up.

Organizational Policy and Plan of Action

Differences of ideology and political strategy within the TPLF leadership were played down during most of the years of the struggle. This might have

---

77 It is still unclear why Young had to avoid this important issue in the political history of the TPLF and even in his subsequent articles on the Front. Young had solid and detailed information about this fact from insiders like Kahsay Berhe, Giday Zeratsion, Aregawi Berhe, etc.

helped the members to focus on just fighting the enemy (*Dergue*) but failed to realize the dangerous direction the Front was leading them in. Differences manifested themselves in the course of implementing political and military policies which were apparently agreed upon by all the members of the leadership. Whenever such differences appeared among the rank and file and seemed to provoke serious discussions, they were blocked by loyal cadres who reiterate the leadership's voice. The contestable acts responsible for the differences were justified as being in the spirit of the TPLF's first general assembly resolution. There were virtually no opportunities to raise and discuss points of disagreement, as such points were considered unimportant and subservient to the main goal of the struggle. If there were debates, they were only among the top leaders of the CC or the politburo. In fact, using this catch-all phrase, the MLLT leaders tried to cleverly construe their position as the generally binding guideline of the organization at large.

As stated above, Manifesto 68 was subsequently dropped, not as a result of debates and discussions among the rank and file members or cadres or even the congress but because of differences within the politburo and external pressure. In 1979 the first TPLF Congress adopted a new programme, devised to correct the secessionist trend that had started to creep into the organization. Yet it would not be far from the truth to say that the TPLF did not explicitly attempt to struggle for a united and democratic Ethiopia during the period between the organization's first and second congresses. Contrary to its publicly stated objective, anti-Amhara propaganda was subtly encouraged within the movement. Cultural events, theatrical performances as well as jokes and derogatory remarks were used to disseminate this poisonous attitude. Fuelling some historical grudges perpetrated by the ruling classes, the Sibhat faction tried to cast doubt on the possibility of living in unity with 'the Amhara'. While they stressed how Emperor Menelik's army pillaged the property of Tigraian people during its Adwa campaign, the damage the same forces had also incurred on the Amhara or Agew peasants was intentionally ignored. These lopsided historical presentations were noted and criticized by friendly organizations like the Ethiopian People's Democratic Movement (EPDM). This does not mean, however, that all the cultural performances presented by the organization were narrowly nationalist in nature. Performances reflecting the class solidarity of all oppressed people were also enacted alongside the former. By condoning anti-Amhara remarks and allowing hostile expressions against an entire group of people within an organization supposedly struggling for a united country based on equality, the MLLT leaders were sabotaging from within the very aim for which the movement was started in the first place. Whenever they found events that served their purpose of fuelling conflict among different nationalities, they magnified it and whenever they came across conditions that pointed to the historical connections of the latter, they chose to ignore and downplay them. Attempts to correct such misconceptions were also discouraged and considered a 'waste of time on marginal issues'.

From the beginning of the first TPLF congress in 1979 until the end of 1985, the communist core, which later turned out to be the MLLT leadership, was also actively resisting any attempt to reconcile the organization's military operation with its political aims. The corrective suggestions put forward at the time were mainly intended to enable the military activities to reflect the broad objective of creating a united country. It was stressed that the military government was making use of the country's total human and material resources to suppress resistance in Ethiopia and Eritrea. The effort to put an end to the power of the military regime thus required the anti-*Dergue* struggle to be waged countrywide. Even though the TPLF was a nationalist movement and as an Ethiopian organization was struggling to create a reformed, united country, it also reserved the right to undertake its military and political activities in all parts of Ethiopia. It was on the basis of this conviction that the TPLF undertook surprise operations in Wollo and Gondar regions in the second half of the 1970s.

Despite efforts to give the struggle a countrywide dimension, the internal intricacies to limit it within the confines of Tigrai became insurmountable over the course of time. When villages like Fersmai and Edaga-Arbi fell to the *Dergue* forces in 1986, the MLLT group would complain of not having defended these places, an argument ignoring the fact that static warfare to defend a territory was not possible for the TPLF, which could only conduct guerrilla or mobile warfare at the time. Due to the sectarian politico-military strategy that isolated Tigrai from the rest of Ethiopia, the fighting tactics of TPLF was affected, and many villages in Tigrai became targets of acts of reprisal by the *Dergue* while other parts of Ethiopia enjoyed relative peace. In a way, this ideology of exclusiveness as stipulated in the Manifesto and the confinement of the military activities to Tigrai alone became more influential in the movement, but with adverse effects. If the strategic goal of the organization was not the creation of an independent republic of Tigrai, there were neither political nor military reasons why the rear and the frontline of the struggle should be confined to Tigrai alone. By isolating the Front from other Ethiopian forces and cutting the movement off from human and material resources it could have mobilized in and from other parts of the country, the MLLT leadership followed a strategy that probably prolonged the war unnecessarily, with devastating consequences for the people it claimed to want to liberate. For the population of Tigrai, the cost of fighting the Ethiopian military regime was high in every aspect.[78] The Manifesto thinking, indeed, was not dominant among the people and rank and file members, but it was the belief of the influential group in the leadership that had the capacity to manipulate policies and strategies of the Front.

'Narrow' Nationalism after the Second TPLF Congress

When the time for a TPLF congress approached, the communist core posed as a guardian of the Ethiopian revolution. That the Tigraian revolution was part and parcel of the Ethiopian revolution and the strategic aim of the struggle was the victory of the Ethiopian revolution were given prominence by them in slogans during the 1976 Fighters' Congress and the 1979 Organizational Congress. These themes were now accompanied by the call to establish a 'united' or common front with other movements for their realization. Activities undertaken in the name of Ethiopia were traced to the cooperation established with the EPDM. Joint measures by the two organizations were exaggerated and praised at every opportunity, as if the then powerless EPDM had an independent existence and enjoyed parity of esteem.

The need to create a common front among the anti-*Dergue* opposition forces was also stressed in the resolution of the second TPLF Congress in 1983. Yet, the same issue was only casually raised in the meeting of the Central Committee, where plans of action should have been discussed in detail. It was not even given the importance that it had received during the general assembly, and the Central Committee did not come up with specific guidelines for its implementation. On the other hand, the group led by Abbay Tsehaye and Meles Zenawi argued against a detailed discussion of the issue, claiming that there were no organizations that qualified for a united front at the time. In the absence of such organizations, talk on how to implement the task would be out of place, they argued. A few members among the leadership contested the views expressed by the communist core and urged the Central Committee still to give the matter the attention and weight it deserved. They maintained that every anti-*Dergue* organization opposed to the intervention of the Soviet Union would be considered eligible to join the front and there were many of them. On the basis of this broad view, they recommended the drafting of a detailed proposal with which to approach other organizations. It was also emphasized that previous calls for a united

---

78 For details see the military campaigns (*zemecha*s) of the *Dergue* in Chapter 4.

front had failed because of a lack of *concrete* suggestions to resolve political differences between potential members.

Eventually it was decided that a renewed call for a common front should be forwarded and an agreement was reached to include the following points in the detailed proposal:

- The aim of the united front would be to remove the *Dergue* and Soviet interventionism and establish a transitional government consisting of representatives of the member organizations.

- The transitional government would guarantee the full respect of democratic rights and pave the way for the creation of a people's democratic state.

- The government would ensure the resolution of the demand for self-determination through popular referendum.

- Any organization engaged in a tangible anti-*Dergue*, anti-Soviet political struggle was eligible for membership.

- The proposal also required that all member organizations support the right of nations to self-determination both in word and deed.

This last point raised debate on how to deal with organizations that partially concurred or rejected out-rightly the right of self-determination and those that did not have a clear position on the issue. Such general responses from different organizations were reported at a politburo meeting during the second TPLF congress in Tekeze in 1983 by Berhane Gebrekristos, who at the same time suggested that the call for a common front '...requires clarity'. A strong attack on Berhane's suggestion[79] came from Meles Zenawi and the issue of the call was left as it was and unresolved. The fact that important points related to the formation of a united front were left open-ended presented ample opportunities to the minority opposition, bent on advancing their group's interests in interpreting matters as they saw fit and delaying the formation of the common front. Since the goal this group wanted to achieve was confined to the province of Tigrai, the broader call for a united struggle with other Ethiopian organizations remained unanswered for a long time (from the 1976 Fighters' Congress to the 1983 Second Organizational Congress). Despite the vague call for the united front, no concrete steps were

79 Berhane's report and suggestion reflected the attitude of opposition organizations towards the TPLF's call of a united front, but it was belittled by Meles, who was backed up by Abbay. Berhane was spared by other CC members, who argued that he '... reported the real viewpoint of the opposition groups. Do you want him to report what was not there?' Meles was then forced to retract his allegation because at this stage of the struggle he had not established himself as a dominant leader and could only push his ideas with different means, working behind the scene Abbay Tsehaye as a shield.

therefore taken. Instead of meeting the political organizations concerned face-to-face and facilitating the creation of an alliance, the section of the CC assigned to undertake this task became engaged in contacting foreign governments and parties to give the impression to these forces that the call for a common front was not given positive response by other organizations at home. Thus they shifted the space of activity for the formation of the united front *outside Ethiopia*. In 1978 the opposition group in the TPLF wrote:

> There is no multi-national organization that could act as central force around which a countrywide struggle is to be mobilized. Besides under the existing conditions even an organization like EPDM which has a relatively better organizational strength and ideological clarity cannot be said to have reached a level of development that enables it to carry on this responsibility.... given this objective condition, it is inevitable that the Ethiopian revolution should be undertaken in a disorganised and spontaneous manner and that this situation is not something that could be changed within a short period of time. (TPLF, *May Day*, April 1978)

Still, from the start of the TPLF, the need to eventually create a united front with other opposition groups had been considered a precondition to expediting the fall of the *Dergue* and to strengthen the struggle for political change in Ethiopia. This goal was not achieved for a number of years because of the emerging separatist agenda of the above-mentioned 'proto-MLLT' group and its hostile and condescending attitude towards other organizations, which understandably had alternative political programs. The proto-MLLT group seemed not only belligerent towards such organizations, but was also reluctant to coordinate the actual struggle on parity even with the only organization with which it declared itself to have had a common strategic goal for years, the EPDM. Several demands of the EPDM to independently operate in Tigrai were rebuffed, and individual EPDM members like Yared Tibebu (Jebesa)[80] who dared to make remarks critical of the MLLT leaders' handling of the relationship between the two organizations were threatened and pressured to resign from their organization. Other fighters who were opposed to the TPLF's unilateralism and demanded a united form of struggle in parity also met with a similar fate. In this manner, the central ideas of the right to self-determination, democracy and ethno-regional autonomy, through which people of different ethnic background or belief could become masters of their destiny and live more harmoniously on the basis of equally recognized rights and obligations, has been derailed due to the blemished interpretation and execution of the issue by the TPLF leaders.

80 Iinterview: Yared Tibebu (Jebesa), Washington DC, 08 August 2003.

Chapter 8

Capture of a Movement: the Role of the Marxist-Leninist League of Tigrai (MLLT)

Introduction

This chapter pursues in more detail the development of the TPLF during and after the emergence of the MLLT, the 'sub-movement' within the Front that gained such a prominent political and ideological role and put its stamp on post-1991 Ethiopia after the TPLF gained state power.

Initially, the TPLF considered itself an organization within the broad spectrum of Marxist movements of the Ethiopian left. With the rapidly growing number of peasant and nationalist members in the Front in the late 1970s, the left-wing elements saw the need to organize themselves to lead the Front in the direction they believed would realize the interests of the 'poor and exploited masses', and in which the right to self-determination of Tigraians would be respected. At the beginning of 1978, a Marxist-Leninist group was uniting around this notion within the TPLF - as a network of revolutionary fighters who believed in socialism as a just and fair system for all. Later on, this group forged an association known as *Merih Baeta* (in Tigrigna: 'leading elements'). All the educated and experienced fighters with a leftist background were listed in the *Merih Baeta* category, since it was assumed that they would all readily subscribe to the National Democratic

Revolution Program (NDR).[81] This elite group constituted a small part of the TPLF's larger peasant army. In due course, the *Merih Baeta* developed into the Marxist Leninist League of Tigrai (MLLT), the antecedents of which were described in Chapter 7. At its formation, the MLLT was declared a party of the so-called communists within the TPLF who were also the leading elements *(Merih Baeta)* in the Front.

On 25 July 1985 the MLLT was formally set up in the liberated central region of Tigrai, in the gorge of the River Worii, in the midst of a famine that took the lives of tens of thousands of people in Tigrai's densely populated highlands. The founding congress convened for thirteen days and the party's organizers (Abbay Tsehaye and Meles Zenawi) argued for the urgent need to create the party at this time. They claimed their intention was to provide ideological guidance and inject fresh political life into the ailing TPLF which, they thought, had lost its sense of direction. Some TPLF members wondered whether this was the real reason for the setting up of the MLLT or whether it was a measure to oust prominent leaders who simply had different views and whose main focus was the success of the struggle as opposed to power-mongering and ideological refinement. Or perhaps elements of both drove them to create the MLLT at this difficult time. From the start, the MLLT was, therefore, highly contested.

The founding congress of the MLLT declared that '…after over 10 years of struggle and preparation, in an atmosphere of deep democratic spirit, a founding congress that was convened in the liberated area of Tigrai from Hamle 5-18, 1977 EC (12-25 July 1985) formed the MLLT'. Although the MLLT's first chairman was Abbay Tsehaye, the chief ideologue and architect of the party was Meles Zenawi, the current Prime Minister of Ethiopia and leader of the ruling TPLF/EPRDF.

As the MLLT captured the leadership of the TPLF in the 1980s and showed itself to be highly influential also in the post-1991 period, we here discuss how the MLLT emerged and managed to control the Front, how it guided the mobilized people of Tigrai, and how it paved the way to seize power in Ethiopia. It provides an interesting though ironic case of the definition and instrumental use of a mobilizing ideology to augment or replace the earlier ethno-nationalist one. It is ironic because the new group emerged appealing to a (universalist) Marxist-socialist ideology but at the same time claiming a solution for Tigrai (i.e., toward 'secession') instead of for Ethiopia as a whole. We also look into the twists and turns the party

---

81 The National Democratic Revolution (NDR) and its variant the People's Democratic Revolution (PDR), core Marxist concepts, were thought to be the defining revolutionary moments leading to a socialist revolution. This was also the Maoist recommendation for underdeveloped countries.

leaders had to make to gain the West's support and still maintain their old ideology.

Leftist Orientation of the TPLF

The MLLT had its inspiration in the radical movements that engulfed the world in the 1960s and early 1970s, including in insurgent and liberation movements across Africa. These tumultuous years were marked by student protest movements around the world against the Vietnam War and by loud cries for socialism. The familiar phenomena of 'imperialism', 'bureaucratic capitalism' and 'remnants of feudalism' were believed to be the enemies of the world's working classes and the peasantry. The anti-colonial movement throughout the Third World was treated as part and parcel of a bigger anti-imperialist wave. Significant numbers of Ethiopian university students from this generation considered themselves as part of the worldwide revolutionary movement and, in many cases, acted not only as catalysts but also as dynamic members of the movement (cf. Balsvik 1985; Fentahun 1990). The Ethiopian students' movement influenced the revolutionary course of events in the then predominantly feudalist and traditional society of imperial Ethiopia.

Although the attempted *coup d'état* to depose Emperor Haile Selassie in 1960 was crushed and its leaders put to death as a lesson to others, it was an inspiration to Ethiopian students and galvanized their movement. Determination to abolish feudalism and the grip of imperialism was growing rapidly while the need for radical change took on a new ideological (Marxist) paradigm. This movement became the basis for the rise of political parties of ethnic and multi-ethnic composition that hitherto had never been heard of in Ethiopia. Radical students started to regroup and published illegal papers such as *Democracia*, *Abyot* (Revolution) and *Ye Sefiw-Hizb Deemts* (Voice of the Masses). In this process, the first multi-ethnic organizations, like the Ethiopian People's Revolutionary Party (EPRP) and the All-Ethiopia Socialist Movement, known in Ethiopia by its Amharic acronym 'Meison' which later became the mainstream leftist organizations of the Ethiopian students' movement and the educated classes, were in the making (Andargachew Aseged 2000).

Overall unrest in the country, spearheaded by the students, gave rise to a spontaneous revolution that broke out in February 1974 and swept the monarchy from its hereditary throne. As there was no organized legal opposition that could have directed the revolution through a transition process, the only organized and armed force – the military – was at an advantage and manipulated the turn of events. The army officers who organized themselves in a committee called the Provisional Military Administrative Council (PMAC), commonly known as *Dergue*, took over state power on 12 September 1974. The *Dergue* swiftly responded to the long-standing call of the people, like 'land to the tiller', and introduced a radical land-reform programme (1975) and also nationalized all industries in the name of the people. The latter was a populist move and basically ignored calls to hand power to the people and refused to allow independent political parties and a free press to operate. In addition, it denied the people their human and democratic rights to organize and express their views freely. Finally, it unleashed its 'Red Terror Campaign' (1977-1978) aimed at violently suppressing opposition movements of any form.

One of the failures of the *Dergue* was to overlook the younger generation radicalized by student movements. To be a left-wing revolutionary and converse on Marxist ideas was the norm in those days, especially for the young intellectuals and students of the 1960s and 1970s. The youth was poised to challenge any power in Ethiopia that did not conform to the perceived 'aspirations of the people' and the revolutionary changes it cherished. Thus, the *Dergue*'s military dictatorship on the one hand and the revolutionary zeal of Ethiopia's younger generation on the other were facing each other, with neither side showing any sign of retreating.

Although Tigraian students were small in number at Haile Selassie I University and other colleges, their involvement in the revolutionary momentum was very significant. Except for the elderly Sihul, who died a year after the start of the armed struggle in 1976, all who forged the TNO (forerunner of TPLF) were young university students in their early twenties and offshoots of the radical Ethiopian students' movement from the 1960s and early 1970s. They espoused Marxism-Leninism as guiding ideology to realize their dream of ending the backwardness and misery of the Ethiopian people and bringing them the 'light of progress'. Parallel to their academic studies, all of them were engaged in reading, discussing and promoting Marxist theory. In fact, they paid more attention to revolutionary ventures than to their academic studies. Many study cells were formed to digest Marxism, and all their activities were fuelled by the desire to start a revolution that would 'remove Ethiopia from the yoke of feudalism and imperialism'. Since they believed wholeheartedly in it as a guiding means of liberating the exploited and neglected masses from their miserable lives, they challenged the autocratic government of Haile Selassie, putting their own lives at risk. With stones and clubs against tear gas and bullets, they fought the police and at times the army in the streets of the major cities of Ethiopia. Many students were killed or injured in the struggles. The cumulative efforts of these 'vanguard' Ethiopian students, together with groups from the working class, the intelligentsia and the army, brought down the government of Haile Selassie. As this revolution progressed without a party or an organization to lead it, it was inevitable that the army, better organized than the rest of the social institutions or classes, would take advantage and seize power. Subsequently, it became evident that the revolution was faltering, and it was at this moment that the TNO decided to take up arms and confront the repression of the ruling *Dergue* regime from the rural frontiers, under the leadership of the TPLF.

Although the TPLF, as its name indicates, was a nationalist front encompassing different social classes, the leadership and the leading elements – later known as *Merih Baeta* – were disciples of Marxism-Leninism and Mao Tse-tung. They believed that a socialist revolution would transform Ethiopian society and that rights to self-determination would be respected. They openly admired what they knew of the socialist countries for the society they planned to build and for the contributions they gave to anti-colonial liberation movements everywhere. However, when the Ethiopian military regime signed an alliance with the Soviet Union, it became expedient for the TPLF to condemn the Soviet Union for collaborating with the *Dergue* in oppressing the Ethiopian people and to look for an ideological justification to explain the Soviets' conduct. In the early days of the struggle, the TPLF had to look for an alternative ally in its revolution. The Chinese model had a ready-made explanation in 'revisionism', which portrayed the Soviet system as a form of imperialist overlordship, namely 'social imperialism'.

Initially, the TPLF leadership considered embracing the Chinese model of a 'New Democratic' revolution. This so-called New Democracy led by a communist party was propagated by the TPLF until the beginning of the 1980s. When the Chinese joined a party with the 'national bourgeoisie' at the strategic objective level, the TPLF condemned them as another form of revisionism and continued to search for a 'truly socialist ally'. Later, the TPLF's leadership shifted to espousing an independent form of Stalinism, with Enver Hoxha's Communist Albania as a model.

Looking at the ideological course the TPLF navigated, the whole objective of the TPLF leadership boiled down to embarking on 'a national democratic revolution [to] pave the way for a planned socialist economy free of exploitation of man by man, in the interest of the masses' (Manifesto of TPLF, February 1976: 25-27). For this objective to be accomplished it was necessary to have a party that could lead the struggle; and this was later to be found in the MLLT. Within a year of launching the armed struggle, a TPLF political department, headed by Abbay Tsehaye, was established. Under this department, a cadre school with Meles Zenawi and others as teachers was created to produce new political cadres. All the well-educated and high-ranking fighters were labelled as leading elements (*Merih Baeta*) and had to attend a number of cadre courses, after which the 'communist core' of the TPLF became functional. As we saw above, it was this communist core that formed the MLLT in July 1985.

Forging a Leftist Party

Why a socialist party? The technological strides the Soviet Union made soon after introducing socialism and Communist China's apparent ability to feed over a billion people and with all the indications of advancing at a comparable pace with developed countries provided the impetus, if not the justification, for the young enthusiasts to fight for socialism. The anti-colonial ideological position and the political and material support bestowed on liberation fronts in many parts of Africa by the socialist camp also bolstered the image of socialism among the students' generation. None of the younger generation seemed to escape this revolutionary fervour. This was also the case with those who started the armed struggle under the TPLF.

From the start of the armed struggle, the TPLF conducted its political activities more or less as a party with strict ideological guidelines rather than a front encompassing all sorts of nationalist trends. In its Manifesto in February 1976, the TPLF stated that: 'The Tigraian national struggle, being essentially a national democratic revolution, has adopted the programme of New Democracy as its program. ... This type of state is to be a transitory one into socialism and provides the necessary political freedom for the masses' (pp. 25-26). And at its first congress in 1979, the issue of creating a party was raised and, without any meaningful debate, all the delegates unanimously agreed on the formation of a party. If there was any uneasiness on this matter, it came from those fighters who had naively taken the TPLF to be a socialist party.

The political department and in particular the cadre school under Meles Zenawi were given the task of organizing the formation of the party. Meles Zenawi was more delighted than anyone when the CC of the TPLF delegated him the responsibility of making preparations to form the party. He found suitable space within the Front to cultivate his own power base without involving himself in the frequent armed clashes. Kahsay Berhe (2005: 77), a strong critic, candidly put it like this: '... Meles Zenawi got the golden opportunity to avoid his [worst] nightmare, i.e., the danger of physical participation in the civil war'. In a trying military assignment at the operations of Adwa and Adidaero, he ducked his duties on two occasions: 'He had the whole time to engage himself in the collection of quotations [and] impress other CC members who had no time for reading' (ibid.) due to the on-going war against rival fronts and the *Dergue*. Also: 'He had the possibility to disseminate his point of view as a teacher of cadres and above all the possibility to train and organize his loyal cadres as his own troops for the struggle of power within the organization' (ibid.). From then onwards, the formation of the proletarian MLLT, was in full swing, with Meles at the centre.

As the head of the cadre school and presiding over its management, Meles determined the school's curriculum, which included an impressive array of Marxist extracts and cadre recruitment procedures. This position gave him the chance to study one Marxist book after another, which in turn allowed him to become the Front's chief ideologue and eventually the head of the future MLLT. More importantly, he was able to overtly recruit MLLT members and, covertly, create loyal cadres for his own power base. Indeed, Meles was organizing himself, creating a power base that would bring him to the top while most of the leaders were preoccupied with thoughts of conducting the war with the *Dergue*.

Theoretical materials from the Stalinist era were selected and translated into Tigrigna to serve as the basic teaching material in the cadre school. Issues like 'democratic centralism' were emphatically articulated and practiced. Anything that did not conform to the Stalinist theoretical framework had no place and was labelled 'reactionary', 'revisionist' or 'bourgeois'. Follow-up discussion materials were prepared and sent to cadres at all levels outside the school and everybody had to internalize what was written and presented. Special discussion arrangements on selected policy-related issues were made for the TPLF's CC at its office in Akmara near the cadre school. At this level, discussions were not managed as they were in the cadre school. Here, they took a different course, which could often be confrontational. In one instance, Meles's deputy, Alemseged Gebre-Amlak, was sent to present a paper on the 'scope and limitations of democratic rights in a proletarian party' in connection with the Marxist concept of the 'dictatorship of the proletariat'. He had the idea that workers should not be allowed to protest and stage demonstrations against their own party because a party is always impeccable and would not inflict harm on its members. However, his view was rejected in the CC's group discussion by referring to the 'Critique of the Gotha' programme (1875) in which Marx himself had argued for workers' democratic rights, including the right to stage a demonstration against their party if they thought it necessary.

While other CC members were mainly engaged in responsibilities related to the war, Meles Zenawi was busy in the cadre school to create a party reflecting his ideals. Abbay Tsehaye, the head of the political department, was supposed to oversee Meles's venture for the CC but lacked the confidence to check him. As the whole affair of party formation became Meles's own domain, it was possible for him to introduce changes at will. The flow of new ideas slowly became his monopoly and any TPLF member who wanted to express an idea had to ask permission from the CC, which in effect meant the department controlled by Meles. This authoritarian practice was later translated into Article 1.2c in the MLLT's Constitution, printed in Hamle in 1977 E.C. (July 1985). If the CC's permission to express ideas was not granted, one had to take the point for discussion through a series of meetings of basic units and a regional conference where at least half of the participants had to support the proposal. This tedious and intimidating process meant that many were inclined to give up trying to get ideas through and avoided incrimination in the process. The TPLF's reorientation of Marxism-Leninism from the Chinese to the Albanian interpretation was also the making of Meles after he read a journal sent by the Union of Tigraians in North America (UTNA). The Albanian conviction regarding the 'Three Worlds' theory put the Soviet Union and the United States of America on the same footing as the 'First World' countries, but considered the former to be more aggressive and dangerous than the latter.

For Meles and his supporters, the Stalinist revolutionary line and the Albanian version of socialism were truly Marxist-Leninist. The Chinese path, which had embraced the national bourgeoisie as a strategic ally in its new democratic revolution, was discarded as a 'revisionist system capitulating to the bourgeois order'. The MLLT was to be constructed on these ideological foundations.

The MLLT's Founding Congress amid Famine

Preparation for the MLLT's founding congress, held from 12 to 25 July 1985, had basically begun already two years before, when a commission, led by Abbay and Meles, was set up by the TPLF's politburo. In 1983, during the TPLF's second congress, Meles, the *de facto* leader of the commission, read out a list of names of about two hundred *Merih Baetas* (leading elements) who would participate in the congress and be the first party members.

Two months before the MLLT congress, the TPLF's politburo convened in Akmara in central Tigrai to review, among other matters, the *Dergue's* attempt of a military offensive and how to counter it; the severe famine that was affecting central and southern Tigrai and how to tackle it; and the preparations for the MLLT's founding congress. No serious time or thought was, however, devoted to the first two big issues, that were going to involve the lives of hundreds of fighters and thousands of people. For the politburo, the preparation of the founding congress was of paramount importance. Hoping to make the majority of the politburo pay serious attention to the famine, Aregawi suggested that the formation of the MLLT be postponed until some time after the famine was over or at least under control. Thousands of peasant families had already deserted their villages in search of food aid and many were exposed to disease and death because there was no one to help them. None of the politburo members had the will or the heart to consider the plight of the people as they were obsessed with the formation of a party – a party that would put them at a vantage point to fully command the TPLF. Aregawi's plea was dismissed as an inopportune if not irrelevant matter. The rationale for devoting all human and material resources to the formation of the MLLT was that once this party was formed, all problems would be tackled in a 'scientific manner and solved forever. This blinded the leaders, who shied away from the harsh realities that had befallen their own people.

A *Dergue* tactical offensive (not a strategic one like the *zemecha*s) soon resumed near the Akmara and Worie base areas, but it faced no serious engagement because the TPLF adopted a tactic of containment with small units. This allowed preparations for the MLLT congress to continue as planned in Tselemti, at the foot of the Semien Mountains. The famine, on the other hand, was having a devastating effect. Amid the complications created by the *Dergue*'s offensive and the worsening of the famine, many peasants, especially in central and southern Tigrai, were dying every day from lack of food and water and related illnesses. The young TPLF fighters, who could have facilitated supplies of food and water to those in need or provided medical attention to the sick, were fully engaged in the upcoming MLLT congress.

Dergue offensives usually lasted for weeks, depending on the magnitude of the rebel counter-offensive, but this time it was over in a matter of days, and government troops returned to their barracks. However, the famine continued to engulf most districts in Tigrai and people understandably turned for support to the TPLF, an organization which claimed to be waging a war on their behalf,. But in vain: the focus of the organization was on Worie, where the birth of the MLLT was to take place. By early 1985, a congress hall that could accommodate well over 500 delegates was carved out in the gorge of the River Worie under Meles's supervision. It was well-camouflaged to protect it from air raids and two brigades were stationed near Worie to repulse any enemy incursion. Logistical preparations for the congress were efficiently executed in advance. While there was nothing to eat for hundreds of thousands of peasants, a variety of foods and different types of local drinks were in abundance at Worie awaiting the arrival of the delegates. The emerging MLLT leadership had organized festivities that were far removed from the situation of the hungry masses.[82]

It was quite a contrast to see the inside of the fancy congress hall in a remote and inaccessible mountainous region of Tigrai where most people lived in dilapidated huts. It was decorated throughout with red ribbons and behind the long podium were large portraits of Marx, Engels, Lenin and Stalin dominating the entire hall. Paintings that depicted fighters coming out of the 'dark' days under earlier TPLF leadership and envisaging a rosy future under the MLLT were hanging here and there. One painting in particular of a man running up to the top of a hill with the message 'Grab the commanding heights' was telling. The message was reiterated and elaborated on with slogans such as 'Let the able ones run, the unable follow and the unfit be discarded'. To 'discard the unfit' meant to eliminate or purge those who differed from the MLLT's ideological and/or political line, and as the slogans suggested, purges and eliminations did indeed take place later on.

The communist force of the Ethiopian People's Democratic Movement (EPDM) and some ten other Marxist-Leninist communist parties from Europe and the Americas were invited to the founding congress. Tamrat Layne, then Meles's comrade-in-arms, led the EPDM delegation. While the German ML party sent a Mr. Kafka as a one-man delegation, the other nine ML parties sent messages of solidarity that were read out on the opening day of the congress. The entire TPLF politburo, all nine of them, sat on the podium, with Abbay and Meles occupying centre stage, as had been the case during preparations. The congress agenda was prearranged. Items for discussion and the resolutions to follow, including the name of the party (the MLLT), were set in advance. Abbay Tsehaye was sitting in the forefront of this drama while the actual stage-manager was Meles Zenawi.

The opening ceremony was ostentatious. Members of the foreign bureau, led by Seyoum Mesfin, had composed a song for the event that heralded the birth of the MLLT and delegates were forced to sing whether they wanted to or not. Indeed there were some silent opponents who were upset about the tragic scenes of famine on one hand and the euphoria of the MLLT founders on the other. The organizing commission began its deliberations to the congress with an evaluation of the last ten years and the performance of the TPLF communist core (although there had been no communist core

---

82 There was some irony here, as these very MLLT founders had condemned Emperor Haile Selassie for the celebrations to mark his 80th birthday in 1972 under impending famine conditions, and Lt.-Colonel Mengistu Haile-Mariam for buying large quantities of whisky to celebrate with his Workers' Party of Ethiopia (WPE) in the middle of the famine in 1985.

as such in this period). As explained earlier, it was the left-oriented TPLF leadership with its eclectic views of socialism that had been leading the movement. The communist core, if it can be so called, began shaping up only after the formation of the organizing commission in early 1983. The evaluation of the performance of the previous ten years was designed to give a sense of purpose and prestige to the MLLT, especially to the efforts of its architects, and conversely to undermine the original TPLF leaders who had brought the organization that far.

The main focus of the evaluation revolved around identifying real or imaginary problems in the TPLF that 'caused its stagnation' and to find someone to carry the blame. In the interview he gave to J. Hammond in *Hagere Selam* later in April 1991, Meles referred to '...the loss of direction in the mid-eighties.... and a period of stagnation set in' (Hammond 1999: 391). Almost all CC members who were presumed to have contributed to the alleged stagnation of the Front were subjected to criticism. Meles came up with the Leninist polemic concepts of 'empiricism' and 'pragmatism' to elaborate the Front's lack of progress and to locate where the fault lay. He argued that the TPLF's Marxist principles had been hidden so that the anti-Marxist western community, where relief aid came from, would not know about them. The TPLF thus failed to develop a strong relationship with its strategic allies, namely Marxist-Leninist parties worldwide, because it did not approach them openly. He called this opportunism and classified it as a mistake of 'pragmatism'. He also related this failure to the TPLF's general tendency to depend on practical experience rather than scientific theory as a guide to all policies. This failure was again labelled as a mistake of 'empiricism' (see MLLT 1985). According to the above approach of evaluation, nobody in the TPLF leadership seemed to escape blame. This appraisal was a long-orchestrated drama designed to pave the way for the emerging MLLT leaders to appear as the redeemers of the TPLF, which was portrayed as inept in advancing the struggle.

Based on the above ideological formulations, Meles had already listed a number of mistakes made by the TPLF leadership and categorized them under the headings of 'pragmatism' or 'empiricism'. On the eve of the MLLT's formation he picked out certain members for reproach. Seyoum Mesfin and Asfaha Hagos from the foreign bureau were his first targets. Although both seemed to concede, neither of them could in fact be singled out as being responsible for the organization's foreign relations, as it had been a tradition in the TPLF leadership to work collectively within agreed guidelines. As no one else was deciding their own policy, those reproached were taken by surprise and could neither defend a pragmatic approach for which they were supposed to be responsible nor challenge the new radical approach Meles introduced. It would on the surface appear that Meles, who had already organized a group of like-minded cadres behind him, stood for the textbook ideas of Leninism but he was simply using them to indirectly attack others who he thought were in his way. It soon transpired that his actual targets of attack were the vice-chairman of the TPLF and the head of the military department. Surprisingly though, in the interview referred to above, Meles gave a different version of the concepts like 'pragmatism' that he used to attack others. 'Pragmatism as I understand it,' he said, 'is different from what we are trying to achieve. Pragmatism is going after what is achievable, not what is desirable. We are going after the desirable, but to us the desirable is desirable because it is achievable....' (in Hammond 1999: 393).

The next part of the appraisal looked into the political principles and positions adopted by the Front and their implications to date. Five major issues were considered to be of paramount importance: 1) the right to self-determination; 2) the strategic enemies of the revolution; 3) the foreign-affairs policy; 4) forging fronts (i.e. alliances with strategic and tactical friends); and 5) the need for a proletarian party. These issues were discussed in the cadre school time and again and positions on every issue were also taken by Meles Zenawi. What remained was to formalize them during the founding congress. Although it was impossible to change the course of the discussion and its predetermined outcome, TPLF vice-chairman Giday Zeratsion attempted to challenge the Meles camp on certain points. 'Whether the national bourgeois is a strategic ally of the new democratic revolution or not, can the petty bourgeois like the proletariat play a leadership role in the transition from capitalism to socialism' (Giday 1979 E.C.:58-59) were issues of debate. Giday could, however, not conduct a normal debate because he was teased and booed by Meles and his followers. In any case, these what now indeed seem quite abstract theoretical issues were irrelevant to the Tigraians' struggle they only created dramatic situation at the time. Famine was killing thousands of peasants throughout Tigrai while the rhetoricians sat in Worii for a month feasting. There were a few fighters who were disgusted with the whole episode of party formation. Some did not take part in all of the discussions and found the occasion inappropriate for serious discussion when the region was in the middle of the famine. Secondly, the Meles group had already hijacked earlier ideas of broadening the struggle to the whole of Ethiopia by creating an all-inclusive united front with independent national or multi-national fronts. Prior to the congress, the alliance with the EPDM was argued to be the first step in that direction although in reality the EPDM was an extension of the TPLF in central Ethiopia and not an independent partner in the struggle. Therefore, the founding congress of the MLLT turned out to be a discussion forum for Meles and his loyal cadres to juggle Marxist excerpts, and was hard to swallow for the majority of delegates.[83]

In light of its self-assigned task of evaluating the ten years' performance of the TPLF 'communist force', the congress took a position on the five issues noted above and elaborated the points in the esoteric Marxist rhetoric of the day as follows (see the MLLT booklet entitled '*Yehiwehat Kominist Hail Ye 10 Amet Guzo Gimgema, Hamle 1977*' (Evaluation of Ten Years' Performance of the TPLF Communist Force, July 1985, MLLT 1985c):

On the right to self-determination, the congress concluded that the Front's position was broadly correct and free of narrow-minded nationalism, yet some mistakes that could be categorized as deviations were noted (MLLT, 1985c: 25-26). Close observation of the controversial Manifesto 68 drafted by Abbay and Meles in which an 'independent Republic of Tigrai' was set as the TPLF's objective revealed that the position was not only one of deviation but also of extremely narrow nationalism.

On strategic enemies of the revolution, the *Dergue* as a fascist class, Western and Soviet-led imperialism as oppressors of all working people and feudalism as a moribund reactionary system were all classified as enemies of the democratic revolution. With regard to the Soviet Union, it was labelled as a social-imperialist force that became an ally of the fascist *Dergue* and tactically became the main enemy at the time (Ibid.: 44).

On the issue of foreign affairs, the policy pursued by the foreign bureau was severely attacked as 'pragmatist' and failing to develop anticipated links with strategic ML friends by focusing on relations with tactical friends who provided short-term advantages like relief aid.

On forging alliances with strategic and tactical friends, a broader front had to be formed against reactionary forces of feudalism, imperialism and bureaucratic capitalism represented by the fascist *Dergue*. The national bourgeoisie was classified as a wavering strategic ally.

On the needs of a proletarian party, the congress approved the formation of such a party in Ethiopia to bring about the 'new democratic revolution'.

On the last day of the congress, a draft MLLT programme and constitution was read out and, without any serious debate, the congress adopted both documents.

---

[83] Interview: Mekonnen Zellelow, 30 July 2003, Abebe Hailu and Gebremeskel Woldu, 07 August 2003, Kahsay Berhe, 27 March 2004, Tesfay Atsbaha, 25 March 2004.

Organizational Restructuring and Take-Over of the TPLF

After fourteen days (5-18 Hamle 1977 E.C. [12-25 July 1985]) of prosaic discussion unrelated to the harsh realities facing Tigrai, the congress elected a central committee (CC) to lead the MLLT. Twenty-one CC members, including Giday and Aregawi, were elected. Almost all of the new MLLT's CC members were former CC members of the TPLF and the fact that Giday and Aregawi were elected by a larger vote than Meles indicated that delegates did not appreciate the difference between the MLLT and the TPLF[84] or even the emergence of the MLLT and its dominance over the TPLF. At the closing ceremony, Meles declared that the 'Formation of [the] MLLT is a great leap forward' and then as a reward for his services Sibhat Nega presented him with a trophy. Both were elated and their cohorts cheered them for the progress they claimed they had achieved, but nobody knew where this progress would take them or how long it would last.

A day later, the 21 CC members of the MLLT and TPLF (in fact the same personalities in both organizations) convened to elect a politburo and a general secretary for the MLLT. Before the election resumed, Meles brought charges against Giday and Aregawi. Close allies of Meles, namely Sibhat Nega, Seye Abraha, Awaalom Woldu and Gebru Asrat, followed suit. They had prepared a range of charges, from 'being an obstacle to the formation of the MLLT' to 'contemplating removing Meles'. The allegations were brought by Meles and his supporters to get rid of their challengers. They could have brought these charges up during the congress, which had been in session just a day before, but they did not have credible charges to convince the delegates, who might have turned down the allegations in an open investigation and further exposed their own motives. As critic Kahsay Berhe (2005: 83) observed, 'To avoid any possible division in the election process, Meles Zenawi chose the plenary session of the CC for the battleground for the expulsion of Aregawi Berhe and Giday Zeratsion'.

The prosecutors, witnesses and judges were the same MLLT leaders and the verdict was predictable. Aregawi and Giday were purged from the politburo of the TPLF and thus disqualified from election to the politburo of the MLLT. The whole process, which lasted less than an hour, could neither be said to be legal nor democratic by any standards. So Giday and Aregawi had no option but to submit to a process they were part of. Sibhat suggested the purges be followed by administrative measures (code words for incarceration or liquidation) under the Front's rules, but Meles

---

84 Tesfay Atsbaha, interview, 25 March 2004.

rejected Sibhat's scheme on the ground that such measures might tarnish the 'blossoming' name of the MLLT. The same evening, the delegates were summoned to assemble and listen to Seyoum reading the CC's decision on the 'exclusion' and 'disqualification' of Aregawi and Giday from both the TPLF's politburo and the MLLT. Except for two or three questions from selected loyal cadres, no discussion was allowed on the matter because, as Seyoum put it, '...the CC had acted within its limits and did not transgress the bounds of the congress'. Aregawi demanded his position be heard but Seyoum denied him the right to express his views or even ask questions like the cadres by stating that everything had been discussed at the CC meeting.

On Meles's recommendations, the new CC approved the politburo members' nominations for the MLLT. The new MLLT politburo and the departments they headed were as follows:

1. Abbay Tsehaye – Secretary General

2. Meles Zenawi – Ideology and Propaganda

3. Seye Abraha* – Military Bureau

4. Tsadkan Gebretensai* – Chief of Staff

5. Tewelde Woldemariam* – People's Bureau

6. Seyoum Mesfin – Foreign Bureau

7. Gebru Asrat* – Socio-economic Bureau

8. Awaalom Woldu* – Socio-economic

9. Sibhat Nega – Socio-economic (nominal TPLF chairman)

10. Aregash Adane* – Alternate Member

11. Arkebe Equbai – Alternate Member[85]

The CC of the MLLT/TPLF continued its meeting for another two weeks to restructure the new organization and plan activities for the coming four years, i.e. until the next MLLT congress. As members of the CC, Giday and Aregawi also had the opportunity to participate in the meetings but with contradictions of ideology and 'pragmatic' policy now transpiring, it became increasingly difficult for them to engage in debate with their opponents. Of the many differences, one outstanding example suffices to illuminate the nature of the contradictions in which the MLLT leaders were bogged down. Although more than one million people were affected by the famine at the time, about 200,000 peasants were instructed to march to Sudan to receive

---

85 The six politburo members marked with an asterisk * were 'purged' in 2001 when Meles as Prime Minister of Ethiopia had a conflict with them over the war with Eritrea in 1998-2000.

relief aid, a difficult journey that would take about two weeks. The peasants were exposed to all sorts of adversities, including aerial bombardment from government MiG fighter planes and attacks from wild animals. Memhir Haddis, a peasant who survived the journey, told Kassahun Berhanu (2000: 82) that 'Several lost their way and ended up as prey to wild animals, were captured by government troops, or succumbed to hunger, thirst and disease in a situation where assistance of whatever kind could not be expected'. Treating it as insignificant news, Seyoum Mesfin reported to the congress that 13,000 peasants died *en route*. He did not even mention that the immediate cause was a lack of basic support from the TPLF/MLLT cadres who at the time were busy with the MLLT congress. As usual, the culprit was said to be nature not man. The irony was that it was the MLLT leaders who ordered the long march to take place so that the famine victims could receive relief aid from Western donors, who they characterized as imperialist class enemies of the first order. No one from the so-called strategic allies was anywhere near the scene.

The worst part of the contradiction was yet to come and was in the allocation of the relief aid collected from Western donors by the Relief Society of Tigrai (REST), the humanitarian wing of the TPLF and now of the MLLT too. By June 1985, REST had received more than US$100 million from donors in the name of the famine victims. Abadi Zemo, the head of REST, handed the money to Awalom Woldu of the TPLF/MLLT's economic department who in turn reported to the CC that was in session for budgetary planning. Meles's proposal for the allocation of the relief aid money was as follows: 50% for MLLT consolidation, 45% for TPLF activities and 5% for the famine victims.[86] Aregawi argued that the allotted amount for the famine victims was too little and should be significantly increased. The Meles group booed and one of them interjected: '…you should understand that if the MLLT is strengthened all problems would be solved scientifically'. Most of them supported Meles and eventually the proposal was put into effect. Opportunism it may appear, it was also the contradiction between an ideology that condemned pragmatic relationships but at the same time made use of the relationship to pursue its own dream at the expense of a starving people. [87]

86 Giday Zeratsion, a CC member of the TPLF and MLLT at the time, interview, 16 March 2004.

87 Before the CC meeting came to a close, once again charges came up against Aregawi and Giday. This time they were related to instigating fighters 'to doubt the good intentions' of the MLLT, followed by a proposal to purge them from CC membership, which was the responsibility of the congress. Meles now had a CC he could drive into any direction, at least for some time. The expulsion of Giday and Aregawi was followed by harassment, defamation and, as Kahsay Berhe (2005: 84) asserts, 'Meles Zenawi

In brief, the process towards the formation of the MLLT was taken as a successful achievement by the communist core of the TPLF spearheaded by Meles and Abbay who, as they claimed in their report of the MLLT congress, '....promoted a broad struggle of ideas in a democratic manner to arrive at such a triumphal stage' (MLLT, July 1985: 86). This was democracy of a special kind, adhering to the Marxist principle of dictatorship of the proletariat and vanguard party hegemony. In such a political structure apart from the party directives that flow from the top there is no free flow of ideas among members. This was the case with the MLLT, where ideas came from the top down and had to be obeyed without question. Free and open debates even in CC circles now became much more limited, as independent-minded members faced purges and later execution.[88] From here on, it was only the MLLT that defined the course of the struggle ideologically, politically and militarily, not only in Tigrai but also in other regions of Ethiopia through 'obedient' organizations. It had herewith completed the take-over of the TPLF

Extension of the MLLT to 'Puppet Organizations'

Article 2 of the MLLT's Constitution stated that 'one of the main objectives of this League is to create a nation-wide Marxist-Leninist party of Ethiopia' (MLLT 1985b: 5). This article clearly defined what the MLLT was planning for a future Ethiopia, and how it was going to execute it was not difficult to comprehend.

In the months preceding the formation of the MLLT, it had become clear that the *Dergue* was losing ground on every front in Eritrea and Tigrai, where its presence was limited to only a few towns. And even there it was in a defensive position. The TPLF controlled all the Tigraian rural areas and most of the towns, from which it launched frequent surprise attacks on the *Dergue*. The morale of the government army was low and troops were

formed a secret commission to oversee the activities of Aregawi Berhe and Giday Zeratsion, including secretly looking into their dairies, interrogating combatants who come in touch with them'. This forced both veteran fighters to abandon the organization they had helped develop and move abroad.

88 E.g., in the case of Teklu Hawaz and Gebrehiwet Kahsay. Teklu was a CC member of the TPLF and a popular fighter who headed the Department of Public Relations for more than ten years. He was one of the few CC members who challenged the MLLT on a number of issues. He was executed in 1989. Gebrehiwet was head of the radio section known as Bado-Bado (00) under the Department of Military Intelligence. He was a brilliant fighter who many times openly ctiticized the ideas of the MLLT ideologues at the TPLF cadre school. He was executed in 1990.

deserting in their hundreds on a daily basis. Crisis in the military hierarchy was deepening, with attempted coups being followed by harsh measures of repression. Some well-known generals like Merid Niguse, Chief of Staff of the Armed Forces, and Amha Desta, Commander of the Air Force, even committed suicide. Kumlachew Dejenie, Deputy Commander of the 2nd Army, fled to the United States. Tariku Ayne and 24 other generals were killed by pro-Mengistu soldiers, some of them having been tried for alleged treason and others without having been court-martialled. In Eritrea and elsewhere in Ethiopia, the whole military structure was weakened from within.

Conversely, the TPLF had grown to be a formidable force with fighting skills that had developed over years of painstaking hard work and experience. The TPLF/MLLT was now in a position to extend its area of operations beyond Tigrai, deeper into central and southern Ethiopia. Militarily it was possible to do so as the government forces had lost their fighting spirit and were only poised to retreat from battlegrounds, as POWs and deserters invariably reported. However, politically it was a totally different matter. The larger territory outside Tigrai was a part of Ethiopia where the TPLF had not even made itself or its programme remotely known. If the rest of Ethiopia knew of the TPLF, this had only come from the *Dergue*, and that would have been negative propaganda which portrayed the TPLF as a bunch of separatist bandits who destroyed bridges, schools and clinics.

Another drawback was its antagonistic relationship with multinational organizations like the EDU and the EPRP, who had a vocal constituency on the conservative and radical spectrum of Ethiopian society, respectively. The fact of both organizations being chased out of Tigrai after a series of battles that took the lives of many young Ethiopians (see Chapter 3) contributed enormously to the negative picture of the Front that the *Dergue* had been painting. The political support the TPLF offered to the separatist movement in Eritrea was another position vehemently rejected by most Ethiopians, and the TPLF was perceived by many as bent on dismantling the unity of the country. The intention of the TPLF/MLLT to expand beyond Tigrai therefore had to be seen in the light of these obstacles.

Aware of its political limitations, TPLF/MLLT leaders had been trying to overcome these setbacks. However, instead of engaging in a political dialogue with the already existing self-assertive organizations to arrive at a solution palatable to all sides, they went for an opportunistic option. By forging organizations of like-minded groups that would not pose a serious challenge to their strategic objectives, they designed a multinational Ethiopian front or party in which the TPLF and the MLLT respectively were the nucleus and dominant forces.

Facilitating the formation of the Ethiopian People's Democratic Movement (EPDM), a splinter group of the EPRP, fell within the strategy of the TPLF/MLLT to extend its grip on the larger part of Ethiopia. For this purpose, the EPDM received the full backing of the TPLF/MLLT. Material, political and diplomatic support was readily available for the EPDM. The EPDM in return promoted the TPLF/MLLT's propaganda and political objectives in the regions the latter could not reach, and had little interest in doing so. Except for some minor tactical issues, the EPDM stood alongside the MLLT on basic principles. Not only did it adopt the main resolution of the MLLT founding congress, but later it created the 'Ethiopian Marxist Leninist Force' (EMLF) within the EPDM, a replica of the MLLT within the TPLF (see Figure 8.1). Like the MLLT and with the same tone, the EMLF declared 'the task of the EMLF is to help raise the class consciousness of the proletariat so that it accomplishes its historic mission of waging a socialist revolution. Besides it shall facilitate the formation of a nationwide ML party under which the working class would be organized' (EMLF Program, 1981 EC: 8-9).

Henceforth, even though the EPDM was declared the strategic ally of the TPLF for the limited objective of the fronts, the EMLF was thought to be an ally of the MLLT in the anticipated socialist revolution. To lead the socialist revolution, a nationwide ML party would be formed from the union of the MLLT and the EMLF. Both the TPLF and the EPDM had gone as far as initiating and later creating a union of the fronts known as the EPRDF (Ethiopian People's Revolutionary Democratic Front). If we follow the pattern, what remains is the formation of a nationwide ML party that gives the 'Revolutionary Democratic' guidance to the EPRDF, with the MLLT and the TPLF, respectively as the core group. E.g., some other organizations, like the Oromo People's Democratic Organization (OPDO) formed in 1990 under the umbrella of the EPRDF, were to follow in the same ideological and organizational mould. This pattern was later set on course nationwide. Meles Zenawi (1990: 24) acknowledged this fact in the *People's Voice* by saying that 'the MLLT programme was in essence not very much different from those of the EPRDF and TPLF'.

When meanwhile in 1985-86 the military feasibility of advancing beyond Tigrai became a reality, Meles Zenawi, whose 'argument revolved around defending the liberated areas in Tigrai, and therefore, waging positional war' (Kahsay Berhe, 2005: 82), changed his mind and initiated the formation of the EPRDF in which the EPDM was picked as a junior partner. Once the EPDM joined the EPRDF, it had no choice but to accept the ideological, political and military dictates of the MLLT, for the former basically depended on the latter in its war and survival requirements.

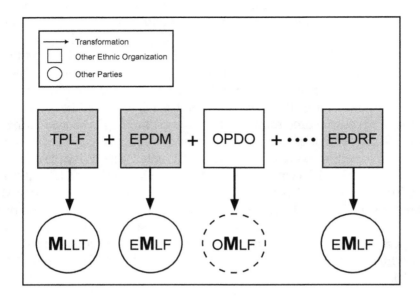

Figure 8.1 MLLT and MLLT-replica inside other fronts

After the EMLF was formed, the TPLF/MLLT had a free ride in realizing their model all over Ethiopia. It could now strike enemy positions anywhere in the country in the name of the EMLF. The south of Tigrai and the adjacent provinces of Wollo and Gondar became immediate areas of operation. As operations were intensified and more territory fell into the hands of the fronts, the EPDM's dependency on the MLLT was growing, for it had neither the physical capacity nor the material resources to manage the 'liberated' areas. The TPLF/MLLT was managing these on behalf of itself and the EPDM, thereby deepening its grip over the later. Success on the military front obviously led to a broadening of the MLLT's political project.

The TPLF/MLLT was also paying due attention to political developments north of Tigrai - in Eritrea - to see if it could initiate the MLLT's broader project. As a party that had the ambition of forging an Ethiopian proletarian party, it had no ideological barrier restricting it from extending its range into Eritrea, to create an Ethio-Eritrean proletarian party. This ideologically driven intention of the MLLT leaders was reflected in their warm relations with the ELF splinter groups, namely the Democratic Movement for the Liberation of Eritrea (DMLE) and the ELF-SAGIM progressive. These groups were opposed to the EPLF and were being groomed in a more or less similar fashion to the EPDM. They had secured the full support of the TPLF/MLLT. Support for the DMLE and SAGIM obviously meant strengthening the position of an alternative ally in Eritrea, as opposed to the EPLF, which in their eyes had embraced 'Soviet social imperialism'. This alignment would eventually lead to ideological conformity which could be the basis for establishing a unitary proletarian party. However, before this grand project matured, the military campaign against the *Dergue* had to be concluded, and indeed the stage was being set for the final showdown.

The imminence of this attracted both the TPLF and the EPLF, the strongest military forces in Ethiopia/Eritrea, to reach an agreement and hasten their drive to power. Meles and Isayas of the EPLF once again renewed ties in order to deal the final blow to the weakened *Dergue*. Confident of the military forces they had amassed, both fronts believed the victory would easily clear their way to power. Their renewed relations became so warm that Meles had to put his project with the DMLE and SAGIM on hold. Yet the logistical support the TPLF/MLLT used to dispense to both organizations continued to flow, with their offices and base areas remaining intact. These confused relationships, bizarre as they may seem today, were calculated moves by the MLLT leaders, to use the DMLE and the ELF-SAGIM - as they used EPDM/EMLF - as ideological partners / stepping stones to power in the new political arenas of both Ethiopia and Eritrea and itself keep the upper hand. Politico-military developments at the time, however, were pressing to consummate the venture undertaken with the powerful EPLF. (See for more details, Chapter 10 below).

After gaining military backing from the strong EPLF in the final march to power, Meles came back to his ideological allies, the DMLE and SAGIM. Voluntarily or otherwise, the DMLE and SAGIM had no option but to accept the deals the MLLT leaders promised. There was no other reason why sworn enemies of the EPLF should be close friends with the TPLF/MLLT. The relationship with the EPLF went well for some time after the *Dergue* was overthrown, only to turn bitter in 1998 at the beginning of a two-year war. The good relationship with the DMLE and ELF-SAGIM, on the other hand, continues to this day. This may indicate their common ideological origin, but also the felt need to balance Eritrean forces against each other.

The Ideological Trajectory of the MLLT since 1985 and the Development of 'Revolutionary Democracy'

In November 1985 (*Hidar* 1978 EC) Meles Zenawi had written a paper entitled '*Afelalayatna ab Gilsti Medrek Nekrib*' (Let's Present Our Differences in Open

Forum) in which he insisted on the need to bring ideological or political differences into the open and discussing them in public. It seemed somewhat paradoxical to blame others for not openly disseminating the objectives and principles of the MLLT in its struggle for proletarian internationalism, as openness and collective decision-making was much more the rule before that after the installation of the MLLT.

Under the leadership of Meles, the MLLT went on to solidify its ideological and political hold on the TPLF and to make its ideology the basis for alliance-building on its own terms.

In 1990 a further organizational development occurred, with the founding of the 'Ethiopian Proletarian Organizations Unity' (EPOU) under the leadership of the MLLT. It was to bring together the MLLT and the EMLF. This was supposed to be the nucleus of a nation-wide Marxist-Leninist organization under the guidance of the MLLT/TPLF. The fate or existence of this organization is not known, but likely is that it was also subsumed under the EPRDF (under TPLF politburo leadership).

Later, the development of the ideology of 'revolutionary democracy' proceeded, and it was kept in place until this day and regularly discussed. As it is an outcome of MLLT thinking and as such still important, I make a brief excursion forward to illustrate this. During a TLPF cadre conference in Meqele in 1994 the leadership, mainly Meles Zenawi, extensively lectured about the concept of 'revolutionary democracy' as an appropriate doctrine that 'had to be firmly grasped' if Ethiopia was to embark on sustainable economic development.

What was the 'revolutionary democracy' that Meles Zenawi was describing at this point in time? The idea of revolutionary democracy originated from the theses of Lenin on 'Bourgeois Democracy and the Proletarian Dictatorship', presented on 4 March 1919 to the First Communist International. Lenin was committed to establishing revolutionary democracy in place of parliamentary democracy, which he defined as 'bourgeois democracy'. Meles Zenawi borrowed this idea from Lenin, who meant a political formula of rule under a politically trained vanguard party representing 'the masses', which would develop national ideological guidelines, consult with the constituency but not accept changes from it, and implement 'the correct policies' from the top down.

Revolutionary democracy was explained in more detail at the recent evaluation of the internal situation of the governing party, the EPRDF, known as the *Gimgema* Papers (Papers of Appraisal/Evaluation, see EPRDF 2001b), a very revealing and defining political document. There the author (PM Meles Zenawi) declared that:

> The world is now cowering to the international network of globalisation. We have to chart our way to develop in this system. ... Even though Ethiopia is now a basket case, it can move stage by stage and achieve a top developed nation status. ... Ethiopia can achieve this if it is guided by 'revolutionary democracy'. Whereas Liberal Democracy is partial wager, a collector of rents, and a representative of the comprador bourgeoisie, 'revolutionary democracy' stands for sustainable development (cited in Milkias 2001: 34-35).

Furthermore, he argued that:

> The only democracy that is possible in Ethiopia is 'revolutionary democracy'. ... When revolutionary democracy permeates the entire Ethiopian society, individuals will start to think alike and all persons will cease having their independent outlook. In this order, individual thinking becomes simply part of collective thinking because the individual will not be in a position to reflect on concepts that have not been prescribed by revolutionary democracy. (ibid.: 36)

One further key suggestion of Meles Zenawi's and the top EPRDF leadership's Marxist-Leninist approach – evident in the above-cited, undemocratic views – was their apparent adherence to Stalinist ideas, in both theory and practice. The Stalinist dictum of the 'right of nations to self-determination, including and up to secession', was emphatically pursued by them from the start. The party also promulgated Stalin's secession option after the take-over of power in 1991, in both the Transitional Charter signed on 22 July 1991 by Meles Zenawi as the transitional leader of the country and in the Federal Constitution, ratified on 8 December 1995 and operative to this day. Article 2c of the Charter and Article 39.1 of the Constitution proclaim that 'Every nation, nationality and people in Ethiopia has an unconditional right to self-determination, *including the right to secession'* (italics added by author). This often-repeated clause is found in Stalin's work on *Marxism and the National Question* (1942). Furthermore, elements of Stalinism can be seen in the purging and persecution before and after 1991 of those with different political views: the executions of Commissar Atsbaha Dagnew (Shewit), Gebrehiwet Kahsay (a head of TPLF radio intelligence), Teklu Hawaz (a TPLF CC member), Alula Gebru (a media officer) and many others are cases in point.

Close observation of the ideological stance, the formulated policies and the practice of executing them in Ethiopia reflect what the MLLT stood for since its launch in July 1985. One is thus inclined to believe that the MLLT in some way still is operative, e.g., as an old-boys' network. In the light of the contentious status of the MLLT, the methodological operations of this organization may be seen from two different angles. On the one hand, to allure Western liberal politicians and donors and keep aid money flowing to the government, the leadership tells the world that they had nothing to do with a Marxist-Leninist party. That was what is done in press interviews and in, for instance, US Congress Subcommittee hearings by party members before the 1991 take-over. This raises the question of how the former MLLT leadership or its successors are able to sway the donor country leaders and democrats who have no stomach for Marxist ideology. No answer will be pursued here. One can perhaps conclude that a hybrid of ideologies - namely the outer trappings of democracy (parties, periodic elections, a constitution) and 'revolutionary democracy', with the latter holding ultimate sway - constitutes the outward political symbolism and rhetoric prevailing in the Ethiopian state. It can also be argued that the MLLT has served its purpose and Marxism has now been officially transformed into 'revolutionary democracy'.

Until the early 1990s, the MLLT leaders were consistent in their Marxist-Leninist ideology and autocratic (if not Stalinist) like methods of policy implementation. As noted earlier, members who put forward alternative views or showed even slight deviations from the established line were treated as enemies, or 'class enemies' as they were called. Even comrades who posed tough questions were condemned as revisionists or thought to have 'reactionary influence'. Those who failed to comply were further labelled 'pragmatists' and/or 'empiricists'. Considering these actions and reactions, one might think that the MLLT leaders were firmly attached to their ideological commitments. But in 1991, with the success achieved on the military front and the ascent to power just beginning, the MLLT membership appeared to make an ideological U-turn. It was not, and still is not clear whether it was a clear denial or a shift in ideological position – it was certainly not made public. In any case, some form of 'pragmatism' and 'empiricism' or, in the eyes of many, naked opportunism, began to emerge, not from the rank and file as such but from the founders and leaders of MLLT, notably Meles Zenawi. Around this time the Socialist bloc, especially the former Soviet Union, was in collapse with the tide of *glasnost* and *perestroika,* and one could assume that the MLLT might have been feeling the impact. However, the same Socialist bloc was still characterized by the MLLT as being 'social imperialist' and 'destined for ruin'. So the fall of the Soviet Union might have been interpreted as a blessing in disguise and may not have influenced the MLLT to seriously shift from its own Marxist-Leninist position.

Chapter 9

The TPLF and the Eritrean Fronts: Backgrounds of a Tense Relationship

Introduction

Primordial components may in large part explain the relationship between the people of Tigrai and Eritrea, through shared linguistic (Tigrinya) and socio-cultural characteristics, but the modern political elite, especially the leaders of the Fronts in both populations opted to tune in to post-colonial developments to define the relationships between the two peoples, and thereby developed quite diverging objectives for their political struggles. Indeed, the desire of both peoples for political freedoms and rights to self-determination was certainly there, but the interpretation of the peoples' needs was left in the hands of the two groups' elites, who wanted to create their separate political domains. The interactions between the Eritrean and Tigraian elites who ran (and still run) the Fronts were complicated by two conflicting factors: the need for close cooperation to fight a strong enemy, the military government, and the urge to come out of the struggle as a dominant force in their own region. For this purpose, ethno-nationalist and nationalist mobilizations coated with exclusivist future political goals were taking place in Tigrai and Eritrea respectively. In this process, the relationship of the Fronts had to pass through numerous twists and turns, at times boiling over to armed confrontation. This in turn had a negative influence on the relationship of the two peoples.

This chapter is devoted to analysing the relationship of the Tigraian and Eritrean nationalist Fronts, which constituted the main forces that brought down the Ethiopian military government in 1991. In both cases, the participation of the ordinary people in the struggle was crucial, yet they could not have a say in the decision-making processes. The competing nationalist outlooks and the impact of the competition on future relationships of the two people on both sides of the colonial divide as well as its effect on the political conditions of the region will also be assessed.

Historical Background

To understand the alternately acrimonious and apparently warm relationship between the TPLF and the Eritrean fronts, one needs to look into the long history of that war-ravaged region and the different perceptions of its history. In the minds of the peoples of both Ethiopia and Eritrea, there is a sense of both intimacy and enmity. It was the combination of old antagonizing factors coupled with current developments and ambivalences that led the former fronts, now the Ethiopian and Eritrean governments, to the war of 1998-2000.

It should be clear from the outset, however, that the interpretations of the region's history – as put forward by the political elites on both sides of the Mereb River – are varied and eclectic. To begin with, it is relevant for the study to contrast the two divergent views of the same historical subject. Let us take two representative assertions. The press and information department of the Ethiopian Ministry of Foreign Affairs wrote in 1976: 'Ever since Ethiopia emerged from the distant horizon of time as a body-politic, its northern part, including the area now called Eritrea, has been at the beginning and at the centre of its development. Ethiopia has never existed without this northern part. Nor has this part ever been identified separately from Ethiopia' (cited in Mesfin Araya 1988: 9). In contrast, the Eritrean Liberation Front's Revolutionary Council wrote in 1989: 'Ethiopia's chimerical reference and legendary claims over Eritrea are, therefore, unhistorical and have nothing to do with the past and present realities in Eritrea and Ethiopia' (ELF-RC 1989: 3).

It is clear that the two positions represent essentially opposed interpretations of the region's history, but behind them laid political objectives that came to the fore in their respective programmes. It is this historiography clouded by objectives emanating from differing political interests that seems to define the volatile history and recent military events in the region. Although the divergent discourses, especially that espoused by the Eritrean fronts, have capitalized on a mutually exclusive evolution of the Tigrigna-speaking people in the same region for the purpose of justifying secession, the historical, religious, cultural and kinship ties of the two peoples divided by the Italian colonial boundary line since 1890 manifest a deeper relationship (see Marcus 1994; Alemseged Abbay 1997, 2004). These bonds are still there and could not be simply erased by the relatively short period of Italian colonialism or by the dictates of a political elite aspiring to create its own 'kingdom'. The same is true for the Afar and Kunama peoples, who live on both sides of the arbitrary Italian colonial boundary. Eritrean independence, as such, is a manifestation of a position adopted by the Eritrean elite for pragmatic reasons and not so much as an historically tenable undertaking. Although the details of the subject are beyond the scope of this book, a schematic historical review of the region in the ancient, medieval and modern periods is sketched below to help understand the present and ponder over the future.

The present people in the northern part of Ethiopia, including Eritrea, are the result of successive waves of migration and subsequent integration with indigenous people. There were several power centres in the region that expanded and contracted with the movements of external and regional adversaries. Some four centuries before Islam was introduced into the region, the Christian Aksumites controlled the area. When Islam emerged, the two religions developed harmonious relations for some time but this did not last longer than the lifetime of the Prophet Mohammed. Concomitantly, certain cultural, linguistic and religious traits of particular significance persisted over the centuries. Sedentary Christian highlanders and pastoralist Muslim lowlanders (many of whom first were Christians) had their separate power centres, beginning with Aksum in the 1st century, later in Yifat and then in Adal after the 8th century. The interplay of religion, environment and language seems to have shaped their cultural and psychic make-up, which in turn influenced their socio-political relationships during their entire existence.

Earlier, between the 1st centuries BC and AD, Aksum emerged as the overlord of the various regional power centres. The Aksumites controlled much of present-day Tigrai, Eritrea and the Red Sea coastal areas and also made several incursions across the Red Sea into southern Arabia. 'The Aksumite campaign into South Arabia is recorded in the inscriptions of Adulis (AD 277-90), which relates how the king of Aksum waged war' (Caetani 1911: 366-67). In its heyday, Aksum was one of the world's great maritime powers, using the port of Adulis, south of the present port of

Massawa in Eritrea. In the words of the Iranian prophet Mani (216-276 AD), cited in Kobishchanov's book *Axum*, 'There are four kingdoms on earth: the first is the kingdom of Babylon [Mesopotamia] and Persia; the second is the kingdom of Rome; the third is the kingdom of the Axumites; the fourth is the kingdom of the Chinese' (Kobishchanov 1979: 59). Kobishchanov goes on, 'From the second half of the III century AD, Axum began to mint its own coinage. The introduction of its own coinage indicates the significance that market relationships had acquired in the Axumite Kingdom' (ibid.: 185). As R. Fattovich said, 'The power of the kingdom [Aksum] derived primarily from the control of the trade from the African hinterland to the Red Sea, through the port of Adulis on the gulf of Zula (Eritrea)' (2000: 3). The old road from Aksum through Yeha in Tigrai and Tokonda and Kohaito in Eritrea to the port of Adulis can easily be traced by ruins and inscriptions that indicate a functioning and stable trade route. 'The archaeological remains dating to this period at Aksum, Matara, and Adulis show the same basic futures and suggest a common cultural pattern stretching from the Tekeze River to the Red Sea coast, ...' (ibid.: 20). Tringali (1965), who conducted pioneering archaeological surveys at forty sites in and around the outskirts of Asmara, found that many contained Aksumite pottery '...correcting the mistaken impression that there was not much Aksumite settlement in the Asmara region' (Kobishchanov 1979: 19).

The Aksumites embraced Christianity during the early part of the fourth century and 'developed their own civilization, as illustrated by their script *Ge'ez*, their number system, *Kutir*, and their calendar, *Awde-Awarih*, which are still in use at the present time' (Belai Giday 1983; Teshale Tibebu 1995; Aregawi 2004), not to mention their splendid architecture seen in the standing obelisks, religious structures and tunnels in Ethiopia as well as present-day Eritrea. The Aksumites translated the Scriptures from Greek into Geez, which served as the country's literary written language for centuries. Aksum 'was not only the religious centre of the country, but the capital of the kingdom' (Budge 1970: 123). Christianity, Ge'ez and the crown became the uniting factors of the Aksumite kingdom in the centuries during which present-day Eritrea was a component. From ancient times, these three factors were the basis of unity and identity for the people of the kingdom, including the Eritrean Christians. Up to this period, relations with the emerging Muslims were harmonious, allowing some of the earliest Muslims who had crossed the Red Sea earlier for fear of persecution to live under protection of the Aksumite king, and in 628 'Mohammed himself, now in authority, sent an emissary to Ethiopia to request the return of his followers' (Henze 2000: 42-43)..

Between 630 AD and 640 AD, a powerful wave of Arabs with the mission of spreading Islam began attacking the Red Sea coastal plains. Early on, the Aksumites resisted by dispatching their fleets and enjoyed some victories. 'The Khalifa Umar al-Khattab is reported to have dispatched a small naval expedition against an Abyssinian fleet in AD 640, but the Arab fleet suffered so disastrously that Umar would have no more to do with the sea' (Caetani, cited in Trimingham 1952: 46). Eventually though, the Arabs continued to penetrate the mainland, and in the 8th century took control of Adulis, the main port of Aksum, thus bringing an end to its maritime trade in the Red Sea area. Throughout the second part of the 8th century, the Arabs continued their assault on the lowland hinterlands, spreading Islam and blocking the trade routes of Aksum with the outside world.

To make matters worse for Aksum, in the first half of the 10th century, a powerful pagan queen, Yodit, emerged from the Agew lands, south of Aksum, and gave another blow to the kingdom in 970 A.D. She burned churches, demolished historic obelisks and disrupted institutions, causing the influence of Aksum to further decline. This eventually gave rise to a new dynasty called Zagwe, which came from Lasta, south of Aksum. They made the centre of their kingdom there and ruled for almost 350 years until they were overthrown in 1270 by Emperor Yekuno Amlak. Despite these problems, the deeply rooted Christian order and political culture remained intact and continued to revive throughout the highlands of Abyssinia as far as Debre Bizen in Hamassien, the monastery along the escarpment overlooking the Red Sea. 'After all, Aksumite civilization was still the dominant political and cultural element up to the medieval times' (Sergew 1972: 267). The same culture, religion and language (Tigrinya) have prevailed to this day in highland Eritrea and south of it in Tigrai, northern Ethiopia. The same is true of the Islamic societies inhabiting the lowlands of the same region. In the areas to the South, the centre of the new 'Solomonic empire' of Yekuno Amlak, Amharic had developed.

Once Aksum fell, the centre of power was forced to shift further southward. From Lasta it moved to Shewa and later to Gondar, leaving behind fractured power principalities. Supported by the Arabs across the Red Sea, Islamic offensives launched from the Kingdom of Ifat and Adal in the Afar lowlands continued to be a menace to the Christian regions. This Muslim attack from the east, although it blocked the spread of the Christian culture and diminished its political prevalence, could not penetrate the high Abyssinian hinterland. Thus the legacies of Aksum continued to operate and provided the basis of legitimacy for later Emperors who were confined to their defensible highland plateaus. Any new emperor had to travel to Aksum, which remained as the ecclesiastical capital of Ethiopia, to be anointed and be acclaimed King of Tsion and of Aksum. The centralized Ethiopian Orthodox Church served as a pivotal force among Christian highlanders and the historic Ethiopian nationhood for centuries to follow.

Throughout the medieval period, the legacy of Aksum was reflected in its written religious literature, religious education, political system and trade, and this remained the basis of a unity and identity of the people of 'Abyssinia'. The *Kebre Nagast* (Glory of Kings) compiled by Yosehak and his team of five writers between 1270 and 1285 and the *Fetha Nagast* (Law of the Kings) produced in 1400 on an earlier Egyptian text were sources of judicial legitimacy and a symbolic-normative measure of the kingdom's stability. The Tigrigna-speaking people of northern Ethiopia were bound together by this heritage and to this day, the majority of the Hamassien, Seraye and Akele Guzay people of Eritrea (estimated to be about 2.5 million) remain Orthodox Christians and speak the Tigrigna language, like their kin in Tigrai (estimated at 3.5 million). Intermittently, they used its common name – Tigrai-Tigrigni (Pan-Tigrinya). Another common name that includes many of the people in the central-north of Ethiopia is 'Habesha', and elderly Eritreans, along with their kin to the south, are often proud to be called Habesha.

From the 16th century, the Ottoman Turks, and later on the Egyptians, occupied the eastern lowlands of Eritrea. The northern defence line of the Aksumite Kingdom was repeatedly attacked from different directions, yet the Emperors always worked to regain the Red Sea coastal territories and ensure access to the sea. Now that the invasion was launched by Islamists against the Christian state, the confrontation took on a religious dimension. Beginning in the reign of Yikuno Amlak (1270-1285), the restorer of the Ethiopian monarchy, and throughout the reigns of Amde Tsion (1314-1344) and Yishaq (1413-1430), all the kings attempted to restore the status of Aksum. Expansion of Christianity was one integral aspect of their mission. Evangelists like Ewostatewos of Geraälta, central Tigrai (1273-1352) and Filipos, the founder of the Debre Bizen monastery (1323-1406) and their followers made tremendous strides in instituting monasteries throughout the region, thereby strengthening the normative grip of the Christian monarchy over their historic domain. Several monasteries were also built in the region now known as Eritrea. Among them, situated in the northern tip of their kingdom is Bizen, not far from Asmara. 'Bizen represented the movement of Christian expansion characteristic of the fourteenth century', (Tamrat 1972: 260). Emperor Zer'a Ya'eqob (1434-1468) upgraded the title and status of the ruler of the region now known as Eritrea and part of Tigrai from *Melake Baher* (emissary to the sea) to *Baher Negash* (sea region ruler). With the intention of re-instituting maritime trade, external relations and control of the coastal region, 'Zer'a Ya'eqob started building his own sea-port at Girar, on the mainland opposite the island of Misiwwa' (Kolmodin, cited in Tamrat 1972: 261).

Like all semi-autonomous regions in highland Ethiopia, the Seraye, Hamassien and Akale-Guzay regions in present Eritrea were ruled by their own rulers under the sovereign power of the Ethiopian monarchy. With the intention of centralizing his kingdom, Zer'a Ya'eqob, as Perruchon (1893: 45-48) said, '...grouped together the districts of Shire, Sara'e, Hamsen and Bur, and placed them under one administration entrusted to the Bahir-Negash'. But this administrative arrangement was to change with the coming to power of another king. Such change could be observed during the reign of Susenyos (1607-1632), when 'the ruler of Hamassien (Mereb Melash) in the early 17th century, a certain Tesfazion Ateshim, was appointed by King Susenyos' (Ghelawdewos 1998: 1, cited in Medhane Tadesse 1999: 4), suggesting that Hamassien was ruled as one administrative district of the Kingdom of Susenyos (1607-1632). It is, therefore, reasonable to conclude that '...in the specific history of highland Eritrea, a consolidated hereditary aristocratic class hardly emerged. The rise of the semi-autonomous status of '*Bahr Negash*' office, (i.e., governorship of highland Eritrea), and its decline since the 16th century is highly indicative' (Longrigg, cited in Mesfin Araya 1988: 39). Furthermore, during the reign of King Iyasu (1682-1706), the Turkish *Na'ib* at Massawa had to pay tribute to Aksum and 'caravan connections were maintained with Massawa via Adwa, with Sudan, and through Gojjam to the southwest' (Henze 2000: 103).

Even during the *Zemene Mesafint,* from 1769 to 1855, (the Era of Princes) when Ethiopia was parcelled among local chieftains and the coastal area was controlled by the Turks, Abyssinian/Ethiopian dominance of the port of Massawa was not severed. *Ras* Mikael Sihul, ruler of Tigrai, his successor *Ras* Wolde Selassie of Enderta and later *Dejazmach* Sebagadis Woldu of Agame maintained their influence over Massawa despite their engagements with bellicose rivals.

In 1855 Emperor Tewodros, who rose to power in Gondar, brought about the end of the *Zemene Mesafint* and the beginning of a unified modern Ethiopia. To realize his vision, he made sure local leaders remained loyal to his throne and paid tribute. The highland regions in Tigrai and Eritrea constituted part of the loyal regions in his kingdom. 'Dejjach Baryaw Paulos, governor of Northern Tigrai, Dejjach Hailu Tewolde Medhin, governor of Hamasen and Seraye, and Bashai Gebrezghi, governor of Akele Guzay respectively paid 35,000, 32,000 and 17,000 Maria Theresa thalers to the state treasury annually' (Bahru Zewde 1991: 32). '*Ras* Wolde Michael, whom the EPLF presented later as the forerunner of 'Eritrean nationalism' was a vassal of the Emperor Tewodros (1855-1868). He conducted all his correspondence with foreigners in Amharic…and gave his children typical Amharic names – Mesfin, Mekonnen, Merid, and so on' (Kindie 2005: 24).

During the second half of the nineteenth century, the Egyptians attempted to penetrate deep into highland Eritrea. Emperor Yohannes IV (r. 1872-1889), who succeeded Tewodros, dispatched his accomplished general *Ras* Alula Engida and under his leadership Ethiopian forces defeated the Egyptian army at the Battle of Gundet in November 1875 and Gura in March 1876. After the defeat and retreat of the Egyptians, the Italians, under the auspices of the United Kingdom, seized Massawa in February 1885. The Ethiopian general, with his seat at Asmara, engaged the Italians for years and finally '*Ras* Alula soundly defeated the Italians at the Battle of Dogali (near Massawa) in 1887, the major setback received by any European power at the hands of an African Army, though only a sample of what was to happen nine years later at Adua' (Hess 1963: 105). Erlich adds, 'His victory over their forces at Dogali in January 1887 was a landmark in their imperialist history' (1996: x). The remaining Italian forces fortified their position at Saati, to which Emperor Yohannes advanced halfway in order to dislodge them. Had it not been for the invasion of the Sudanese Mahdists in the northwest of the country, which forced him to change his former plan, that advance might have brought an end to the Italian presence in the region. To the relief of the Italians, Yohannes died at Metemma on 9 March 1889 while fighting the Mahdists. Soon the re-enforced Italian army began encroaching on the highlands of Serae up to the River Mereb, and in January 1890 the Parliament in Rome declared this part of Ethiopia and the adjacent lowland regions a colony to be called 'Eritrea', going back to the old Roman name Mare Aerythreum (Red Sea). Thus began the colonial history of Eritrea, a precursor of Eritrean nationalism. The 1890 Rome Declaration set the political geography of what is now known as Eritrea and the nationalism that has appeared since then.

The Italians were not content with only occupying the region they named Eritrea. Their aim was to colonize the whole of Ethiopia. Thus they continued their encroachment on the hinterland until they were stopped at Adwa in 1896 by the united Ethiopian forces under Emperor Menelik. They were then contained in Eritrea for the next four decades until 1935, when they again launched their invasion of Ethiopia, which lasted until their defeat in 1941. During these years of war and occupation, Eritreans in their thousands fought against the invaders like any other patriotic Ethiopian. Studies conducted by Salome Gabre-Egziabher (1969), Seifu Abbawollo (1960), Gerima Yafere (1956), Tadesse Mecha (1951) and Alazar Tesfa-Micael (1948) to mention but a few, give a lengthy list of Eritrean patriots who fought for the independence of Ethiopia, of which Eritrea was a component.

After the cession of the present Eritrean region to Italy in 1890, relations between the people on both sides of the imposed border remained intact but latent, as they fell under separate administrations. The Eritrean regions of Hamassien, Seraye and Akele Guzay in the northern highlands, the Afar in the eastern and the Kunama in the central-west lowlands remained connected with their kin on the Ethiopian side of the border. After all, ethnically they were the same people; they spoke the same language, had shared the same history for centuries, and also continued economic relations.

With the defeat of the Italians in the Second World War and without the consent of the people, the British took over Eritrea and ruled from 1941-1952. But after a diplomatic fight, Emperor Haile Selassie succeeded in claiming back Eritrea by a federal arrangement under his crown from 1952-1961. The federation, however did not last long.[89] Against the provisions stipulated in the federal agreement, 'By 1955 the federation was de facto dismantled. In place of Arabic and Tigrigna, Amharic became the official language. In 1959 the Eritrean flag was removed' (Mesfin Araya 1988: 170). Except for negligible numbers of Christians like Woldeab Woldemariam who envisaged a secular autonomous Eritrea and a few Muslims like *Sheikh* Suleman Aldin Ahmed who joined the unionists, the population was divided into two major blocs largely on the basis of religion with Christians mostly approving union and Muslims opting for separation. Supported by the unionist block which had 32 of the 68 seats in the federal parliament and against the advice of his far-sighted Prime Minister Aklilu Habte-Wold, Emperor Haile Selassie dismantled the federation and declared Eritrea to be the fourteenth province of Ethiopia in 1962. With the gradual break-up of the federal arrangement, the Eritrean Liberation Front (ELF) was formed in 1961 in the Muslim-inhabited western lowlands. Hamed Idris Awate, formerly a junior officer in the Sudanese army and on-and-off a bandit (*shifta*) preying largely on the Kunama, joined later and made it an armed insurgent group in 1962. 'By mid-1964 ... first foreign assistance came from Syria' (Osman Salih Sabbe, cited in Habte-Selassie 1980: 64), which was indicative of an emerging Islamic alliance. As the ELF remained Islamist for some years to follow, followers of Woldeab and some liberal Muslims opposed to the ELF came together to form a secular movement which later evolved as Eritrean People's Liberation Front (EPLF) in early 1972. It was this EPLF that forged an alliance with the TPLF to finally overthrow the Ethiopian military junta.

In a brief period of about 65 years (compared with their long history sketched above), the Eritreans experienced Italian colonialism, British

---

89 For a fascinating history of the Federation, see Tekeste 1996.

'trusteeship' and finally federation with Ethiopia – a period of political discord and unrest rather than a stable evolution that could revive their historic and historical identity. It was in the middle of the period of federation that the old dichotomy in Eritrean society began to emerge. As we saw, the Christian highlanders mostly opted for unity with Ethiopia while the Muslim lowlanders wanted to stay outside it. Some were liberal Muslims, others die-hards and still others pro-Italian, while the Christians fell into one unionist organization. As the unionists looked for support from their kin in Ethiopia, many of the Muslims yearned for not only political but also spiritual sustenance from the Arab world. Initially Egypt intended to subsume the region; later support was given by Syria, Libya and Saudi Arabia.

Reciting the long history of the region, the Tigraians in Ethiopia saw the Eritrean people and the land as part of their joint history. This link is based, among other relations, on the fact that 'Eritrea was an integral part of the Ethiopian Empire for centuries with the exception of the period of Italian and British colonial occupation and the federal years' (Addis Birhan 1998: 31). True, as Tesfatsion Medhanie (2007: 132-133)[90] wrote 'History has been badly abused in the course of the liberation struggle. It has not merely been misconstrued, but has also become the subject of fraudulent discourse'. Although influenced by elite politics which emphasized exclusiveness at times and parochialism at others for the sake of sectarian interests manifested by both the Tigraian and Eritrean elite, there is still great affinity between the divided peoples, as the longstanding cultural, religious, linguistic and kinship ties kept on revitalizing the historical bonds. Tigraian sympathy and support for the Eritrean cause, though short of secession, emanate from the sense of tangible affinities and of belonging to the same historical roots, and later, when Tigraians began to challenge Amhara national domination, it was expedient for them to forge closer cooperation with the Eritrean fronts. The TPLF enjoyed a warm reception and hospitality from Eritrean peasants in the adjacent regions of Seraye and Akele Guzay. The forces that worked against the unity of the Ethiopians and the Eritreans apparently found the affinity of the divided people a liability in their project. Despite this affinity and to promote the forging of an independent state, the Eritrean elite portrayed Ethiopia as a colonizer like the Italians, and their movement as an anti-colonial struggle '...to reconstitute itself as the new ruling class'

90 In this book Tesfatsion Medhanie critically discussed how Eritrean writers like Tseggai Isaac (2001) distorted history. For instance, the defeat of the Italians who ventured to occupy the whole of Ethiopia by the combined Ethiopian forces, Eritrean patriots included, under Menelik at Adwa 1896 was presented as the defeat of Menelik, who 'forfeited' Eritrea to Italy while Eritrea was already in the hands of the Italians long before the Adwa war.

(Mesfin Araya 1988: 32) in a separate state of Eritrea. And ultimately, in 1991, through an EPLF-sponsored referendum, this class achieved its goal, the independence of Eritrea. Of course, as Tesfatsion Medhanie (1994: 57) observed, 'There were many who felt there was no environment which allowed opposition groups, especially those who may not favour Eritrean independence, to organize themselves and freely campaign for their positions'.

Launching the TPLF and the Eritrean Connection

When the seed of the Tigraian national movement sprouted at the campus of the Haile Selassie I University in the early 1970s and the Tigraian National Organization (TNO) was formed it was expedient for the Tigraian group to forge relations with their Eritrean counterparts. The TNO sought contact with the two Eritrean fronts simultaneously, the EPLF and the ELF, through their members at the Haile Selassie I University. For the TNO members, it was not difficult to contact EPLF activists and because of its leftist stance it had some sympathy among the radical students at HSIU and they were easily identifiable. Both sides knew each other from a distance, particularly regarding the question of nationalities and self-determination in Ethiopia, and also because of their common language, Tigrigna. However, tracing ELF activists was not so easy because their supporters were found mainly outside the university campus and working more covertly.

Amid this radical activism and through his individual efforts, Teklai Gebre-Mariam ('Aden'), of Eritrean parents born in Adwa, Tigrai, managed to contact the ELF and enlisted in 1973, but his involvement was short-lived. To his dismay, the outspoken 'revolutionary' Teklai-Aden found the ELF far below his expectations, as he found it as bogged down in deep crisis fuelled by religious and regional animosities. He abandoned the Front and returned to his home in Adwa, where he was welcomed by militant Tigraians who were waiting for first-hand information on the fronts. Unexpectedly, he took a dim view of the dominant Islamic stance within the Front. His assessment of the ELF negatively influenced Tigraians who had started forging a political organization to fight the regime and were seeking collaboration with the ELF. Ignoring Teklai Aden's assessment of the ELF, some of the activists, for example Amare Tesfu and Tekeste Wubneh, went to Eritrea and contacted ELF officials in their turn. At that time, a group of Tigraians led by Yohannes Tekle-Haimanot and Gebre-Kidan Asfaha were forming the TLF and being trained by the ELF. Amare Tesfu and Tekeste Wubneh joined the TLF on the ELF's recommendation. The other group, which subsequently formed the TNO, went its own way and established relations with the EPLF.

Although it was known that another Tigraian group, the TLF, was training and operating with the support of the ELF, the TNO group was keen to maintain cautious contact with both Eritrean fronts. This was not without reason. The TNO was aware of the fact that the ELF had a wider area of operation, including along the borders with Tigrai, which could serve as a safe zone of retreat if the enemy's offensive in Tigrai would be unbreakable. The EPLF, on the other hand, which in general seemed to be an ideological match for the TNO, was already supporting another Ethiopian organization, the EPRP. This situation left the TNO uncertain about its relations with the EPLF. So, the leaders of the TNO found it expedient to recognize both Eritrean fronts as legitimate representatives of Eritrea and pushed to establish relations with both. However, this strategy had difficulties because these Eritrean movements were in furious conflict. Under such circumstances each front wanted to support an organization that represented its organizational interests and could be an ally against its rival.

The formation of the TLF and its apparently warm relations with the ELF drew the EPLF and the TNO together. The TNO approached the EPLF through the intermediary of clandestine EPLF cells in Addis Ababa. Without any sign of hesitation or complaint, the EPLF agreed to train recruits and provide armaments and ammunition for the future front, the TPLF. It appeared that the EPLF was desperately looking for an ally amongst the Ethiopians. Mahari Tekle (Mussie), a Tigraian by origin and a fighter in the EPLF, became the contact person and, as he revealed later on, he intended to pursue the cause of self-determination in Tigrai. Furthermore, the EPLF consented to his demand to join the nascent Tigrai Movement. It was common for young Tigraians who found themselves at odds with the government of Haile Selassie to join an Eritrean front to fight, and many such fighters joined the TPLF at a later stage.

The organizers of the TNO co-opted Mussie into its ranks and made him a member of the founding leadership of the TPLF which led the organization until a fighters' congress was held. On 18 February 1975, the leadership and some recruits went to Dedebit in rural Tigrai and launched the TPLF-led national armed struggle (see Chapter 3). The launching of the TPLF in Dedebit was also a message to the Eritrean fronts making it clear that the Tigraian movement, with or without their help, would advance.

TPLF and ELF Never Went Along Well

The formation of the TPLF, which had established warm contact with the EPLF in a short period of time, was not good news for the ELF. Its rival front, the EPLF, which was contained in the northern terrains of Eritrea, had now found an ally in the south which would share the opportunity of wider mobility that the ELF had monopolized so far. From the beginning, the ELF showed its aversion to the TPLF by turning down all its efforts to establish good relations. In April 1975, just two months after it was established, the TPLF dispatched a delegation to the ELF Seraye administrative unit (better known as No. 9) and made known its intentions to set up working relations with the ELF. This initiative was conveyed to the highest bodies in Barka, their base area. Soon after, the ELF held its 2nd National Congress, which delegates of the TLF and representatives of *Ras* Mengesha Seyoum (later the leader of the EDU) attended. The TPLF was not invited, despite its efforts to maintain contact. Not discouraged by the rejection, the TPLF made extra efforts to contact the TLF and through that endeavour tried to ameliorate relations with the ELF. It was also thought what had begun as good relations with the TLF would help contribute to fixing the gap the ELF had created and forge better relations with the latter.

In November 1975, relations with the TLF itself suddenly ended. After news of the atrocities committed by the TLF against its own members began to spread like wild-fire, rank and file members of the TPLF, among them Meles Zenawi, Yemane Jamaica and Sibhat Nega, started agitating for action to be taken. The TPLF leadership then called an emergency meeting to discuss the matter and because the situation was getting out of hand, it was left with no option but to take action against the TLF. The TPLF forcefully subdued the TLF and put the surviving leaders under arrest (see Chapter 4 for the details). It was an unexpected turn of events for all parties, the TLF, the ELF and the TPLF itself. A few days later, the TPLF, confident of the righteousness of its measures against the TLF, informed the ELF and invited them to assess the episode for themselves. The ELF sent two of its senior officials, a central committee member and a division commander, to Tigrai to discuss the matter with the TPLF's leadership. They also had the chance to talk about the matter in private with the TLF leaders under arrest. The delegation had nothing negative to say about the drastic measures taken by the TPLF. The TPLF demanded that the outcome of their investigation be reported in written form to all ELF members so that relations at all levels would be comradely. But top ELF leaders, who feared the exposure of their involvement in the TLF misdeeds, never released any such statement. It should be recalled that prominent members of the TLF, like Tekeste Wubneh, Yohannes Andebirhan, Berhe Tewldebirhan and Teklai Gebrezgi, were executed with the consent of Salih Shume and Mohamed Kiduwi, both leaders of the ELF at the administration unit no.10. The ELF delegation must have been embarrassed by this and related facts which the TLF leaders revealed.

For the moment, the discussions seemed to have cleared future relations between the TPLF and the ELF. In fact, the ELF dropped the issue of the TLF and the question of the prisoners, altogether and began to focus on future cooperation. As a goodwill gesture, it also granted its consent for the TPLF to retain the arms it captured from the TLF. These firearms initially belonged to the ELF, which had every right to claim them. Such ELF moves were thought to be signs of bridging the gap with the TPLF, but it was not clear how the relationship would develop, for the ELF's top policy engineers were based far away in the Barka lowlands and would not be expected to change their attitudes towards the TPLF as long as the latter's contiguity with the EPLF was not severed.

As a matter of fact, the initial warm relations between the TPLF and the EPLF had been one of the reasons for the bad relations between the TPLF and the ELF. From the outset, the EPLF had portrayed itself as a revolutionary front that would embrace and work with the Ethiopian revolutionary left, and was accommodating the EPRP and the TPLF. The first TPLF recruits were trained and armed by the EPLF, an initial indication of a serious alliance. Two long-time EPLF fighters – Mussie and Yemane Kidane (a.k.a. Jamaica) – who were both Tigraians by birth, were transferred to the TPLF for good. Mussie in particular was instrumental in maintaining the relationship with the EPLF when it experienced problems. The organizational name TPLF resembled that of the EPLF as did the TLF that of ELF. In the ELF camp, the rhetoric surrounding class struggle, socialism and dictatorship of the proletariat entertained by both the EPLF and the TPLF created the suspicion of a rising unified revolutionary force. This was happening at a time when the ELF was claiming that it was the only legitimate representative of all sections of Eritrean society. On top of that, the ELF's perception of the EPLF as an organization of Tigrigna-speaking highlanders from Eritrea who were ethnically the same as the Tigraians in Ethiopia decisively shaped its attitudes towards the TPLF as an ally of its rival, the EPLF. Besides, the permanent presence of ELF cadres along the borders with Tigrai and their confrontational dealings with Tigraians living there was another area where relations were difficult. TPLF-ELF relations were, therefore, strained from the beginning by many factors and remained fragile all along, sometimes even turning violent.

For the top ELF officials, who were always seeking surrogate organizations in Ethiopia, the liquidation of the TLF in itself was understandably annoying. From then onwards, the ELF invariably supported any organization in Tigrai that was in some kind of armed conflict with, and could potentially weaken, the TPLF. In 1976 and 1977, the ELF provided the Tigraian Movement Coordinating Committee (*Teranafit*) and its umbrella organization the

Ethiopian Democratic Union (EDU) with military information on the TPLF. Since the operational areas of both the TPLF and ELF in many cases overlapped, it was possible for the ELF to pass sensitive military information to the *Teranafit* and the EDU on the mobility and strength of the TPLF. This had happened on several occasions, as the TPLF's radio interception unit could prove, and indeed was a 'stab in the back' of the TPLF.

Later, in 1978, the TPLF destroyed the *Teranafit* by waging a counter-offensive and also evicted the EDU from Tigrai. It seized armaments and ammunition from both adversaries that bolstered its morale and strength. The TPLF became a formidable force in western Tigrai and began full mobilization of the people without encountering any resistance from its former rivals, the *Teranafit* and the EDU. Once again, the ELF did not have any choice but to accommodate the TPLF, and relations between the organizations appeared to improve. By the end of 1976, the TPLF had managed to establish formal relations with the ELF but they only lasted for a brief period. This time the ELF gave the TPLF few arms and ammunition, which the TPLF needed but was not desperate for. It also lifted restrictions on the TPLF outlet to Sudan through western Eritrea. The ELF also assisted the TPLF on the diplomatic front, introducing it to Arab regimes such as Saudi Arabia, Syria and Egypt, which offered advantages to the TPLF. However, friendly relations did not last long. Despite the support the ELF was providing, the position of the TPLF as far as the EPLF (the former's rival) was concerned did not falter and this must have annoyed the ELF. 'The ELF also endeavoured to get the TPLF to accept its political positions over those of its rival, the EPLF, something the TPLF was reluctant to do', (Young 1997: 113). The administration of Eritrean peasants who settled in the Tigrai region was another source of continuous disagreement which the ELF took as provocation. When the TPLF began to execute its land-reform policy which favoured poor peasants, Eritrean landlords living near the borders were seriously affected. The ELF stood up on behalf of these landlords and worked covertly and overtly not only to frustrate the land-reform policy but also the TPLF's entire politico-military venture. It defended and offered sanctuary to feudal Eritrean or Tigraian elements opposed to the land reform and committed acts of reprisal against members of the TPLF or even ordinary TPLF sympathizers. The ELF protected such opponents of the TPLF by claiming that they were members of its organization. Repeatedly, its units obstructed the mobility of TPLF members or vehicles travelling to or from the Sudan through their territory.

In the middle of all these tense circumstances, war broke out between the TPLF and the EPRP in April 1978. Once again the ELF was quick to grab the opportunity and use it against the interests of the TPLF. The EPRP army, which was operating in Tigrai, was defeated and driven out of its base area in Alitena and Assimba by the TPLF in a matter of days and fled to the ELF-held territory of Shumezana in Eritrea. It was unexpected for the ELF to act as a host for the EPRP because they had no formal relations and until then, the latter was known to be an ally of the EPLF, the ELF's arch rival. But all of a sudden, the ELF gave the EPRP sanctuary in its base area near Augaro in western Eritrea close to the TPLF area of operations. The cooperation between the ELF and the EPRP put the TPLF under a serious threat of war. The TPLF wrote a number of letters of reconciliation to the ELF and in May 1978 leaders of both the ELF and the TPLF met in Barka. They agreed to work together and not interfere in each other's administrative territory. They spelled out their differences, particularly on the nature of the *Dergue* and the Soviet Union – the ELF considered the *Dergue* and the Soviet Union as 'truly socialist' and 'progressive' forces, while the TPLF held that both were anti-democratic and anti-revolutionary. Yet they agreed that such differences should not hamper the progress of their cooperation as long as they were fighting against both of them. Subsequently, they went as far as putting together their forces to challenge the *Dergue*'s biggest military campaign on the Shire front in May 1978.

At this time, the ELF rearmed the EPRP and began supporting the latter's plan of establishing itself in Wolkait in western Tigrai. To accomplish this, the ELF had to escort the EPRP through TPLF-held territory in western Tigrai where it had created popular support. At the end of 1979, three ELF battalions under Tesfay Tekle, a member of the ELF revolutionary council, joined the EPRP forces to cross to Wolkait but they were attacked by TPLF forces at Moguee and forced to return to Eritrea. Reinforced by another fresh brigade, the joint forces of ELF-EPRP advanced to Sheraro, the popular base of the TPLF. But on 6 April 1980, they were intercepted by TPLF forces in the hilly terrain of Gemmahlo and suffered a heavy defeat. The troops of both defeated fronts were in disarray, each blaming the other for what had befallen them, although it was the endurance coupled with the TPLF's better fighting tactics that brought about their defeat. Thereafter, the ELF refrained from attacking the TPLF in the western part of Tigrai while the EPRP made a long march of retreat to reach remote areas of the Wolkait region. The EPRP had difficulty reviving its forces and was then engaged in a survival strategy. The implication of this war was that it frustrated attempts by the EPRP to launch an operational zone in western Tigrai and Wolkait and to open a corridor from its bases in Gonder to ELF territory in western Eritrea and eventually to Sudan. Once again, the TPLF proved to be invincible in the eyes of its adversaries.

By November 1980, furious ELF units operating across central Tigrai launched another surprise attack on the TPLF base area in Belesa-Maihamato. They chased away the few guards they encountered and looted the small base area before returning to their own territory. This was an unprovoked attack, and the TPLF was in no position to and had no intention of declaring war on the ELF. By this time, the former had emerged as the only formidable armed resistance force to the *Dergue* in Tigrai. The destroying and eviction of the TLF, the *Teranafit*, the EDU and finally the EPRP was, however, a message that the ELF had to consider seriously. The fact that it was now left without proxy organizations in Tigrai indicated its isolation. Confrontation between the TPLF and the ELF from then onwards became direct and had to be resolved one way or the other.

The TPLF and ELF operational areas were adjacent. The ELF operated in many parts of Tigrai for military and economic reasons. The border claim and counter-claim and the exclusive right to operate in the border territories continued to be a constant problem in relations between the organizations. The policies on land, trade, the mobility of people and the forceful extraction of material contributions and recruits from Eritreans living in Tigrai continued to cause strain between the TPLF and the ELF. The ELF's border security officers declined to discuss seriously the problems with TPLF cadres and seek solutions to the problems. The ELF wanted to impose their way and in the final solution resorted to killing TPLF cadres and trying to overrun their base areas. Conflicts became frequent, nerve-racking, and sometimes bloody. The ELF created a situation that was unbearable for the TPLF and even more so for the people of Tigrai along the borders, and, day in day out, they urged the TPLF to do something about it and to drive away any ELF unit. The TPLF had thus many reasons to remove the ELF.

At the very beginning of 1981, the EPLF, which since its formation had been in a similar – if not more hostile situation – with the ELF, sent a delegation led by Sibhat Ephraim, a politburo member, to the TPLF to try to resolve the lingering problem with the ELF. By this time both seemed to have had enough of ELF provocations and they agreed on organizing equal numbers of forces to deliver a decisive blow to the ELF. In mid-1981, combined TPLF-EPLF forces began their offensive from the Afar lowlands, the eastern base area of the ELF and swiftly advanced on the central and western bases. Without joint action, the war with the ELF would have remained an impossible task for the EPLF alone. Weakened by internal squabbles and stretched over a wide area in small units, the ELF was in no position to pose any meaningful resistance. In less than two weeks, the entire ELF force was forced to leave Tigrai and Eritrea and flee to Sudan following the impact of the joint TPLF-EPLF attack. Nharnet Team, an ELF sympathizer, described the situation as follows:

> The aggression on the ELA [ELF army] started and the TPLF
> of Ethiopia joined in the fratricidal war declared by the EPLF
> that lasted till 10 August 1981. The ELA was forced to withdraw
> to the border areas in the Sudan where it faced many problems.
> During that fateful period of 1980-81, the ELA lost 1458 fighters
> martyred mainly in the destructive war provoked by the EPLF/
> TPLF alliance (Nharnet, 2005: Part VIII).

TPLF-ELF relations had been rocky from the start and continued to be so despite the conciliatory gestures made by the TPLF. At last it had led to this bloody confrontation in which the ELF was defeated and ceased to exist as a viable organization. The defeat of the ELF opened up the opportunity for the EPLF to control rural Eritrea without a rival. The TPLF too had nothing to fear from behind for some time to follow. This was also a relief for the Tigraians living along the borders. Afterwards splinter groups formed, made up of dispersed ELF members, and they vowed to continue the struggle for independence. They were against the rival EPLF and even those who looked to espouse Marxian ideology took no time to establish a relationship with the TPLF. Later, the TPLF began to support the Eritrean Democratic Movement (EDM) and the Eritrean Liberation Front Central-Command (ELF-CC), better known as *Sagem,* as a countervailing force to the EPLF. A new alignment that would complicate relations with the EPLF was in the making.

The TPLF and the EPLF: Cupboard-Love Relationship

From the beginning, the TPLF-EPLF relationship was an amorphous connection, but on the side of the militant Tigraians, who counted on historical, cultural and kinship ties, it was believed the new relationship with the EPLF would work. There was the perception among TPLF members that the EPLF elite was well-educated and could articulate and extend the long-standing relationship between the two peoples beyond what Italian colonialists had created in the 1880s and 1890s. However, considering the attitude of the EPLF that transpired in due course, it was by and large external circumstances, i.e., the pressure of a common enemy that propelled the relationship to work. Yet unlike the larger section of the ELF that was from the outset influenced by Islamist lowlanders, the EPLF had a clearer picture about cultural and political developments in Ethiopia in general and in Tigrai in particular, largely because of their affinity and exposure to kin across the Mereb River. Contacts between EPLF activists and militant

Tigraians had started much earlier, during the Ethiopian student movement of the early 1970s.

When the militant Tigraians were confronted in 1974 by an aggressive military force, the *Dergue*, that sought total obedience from everybody, they were in outright defiance and searched for support in order to launch armed insurgency. It was imperative for them to look for such support from the EPLF. But EPLF leaders, on the other hand, were hoping to find an ally in Ethiopia that could cooperate in expanding their theatre of operations. It was a time when the EPLF was badly in need of support from Ethiopian sympathizers in its efforts to dislodge the remaining government forces concentrated in a few towns in Eritrea. The well-publicized news of ELF-TLF joint operations inside Ethiopia in early 1975 must have motivated them to quickly link up with a Tigraian front. These circumstances led the TPLF – EPLF relationship to start before it had had time to conduct formal discussions or agreements. There seemed to be enthusiasm in the EPLF camp for supporting a Tigraian movement at this juncture, which led to the forging of working relations between the two fronts.

After the initial connection was established, modalities of cooperation were expected to be set and political positions discussed and agreed upon, but the EPLF instead offered in advance to train as many recruits as the TPLF could mobilize. It was an attractive offer the TPLF could not afford to waste. It focused on seizing the opportunity and on finding recruits to be engaged in fighting the enemy. The formalities that would define the relationship between the two organizations were therefore ignored and informal contact became the defining aspect of the relationship.

Initially the cooperation appeared to go smoothly, but the EPLF's support for the TPLF did not match the latter's expectations. Many reasons could be attributed to this shift of attitude on the part of the EPLF: perhaps because the relationship was not based on a formal agreement, or existing relations between the EPLF and the EPRP might have created reluctance of the EPLF towards the TPLF, or perhaps supporting a struggle for the self-determination of Tigrai might have set an unwanted precedent for Eritrea.

The EPRP was then considered the strongest revolutionary party and indeed had huge numbers of followers all over Ethiopia. It was also widely believed to assume power sooner or later. The EPLF too seemed to believe this. For the EPLF, its relationship with the EPRP was thus much more important, as the latter claimed to represent the whole of Ethiopia. And when compared with the EPRP at that time (1975-76), the TPLF was just a small ethno-nationalist movement with fewer followers. However, there were some sticky political problems for both the TPLF and the EPRP regarding

Eritrea. While they recognized the struggle for the Eritrean independence as genuine, they had differences as to whether the case was a 'colonial issue' or not. Without conducting the necessary study or having appropriate discussions, the TPLF held the view that the Eritrean case was a 'colonial question', as the EPLF wanted it be. It was probably an opportunistic stand, designed to outflank the EPRP from the privileged position the EPLF offering it. Without understanding the consequences that were to haunt it in the discourse of Ethiopian political history, this position continued to be the stand of the TPLF for years to come.

Another concern of the TPLF was what the removal of the TLF from the scene, which took place as early as November 1975, would mean for the EPLF. The ELF's wider mobility, supported by a proxy organization in Tigrai, might have prompted the EPLF to initially look for its own proxy organizations in Tigrai to counter its rival. But once the TLF had been dissolved, the EPLF had less need to worry about the ELF's activities gaining ground in Tigrai and beyond. That situation appeared to reduce the TPLF's importance for the EPLF and gave more weight to its relations with the EPRP.

Towards of the end of 1975, differences between the EPRP and the TPLF surfaced when they were operating in the same territory and trying to mobilize and organize the same people. News of rivalry between the two was also coming from the towns. On the initiative of the TPLF, leaders of both fronts met in Marwa in January 1976 to look into these encounters and consider possible remedies (See Chapter 5, section *Words and Bullets – Battles with EPRP*) The TPLF presented a suggestion that it thought would benefit both organizations and avoid them overlapping and clashing. The TPLF requested that the EPRP operate in regions of the country that the TPLF could not reach. By implication, the suggestion was recognition of the TPLF as the viable front that could take care of the struggle in Tigrai against the common enemy, the *Dergue*. As we saw earlier, the demand infuriated EPRP delegates and they broke off the meeting and enmity was created. This was a concern for EPLF leaders, but their main worry was that a fragmented or ethnically based movement in Ethiopia might weaken a viable future ally - the EPRP. Eventually, TPLF military action, like that launched against the TLF, would deprive the EPLF of an ally expected to seize power in Ethiopia and the anticipated acquiescence to handle the Eritrean question would evaporate. The EPLF continued to exert pressure on the TPLF to come to terms with the EPRP and in a letter to the TPLF, the concerns of the EPLF were clearly stated, with an underlying warning note. For strategic purposes, the EPLF stood beside the EPRP and influenced by their leader's desire to work with the EPRP, EPLF top cadres urged Ethiopians, and especially Tigraians in Eritrea, to join the EPRP and not the TPLF.

In the first half of 1976 the TPLF unexpectedly had released its controversial manifesto, better known as Manifesto 68 (see Chapter 5). In this handwritten document, the TPLF declared that its struggle was for Tigrai's independence from Ethiopia, which was basically the same claim the Eritrean fronts had put forward for their region. Earlier this position had been entertained by the TLF but it was vehemently rejected by the TPLF on the grounds that there was no historical or political justification for it. It was a surprise to many fighters to see their organization come up with such an unwarranted claim. The EPLF also opposed the TPLF manifesto for independence on the grounds that Tigrai was an integral part of Ethiopia and there was no justification for secession from Ethiopia. At this time, the EPLF was reluctant to support separatist movements in Ethiopia, not just as a matter of principle but for various other motives as well. First, supporting separatist movements might have given the Ethiopian regime extra ammunition to accuse it of working against Ethiopian unity and for fragmentation. Second, it feared that the growth of separatist movements in Ethiopia might blur the alleged distinction between Ethiopia and Eritrea as two different political entities and the propaganda line it held to that end. Henceforth, EPLF support for the TPLF seemed to be conditional, i.e., the TPLF's subordination of its programme to that of a unified Ethiopia through the right to self-determination. Although the EPLF position in this case appeared quite palatable to many Ethiopians, one could not conclude for sure that it was adopted as a matter of principle, given their presentation of Eritrean history as having no connection with Ethiopia. Also, in light of the EPLF's continued support for secessionist organizations like the OLF and the ONLF, that stand would seem to have been an act of opportunism rather than a matter of principle.

The politico-military developments in Tigrai between 1975 and 1977 had not been conducive to cultivating good relations between the TPLF and the EPLF. Tigrai then became the operational field for several anti-*Dergue* fronts, among them the TLF, the TPLF, the *Teranafit*-EDU and the EPRP. Ethno-national or multinational groups were all seeking the backing of one or the other or even both Eritrean fronts. The radical TPLF was involved in armed conflicts with almost all the fronts in Tigrai – the TLF, the *Teranafit* and the EDU. While these had the ELF on their side, the TPLF had only the nominal support of the EPLF, which was simply watching events take their own course. The TPLF had already managed single-handedly to deal with its two rivals. Later, when the war rhetoric between the EPRP and the TPLF was increasing, the EPLF manifested its worries by dispatching a letter of warning to the TPLF, threatening to sever relations – a threat that did not worry the TPLF. As a result, the EPLF turned a deaf ear to the TPLF's request for assistance, while the former's relationship with the EPRP remained amicable and supportive. In its turn, the EPRP reciprocated by declaring its support for the EPLF. In their joint statement of 3 March 1976, it was stated that: 'The EPRP unconditionally supports the Eritrean people's struggle for their independence. It as well supports the political and armed struggle waged by the EPLF for the independence and liberation of the Eritrean people.' Whether the term 'colonial' fitted the Eritrean question in relation to Ethiopia remained controversial, and the EPRP pledged to '... study the question and take a stand accordingly'. On the other hand, the EPLF maintained its benevolent and opportunistic stand towards the EPRP until the latter was driven out of Tigrai by the TPLF.

After the TPLF having defeated the TLF, EDU and *Teranafit*, its confrontation with EPRP that had been brewing at the isolated cadre level, moved to organizational level. In April 1979, war broke out and in a matter of a few days the TPLF drove the EPRP out of Tigrai. The TPLF came to control the entire Tigraian countryside. The EPLF may have been disappointed about the loss of a potential ally, but there was nothing it could do except to continue building an alliance with the rising TPLF. Cooperation between the EPLF and the TPLF became not only possible but essential, with the *Dergue* receiving massive military assistance from its ally, the then Soviet Union, and with a series of offensives imminent. However, close cooperation did not materialize until the point when the *Dergue*'s invasion threatened their very existence.

In 1977, Somalia had invaded the eastern regions of Ethiopia. The Ethiopian military regime was caught by surprise because its attention was on the northern rebels. The *Dergue* decelerated its military engagement against the revolt in Eritrea and the newly emerging rebels in Tigrai. It mobilized against the invasion of Somali forces, which was much easier to deal with by pursuing conventional warfare. It was also easier for the *Dergue* to mobilize Ethiopians regarding the invasion of Somalia than the rebellion in northern Ethiopia. It raised a huge army and secured armaments from its allies in the Eastern Bloc, particularly the Soviet Union. In a series of decisive engagements the Ethiopian army repulsed the invading Somali armed forces. The Ethiopian army's morale was high and after the victory the *Dergue* immediately switched its offensive military force to the northern rebel movements, mainly targeting the Eritrean fronts. For the *Dergue*, the TPLF was not yet a serious threat at the time and it was thought it could be easily squashed on the way to Eritrea.

With the cooperation of the TPLF in Tigrai, the Eritrean fronts made desperate attempts to contain the *Dergue's* massive offensive but were not able to halt it. The EPLF made a strategic retreat from previously held territory and dug trenches in Sahil, in the northern tip of Eritrea. The *Dergue* pursued the EPLF and threatened to break its well-entrenched line of defence in Sahil, where Nakfa was the only town not to have been captured by the *Dergue*. The EPLF army stood firm in the rough terrain in Sahil and repulsed a series of government attacks supported by air power. But it was not clear how long it could sustain this offensive and what the point was of fighting a pitched battle against a force whose material and human resources were far superior. As a result of repeated engagements, the EPLF line of defence was growing weaker with every passing day and towards the end of 1979 it was desperately looking for fresh recruits to replenish its army. The EPLF was in need of support from the TPLF for its own survival and was forced to revitalize the ailing cooperation with the latter. It presented a request to the TPLF for immediate military support and for access to the Eritrean community in western Tigrai to find recruits. The TPLF was willing to cooperate as long as the common enemy was weakened or engaged in Eritrea – an enemy force which could have created havoc had it been deployed in Tigrai. From a strictly military point of view, it was also to the TPLF's advantage to contain and weaken the enemy outside Tigrai in Eritrea, but it did not agree with the static military strategy the EPLF had adopted in confronting the *Dergue's* forces and made this clear to the EPLF. The TPLF decided to offer calculated support that could be called off at any time.

It would have been expedient for both the Eritrean fronts, the EPLF and ELF, to forge an alliance and challenge what they called an enemy of Eritrean independence. Instead, they were tied up in self-destruction and ironically bargaining and even seeking an alliance with their so-called occupiers or colonizers under the auspices of the former Soviet Union and East Germany. In the early 1975 and from a stronger bargaining position, the ELF had proposed a union with the EPLF, believing that it could harness and integrate the then smaller EPLF. The EPLF rejected union and demanded only an alliance or united front whereby both organizations retained their separate identity and independence. As of 1979, the balance of power had shifted in favour of the EPLF when a large number of Eritrean youth, provoked by aggressive treatment by the *Dergue*, had flocked to it. In a new twist of events, the EPLF adopted the policy of union it rejected earlier – a union based on its analysis that the Eritrean field could not accommodate more than one army. The EPLF thus indicated its plan to dominate the Eritrean scene either through 'voluntary' union on its own terms or by using the firepower it now possessed. To accomplish this strategy, alliance with the TPLF was crucial for the EPLF.

Towards the end of the 1970s and at the beginning of the 1980s with the *Dergue* securing the full backing of the entire Eastern Bloc, political events in Ethiopia and Eritrea were changing swiftly, and the TPLF and the EPLF were being cornered on different fronts and needed each other more than ever before. One was looking for support from the other in exchange for what it could offer. The TPLF could provide the EPLF with a much-needed army in its military engagement against offensives by the Ethiopian regime and could also enter into an alliance against the ELF, as mentioned earlier. It could also provide access to the Eritrean community in Tigrai, which the EPLF badly needed, in order to find recruits and economic support. In a planned venture, the TPLF then cooperated with the EPLF in recruiting young Eritreans in Tigrai and opening the border areas for the EPLF army. The TPLF itself was in dire need of armaments, ammunition and training assistance in the short term, and diplomatic support in the long run. It had also had enough of ELF's aggression and one way or another wanted to resolve its conflict with it. In all these aspects, the EPLF now showed a readiness to cooperate with the TPLF.

Unprecedented warm relations and cooperation between the two organizations began in all fields – propaganda, joint military operations, the exchange of information and material, and diplomacy. The EPLF trained and armed thousands of TPLF recruits in its training facilities in Sahil and also instructed its offices abroad to cooperate with TPLF functionaries or even agitate on behalf of the TPLF if cadres of the latter were not available. EPLF's bureaus abroad became stepping stones for TPLF diplomatic missions. The TPLF reciprocated by fighting alongside the EPLF on the Eritrean war fronts. In 1979, when the EPLF decided to chase the ELF out of Eritrea once and for all, it asked the TPLF if it would form a military alliance. Agreeing to the EPLF military blueprint, instantly sanctioned in early 1980, the two organizations launched an all-out offensive against the ELF. The ELF fled to Sudanese border and disintegrated.

In 1982, the *Dergue* unleashed one of its biggest military offensives – known as the Red Star Campaign – against the EPLF. It targeted the EPLF base area of Sahil and so the EPLF turned to the TPLF for help. The TPLF responded positively to the EPLF request for military assistance in the Red Star offensive, not just for its own sake but also for its own survival and to curb the *Dergue*'s campaign before it would roll into Tigrai. With such pressing concerns, the TPLF in that year sent a contingent of three brigades to the EPLF trenches in Sahil. The assistance of the TPLF fighting forces was critical to the EPLF in its fight for survival and the *Dergue*'s offensive was subsequently foiled. That trial of strength and endurance, coupled with Ethiopian leader Mengistu's mistaken desire to 'command the last push' himself, marked the turning point in the government offensive. Without the assistance of the TPLF, this would not have happened and perhaps the fate of the EPLF – and that of the TPLF for that matter – would have been uncertain. In any case, both fronts would have been forced to adopt the guerrilla tactics of the early days.

This warm cooperation between the TPLF and the EPLF seemed promising, but this would change as differences in military strategy resurfaced and ideological divisions came to the fore. Differing points of view on the nature of the Soviet Union, the question of nationality, and the military strategy to be applied for combating the *Dergue* were the most significant points of enduring disagreement. The EPLF believed the Soviet Union's Communist Party (CPSU) to be a genuine party and it saw the Soviet Union as a socialist state, arguing that domestic relations were socialist and there was no exploitation. The Soviet Union's intervention in the Horn of Africa was an isolated misguided foreign policy that could be rectified any time. In general, according to the EPLF, the Soviet Union was a strategic ally of oppressed peoples throughout the world. The TPLF, on the other hand, argued that, after Joseph Stalin, the CPSU had become a revisionist party and the Soviet Union was no longer a socialist state. Instead it had become an imperialist power that oppressed and exploited common people everywhere it set foot. Fundamentally similar to US-led western imperialism, it was in their view a dictatorship of state capitalists that had to be dislodged from its autocratic position by the cooperation of the working classes in every country. For the TPLF, the only truly socialist country at the time was Enver Hoxha's Albania. On this issue, the gap between the TPLF and the EPLF was wide, but the EPLF preferred to downplay it by writing in their journal *Adulis* (1985: 8), 'For all these reasons, the 'social imperialist' nature of the Soviet Union should not be a touchstone that divides Ethiopian organizations and the EPLF into two antagonistic camps'.

On the question of nationalities, the difference was also great. Self-determination of a nationality for the TPLF meant the inclusion of the right to secession. Even after becoming the government of Ethiopia, the TPLF, as a core element of the ruling EPRDF, adhered to its secessionist stand (see Article 39 of the 1994 Ethiopian Constitution). However, for the EPLF, 'The demand for the secession of Ethiopian nationalities has neither an historical nor an economic basis; nor is the extent of the prevailing national antagonism so acutely sharp as to justify it' (ibid.: 4). The details of this position were broadcast on EPLF radio – *Dimtsi Hafash* - in January 1985 on three consecutive days, to which the TPLF responded in March 1985 in a twenty-two-page article under the sarcastic headline '*Abi Zila Nikidmit*' (Great Leap Forward). In it, the TPLF openly but bitterly criticized the position of the EPLF, as if they had been enemies throughout.

On the military front, the EPLF pursued positional warfare. Before 1977, it had used mixed strategies of positional, mobile and guerrilla warfare but after the *Dergue*'s military offensive in 1979, the EPLF army was pinned down in its trenches in the Sahil region of northern Eritrea. Guerrilla and mobile operational warfare was abandoned. The TPLF saw the EPLF's military strategy as fatal to the Eritrean movement. The Ethiopian military regime, having much greater human and material resources under its control, could drain the strength of the Front in positional warfare. The TPLF argued that the confinement of the EPLF to the trenches weakened its ability to mobilize the people and adopt a flexible military strategy appropriate for the struggle. It argued that the EPLF should abandon its positional warfare and, to compensate its shortage of human and material resources, should adopt a mobile strategy of challenging the stronger enemy.

However, these differences were not by themselves the only cause of bad relations and confrontations. The stronger and more experienced EPLF had always expected to impose its will on the younger and less-experienced TPLF, although the latter would not move from its organizational position. This attitude, which provoked and kept alive an uneasy relationship between the two fronts, had already emerged in meetings of both leaderships but since they were badly in need of one another in the face of a common enemy, they suppressed their inimical attitudes and continued to work together. By this stage, the TPLF had developed a large army that would play a critical role in major engagements, such as foiling the *Dergue*'s Red Star Campaign. A development on the other side was the establishment by the TPLF of the Marxist-Leninist League of Tigrai (MLLT) (see Chapter 8). This led to TPLF talking about its 'superior' ideology. It now became obvious that the confrontation was between the elites of the two fronts that both wanted to dominate the political scene and clear their way to power, as events subsequently proved. It was, however, the leaders of the MLLT who appeared to be more provocative than the elites on the other side, as evident from the former beginning to publish polemic articles and generate unrest. They later even released one (in November 1986 in Tigrigna), under the title '*Afelalayatna ab Giltsi Medrek Yekreb*' (Let Our Differences be Public). In their drive to put the TPLF under party control, the founders of the MLLT had begun to question all the organization's existing positions and achievements, including its relations with the EPLF. The motive appeared to be to undermine the then TPLF leadership and provide an alternative.

The organizers of the MLLT were also sowing discord among TPLF and EPLF fighters. They instructed the TPLF's political commissars in the EPLF trenches in Sahil to discuss the differences between the two organizations. Except on matters of military strategy, the additional political and ideological rhetoric had no bearing on the struggle and was irrelevant to the ordinary fighting force and the people. Since the fighters in neither organization had the right to form and express their own opinion, the discussions instigated had nothing to do with enlightenment. Fighters in both fronts were simply supposed to reiterate what they were told by their respective ideologues. Deviation from this norm was fatal. Thus the confrontation was spreading from top to bottom, with each side mobilizing its fighters for its own opportunistic cause.

In these tense circumstances, the withdrawal of the TPLF contingent from the Eritrean trenches was completed by the beginning of 1985. It was a grim time and probably a blow to EPLF morale, since it now had to withstand other *Dergue* onslaughts without the help of the TPLF army. Months later, the EPLF retaliated in a series of harsh measures that infuriated not only the TPLF but also many Tigraians:[91] it blocked the TPLF's only outlet to Sudan through western Eritrea in June 1985, at the time when drought was affecting most of Tigrai and thousands were dying of starvation. This route was the only one used by the TPLF and international aid organizations for deliveries of humanitarian aid to the famine-stricken Tigrai region. The EPLF also unexpectedly closed the popular *Dimtsi Woyyane* (Voice of Revolution), a TPLF radio station operating from EPLF territory in Sahil. These measures were too harsh and too obvious to hide from the public, as had been the practice of the TPLF with questionable measures in previous years. This time, the subtlety of downplaying serious public issues, especially in the eyes of the people whose sons and daughters were suffering to defend the frontlines of the EPLF, did not work and from then on the TPLF was forced to exercise self-reliance in everything it did. It soon mobilized peasants in their tens of thousands to build a road to Sudan and in just three months an alternative route through the rough terrain of Wolkait, southwest of Eritrea, was opened.

In mid-1985, the leaderships of the two organizations held a meeting, ostensibly to discuss and solve their differences. However, they never came up with a solution to the key differences and merely agreed to inform their fighters about the differences, which was a recipe for further confrontation. Both fronts continued their propaganda campaigns against each other in publications and public gatherings. The TPLF/MLLT went further and

91 Tesfay Atsbaha, interview, 25 March 2004

appealed to the Eritrean people to reject the EPLF's path of struggle, which it thought would end up in betraying Eritrean independence. It declared:

> 'These ordinary liberation organizations [EPLF and ELF] could not bring the right solution to the complex situation. They have created a situation whereby the Eritrean people could not mobilize itself to carry on the struggle. ... Therefore, by getting rid of these obstacles, and to establish a new people's Eritrea, it is compelling to create a capable organization, which could give scientific leadership', (TPLF 1979 EC [= 1986]: 289-91).

This declaration was accompanied by a book of 151 pages entitled *Biret hizbi Eritrea kulkul Afu Ayidefaen* (Never Will the Gun of the Eritrean People Hang Down) published in 1986; it argued that only the gun would solve the Eritrean national (independence) question. This was also in response to the Eritrean scholar Tesfatsion Medhanie who, in his book *Eritrea: Dynamics of a National Question* (1986), had proposed a peaceful resolution of the Ethio-Eritrean conflict.

In 1986 also, a booklet entitled *Ye-Eritrea Hizb Tigil - Keyet Wediet* (The Eritrean People's Struggle – From Where to Where, 1979 E.C.) was prepared by the TPLF/MLLT to motivate people to form a 'truly democratic', 'scientific' and 'capable' organization that could lead to the independence of Eritrea. ELF splinter groups, such as *Sagem* and the Democratic Movement for Liberation of Eritrea (DMLE), were offered generous material support in a bid to form an alternative Eritrean organization that would replace the EPLF and could cooperate with the TPLF/MLLT. The TPLF/MLLT leadership went too far in their relations with the EPLF by inviting the latter to open and confrontational ideological debate.

The embittered relations and erratic confrontation between the TPLF and the EPLF lasted for about four years (1985-1988). Had the *Dergue* refrained from exerting military pressure, it is likely that they would have gone to war against each other, as happened later in 1998. Their hostility was a blessing in disguise for the *Dergue*, which gained time. Amicable cooperation not only could have brought down the *Dergue* sooner, but could also have led to more fraternal cooperation between the two peoples who might have rekindled historical relations. Knowingly or unknowingly, they were also the source of additional misery for the two peoples, caught between at least three rival warring factions. In this chaotic situation, the MLLT became the ideological vanguard of the TPLF and came to control further political developments in the region. The EPLF meanwhile prevailed in the whole of Eritrea.

Towards 1988, as the *Dergue*'s strength began to subside rapidly and the road to power became apparent, the two fronts set their ideological rhetoric aside, at least temporarily, dropping all propaganda attacks and accusations against each other. As Gilkes and Plaut (1999: 10) put it, 'Despite this rupture, the imperatives of war continued to drive the two movements back into each other's arms'. The TPLF and the EPLF resumed relations following a four-day meeting in Khartoum and issued a joint communiqué in April 1988 that they would fight the *Dergue* together. Once again relations between the two fronts warmed, as if past confrontations had not led them to the brink of war. They began to hail their renewed relationship not out of principle or sincerity but '...basically because of the dictates of military realities in the face of a common enemy and with the operative logic of 'an enemy's enemy is my friend'' (Aregawi, 2000: 117). The question, however, as to what would happen to both Fronts when that common enemy would have gone remained unanswered. The pattern has prevailed to this day.

Ethiopia and Eritrea under the TPLF and the EPLF Respectively

As the *Dergue* was gradually losing ground, for the TPLF and the EPLF, the bells of victory were ringing, thanks to the thousands of young fighters who had committed their lives to the struggle for change. The alliance forged in 1988 looked as though it would hold at least for the near future. Optimistically, they began to launch joint operations under a joint command. The *Dergue* faced multiple defeats and its strategic initiative seemed to have gone for good.

After a series of joint campaigns, in May 1991, both armies marched on Addis Ababa and Asmara respectively and removed the ruling regime from power. A small EPLF contingent also joined the TPLF on its march to Addis. The EPLF formed the Eritrean Provisional Government in Asmara and the TPLF, together with the junior partners that formed the EPRDF,[92] namely the Ethiopian People's Democratic Movement (EPDM), the Oromo People's Democratic Organization (OPDO), the Southern People's Democratic Organization and the Oromo Liberation Front (OLF), which was not part of the EPRDF, formed the Transitional Government of Ethiopia in Addis Ababa. The former fronts became new governments in their respective domains and assumed different political responsibilities. Now they were confronted with the challenging reality of delivering what they

92 The junior partners were formed by the support and guidance of the TPLF basically in the interest of the later that badly needed the multi-national image to execute its agenda in Ethiopia.

had been promising during the years of struggle – democracy, freedom, rule of law, peace, progress, etc. But concern no. 1 was to retain and solidify their power, which came from the 'barrel of the gun', and was to be maintained by the same means. The EPLF and TPLF signed military accords, after which secretive and dubious cooperation between them continued on the state level.

A study of the pragmatic and sometimes opportunistic relations established during the armed struggle that continued after the two Fronts seized state power in Addis and Asmara in May 1991 would be worthwhile, but the history of their relationship after this juncture falls outside the scope of this thesis. However, it can be said that many problems of the region today are rooted in the immediate past and the events described here.

After the take-over of power in 1991, neither the TPLF nor the EPLF were democratic and both lacked the confidence to accommodate other well-known political forces that had fought against the *Dergue*. It led them to a systematic effort to rule alone, co-opting others, ignoring the civil society forces in their respective countries and denying them a space to operate. They neither sufficiently trusted their own people nor allowed them to exercise basic rights freely or work with similar national organizations. The TPLF after May 1991 began to dismantle all institutions of state power across Ethiopia, which had never been its political domain during the struggle, as its strategic objective was exclusively defined as self-determination for Tigrai. It relied on its Tigraian guerrilla army and its alliance with the EPLF to settle in power and to stabilize the Ethiopian political arena. To that end, the TPLF also had to appease the demands of the EPLF, which extended from the political to the economic domain.[93]

Due to its heavy-handedness, the EPLF created opposition in Eritrea and made the road ahead tough for itself. Splinter groups of the former rival

93 It is interesting to note that the two organizations (TPLF and EPLF) possessed huge amounts of capital that had been amassed partly from the contributions of the people to the struggle and partly from humanitarian aid consigned to famine-stricken population in both areas. As a result of this accumulated wealth, the investment and business firms of the two organizations came to dominate the economic activities of their respective countries, but still the unfair relationship put the Ethiopian economy at a disadvantage. Individual investors found it an uphill struggle to compete with organizations that had state protection and enjoyed tariff and tax exemptions. The Eritrean business community and above all, the EPLF business empire, transferred a huge fortune from Ethiopia for domestic consumption and exports from which Ethiopia could have benefited for its growth. The EPLF had been running a currency market in Asmara and had been exchanging the common currency, the Ethiopian *birr*, for the US dollar at 1 to 7 while the official exchange rate at the time was at most 1 to 5.

ELF emerged in the western lowlands, adjacent to Sudan, to fight it. These regrouping fighters had longstanding ties with the Muslim communities in the lowlands and with part of the Christians in the highlands of Eritrea.

Because of the volatile circumstances both fronts had to face, they were forced, as in the past, to turn to each other for help. Once again, relations between the two organizations became deeply interlinked in the interests of survival and continuity. They were also confronted by an as-yet-unresolved political crisis triggered by the sensitive process of the secession of Eritrea from Ethiopia and the related border issue, the consequences of which have been with us ever since.

Eritrea separated from Ethiopia politically in 1991 but in terms of trade, currency and overall socio-economic activities it remained united with Ethiopia. Generally, the following years showed that the two economies were intrinsically connected. The impotence of party leaders in resolving their differences amicably and the dominance of party economic investments over individual entrepreneurship are responsible not only for the deep all-round crisis the people are facing but also for the fratricidal wars that took tens of thousands of lives. The cause of the wars was presented as a 'defence of territorial integrity' because this was the easiest way to mobilize the people, but this broad and often vague claim is undermining, if not hindering, talks on relevant issues and prolonging the conflict.

Chapter 10

Consolidation of the TPLF: Forging Power through Social Change

Introduction

'Let the masses be conscious, organized and armed' became the TPLF's motto[94] after it had defeated its rival fronts (the TLF, the EDU and the EPRP) in rural Tigrai, and the battlefield was clear for direct confrontation with the ruling *Dergue*. Before engaging in the decisive battles though, the TPLF considered it crucial to regiment the region's people into a manageable setting so that they would adhere to the political discipline required in circumstances of war. After all, the TPLF depended solely on the people for human and material resources to support its costly war project against a regime that had the backing of the Soviet Union. With the Front's seemingly good intentions and the hope that the war would bring an end to their misery, the people had no other option but to adhere to the TPLF's projected aims *sine qua non*. This chapter considers the processes by which the TPLF managed to

---

94 This motto was conducted in a form of campaign that involved most of the TPLF departments and mass associations. It was, to some extent, of a similar kind as the Cultural Revolution of China. After this campaign the TPLF affirmed its prevalence in rural Tigrai.

muster and direct the people in its war efforts that brought down the *Dergue*. It also examines the social-revolutionary measures introduced, ostensibly to transform local society from feudalist bondage, thereby creating a situation of 'movement hegemony'.

Peasant Associations

Two fundamental considerations shaped the TPLF's mobilization and organizational policies. Firstly, the TPLF wanted to isolate Tigrai from the regime and the multinational movements operating within Tigrai. As an organization fighting for the right to self-determination for the people of Tigrai, the TPLF saw it as imperative to claim and realize a *power monopoly* in Tigrai. From the beginning, the TPLF claimed to be the vanguard or true representative of the people of Tigrai. This stand was a basis for creating relations with other Ethiopian multinational movements. Initial discussions with the EPRP in early 1976 collapsed among other things due to the TPLF claim that it was the sole legitimate representative of the people of Tigrai and that the EPRP must endorse this claim if it wanted to operate in Tigrai in a manner that would not jeopardize the TPLF as self-proclaimed vanguard of the Tigraian struggle for self-determination.

In the second half of the 1970s, as described earlier, there were rival organizations in Tigrai competing with the TPLF that wanted to establish primacy. None of the fronts (the TPLF, the EDU or the EPRP) then had been able to impose their will on the people and each was afraid that the rival organization would exploit dissatisfaction. In the districts of Agame and Adwa, where the TPLF and the EPRP operated side by side, and in Shire, where the TPLF and the EDU operated in a confrontational manner, the people felt relatively free to express their opinions and reject policies that they believed did not serve their interests. For the people, the presence of competing organizations at the time was a blessing in disguise, but it aroused the indignation of the TPLF, which worked towards forced retreat of the other organizations.

Secondly, after having seen the Chinese and Vietnamese experiences, the TPLF wanted to organize the people in order to be able to *mobilize and control* them. Experience was gained from studying these revolutions and other countries where protracted armed struggle showed the importance of mass organization in the mobilization of the people and the creation of mechanisms to control and suppress deviants, who were considered to be serving the enemy (the *Dergue*) or rival forces. The insurgent war required, as they saw it, a predictable and passive home front following the vanguard.

At the early stages of the struggle, neither the TPLF nor the EDU or the EPRP were able to call for compulsory meetings of the people. They, instead, used to go to places where people gathered freely for social purposes, such as churches, burial ceremonies, market places and sometimes neighbourhood meetings, and used these as a forum (fora) to explain their goals. Force was never used in these gatherings. Persuasion was the only acceptable method to direct people - as the TPLF and the EPRP had to respect the rights of the people to be administered by the organization of their choice.

During the first one or two formative years, the TPLF was unable to attract sufficient young men and women to enlist in its army. The *shimagles* (or elders), who traditionally speak for the community, approved the TPLF's conduct and the discipline of its army but they cautioned their sons and daughters against its propaganda. Through songs and by way of informal discussions, the TPLF cadres presented themselves as the legitimate sons and daughters of Tigrai, claiming that the other fronts did not belong there. As an oral genre, *Wodi-Tigrai* (literally, the 'son of Tigrai') was used by the TPLF rank and file as the rhetoric formula in its daily encounters with rival elements. The others reciprocated by accusing the TPLF of fostering 'narrow nationalist sentiments' in its members, which was in a way happening, although the others too had their own domineering attitudes.

As the TPLF had no external relationships to generate support, it was totally dependent on the local population for human and material resources, more so than the EDU and the EPRP. The latter two were receiving substantial external support in addition to what they earned from the local population. On top of that, or because of it, the TPLF had to bear the extra burden of mobilizing the people of Tigrai against the state and all the forces that seemed to stand against the self-determination and who leaned towards a strict unitary view of Ethiopia. The TPLF worked hard to prove its slogan 'Vanguard of the Tigrai nation' by developing populist mobilization rhetoric. The struggle to resolve the impasse was complicated by the presence of the EDU and the EPRP in Tigrai. It was, however, during this brief and tumultuous period of competing forces that the people experienced relative freedom of expression and the right to support a front of their choice – a relative freedom which later vanished with the TPLF's domination in the military and political fields. As explained in Chapter 5, the TPLF removed the TLF, EDU and the EPRP from Tigrai between 1975 and 1978 and became the only force in Tigrai opposing the *Dergue*. The line of confrontation in Tigrai came to be between absolute unity, as hailed by the *Dergue*, and self-determination, represented by the TPLF, with lip-service to unity.

The victory of the Ethiopian armed forces over the invading Somali army in 1978 had given the regime respite to mobilize its forces against the movements in the north. Land reform, the successful repulsion of the invading Somali army from Ethiopian territories, and the organization and arming of the people in the towns and cities as well as in most parts of the central region in the South enabled the *Dergue* to wipe out the democratic movements in the centre and muster forces to confront the insurgent movements in the north.

The consolidation of the *Dergue* denied the TPLF its material and human resources in the cities and towns of Ethiopia. The flow of new recruits and the trickle of material support from the urban areas to the TPLF dramatically slowed down. On top of this, the TPLF lost many of its combatants in fighting with the EDU, EPRP and the regime. At the same time, the TPLF had to fill the vacuum created by the removal of the EDU and the EPRP. A combination of uphill undertakings made the struggle of the Front very difficult, and the wars and the hard living conditions even caused desertions among TPLF members to the *Dergue* camp. It desperately needed new recruits to replenish its army and guarantee their continuous flow in the future. The TPLF was to place the burden on the peasant society.

On the other hand, the removal of the rival organizations, the EDU and EPRP from Tigrai created two important conditions for the consolidation of the TPLF. Firstly, EPRP's and EDU's absence terminated TPLF (potential) members' exposure to the propaganda of these multinational movements. The crack in the TPLF's CC that appeared in 1976 on the Tigraian national question remained perhaps because of the fact that the monopolization of power in Tigrai by the TPLF satisfied the secessionist elements in the leadership who wrote the 1976 manifesto. They believed that controlling the people was a step in the right direction and that it strengthened their aspirations. The immediate task therefore became the mobilization of the people for the TPLF cause, which in a way did not contradict their sectarian, if not secessionist project.

Secondly, the confrontation in Tigrai became one between the TPLF and the *Dergue* regime alone. People in Tigrai outside the regime's control lost the right of choice that they had enjoyed when other organizations operated in Tigrai too. Following this development, the TPLF launched a massive campaign with the aim of 'agitating, organizing and arming the people'. With the motto of 'liberation', it became easier and more expedient for the TPLF to coerce the people and put them in the respective organizational blueprints provided by the movement, most of which were reproduced or copied from like-minded liberation fronts or regimes with a similar ideology.

People's associations that had been previously constituted in some form by the EDU and the EPRP were taken over by the TPLF. A series of *gämgams* (evaluation procedures) were carried out to weed out or suppress EDU and EPRP sympathizers. Large meetings were organized with the aim of exposing those who sympathized with the EDU and the EPRP and assessing the depth of their involvement in these organizations. Such procedures of scrutiny went on until 1991. There was an atmosphere of terror for the individuals concerned because their relations with the EDU or the EPRP were made public. Fighters from all the organizations frequently used to visit peasants and spend the night in their houses either to politicize them or to seek food and accommodation. For many individuals, the safer way was to make the necessary 'self-criticisms' and redefine their allegiance even if they did not like it. For others, silence seemed the better choice and they remained undetected, keeping their original views.

The second part of the *gämgam* process was criticism. The chairing cadre or any TPLF sympathizer could direct his criticism against anyone suspected of being a supporter or a member of the EDU or the EPRP. The accused had little chance to defend him/herself. Arguing that s/he had done no wrong being an EDU or EPRP sympathizer was tantamount to admitting a grave mistake. The fate of those who denied their connection to the EDU or the EPRP lay in the hands of the TPLF – they could be set free or sent to prison for further interrogation.

The TPLF-liberated/controlled areas also underwent sweeping changes in social mechanisms or procedures introduced by the Front to organize and control the people. The project of 'agitate, organize and arm the people' was meant for this purpose, and trained cadres (*kifli hizbi*) were placed in every liberated *woreda* (district) to carry out this revolutionary project. Persuasion was replaced by disguised coercion in the name of 'the revolutionary duty for the struggle'. The TPLF organized countless meetings and seminars to convince at least some of the people and in order to impose the will of the movement. The people did not have the right to choose the agenda or pass a decision against the will of the Front. From the beginning, there were people committed to the cause of the TPLF but there were still many others who for one reason or another did *not* establish close relations with it. Their motives for cooperation could be political conviction, their loved ones being in the Front or because they had benefited in some way from the presence of the TPLF. The TPLF used these persons as a stepping stone to organizing the people in various manageable associations and to mobilize them for the war effort.

A policy of organizing the people according to profession, sex and age became compulsory. Peasants were ordered to gather and form a 'mass association', membership of which was obligatory for all peasants in the locality concerned. The constitution was prepared by the TPLF and presented for discussion and adoption as the constitution of the association. Election of CC members to the association finalized the process.

The largest and politically the most important associations were the *peasant associations*. All adult peasants, including women and the upper sections of the youth (young families), were obliged to enlist. With the growth of the TPLF, the consolidation of the mass associations and the subsequent *baitos* (people's council), persuasion was gradually replaced by orders and coercion.

The peasant associations became a mechanism for control and mobilization of the people for the armed struggle. They performed civil administration according to TPLF guidelines, with direct supervision by the *kifli hizbi*. In every *tabia* (village) in the liberated areas there was also a *tabia baito* with all its committees. The *baitos* confirmed all the laws and directives presented to them by the TPLF. The TPLF mobilized the peasant associations as well as other associations to secure confirmation of the rules and regulations and their application by the *baito* organs.

In Tigrai, as tradition dictated, the community elders (*shimagle*) speak for the entire community. The status of *shimagle* was an individual's achievement. People with wisdom, integrity, honesty and impartiality were accepted as *shimagles* in the community and they had a broad role, from settling family and community disputes to resolving armed conflicts. Some *shimagles* had tried to mediate between the TPLF and the regime or the EDU and the EPRP. In the face of such an experienced and deeply rooted institution, it was difficult for the TPLF to steer the peasantry at will. The formation of the peasant associations included young adults and women who were at the same time members in the youth and women's associations, as well as the *shigweyenti* (peasant cadres), who were members of their respective association and became a force against the *shimagles*. The roles of the *shimagles* were gradually undermined by these new structures, to which the *shimagles* rarely belonged. The traditional institution of *shimagles* which had been effectively mediating between forces in conflict thus had to give way to the new revolutionary arrangements.

Land Reform

The land-holding system in Tigrai differed in many ways from that in other parts of Ethiopia, where peasants had often been denied possession of their land and where past emperors had granted large expanses of land to their active and retired officials and soldiers for their service to them and the country. Peasants often had a status near to serfs. As in feudalist systems elsewhere, big landlords, most of whom were absentee owners and not native to the region, demanded from a half to three-quarters of their peasants' annual produce. The landowners together with the assimilated native landlords formed and consolidated what became known in the South as the *neftegna* (warrior, gun bearer) settler stratum and the economic basis of the ruling elite of Ethiopia

In Tigrai, a historic heartland of the Ethiopian state, it was different. Traditionally and until the emergence of movements like the TPLF, there had been two types of land-holding system in Tigrai. One was the *risti* system, in which every Tigraian was entitled to a piece of land by virtue of his/her descent from a common ancestor. *Risti* landholders had the right to pass on their land to their offspring. This land-holding system led to endless fragmentation of the land in northern Ethiopia, and the subsequent division and redistribution of land among heirs led to complex land disputes (cf. Bauer 1985). Parcels of land became smaller and more spread out and land became fragmented to the point that it decreased in productivity because of its size and scattered position.

Moreover, land inheritance brought about litigation over claims and counter-claims concerning land. Land disputes were expensive and time-consuming, with those in government and church positions and rich people being the main beneficiaries, while the peasants were often disadvantaged and found themselves destitute. Those claimants who were in government positions in the urban areas were able to amass more land than their kin. Like the feudal lords, the church also possessed large tracts of land known as *risti-gulti*,[95] a system that excluded many migrant newcomers and minorities. A fair distribution of land under the *risti* system did not appear possible without changing entirely the system of ownership. Putting an end to this system was a popular demand in Tigrai.

Unlike the *risti* system, the second land-holding system, known as *deisaa* (community ownership), was based not on blood relations or descent from the common forefathers of the community, but on membership in the local (territorial) community and taking part in community obligations. Every member had the right to a piece of land by virtue of his/her membership of the community. Land was not inheritable in this system and when a landholder left the community or died his/her land went back to community ownership and would be available for redistribution.

---

95 'As the theoretical owner of all land, the emperor assigned *gults* or fiefs to worthy followers' (Marcus, 1994: 19), the Church as an observant ally included.

Land in the *deisaa* system was redistributed at regular intervals, usually every seven years, to accommodate the needs of young families and newcomers to the community, who often suffered due to delays in redistribution. People in positions of power and influence amassed large areas of fertile land through bribes and promises of money lending for poor peasants. The *deisaa* land-holding system began to lose its initial egalitarian character and gradually fell into the hands of the powerful who managed to control the best land at the expense of others.

Land under the *rist* and *deisaa* systems could not be sold or transferred. Land for Tigraians was not only an economic asset but also a sign of status and a defining parameter of one's identity. It was a 'birth certificate' for an individual and testified to his/her birth in the area. Therefore, in theory if not in practice there were only few landless peasants and absentee landlords in Tigrai. The state and the church, which claimed a third of the land each, did not abuse ownership of *rist* and *deisaa* land. *Riste-gulti* rights were simply imposed on the general *rist* and *deisa* rights.

Emperors and their officials used to grant land as *gulti* to officials and churches, and especially to monasteries for their services and upkeep. *Gulti* rights did not bias *rist* and *deisaa* rights. *Gulti* was also superimposed on *risti* and *deisaa* rights. *Gulti* was also granted to servants of the state and the Emperors in lieu of salary and pension. The *gulti* holder collected taxes on his *gulti* and passed part of it on to the state and retained the rest for him/herself. Any *gulti* holder had the right to demand services and expect gifts from the peasants on that land. This system was abolished in the 1960s by the late Emperor Haile Selassie, but vestiges remained in isolated cases. Only church *gulti* existed at the time of the collapse of the Emperor's reign in 1974.

Many of the monasteries in Tigrai owned large *gulti* lands and the church was entitled to part of the produce of the peasants who farmed the *gulti* land. A minimum of 20% of the peasants' produce went to the *gulti* holder. The monks and nuns in the monasteries did not offer services directly to the peasants except their religious activities as (perceived) guardians of the moral order and worldview, including prayers for good harvests, peace and long life for the Emperors. The vast majority of the people on *gulti* land probably did not even know where the *gulti*-holding monasteries were, let alone benefit from the offerings they made. Every village had a parish church and priests, and a few monasteries offered services in the villages in their immediate vicinity. Generally, the peasants saw church *gulti* as simply unjust.

Unlike the monasteries, all parish churches were supported and maintained by the community concerned. Each church had its hierarchical administration. The *gabaz* (the administrator of the church) could be a priest or a layman and he would organize the church land and other properties. In the countryside, the people allocated tracts of land for the upkeep of the church and for the services of the priests. These particular sections of land were called *rim* and were neither inheritable nor for sale. It was distributed among priests in active service.

Tekeste Agazi (1983: 6) gives a general picture of land holding in Tigrai just before the revolution:

> ...25% of the peasants had little or no land. Those who owned land had very small holdings: 45% had less than a hectare, 23% between half and one hectare and 21% between one and two hectares. A very small group of people, usually those in positions of power, and the church, owned a great deal of land. In addition 25% of the farmers were renting all or part of the land they farmed, and sections of the Tigrean people had no land rights. These included Moslems in certain *awrajas*, some women and immigrants.

In 1975 the *Dergue* proclaimed the nationalization of all land, thus implementing the revolutionary student slogan 'Land to the tiller'. This proclamation abolished all church *gulti* rights and the peasantry on church *gulti* land understandably were then no longer willing to continue to deliver part of their produce to the churches and monasteries. The monasteries thus lost their rights to their *himsho* (a fifth of what was produced on the land) and absentee landlords lost their rights to the land they claimed as *risti*.

Right after the military regime's land proclamation, the peasants in Tigrai wanted it to be implemented, and peasants in areas under *Dergue* control formed committees that redistributed land. However, a few hours' walk from the garrison town of Adigrat, the EPRP also began to redistribute land, a development that created substantial political pressure on the TPLF to move fast in implementing land reform ostensibly to benefit the poor peasants. Later, the TPLF admitted that people's pressing demands for land reform, the *Dergue*'s attempts to mobilize the people on the issues as well as the EPRP's land reform efforts in its liberated areas in Tigrai forced it to launch its own land reform, long before it had trained *cadres* and made the necessary preparations for it (TPLF, September 1977 EC.: 9).

On this issue the TPLF stood, in principle, for the nationalization of land but was lagging behind the *Dergue* and the EPRP in land-reform policy, but when it did start land distribution, it is fair to say that it made it an instrument for mobilizing people who otherwise would have rallied behind the EPRP or the *Dergue*. Thus, land reform was hastily conducted by the

TPLF: not primarily for its own sake but to rally the people behind its war project. The TPLF justified such a policy by rationalizing that the fate and long-term interests of the people depended on the victory of the TPLF's armed struggle.

Land distribution in the liberated areas was thus influenced by the need to make available material and human resources. Firstly, land was granted to people who lived in the liberated areas but were not engaged in farming and were not expected to do so in the future. These people included manual workers, merchants, prostitutes, sellers of homemade liquor, small retailers and goldsmiths. These working-class people and craftsmen generally lived in the towns. Hired labour was also tolerated. Land grants to these people were politically motivated, as these groups would not have been eligible for land under the *Dergue*'s land policy. That privilege they owed to the TPLF and in return the TPLF demanded their loyalty and their contributions in one form or the other.

Secondly, land was used to reward those who supported and contributed to the armed struggle. It was initially declared that land would be divided among families according to their size. For instance, students who went to school in the towns and cities depended on their families, who could therefore claim land on their behalf. The TPLF imposed political criteria to exclude those who were believed not to support the struggle. Land clearly became an instrument for mobilization and surveillance of the people, and access to land was, in effect, under the TPLF's control.[96]

In many *tabias* (village units), land was put aside allegedly for communal use. The people of the respective localities farmed the so-called communal land and passed on produce to the TPLF. This produce from the communal land went either directly to the TPLF or was used as provisions for TPLF-related conferences and congresses of the associations and *baitos*. For example, in 1976 E.C., the peasants of Zana farmed 50 hectares of arable land and handed the produce over to the conference of the *woreda baito* (TPLF September 1977 EC.: 179-80).

The abolition of the land-holding system of *risti* and *deisaa* certainly had popular support among the people. The peasants hoped to avoid the expensive land disputes and court cases of the *risti* system and the delays of

96 This system of land control and using it as an instrument of mobilization and surveillance of the people continued after the TPLF seized power in 1991 in the name of EPRDF. Article 40.3 of the Ethiopian Constitution that was ratified in 1994 declared that, "The right to ownership of rural and urban land, as well as all natural resources, is exclusively vested in the state and in the people of Ethiopia. Land is a common property of the nations, nationalities and peoples of Ethiopia and shall not be subject to sale or other means of transfer."

redistribution in *deisaa* which affected newcomers and young families. The TPLF slogan 'The land belongs to the community/people' was understood by the peasants as communal ownership and not state ownership. It should be noted, however, that in the early stages of the TPLF's struggle, i.e. before its consolidation, the land-reform process was carried out after obtaining the partial consent of the people to distribute land and after the parameters for distribution had been discussed in public. There were, therefore, different land-reform approaches and techniques in different *tabias* and *woredas* at different times. The TPLF could not impose its land-reform policy due to a lack of power and concern about losing the confidence of the people, who at the time had the option of switching their support for the regime in power or the rival front EPRP.

Such an opportunistic and varied land-reform policy had drawbacks. Frequent redistribution of land reduced the peasants' motivation to care for it, and reduced investment had consequences for the future land economy. Whether land reform led to an increase in agricultural production is not clear, because recurring drought had left the land dry and unproductive. Giday Zeratsion, the former TPLF CC member and the late Meles Bezabih, the former TPLF official in charge of agricultural development in 1984 reported[97] that the TPLF's land reform did not lead to an increase in production, but Sibhat Nega, the TPLF CC member in charge of the Socio-Economic Department, disputed this allegation on theoretical grounds, arguing that peasants put more effort into production if the land and the produce belonged to themselves than if they were only tenants. According to Sibhat, the nationalized or state/front owned land belongs to the peasants. He also claimed that an increase in production could have been realized had there been no drought and accused Meles Bezabih of denigrating TPLF policies, for which he was incriminated until he resigned from the organization.[98]

Agricultural development involved not only the change of hands of land based on a fair redistribution but also the introduction of technological innovations, better methods of farming and market opportunities. Without a comprehensive plan to address all the variables associated with land reform, land distribution in itself would not bring about the outcome the people had hoped for. The liberated territories in Tigrai were isolated from the urban areas and the peasants therefore had no market possibilities. Farming methods and equipment were archaic. The very limited veterinary services and rare credit opportunities previously provided by the state were

97 The report of Meles Bezabih was presented at a TPLF CC meeting in 1984 at Akmara in the presence of author of this book.

98 Interview, Giday Zeratsion, Oslo, 16 March 2004.

discontinued, and the TPLF was not in a position to provide an alternative since its main preoccupation was the war effort against the *Dergue*.

Both the drought and the war obviously had a negative influence on production, but to put the blame solely on these factors, as the TPLF CC did in 1985 during the MLLT founding congress, would be wrong. Firstly, the forms of tenancy, which did not encourage farmers to work hard for limited years, were not abolished in the liberated areas because land was granted to almost everyone, including those who were not engaged in agriculture.[99] Secondly, the fact that land was distributed and redistributed at short intervals discouraged the peasants from investing in it. Since the peasants were unsure whether the land would belong to them in the coming years and could not give it the necessary care, its quality deteriorated. The influence of the TPLF land policy on agricultural production was therefore minimal.

Land reform, however, indirectly helped produce a big number of fighters for the armed struggle. Almost everyone in the liberated area had a claim to a plot of land, which generated a sense of equality among the people. But to actually receive it and retain it depended on the consent of the TPLF. It used land as a positive and negative incentive in mobilizing people for the war project. Land and its management was thus a crucial link between the people and the TPLF's strategic aim.

Women's Organization: A New Phenomenon

From the beginning, the TPLF recognized the importance of organized constituencies in the protracted armed struggle. As a matter of principle, in the national struggle no social group was to be ignored and each was expected to contribute something in the fight. Women were seen as the most oppressed section of society in Tigrai and indeed their oppression was multi-faceted. During the initial period of the armed struggle, mobilizing and organizing them was difficult and slow. The first woman fighter, Kahsu (Martha), joined the front some eight months after the struggle started. The male-dominated cultural attitudes in Tigraian society that confined women to the house, coupled with the nature of the guerrilla movement, hindered the TPLF from enlisting women fighters and forming women's associations.

But the need to mobilize women's associations appeared when village elders – together with the wives of militia men – exerted pressure on the militia to allow them to reduce the amount of time they were expected to spend caring for their families. In Tigrai, a parochial society, it was difficult

---

99 According to the report of the Foreign Relations Bureau of the TPLF (1979: 10), over 2.2 million Tigreans became 'owners' of land.

to address women's issues in public because when the TPLF conducted propaganda work among assembled groups of people, the women were either not there or could not express their opinions in the presence of their spouses. The TPLF was thus forced to form separate forums for women to expose them to its propaganda.

The few educated women fighters who had already joined the Front focused on this problem. The male and female cadres of the TPLF in the mass mobilization bureau gradually succeeded in organizing women at various levels, and the female fighters became part of the peasant women's community. In the beginning it was difficult for the village women to even differentiate between male and female TPLF fighters as their hairstyles, footwear and clothing were similar. The female cadres had to uncover part of their clothing to show the peasant women that they too were women like them. They also worked in the kitchens, fetched water, gathered firewood with the village women and together attended local cultural ceremonies at which the Front's political programme was presented. As insiders, they were able to mobilize the women and, consequently, the whole family and the community.

Another factor that facilitated entering the women's domain was the monkish behaviour of the TPLF fighters. Sexual contacts between the fighters and between fighters and peasant women were prohibited. Sexual violence, which was rampant in this semi-feudal society, was declared a crime punishable by death and from then on, peasant women had no reason to fear offences such as rape by male fighters. Equally, the male peasants had no reason to question the faithfulness of their wives and daughters when they lived and worked with male fighters. The confidence of peasant women in the male fighters thus increased dramatically.

A growing enthusiasm emerged among the women about their new rights, something that had previously been unheard of. They got the chance to discuss social issues in public which had hitherto been a male domain. It was also new for women to communicate with the authorities and present their own cases themselves. The presence of the women cadres increased the confidence of the women in the community and the communication between the people and the TPLF. In the past, women had been represented in public places like courts by their husbands or male relatives and acquaintances. Now, they could represent themselves in a real sense. Women became not only entitled to seek justice on their own account but also to dispense it. Aregash Adane, the female member of the TPLF's CC confirmed that 'In the *baitos* [people's assemblies] they share the activities on an equal basis with men. Their number is more than 30% overall. This is good, considering the backwardness of the culture' (quoted in Hammond 1989: 136). This achievement was a revolutionary step forward that uprooted the former male chauvinist culture and the women were grateful to the TPLF for these new rights. Some even composed songs of praise and encouraged entire communities to sing with them. Youth and children saw their mothers' attitudes towards the TPLF and followed suit.

In addition, women were beneficiaries of the TPLF's land policy. Unmarried or widowed women received land and women were entitled to a half of the family's land if divorced. Land reform made them economically independent of their husbands and marriage, which had previously been arranged by the family, became a voluntary association. Women in the small towns who lived off retail trade, the sale of homemade beverages and prostitution were all given land. Most of these women were victims of the *risti* and *deisaa* land systems and, as women, it was difficult for them to claim and share land in the old system. They had fled to the towns in the grim hope of being able to keep their alive. The right to land under the TPLF land policy was more than an economic benefit for them: it was recognition of their human rights and made them equal to men. They perceived this newly won right as the social justice they had been denied for so long.

TPLF cadres organized political seminars for selected women at the *tabia* and *woreda* level. Many of those who absorbed the political training were helpful in forming and mobilizing women's associations. As of the 1980s, these were set up in many of the *woredas*. Women played a part in all community activities as administrators, judges and assembly members. And as they became economically independent, their support for the TPLF grew steadily. The TPLF women's associations became a strong force in the TPLF's campaign to oppose early marriage for girls because it was women who had been suffering in many ways from the widespread practice of child marriage in Tigrai.

The old system of socio-economic and gender suppression changed, and victims could now hope for a better life. Family relations became more open and were based on a free choice of partners and no economic subordination. These new liberties aroused enthusiasm and many women became fulltime campaigners for the TPLF as their participation in all fields of public life grew steadily.

With progress in the armed struggle, however, the rights and aspirations of women in the liberated areas had to endure many ups and downs. As more and more men were enlisted in the army, the number of marriages in the liberated territories dropped dramatically. An article in the TPLF constitution that forbade sexual relations between fighters and between fighters and the civilian community was extended in the 1980s to include married spouses, if one or both of them was a TPLF member. Those men who joined the TPLF leaving their wives and children at home were not allowed to see their families. In this way, the TPLF annulled all existing marital contracts between fighters and between the community and fighters.

Many young women in the liberated areas were in a dilemma. Some wanted to go to the urban areas to look for a better life, while others wanted to join the TPLF army. But both options were unrealistic in the circumstances. The TPLF prohibited the movement of people, especially young women, to government-occupied cities and towns but it could not accept all the women who wanted to join the TPLF army. It argued that the army could not absorb everyone who applied for enrolment without reducing its fighting capacity, a position that was unacceptable to women in and outside the Front.

The mobilization of women was effected mainly by the TPLF women fighters. They were over-represented in the cadres, the department responsible for the organization of the masses. In 1983, the TPLF decided to place the women fighters in a separate organization in order to tackle the growing dissatisfaction among women in the liberated areas. It was supposed to take over formal leadership of the Women Fighters Association (WFA). At that time the women in the liberated areas were threatening to resort to demonstrations for their rights and for equality. The new committee was chaired by Aregash Adane, a social work graduate and then a CC member. The motive for organizing the women fighters in a separate organization was to centralize the mass association of women in the liberated areas.

In line with this, the TPLF also established two schools for women, called 'Martha' and 'March 8'. The first was exclusively for female TPLF fighters, the second was for women fighters and civilian women cadres in the Front's mass associations. The establishment of these schools in 1983 was part of the process of creating the Tigrai Women's Association under the control of the TPLF.

The project of bringing the women associations directly under the TPLF structure was a reverse of a prior promise that the local mass association of women would be organized on their own in zone, regional and higher levels and would remain independent. The TPLF wanted to subordinate the women's mass associations to the direct control of the TPLF fighters' association. This denied women their rights to an independent association so it was an uphill struggle for women fighters like Aregash Adane and the male fighters who supported their cause.

The TPLF leaders, especially after the take-over of the MLLT, argued that the rights of women were achievable only after the victory of the ongoing revolution. All women's activities had to be subordinated to the armed struggle and the congress passed a resolution condemning feminism in the TPLF.

The extensive organizational network of women nevertheless became a formidable force in the war against the regime. As of 1984, the women's associations were put under the WFA of the TPLF. Massive campaigns were set up to mobilize and control women in the liberated areas. Women made up about a third of the TPLF army and hundreds of female peasant cadres were engaged in organizing the people and mobilizing resources for the army. The TPLF provided young women in the associations with texts for songs that praised those young men who joined the TPLF and humiliated those who did not.

There were also attempts by the TPLF to train women to replace men in the production process. Men and women peasants worked together on their farms as well as at home. But there were special tasks exclusively for men and for women. Ploughing and threshing remained the exclusive domain of men, while cooking was a task for the women. The TPLF was worried about a possible decrease in agricultural production because more and more young men were joining the TPLF. It therefore wanted to train women to take over the male role of breadwinner in their families. But this was an ambitious task, which required good planning and the technological support that would replace the enormous burden the women had to shoulder both in the house and outside. The project was abandoned because of the looming protests of the people.

The Youth: Cadres and Cultural Troupes

The TPLF's first recruits were students and young civil servants from the towns and cities, where Tigraian nationalism sprouted in the wake of the 1974 revolution. The wanton measures of the *Dergue* regime contributed to this flow of youngsters. As Merera Gudina (2002: 171) wrote: 'The massive military repression, especially the unleashing of the 'Red Terror', became the unintended catalyst to drive the Tigrayan youth to the TPLF side'. The peasantry was not concerned with Tigrai's relations with the rest of Ethiopia. There was only a small non-Tigraian minority living and working in Tigrai and there had never been any conflict between Tigraians and those from outside Tigrai. Some of the peasants who were trained by the EPLF dropped out immediately after they returned to Tigrai.

Nevertheless, the TPLF was able to establish good relations with the people, based on the respect the TPLF showed them, their liberation from local bandits by the TPLF and the TPLF's efforts to dispense justice in civil disputes, which had been rather inaccessible and expensive for the people under preceding regimes. The people accepted the TPLF mainly because in comparison with the situation under the previous regimes, it made their lives more peaceful and had put an end to the *shiftas* who lived by plundering them. However, there was little commitment by the people to the wider goals of the TPLF, and the rural youth (as opposed to the urban youth which was inspired by revolutionary ideals) showed limited interest in joining the TPLF, a situation that continued until 1979.

In due course and for a number of different reasons, the TPLF began to face a shortage of new recruits. The *Dergue* obtained political, diplomatic and, above all, military support from the Soviet bloc and consolidated its power in the administrative centres of the country. Fighting the *Dergue* appeared impossible for the peasant youth. The major multinational opposition organizations lost hold in the cities and towns under the impact of the Red Terror Campaign (1977-78). The flow of recruits from the towns to the TPLF also declined and at the same time the TPLF lost many of its fighters in wars against the EDU, the EPRP and the *Dergue*. The growth of the TPLF army slowed markedly in 1978-1979.

In addition, the TPLF was emerging from its 1978 internal crisis, which the leadership attributed to the 'petty bourgeois nature' of its rank and file. Many fighters were implicated in the crisis, imprisoned and, in some cases, killed. A significant number deserted, fearing for their lives. The TPLF desperately needed new sources of recruitment and was only left with the option of mobilizing the peasant youth. The TPLF tried to recruit as many peasants as possible to neutralize the student-dominated army and after the drastic decrease of the flow of new recruits from the towns, recruiting peasants became a question of life and death for the TPLF. It thus launched a systematic campaign to mobilize the youth to its cause.

Part of this was a new demographic policy. It pressed the *baitos* to increase the allowed marriage age, which was accordingly raised as high as 26 for men and 22 for women. In some *tabias* (villages, hamlets), marital status was the main criterion for claiming land, while in others, age was one of the criteria. In effect, land determined marriage because it was the main economic base to establishing a family. In *tabias* where age was a criterion, young adults below the age level could not marry because they could not support themselves and their families without land. Delaying marriage meant young people had to wait longer to get land. The TPLF had ample opportunity to manipulate the youth who were trying to get married and get land, or get land to get married. Family responsibilities prevented men from staying away from their homes and their land for a longer period of time. Fathers had to earn to support their families. But delaying marriage left the young adult without a family to look after. The fact that young unmarried adults did not own land meant they could not produce and save for the future. Thus, the young adult was separated from family and land, their only means of production. These two factors were the most important ones that tied Tigraian peasants to their home and their land.

After isolating the youth from family and land, the TPLF launched a campaign of organizing *youth associations* throughout the liberated areas. It was conducted in such a way that resisting appeared tantamount to 'betrayal of the nation of Tigrai'. The youth associations became the instruments for engaging the youth in logistical tasks and became the breeding ground and preparation for joining the TPLF's army.

The TPLF used many instruments to attract the youth into joining the army or even pressurize them to do so. One such instrument was the organization's cultural troupe, codenamed 01, which had special branches for the regions. The cultural troupe toured the *woredas* and *tabias* to 'agitate' the youth and the cadres organized cultural events for them. After each scene, one of the cadres called out a slogan such as 'I shall fight for Tigrai', 'Let us stand for our rights' and 'I will join the TPLF army!' The entire group had to repeat it. This was interpreted as a declaration of intent to join the army. The *kifli hizbi* used such pronouncements to humiliate those who failed to enlist in the TPLF as 'opportunist'.

Another method of arousing the youth was that of selecting slogans that appealed to the manhood of each young adult. At the end of every youth mass rally, the cadre called out slogans designed to encourage the youth to join the TPLF. Such slogans included: 'The hero for his land, the coward for his belly!' The selected slogans were echoed from among the youth. The TPLF usually assigned selected youngsters to work in their respective associations before they were sent to the training centres. Since this arrangement was secret, the new recruits pretended to speak on behalf of the youth.

Discussions in the youth associations and other youth gatherings revolved around the armed struggle. Other issues of youth and community had no place in the discussions and policies and those who raised social and economic issues were viewed as traitors to the Tigraian cause. One of the methods the TPLF used to mobilize the youth was drama. Those who had joined the Front, including those who promised to do so, were portrayed as 'the true heirs of the heroic forefathers', and the others were branded as the 'humiliation to the people and history of Tigrai'.

TPLF efforts to mobilize the youth were successful. However, as the number of peasant combatants overtook those from the cities and towns, the effect was that the majority of the combatants now were illiterate. This became a handicap for the TPLF, as it became difficult to find enough literate combatants for the ever-expanding communication and command posts. The Front tried to satisfy the demand for literate combatants by training young combatants in its training centres. These combatants were selected to fill gaps in units such as radio communication, unit commissars, mass organization and foot doctors. Alongside this, a literacy campaign was waged in all units and departments of the organization, but the need for literate combatants was still not satisfied.

In a further endeavour to boost its army, the TPLF turned its schools in the liberated areas into political and literary training centres. Initially, the schools were established by the TPLF and financed by international aid agencies and Tigraians in the Diasporas but faced with the total closure of all state schools in the liberated territories, campaigning against the deterioration of education conditions was required. The peasants sent some of their younger children to school but the older boys and girls were needed to help in the farms. Therefore, the schools served the younger children, and only seasonally did the young adolescents attend classes.

There were not many qualified teachers in the liberated territories. Those who had taught in the state schools in these areas either fled to the towns or joined the TPLF or other movements. The TPLF gave political and academic training in its training centres to men and women in the liberated areas with some educational background. These trainees were then assigned to schools as teachers. By 1985 there were about 674 TPLF-trained teachers and 58 primary schools with 19,800 pupils (TPLF 1978 E.C.: 138-39). But this still did not solve the immediate needs of the TPLF.

Its motto that all human and material resources should serve the interests of the war project was applied to the education system. As of 1983, the Front changed the schools' admission policy and only young men and women who could be called up to join the army attended school. The schools became political and educational training centres for TPLF departments and army units.

To intensify its propaganda work, the TPLF established a boarding school in 1983 for selected young and fresh recruits as well as the younger members of the army. Students in these schools could be placed in TPLF army units or departments at will. By 1985, there were about 2,000 youngsters in boarding schools (ibid.: 140) that were mainly run by TPLF combatants and where training was intensive and comprehensive. Young combatants were however also admitted to these schools to increase their academic capabilities in general.

Alienated from land, discouraged from establishing families, denied the right of mobility, forcefully organized and controlled by the TPLF, bereft of any perspective and life outside the TPLF, the Tigraian youth saw their predicament as a corollary of ethno-national oppression as they were mobilized to shoulder the brunt of the armed struggle in Tigrai. It was this situation that helped the TPLF army to grow against all odds.

'Neutralizing' the Church and Mobilizing Muslims

The Church

A combination of factors made relations between the TPLF and the church difficult. Firstly, the Ethiopian Orthodox Church had been at the centre of the villages' social life for centuries. Weddings, christenings (baptisms), burial rites and mediation in conflicts between neighbours all took place via the church, and there were substantial numbers of priests in every parish who performed church services. Each household had a priest as its religious 'father' who took care of the spiritual life of the family and was called for special life-cycle events to give his blessing. In every community the Church was connected to each household in this way.

Secondly, the church constituted a link between the people and the state. It had always stood on the side of past emperors, who furthered the existence, expansion and unity of the Ethiopian Church. It was organized hierarchically from the village to the national centre and as an embodiment of spiritual and socio-cultural life. The institution of the church had always played a crucial role not only in community life but also in mediation between rival forces and even between the state and rebels. The church taught its followers to respect their allegiance to the Ethiopian state and was, in effect, a school for national consciousness, using national symbols such as the flag in all religious and social events. No church ever conducted major ceremonies without hoisting the Ethiopian flag – an act also regularly observed in the Ethiopian army.

Thirdly, the church was the core legitimizing body for any emperor who ruled over Ethiopia. It had been a tradition in Ethiopia that emperors had to be anointed in Mariam-Tsion, the Holy Church of Aksum in Tigrai. They repaid the support of the church by granting *gulti* land to monasteries. The monasteries and the *gädams* then claimed at least a fifth of the produce of the *gulti* land.

The local people were also allocated land for the upkeep of the church and priests were compensated for their services. Land was the most important incentive and encouraged many young men to invest time in going to church schools to become priests. All priests in active service in a parish received *rim* land for their services. The administration of the land and the church was in the hand of a *gabaz*. The *gabaz* could be a priest or a layman selected by the community and approved by the church.

After the collapse of the monarchy and the military takeover of power in 1974, the state-church alliance came to an end. The *Dergue* proclaimed socialism and nationalized all church land. *Abune* Tewoflos, then the patriarch of the Ethiopian Orthodox Church, was imprisoned and later murdered by those in power. By 1975, the church was cornered by the Marxist military regime, the left-wing armed struggles and the national movements in the north. The church initially saw hope in the Ethiopian rightist movements, especially the EDU, which was involved in armed resistance in Tigrai and Gondar, but nothing ever materialized.

The pragmatic TPLF understood the church's role in village social life and its support for the unity of the country. It also understood a possible alliance between the Church with forces that stood against socialism and nationalization of the land as well as against separatism. The church was viewed as a force standing in the way of the TPLF but one that should be handled with caution. The TPLF had never been anti-religion as such, although its Marxist ideology called for that. Nevertheless, there was no doubt that that it wanted to subordinate the church to its cause.

The TPLF therefore took a series of coordinated steps to neutralize the church's influence. The first was, to uphold the *Dergue's* measure of nationalization of church land, which denied the church its economic power and frustrated hopes of resurgence among the rightist multinational movement in Tigrai, such as the EDU. The centuries-old economic status of the church was broken and it was forced to enter into new social contracts with its followers. *Gulti* land was no longer controversial and, as far as the *rim* was concerned, the peasants saw it as a fair compensation for parish priests for their services: the nationalization of *rim* land met resistance not only from the church but also from the community. During the first phase of land distribution, many localities refused to distribute *rim* land. Threatened by mass resistance, the TPLF tolerated the continued ownership of *rim* land in such localities and in fact used it as a means of justifying its recognition of the importance of the church.

The second step was to try and move the socio-economic focus of life from the church to the *people's assemblies.* All administrative and social activities were taken over by the associations and the *baitos* and even church affairs such as the rights and obligations of the church and its followers fell under the jurisdiction of the assemblies. The capacity of the church to mobilize and influence the people waned. The church lost its status as mediator in conflicts, rights over spiritual and familiar issues because the new political authorities did not support it.

Thirdly, the TPLF launched a series of conferences or 'seminars' for selected parish priests in 1979 to win them over. The underlying motive of the seminars was to isolate the church in Tigrai from the wider Ethiopian church in order to foster Tigraian nationalism along the lines of the TPLF's strategic objective. Suppressed Tigraian nationalism was invoked to challenge the dominant Ethiopian Orthodox Church. The initial *woreda* seminars for priests were conducted by an eloquent TPLF fighter, Gebre-Kidan Desta, a graduate of the Theological College at Addis Ababa University. The themes of the seminars were to replace the Ethiopian Church's authority by a TPLF-minded church and the language in the church with Tigrigna and, ultimately, to further Tigraian nationalism and identity.

This process involved the mobilization of parish priests and ordinary Christians to isolate them from the church's national hierarchy. To weaken church authority, an intelligence group was formed under Sibhat Nega to infiltrate the well-established monasteries in Tigrai, such as Debre Damo, by planting TPLF members camouflaged as monks and influencing church activities in the interests of the TPLF.

In 1987 and 1989, regional and national conferences for priests were organized by the TPLF in liberated territories to reshape the Tigrai Church in line with the TPLF's programme. A separate secretariat of the Orthodox Church was formed in the liberated areas of Tigrai and was supposed to operate under TPLF guidelines. Practically, the Ethiopian Church was divided in two separate secretariats, one under the regime and the other under the TPLF. Both worked in Tigrai until 1990, when the TPLF overran Meqele, the capital of Tigrai. The regime's secretariat fled Meqele for Dessie and the secretariat in the liberated territories entered Meqele and operated there until the TPLF seized state power in 1991.

Muslims

Muslims in Tigrai constituted a substantial minority. Although an earlier estimate stated that 'Tigray is 70% Christian and 30% Muslim in broad terms' (Hammond 1989: 102), the 1994 National Census data concluded that the number of Muslims was 4-5 % (CSA 1998: 132). In traditional Tigrai, Muslims had less chance to acquire land than Christians and were discriminated against. Most of the Muslims specialized in trade and handicrafts and today the Muslim community in Tigrai controls a large part of the business and service sector of the economy. Consequently, the majority of Muslims in Tigrai live in towns. Those in the countryside were engaged in farming, retail trade and handicrafts and lived in small settlements all over Tigrai. There was little intermarriage with the Christians and as the kingdom was exclusively Christian, the Muslim enclaves were under constant harassment by the authorities. Muslim settlements remained relatively unchanged for centuries although mobility was possible from one settlement to another or to the towns. In most cases, Muslim weavers who worked in Christian areas could not get land for dwelling and workplaces and had to find shelter and work space from their Christian hosts.

The Muslims in Tigrai did not shed any tears following the collapse of the Christian monarchy in 1974. Both the regime's land proclamation and the TPLF's land policy in the liberated areas were a milestone achievement for Muslim highlanders in the struggle for equality and a better livelihood. Under the TPLF land policy, the amount of land granted to individual households depended on the number of mouths each household had to feed. Boundaries were redrawn between neighbouring villages and *woredas* to balance relations in neighbouring localities, and the hitherto isolated Muslim enclaves could now claim more land.

Muslims in towns in the liberated areas were not entitled to own land because like other town dwellers they were not engaged in agriculture. Only those involved in farming received land. But the TPLF granted land to most people in the towns, including Muslims, to win support. The claim to land and its possession was a source not only of income but also of prestige and status.

The TPLF avoided involvement in several thorny issues raised by the Muslim community. One was marriage under *Shari'a* law. Many Muslim women raised the issue of unfair marriage and divorce practices in Muslim society in Tigrai in the women's associations in which both Muslims and Christians participated. The TPLF avoided the issue by indicating that they would tackle the problem in the future.

The participation of the Muslim community in the mass associations and *baitos* increased dramatically and many Muslim women assumed leadership positions in the associations. This was indeed experienced as a step forward and the TPLF saw the long-oppressed Muslim community as a readily available ally in the struggle and invested time and effort in mobilizing them. To make the Muslim community feel that they were well-represented in the TPLF, many Christian combatants adopted Muslim names. Participation of Muslim youths in the army was also growing as the struggle progressed.

The People's Council (Baito): Reconfiguration of Local Administration

In the Imperial era, the absence of effective, accessible and affordable civil administration in the countryside was the most important issue for the peasants in Tigrai. The administrator, the police chief and the chief judge constituted the three most important state representatives in the *woreda,* which was made up of a district of seven to fourteen *tabia* (villages). These state organs were not in a position to provide the necessary services for the people in the entire *woreda.* For many, they were neither accessible nor affordable and those who sought justice had to finance the court costs themselves. Distance was also a problem: most people had to walk a day or more to see a judge.

In addition, in most of the remote areas organized bandits reigned over the people. They terrorized the local people at night and state officials during the day. And in remote villages like Shimelba, strong bandits such as Alemshet Tewolde even effectively ruled during the day. State officials sometimes had a tacit agreement of coexistence with the leaders of the bandits, and they often mediated between bandit leaders and the state. It was not uncommon to see a one-time bandit leader later occupying a state post in Tigrai. Towards 1978, the TPLF through an extensive campaign, had brought an end to banditry in rural Tigrai. It had called on the bandits to lay down their arms and return to civilian life or join the TPLF. Many complied and surrendered their arms to the TPLF and those who defied the call were hunted down by TPLF units, supported by the peasants.

As soon as it liberated territories from government control, the TPLF formed local administrations at the village (*tabia*) level and the people elected a committee to replace the abandoned state organs. They adopted a constitution (*sirit*) with the support of the TPLF and the committee appointed a 'village keeper' (*kodere*) from among the people. The *kodere* was responsible for getting all sorts of provisions (food, drink, donkeys for transport and individuals to carry fragile materials) from the people for TPLF units or individuals with a TPLF mission whenever they came to his *tabia*. The TPLF militias usually served as police and liaison officers between the TPLF leadership and the assembly.

TPLF cadres organized and supervised the local administrative organs, the core institution of which became the *baito,* the 'people's council'. Initially, the basic organs were the *firdi baito* (tribunal), the chairman of the *tabia* assembly (the hamlet or village meeting), and the militia. For the first time in rural Tigrai, justice and administration became accessible and free to all, as individuals were able to obtain justice in their own neighbourhood without having to travel long distances or pay court fees. Moreover, decisions by the *baito* were subject to reconsideration if flaws were detected and when the TPLF cadre, usually the *kifli hizbi*, found it necessary. Whenever disputes arose between *tabias*, a mass gathering was called at which village shimagles took centre stage and the kifli hizbi was the moderator. Cases were settled by general consensus.

As the TPLF managed to defeat the rival organizations and push them out of Tigrai in contested areas, the people were confronted with either the TPLF or the *Dergue*. They did not have a choice as to who ruled over them: it was decided by means of fire power. In the semi-liberated areas where the *Dergue* and the TPLF ruled alternately, the TPLF formed assemblies. When the regime's forces intruded, the TPLF assemblies suspended their work and their officials either went underground or retreated to the liberated areas. Where the regime recaptured a town and reinstated its administration, the TPLF *baitos* moved their seats to the surrounding countryside and continued to operate. The *baitos* in such zones, for example Sheraro and Idaga-arbi, were prone to attack by the *Dergue*. The regime targeted the *baito* officials in particular and the communities often became engaged in pitched battles. Many of them lost their lives and property, and still others had to join the Front as fulltime fighters.

The recurring shifts in authority in the towns and villages had long-term repercussions for the rights and mobility of the people in the areas involved. On the one hand, people's livelihoods were constantly being destabilized and their mobility hampered by the war situation. On the other, each side demanded absolute loyalty from the people under its control in fighting against what they both called 'the enemy'. The limited freedom the people had because of the presence of rival movements operating in the same area was slowly being eroded by the military situation. In the final resort, the TPLF prevailed in large parts of Tigrai and began to act as a quasi government, with Tigrai becoming almost a separate state.

The TPLF's guiding motto, 'Let the masses be conscious, organized and armed', dominated all socio-economic and political life in the liberated areas of Tigrai. Existing structures and authorities were consolidated and were assigned new tasks, as we saw in the case of the village assembly, restructured and renamed the people's council, the *baito*. This institution existed in traditional society (see Aberra 2000: 45) as an elected local assembly of tax-paying, land-holding people and authority figures, but underwent changes. It became the assembly through which local people were organized and expressed political decisions guided by the TPLF. The *baito* was an assembly based on membership from a number of villages and hamlets (*tabia*), and from the district (*woreda*) was extended to a zonal (*zoba*) level. The *baito* was the central organ in a structure of local units.

The figure below presents the structure of the *baito* as created by the TPLF.

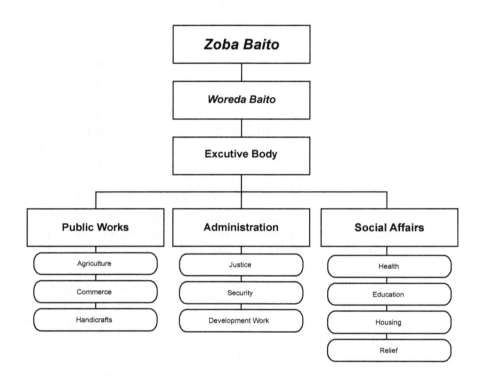

Figure 7.1 Structure of the *Baito*

The TPLF brought together all the *tabia* mass associations to form *woreda* mass associations. Representatives from the *tabia* associations created the respected *woreda* mass associations and it became easier for the TPLF to mobilize and control the associations. The organization of the mass associations at *woreda* level was the final step to setting up the *woreda* people's assembly, the *baito*. A *woreda* assembly was formed by a founding congress composed of delegates from the mass associations in the respective *woreda*. 'In this manner, *baitos* were created in 33 *woredas* and 3 towns' (TPLF 1978 E C.: 73). Several *woreda baitos* convened at zone (*zoba*) level when the TPLF deemed it necessary. *The Zoba Baito* was guided by the Mass Organizations' Department in the TPLF's politburo.

The *woreda baito,* alternatively called the People's Revolutionary Assembly or Council, consisted of the committees for public works, administration and social affairs. The committee for administration was entrusted with the task of ensuring the security situation in the area and assigned patrol groups at strategic spots to monitor enemy movements. The members of the patrol group were usually unarmed peasants working in shifts, and all able-bodied adults took part in this activity.

Militia forces, known locally as *woyenti,* were reorganized at the *zoba* (zone) and *woreda* (district) levels as a defence and combat force of local communities. The TPLF promised members of the militia and other cadres in the mass associations that the people in their respective localities would be able to farm their land and take care of their families when they were away from home on organizational missions. The *baito* administrative branch carried out this pledge. For example, Senayt Adhanom, a peasant woman from Sheraro, stated: 'I have no oxen but because my husband is a fighter, I got them from the people' (quoted in Hammond 1989: 78). The militia engaged the enemy sometimes on their own and sometimes alongside the TPLF regular army units, while other functionaries in the mass associations spent more of their time on organizational activities.

Due to concerns about intelligence leaks, people were not allowed to move about in the liberated areas without a pass. With instructions from the security section, the *tabia baitos* were responsible for issuing these permits and any individual who wanted to travel from one *woreda* to another had to obtain a valid written permit with the TPLF seal on it. Failure to do so would result in the subject being placed on a suspect list as an enemy agent.

The public works (or economic) committee of the *baito* procured material resources for the armed struggle. The committee mobilized and coordinated people to farm communal land and land that belonged to the TPLF. It organized the harvesting of produce on this land, campaigned for fundraising on behalf of the TPLF and was one of the instruments for regulating trade and collecting taxes for the TPLF.

The justice department constituted the *woreda* court. It took care of civil peace and adjudicated in civil disputes between community members. Resolution of all civil disputes in communities was entrusted to this section of the *baito.* The TPLF, through its cadres, supervised the performance of the committee and now and then called public meetings and scrutinized the activities of the justice committees. People who felt they had not received justice could present their grievances to a court headed by community elders (*shimagle*) and the TPLF *kifli hizbi* who had the final say on all matters.

The TPLF recruited and trained thousands of cadres from the areas under its control and from all sections of society, the majority of which were with peasant background. These cadres were known as *Shig-weyenti* ('torch bearers of the revolution'). The individual *Shig-weyanay* operated in his/her own association and in the *baitos*. Through those cadres, the TPLF was able to control the activities of the *baitos* and the society at large. In the first instance, they were constituted by delegates from the mass associations in which the *Shig-weyenti* were active members. TPLF cadres also led and controlled the mass associations and since the *Shig-weyenti* had direct contact with the TPLF, they were informed as to what was at stake and given directives on how to respond accordingly.

The tasks of the *baitos* were to implement the TPLF's war policies and were organized in such a way that they could generate the maximum contribution to the movement's project. TPLF control of the *baitos* was mainly from above, as the structure indicated, and through its directives, while the mass associations were the means of mobilizing and controlling the people. Their representatives were pooled to form the *woreda* people's assemblies, ending up as a TPLF department as in government bureaucracy.

The *baito* was elected by the people directly and according to some observers 'independent of the TPLF' (Hammond 1999: 82), but that was just rhetoric. Hammond could have noted that, as the TPLF itself had stated ((TPLF 1978 E.C.: 73-74): 'The *baito* is the foundation of the future people's government and would be led by the dictatorship of the workers, poor and middle peasants, using the principle of democratic centralism'. To make sure the formation of the *baito* and its subsequent activities did not contradict its ideological and political line, the TPLF conducted 'assessments' (*gämgäm*) and 'rectification (*tsereyet*) among the people, the associations and future *baito* candidates as part of the consolidation process. In the course of years, hundreds of peasants were accused of collaborating with the enemy or of acting against the armed struggle. Many were interned and others were killed. Members of the CCs of the associations and of the people's councils who were not in favour of the TPLF were purged.

The continued allegiance of the members of the *baitos* was assured by the TPLF's principle of democratic centralism, originally a Leninist tenet combining party democracy with strict hierarchical methods of execution of party decisions. The TPLF's organizational work was controlled at all levels according to this principle of democratic centralism. Deviation from TPLF policies and directives by any association or assembly was practically impossible and dissidents were subject to recall by their respective associations. Even a unanimous decision by the *baito* assembly had no validity if it went against the interests of the TPLF as determined by democratic centralism.

The TPLF could dismiss the entire assembly or have all its members recalled by their organization.

The TPLF's authority in the liberated areas thus took hold. No rival ethnically based or multinational movements were operating in Tigrai by 1978. Every member of society was organized in every possible way on the basis of age, sex, occupation or religion. With the establishment of the *baitos* in most of the *woredas*, the TPLF became a quasi government and Tigrai almost a separate state. TPLF slogans became decrees and its propaganda was strictly observed like a law. The main programme was to win the war and all activities and human and material resources had to be mobilized for this aim. The mass associations and the assemblies (*baitos*) basically came to function as appendages of the TPLF. They could not independently serve the people that they represented by putting pressure on the TPLF, an organization they called *Widebna* or *Wideb*. The mass organizations thus inevitably became tools of the TPLF.

Chapter 11

Turning Point: The Fall of the *Dergue* and the Triumph of the TPLF

Introduction

In this chapter I discuss the end game of the military confrontation of the TPLF with the *Dergue* regime since the mid-1980s to 1991. This will be accompanied by a brief assessment of the conduct of the TPLF elite in its initial moments in power, and which are a direct reflection of the history of the movement presented in the previous chapters.

Sapped by its efforts to control and rule Ethiopian society by force, thereby isolating itself from its own people, the *Dergue* faced mounting defeats at the hands of the insurgents in Tigrai and Eritrea. It reached a stage where it could only make moves to buy time. The two fronts, the TPLF in Tigrai and the EPLF in Eritrea by the mid-80s had become large and competent enough to challenge the government army, then one of the largest in Sub-Saharan Africa, in conventional warfare. Mustering a huge quantity of weaponry, including T-55 tanks and heavy artillery captured from previous engagements with the *Dergue*, both Fronts were poised to bring the war to its final stages in 1990. The OLF's less spectacular activities in the southwest and the simmering opposition of the Ethiopian people in general had also caused the *Dergue* to falter elsewhere in the country.

The *Dergue*'s own terms of engagement, military confrontation, did not help in the face of the thrust of the insurgent movements, as it has lost its domestic legitimacy and made the ordinary people weary from the violence, the lack of democratic governance and the continuous 'sacrifices' to be made. The fronts were encouraged and supported by most of the local population as they advanced towards the centre of the country, the last stronghold of the military regime (cp. Young 1997; Hammond 1999; Kassahun 2000). As in late 1990-early 1991 the *Dergue* failed to come to grips with the insurgent attacks, there was intervention of foreign powers to mediate for peaceful transition of power, but that was too late to save the *Dergue* from defeat. The TPLF and its junior partners constituting the EPRDF, seized power in May 1991, and the TPLF elite, dominating the scene, began to implement policies that would shape the future of the country.

Ethnic mobilization evidently enabled the elite of the TPLF to build its force and dislodge the well-established *Dergue* regime, but the ethnically mobilized populace in the North was not in a position to influence the new power holders. The dominant posture of the TPLF over the guidance of the struggle, as discussed in previous chapters, continued to prevail after it seized power. This in turn has created a new relationship between the political elite and the people on the one hand and between the new power holders and Ethiopian people in general and between them and the country's ethnic groups in various states of mobilisation on the other.

The Dergue Falters[100]

In 1987 of the twenty-five combat divisions the *Dergue* commanded, thirteen – including two mechanized divisions – were deployed in Eritrea. According to a TPLF military intelligence report of February 1987, this force then constituted 71,500 men and was called the Second Revolutionary Army (SRA). It was classified into four *Ezze* (commands) with three to four divisions under each *Ezze*, out of which the *Nadew* (Demolish) *Ezze* led by the revered General Tariku Ayne was the strongest. It was based in Af-Abet, facing the steep Nakfa hills where the EPLF's pronged trenches were located. 'Even though the operation in Eritrea was headquartered in Asmara, Af-Abet was actually the command centre and the largest military garrison in Ethiopia with the heaviest and most sophisticated armaments' (Dawit 1989: 364). *Nadew* was entrenched in the strategic terrain of Af-Abet, between the

---

100   This became the overriding view not only of the insurgent movements but also of the ordinary people, foreign observers including the regime's own army officers and rank and file.

Sahil lowlands, the EPLF's strong-hold, and the more populated highlands under the control of the *Dergue*. The other three *Ezzes* were dug in at Keren (not far from Af-Abet), Asmara and the port of Massawa. All were in a defensive position, appearing to have lost the will to fight.

As the army was losing ground every day to the EPLF, the Commander-in-Chief of the Ethiopian Armed Forces, president Mengistu Haile-Mariam, visited Af-Abet in early February 1988, 'allegedly to boost the morale of the soldiers but intent on punishing those responsible for the failure' (Gebru Tareke 2004: 249). On 15 February he ordered the execution of General Tariku and the demotion of General Kebede Gashe, commander of *Mekkit* (Challenge) *Ezze*, and many other high-ranking officers. The execution of General Tariku Ayne caused great distress and panic in the entire armed forces (Dawit Shifaw 2005: 180; Teferra 1977: 286; Dawit 1989: 365).

The EPLF then saw that the moment to strike was ripe. A month after the execution of General Tariku and following the shockwaves this had sent through the armed forces, the EPLF launched a condensed attack upon Nadew *Ezze* at Af-Abet from 17 to 19 March 1988. To the shock of every *Dergue* officer, the strategic garrison town of Af-Abet fell into the hands of the insurgents. Major Dawit (1989) described the scene as follows:

> In less than 48 hours, rebel forces numbering only 15,000 overran 30 miles of defence line, destroying an elite force of close to 100,000. … Over 5,000 troops surrendered to the rebel forces; 10,000 were killed; thousands crossed the border to Sudan, and the rest ended up in Keren where they were stopped by pleading officers and cadres. Lost to the rebels were over 50 Soviet-made T-55-tanks, several 'Stalin Organ' rocket launchers, artillery weapons and trucks in the hundreds, thousands of small arms, millions of rounds of ammunitions … In an effort to regroup, Mengistu ordered the evacuation of all troops in Tessenei, Agordet, Barentu and Marsa Teklai. Thus the rebels got control of almost half of Eritrea in one 48-hour battle, and were now equipped with the latest Soviet weapons (ibid.).

Owing to the government army's organizational failings and the determination of the insurgents, Af-Abet fell into the hands of the EPLF. One Ethiopian army Major-General Fanta Belay observed then that: "…the fall of Af-Abet was the secession of Eritrea" (cited in Teferra 1997: 286). This prophecy would come true in a couple of years but not immediately. The *Dergue*'s rearguard was still intact, which enabled it to prolong the war, so something was needed to deplete its resources and support there if it was to be defeated for good. The *Dergue*'s rearguard access vis-à-vis that of the TPLF and its impact on the theatre of confrontation – the fronts of both warring forces – had until then been affecting the war in favour of the former (see Chapter 6, section 'Debate over military strategy').

Next to developments in Eritrea, the TPLF was active in its offensives in Tigrai, seizing town after town from the government army. At this point, the TPLF and the EPLF were still at loggerheads (from 1985 until early 1988) and coordination by consent was not possible. The *Dergue*'s dismal situation, however, prompted the TPLF to go for a major offensive. The Shire-Enda Selassie operation once again had to be repeated. Had there been amicable relations between the EPLF and the TPLF and with unarmed anti-*Dergue* forces who were involved in invisible sabotage and offensive actions from the rear, the *Dergue* might have collapsed much earlier.

Shire is the western district of Tigrai and was where the TPLF was founded and began its armed struggle. The TPLF had cultivated strong popular support in this region, which extended up to Dejena in Wolkait and across the Tekeze River, and its major base area where it had established training schools, medical centres, firms and a radio station. The district capital, Enda Selassie, had been a town of contention between the *Dergue* and the TPLF since Mussie, the TPLF's first commander, was incarcerated there in July 1975 and set free in the young Front's very first operation. Ever since, the *Dergue* had kept an eye on this region and on Enda Selassie in particular. A number of offensives in the form of *zemecha* (campaigns) directed at destabilizing, if not annihilating, the TPLF had been launched from Enda Selassie over the last thirteen years, but none had been able to prevent the TPLF from gaining strength. The TPLF was now preparing to upset the balance forever. The *Dergue* was compelled to fully focus on the TPLF. 'Hitherto, it [the *Dergue*] believed that the defeat of the EPLF would lead to the easy eradication of the other armed groups. Now it concluded that without the elimination of the TPLF, the Eritrean rebellion could not be extinguished' (Gebru 2004: 257). The TPLF's military activities beyond Tigrai into the neighbouring provinces of Gonder and Wollo on one hand and the blockage of land transport between Addis Ababa and Asmara on the other would naturally result in the consideration of a strategic shift, but appeared to be too late. By then, the TPLF had reorganized into seven divisions, its manpower estimated at 56,000 (ibid: 260), and was supported by mechanized brigades and artillery units in addition to thousands of local and militia forces.

In April 1988, the *Dergue* established the Third Revolutionary Army (TRA) by combining its forces from the provinces of Wollo and Gonder. A month later, it declared a state of emergency in the whole of Tigrai, with

Sergeant Legesse Asfaw, a person no less ruthless than Mengistu, as Chief Martial Law Administrator. With its headquarters in Meqele, the capital of Tigrai, the TRA launched several campaigns to regain strategic heights and towns relinquished to the TPLF. From June to August, the TRA's 604 Army Corps moved to recapture the towns that had surrendered earlier and managed to do so. But after being attacked at Dansha it was forced to retreat in disarray to Enda Silassie. It was during this campaign, on 22 June 1988, that Legesse ordered the aerial bombardment of Hawzien. This attack, conducted by helicopter gunships and MiGs, resulted in 1,800 civilian deaths, the worst single atrocity of the war since the start of the ELF insurrection in 1961 (De Waal 1991: 258).

TRA efforts to maintain its supply line between Eritrea and Tigrai were frustrated by the defeat of its contingent at Rama on 29 September 1988. While the TRA was expecting a joint operation with the support of the SRA's 10th Division, the TPLF captured Dabat in January 1989, thus controlling the road to Gonder. Not knowing where and when to confront the rebels, the TRA moved to regain towns in central Tigrai in early February 1989. However it was caught by surprise in the hills of Selekhlekha and swiftly retreated to its trenches, breaking the chain of command.

In its final attempt to prevail over the region of Shire, the TRA moved its headquarters to Enda Selassie and regrouped, under its command, divisions from the 603 and 605 Army Corps, the entire 604 Army Corps and the 103rd commando division. With this huge concentration of forces, it was able to regain towns southwest of Shire, like Dabat and Debark on the way to Gonder, in early February 1989. This concentration of forces was part of the TPLF's plan to upset the stalemate by launching a major offensive.

In the event of posturing to launch a strategic offensive and snatch the initiative from the enemy, both the TPLF and EPLF calmed down their bickering momentarily as before, opened their eyes again for rapprochement and met in Khartoum. 'The two fronts resumed cooperation in 1988, but not on such close terms as before the breach of relations in 1985' (Tekeste Negash and Tronvoll 2000: 20). More than anything else, their dream was military victory and amid the incessant battles, the renewed relationship was going to serve them well, albeit for a short time and for a limited objective.

Four divisions of the *Dergue*'s army – the 4th, 9th and 16th divisions and the 103rd commando division – had congregated in and around Enda Selassie, occupying the commanding heights of Mt Qoyetsa, Mt Atarit and Mt Dembelailay, all of which are above 2000 metres. The decisive assault on the concentration of the TRA corps in Enda Selassie began on 15 February 1989 by making flank attacks on positions in Selekhlekha, 30 km southeast and on the commanding heights. As Hayelom Araya, the TPLF's cardinal commander put it, 'The strategy of the rebels was to hit the isolated units piecemeal first, seize the strategic heights, and then cut off the two divisions from their main headquarters at Indasilase, encircle and demolish them with one concentrated attack' (in Gebru 2004: 265). That was exactly what the insurgents did in Shire-Enda Selassie, but it was not an easy battle. Fighting raged on three main flanks of the enemy when two EPLF mechanized brigades came to support the TPLF and tilted the balance in their favour. It was a vital contribution but did not bring the battle to an end. 'Still, the unit refused to budge, effectively directing its tanks, artillery, ... Unable to break the impregnable defence, the guerrillas shifted the line of attack' (ibid.: 267). Yet, as Young (1997: 164) observed, 'The presence of the EPLF brigade represented both the result in tangible form of the recent unity agreement and the TPLF's continuing weakness in the sphere of heavy artillery'.

The perseverance of the insurgents, coupled with the flexibility of their tactics, disoriented and demoralized the TRA's fighting spirit. They surrendered the commanding heights one after the other. Gebru (2004: 268) describes the scene:

> Pandemonium turned into fright when the command and control centres of the Corps and 4th Division were hit almost simultaneously, precipitating the breakdown of the chain of command. In the ensuing confusion and turmoil, over 200 trucks as well as armoured cars rushed south towards Gondar with some guerrillas hard on their heels. The 604 Corps had crumbled. The TPLF had prevailed.

Finally, on the afternoon of 19 February 1989, the battle of Enda Selassie came to an end and, according to Gebru and Young, '...close to 12,000 *Dergue* soldiers were killed or taken prisoners' (ibid.: 269, 1997: 164). During a mop-up operation on the way to Gonder, two generals – Addis Agilachew and Hailu Kebede – were found dead. They had presumably committed suicide.

The immediate effect of Enda Selassie was unexpected even for the TPLF, which had started up operations with limited numbers of men and needed time to reorganize its forces for the following phase. The next day, the *Dergue* withdrew its forces from the towns of Humera and Adigrat to Gonder and Meqele, the capitals of Gonder and Tigrai respectively. A week later, on 25 February 1989, a dramatic evacuation from Meqele took place. All government officials, accompanied by 20,000 troops, hurriedly left Meqele bound for Dessie, the capital of Wollo Province, south of Tigrai.

Within a week, no traces were left in Tigrai of the government army. 'In February 1989, a victory at Enda-Selassie by the TPLF left it in control of the whole of Tigrai', (Clapham 1991: 465). The people of Tigrai were spared further ground onslaughts but the aerial bombardments continued. Tigrai was 'liberated' as the nationalist leadership of the TPLF had envisaged it would be, but this did not mean the end of the war.

President Mengistu Haile-Mariam, the Commander-in-Chief, was in a state of shock and his regime was disintegrating. He immediately forged a team to investigate the fall of Enda Selassie and in his directives, Mengistu lamented:

> A huge army has fallen, scattered or surrendered within days and hours in a manner that is beyond belief. Quantities of weapons and property that will profoundly impact on the unity and survivability of the state have fallen into the enemy hands. It is no exaggeration to say that this lamentable [episode] will occupy a disgraceful place not only in the history of Ethiopia's struggle, but also in world military history. We are now in a situation where it is impossible to predict what the eventual outcome will be. (in Gebru Tareke 2004: 269-70)

It was not impossible to predict the eventual outcome after the SRA's defeat at Af-Abet in March 1988 and the collapse of the TRA at Enda Selassie in February 1989. The two strongest armies of the regime, the TRA in Tigrai and the SRA in Eritrea were in irreversible retreat. The balance had shifted in favour of the insurgents and the government army had been forced from an offensive position into a defensive strategy. The situation in the *Dergue*'s camp was aggravated by the retreating troops that were spreading waves of fear. One part of the defeated army, which was not under any chain of command, was estimated to be about 6,000 strong (ibid.: 268) and was spreading panic as it retreated to the provinces of Gonder and Wollo, where it was forced at gunpoint by commanders to stop, regroup and fight back. But the *Dergue* was already in hot water. Released POWs from previous battles had spread news of the resoluteness of the rebels and the inevitable expansion of the war into the central provinces. Some of the POWs had even joined the TPLF to fight the military regime. On 12 January 1989, a former senior navy lieutenant, Dawit Shifaw (2005: 195), who was re-indoctrinating 4,475 freed POWs in Tatek Military Base near Addis Ababa, wrote:

> Another war that the Tigraian rebels were waging at this time was releasing the prisoners of war in thousands. ...They [former POWs] told me that after listening to the indoctrination of the

TPLF in prison camps some of the POWs voluntarily joined the
rebel forces to fight against their own government.

This reflected the state of mind of the *Dergue* army after fourteen years of
protracted war against the rebels and, even more so, the retreating defeated
troops. To make matters worse, Legesse put the blame on the commanders
and sent many to prison for failing to win the battles in Tigrai. Mengistu
showed no mercy when dealing with them. 'Such irrationalities of Legesse
and Mengistu annoyed most of the Ethiopian generals who attempted to
overthrow the dictator on May 16, 1989' (ibid.: 201).

The Descent of the Dergue and the Ascent of the TPLF

This coup attempt was another blow struck at the centre, this time from the
generals of the *Dergue*. On 16 May 1989, Mengistu Haile Mariam flew to
the German Democratic Republic (GDR) in an attempt to acquire more
weapons. As usual, high-ranking generals and ministers were at the airport
to see him off. Immediately after Mengistu took off, the generals headed
straight to the Ministry of Defence and executed what appeared to be a
well-planned change of leadership in a *coup d'état*. The meeting was well
represented by top generals from every branch of the armed forces. The
former Commander of the Air Force and, at the time, Minister of Industry,
Major General (M/G) Fanta Belay, the Minister of Defence M/G Haile-
Giorgis Habte-Mariam, Commander of the Air Force M/G Amaha Desta,
Chief of Staff of the Armed Forces, M/G Merid Negussie, Chief of
Operations, M/G Aberra Abebe, Commander of the Ground Forces, M/G
Hailu Gebre-Michael, Commissioner of Police, M/G Worku Zewdie and
the Commander of the Navy, Rear-Admiral Tesfaye Berhanu met and began
discussing the details of their plan to dethrone Mengistu. It looked as if they
had been waiting for this moment, but as it proved later on it was not well
organized. Two hours later, they found themselves surrounded by Mengistu's
special guards. It so happened that the Defence Minister, Haile Giorgis, was
among Mengistu loyalists and he had some how slipped out of the meeting
only to reappear with Mengistu Hailemariam's aide-de-camp, Captain
Mengistu Gemechu and No. 2 Chief of Security Tesfay Wolde-Selassie who
led the elite force to abort the *coup d'état*. Incidentally, in the shoot-out, it was
General Haile-Giorgis who became the first victim and died instantly. M/G
Amaha Desta and M/G Merid Negussie took their own lives on the spot.
The *coup* failed miserably and the other plotters were either killed or taken
prisoner. General Kumlachew Dejenie, Deputy Commander of the SRA,

who stayed outside the meeting in Addis Ababa and M/G Demissie Bulto, Commander of the SRA in Asmara, made efforts to reverse the situation but it was too late. Mengistu's confidantes were after the rebellious officers. Mengistu himself called off his visit and arrived in Addis Ababa on 18 May 1989 and continued the hunt for the plotters and their associates. According to Mengistu, in Asmara alone, '11 generals and 27 other officers were killed while 7 generals and 133 other officers were detained', (Dawit, 2005: 218). The Ethiopian army was badly impaired as it had become evident that the onslaught continued not only from the side of the insurgents but also from within its own hierarchy, which was equally damaging.

The soldiers retreating from Tigrai had been forced to regroup in Dessie and Gonder for some months in the grim hope of fighting back. The *Dergue* was rushing in soldiers who had been forcefully conscripted into the demoralized army in an effort to stop the advancing TPLF fighters, who were now more highly motivated than ever. The TPLF's motivation, however, had a downside to it: some of the fighters began raising the point of fighting outside Tigrai, a rerun of their previous ethno-nationalist orientation that focused on the liberation of Tigrai. Just a year before, their leaders had been bent on this idea and were agitating for the fighters to follow suit. In its propaganda for the year 1979 E.C. (1987/1988), which was prepared by Meles Zenawi and Abbay Tsehaye, the TPLF had declared that every member of the League (MLLT) and the Front had to take part in a campaign 'to avoid the confusion created in the relationship of the ethno-national question to the Ethiopian revolution and rectify the de-motivating view to the ethno-national question' (TPLF, 1979: 2). In this campaign, the entire TPLF membership had been encouraged to embolden ethno-nationalist consciousness as opposed to a pan-Ethiopian vision. Now that it had to fight the *Dergue*'s vast rearguard, which had hitherto been ignored because of the prevailing ethno-nationalist view, the TPLF leadership was confronted with the daunting task of 'de-agitating' its forces while pursuing the strategy of decapitating the *Dergue* from behind – a strategy it adopted only reluctantly. To advance this strategy, early in 1989 the TPLF had forged the Ethiopian People's Revolutionary Democratic Front (EPRDF), out of organizations it helped to form. These were the Ethiopian People's Democratic Movement (EPDM), a splinter group of the EPRP, the Oromo People's Democratic Organization (OPDO) and the Ethiopian Democratic Officers' Revolutionary Movement (EDORM). The last two were created from among the POWs taken by the TPLF.

In the months of March, April, May and June 1989, the TPLF in liberated Tigrai while the *Dergue* forces in Dessie and Gonder outside Tigrai were reorganizing and beefing up their forces for imminent confrontation.

The TPLF's aim was to advance to central Ethiopia to the rear of the *Dergue*, while the *Dergue* was keen on recapturing its positions in Tigrai. Amid resounding rebel victories, the *Dergue* intensified its forcible recruitment of youth from schools, markets and the streets across the country and after a short training programme deployed them to the fronts. Such hasty and irrational planning was an act of desperation and was not able to help the army regain its morale or fighting power and stop the advancing TPLF. Nevertheless, there were a number of engagements triggered by the drives of both sides to gain more ground before the main offensive commenced.

It was at this time that the TPLF rank and file began raising questions about fighting outside Tigrai. The whispering campaign spread, recalling the ethno-nationalist agitation of the leadership, and many fighters began running away from their regiments to their villages. The reactions of civilians in some towns outside Tigrai were not encouraging either. 'In response, some 10,000 fighters virtually spontaneously withdrew and returned to Tigrai' (Young 1997: 166-67). The leadership had to halt its movement south of Tigrai and reorient the fighters because they, as Ethiopians, had the duty to get rid of the enemy anywhere in Ethiopia – a task which was ridiculed for many years but without which the victories in Tigrai could not be sustained. Parallel to this reorientation, the TPLF leadership deployed squads to hunt for those who ran away from the war front, forced their parents to hand them back and put some of them in jail. The situation was brought under control following these measures.

By the end of July 1989, the TPLF had taken the initiative again and launched its offensive outside Tigrai on two prongs, the Dessie and Gonder fronts, following the mountainous central highlands that stretched all the way to Addis Ababa. The choice of that route was of immense tactical advantage. Militarily, it reduced the effect of the *Dergue*'s air superiority and also forced the enemy into engagement outside its trenches and away from its supply lines. By now, the TPLF also had a political edge over the *Dergue*. The local people had been at loggerheads with the *Dergue* for a number of years, and were therefore in favour of the insurgents who were presenting themselves now not as TPLF but as the EPRDF (Ethiopian Peoples Revolutionary Democratic Front) that had recently been forged precisely for this strategic purpose. Six TPLF divisions, namely Alula, Aurora, Agazi, Maebel, Mekdela and May-Day, each with roughly 3,000 combatants including about 400 fighters from the EPDM were deployed on the fronts. Stretching from Wollo to Gonder, the *Dergue* on the other hand had five divisions (the 3rd, 4th, 7th, 17th and 25th) with up to 15,000 soldiers in each. Because of the intensity of the war and the heavy casualties on both sides, the number of troops fluctuated, at times dropping abruptly until fresh recruits and reinforcements arrived.

With the TPLF/EPRDF on the offensive, fierce battles raged in the mountains and gorges of Wollo and Gondar. From September 1989 to May 1990 there were running battles. Places such as Nefas-Mewcha, Guguftu, Ataye, Mahil-Meda, Lemi, Kimer-Dingay, Debre-Tabor, Alem-Ketema and Meragna witnessed heavy fighting, and in almost all cases it ended in defeat for the *Dergue*'s forces. Yet, in the Battle of Meragna that lasted for three days in early June, the *Dergue*'s 3rd Division had the upper hand and inflicted damage on the TPLF. Seare Mekonnen, commander of the TPLF Aurora Division recalls:

> We were once pushed by the 3rd Division to a point where we could not even retrieve our wounded comrades. *Meswaetinet* [= 'sacrifice', 'martyrdom' A.B.] became a daily scene. The enemy encircled us and caught some of our fighters. Finally with the arrival of Alula [TPLF Division] to our side, we launched a counter-offensive and destroyed the 3rd Division and captured its commander Colonel Sereke Berhane. We also found our dead comrades soaked in blood after they were tied and pushed down a steep cliff. (*Woyeen*, 1990: 3)

Such was the frenzy and cruelty of battle. The *Dergue* undoubtedly fought resolutely at this battle but, finally, the tactical manoeuvrability and endurance of the insurgents determined the outcome. According to Commander Seare, his Aurora Division had 3,000 fighters while the *Dergue*'s 3rd Division had 15,000 soldiers (ibid.), a ratio of 1 to 5. But what mattered in such encounters was not the sheer number but the will to fight and the ability to endure hardship. In his report to the Ethiopian Defence Minister, Brigadier General Abebe Haile-Selassie confirmed that the tactical excellence of the insurgents was beyond doubt.

> The bandits had effectively utilized the guerrilla [Maoist] stratagem. For instance, to strike at Debre-Tabor they pulled together all their forces from the Wollo Front. To launch an attack at Weri-Elu and Alem-Ketema they left South Gonder empty. To destroy the Lion 3rd Division, they amalgamated all their forces in Northern Wollo and Northern Showa. ...We saw this repeatedly and should have pondered over it.[101]

101 The report of Brigadier-general Abebe Haile-Selassie is cited in the book *Teraroch Yanketekete Tiwled (Amharic)*, Mega publishing enterprise, 1989 E C., p. 193.

In the eyes of the general, the 'bandits' had become a menace not only to the army under his command but also to the national military government itself. Following these events, the port of Massawa fell into EPLF hands in 1990, while the *Dergue* was expecting attack on Keren after Af-Abet. By the end of March 1990, the TPLF rebels had seized Bahir Dar, the biggest town in the province of Gojjam, which was also an air base from which the *Dergue* flew its sorties to Tigrai and Eritrea. Now the remaining fighter planes had to be moved to Debre Zeit, southeast of Addis Ababa. The whole army was in retreat, with some of the retreating troops having reached Wollega Province, south of Gojjam and west of Showa.

Futile Peace Talks

Pressed by the advance of the insurgents to the seat of his government in Addis Ababa, Mengistu Haile Mariam took a U-turn in ideology and in the political line he held. He had seen the Soviet Union, his main backer, turning to a non-Communist path the year before. With the Cold War coming to an end and the US emerging as the only super power, he was left with no choice but turn to the West. In a national speech on 5 March 1990, he declared that socialism would not work in Ethiopia and his party, the Ethiopian Workers' Party, should be changed to the Ethiopian Democratic Union Party (EDUP). This was clearly a message, if not an act of rapprochement, aimed at Western powers. His calculation, understandably, was to at least neutralize the West, which had directly or indirectly backed the insurgents during the Cold-War era. It was also a conciliatory call to the people who were suffering under his dictatorship. He even sent out emissaries to contact political organizations previously banned by his government, like the EPRP and groups of former TPLF members. Five factions of the ELF were also contacted in Khartoum, Sudan but these last-minute peace efforts were never taken seriously by any side, as the *Dergue* was near collapse.

With the Italians as mediators, peace talks began in Rome towards the end of 1989 between representatives of the TPLF and the *Dergue*. Parallel talks were also going on between the *Dergue* and the EPLF, but none came even close to bearing fruit, simply because their positions were irreconcilable and there was no culture of peaceful engagement for reaching a settlement acceptable to both sides. In addition, the insurgents saw no point in negotiation with the *Dergue* so close to collapse. In his conversation with Paul Henze in early April 1990, the EPRDF leader Meles Zenawi (1990: 16) said, 'We think the *Dergue* is too weak to be a partner in serious negotiation. The same is true, I think, with respect to the EPLF. The *Dergue* has to be eliminated. We cannot compromise with it.' While President

Mengistu was delivering his nationwide speech of mobilization for a final showdown on 19 February 1991, EPRDF forces were closing in on Addis Ababa. Mengistu portrayed himself as emperors Tewodros and Yohannes IV, who would fight to the last for what they believed in, only to escape days later by helicopter to Nairobi, Kenya on what was supposedly a visit to a militia training centre in the south of Ethiopia. Finally, on 21 May 1991, Mengistu showed up in Harare, Zimbabwe, where he requested asylum. The Council of State immediately called an emergency meeting and appointed Lieutenant General Tesfay Gebre-Kidane as acting president and Tesfaye Dinka as prime minister. Abandoned by their Commander in Chief, there was nothing the new leaders, and for that matter the entire army, could do. The new leaders hoped for a negotiated end to the catastrophe and an immediate ceasefire. What could a rump government do in the face of a mighty force? All indicators from diplomatic circles, NGOs and local and foreign journalists showed that they were prepared to surrender.

The US, which had been following events in Ethiopia closely through former President Jimmy Carter who was mediating between the two sides in his role as head of the Carter Centre, now assigned its Assistant Secretary of State for African Affairs, Herman Cohen, to mediate at a conference in London. The warring forces, the TPLF, the EPLF and the OLF on the one hand and the *Dergue* on the other, were invited to peace talks that could have allowed a smooth transition of power. However, given their track record and with all parties having settled matters so far with the gun, it was futile to consider a peaceful settlement at the eleventh hour. Giving the platform of peace talks only to the armed contestants, while opposition groups who chose a peaceful path of struggle were marginalized in negotiating the transition, was a short-sighted exercise. This approach of settling conflicts or the transition of power only emboldened armed groups instead of civilian power. No wonder then that the London peace talks impacted negatively on future events in Ethiopia.

On 27 May 1991, the day the London conference was to convene, EPRDF forces completely surrounded Addis Ababa and other contingents marched further south and reached Jimma and Gambella, deep in the southwest. In the capital, the army commanders had no control of their troops, who started roaming around in groups. The doors of Alem-Bekagn, the capital's main prison, were opened and prisoners could walk free. The acting president, General Tesfaye Gebre-Kidan, was in contact with Robert Houdek, chargé d'affaires at the US embassy in Addis Ababa, to hear about developments at the London talks and seek advice on how to act amid the deteriorating situation in Addis Ababa. The London talks were more of a bilateral and consultative exercise between Herman Cohen on the one hand and the other parties on the other, with the TPLF and the US suddenly appearing to be on better terms. 'To any honest observer', Tesfatsion Medhanie (1994: 110) noted, 'there was something strange in the cordial relations between the US and the EPRDF, which, till some time before the talks, was espousing the Albanian variant of Marxism-Leninism and 'Stalinism''. The next day, 28 May 1991, TPLF/EPRDF forces triumphantly entered Addis Ababa. There was no meaningful resistance to deal with and this marked the *Dergue*'s final day in power. After spending the night at the American Embassy in Khartoum, the MLLT's founder and the TPLF/EPRDF's leader arrived in Addis Ababa on 1 June 1991 to replace Mengistu Haile Mariam.

Many factors had contributed to the military success of the TPLF/ EPRDF: the experience and example of insurgent movements around the world, the precedence set by veteran fighters like Sihul, the strong desire to create an egalitarian society among people of a marginalized province, a guerrilla army that was highly motivated, taking inspiration from the history of its forefathers, the successful mobilization of ordinary people, early victories over rival organizations, the intermittent involvement of the EPLF, and the growing unpopularity of the authoritarian, deeply undemocratic *Dergue* government generating revolt and sabotage across Ethiopia, and even inside its own army. Not only morale and material support but also the participation of the ordinary people at crucial moments of the war had emboldened the tenacity of TPLF fighters and other insurgent groups. Thus the endurance exhibited under harsh battle conditions, the conformity to centralism and strict discipline maintained throughout the duration of the war were high compared to the government army. The insurgents considered themselves as liberators of the Ethiopian people. They had marched deep into the heart of the country, incurring heavy costs of human and material resources, but had unseated the military regime, and saw themselves as the rightful rulers to open a new chapter in the country's history.

The TPLF/EPRDF's Initial Moments in Power

With the nominal participation of the Ethiopian People's Democratic Movement (EPDM) – that later changed its name to Amhara National Democratic Movement (ANDM) – and the Oromo People's Democratic Organization (OPDO) as junior partners in the EPRDF, the TPLF's task of toppling the *Dergue* had come to a successful conclusion. The President and Commander-in-Chief of the Armed Forces, Mengistu Haile-Mariam, had fled to Zimbabwe, and the government army was dispersed all over the country. The TPLF/EPRDF fighting force automatically assumed the role of a national army under the command of Meles Zenawi, who had so far shown no commitment to Ethiopian nationalism. As he ascended to power, the more complex and challenging political task of governing a diverse society began. Nobody knew which path the TPLF would follow as it tried to find its way in new political territory. Itself an organization claiming to represent only one of the over 80 ethno-linguistic groups in Ethiopia, the TPLF was confronted with the sensitive and complex task of controlling a diverse society with which it had only limited interaction because of its entrenchment in an ethnic or ethno-regional programme.

Given the ethnic diversity of Ethiopia and the longstanding emphasis on the ethnic stance that the TPLF pursued to gain power, there was real concern among large sectors of Ethiopian society that ethnic polarization and confrontation would emerge and that this perilous dimension might spoil the country's entire political environment. With an authoritarian outlook embedded in its ideology and a triumphant military force under its command, the TPLF/EPRDF was poised to define the future of Ethiopia on the basis of ethnicity. Alternative approaches to the post-*Dergue* political set-up were already threatened by the sounds of the gun which came with the new power holders. As Kefale Mammo (2004), former President of the Ethiopia Free-Press Journalists' Association, recalls '...anybody with a different view from that of the insurgents who called themselves 'ethnic liberators' was labelled 'remnant of the *Dergue*' and therefore should be hunted down. This war of nerves and the ethnic liberation propaganda were the greatest preoccupation of the national radio and TV everyday.' Kibret Mekonnen (2005), the then editor of *Aemero*, also attested that 'by declaring the establishment of [a] 'peace and stability' special force, the TPLF/EPRDF silenced the voices of the civic organizations and the emerging opposition parties. Ethnicity took on an elevated political role and people began to look for their ethnic trenches so as to safeguard their interests or fight back their real or perceived adversaries. When people are pushed to interact on the basis of ethnicity, extreme and irrational ideas can find fertile ground. As Esman has said (1994: 15), 'The more politicised ethnicity becomes, the more it dominates other expressions of identity, eclipsing class, occupational, and ideological solidarities'.

Wrangling over Power: Events Leading to the July 1991 Conference

One of the agreements reached in the US-backed London talks in May 1991 between the TPLF and the OLF was the convening, within a month, of an 'all-inclusive national conference' in Addis Ababa that would establish a Transitional Government to pave the way for democratic elections. The

TPLF and the OLF took the initiative of drafting a Charter on the basis of which Ethiopia would be administered for a transitional period of two years. Meles Zenawi of the TPLF/EPRDF and Leenco Lata of the OLF were responsible for formulating the content of the Transitional Charter and notably the Eritrean 'EPLF role in the anticipated transitional arrangement was often defined as that of a quasi-partner' (Leenco 1994: 14). He went on:

> ... the EPLF offered to host a meeting in Sanáfe, Eritrea, in late June, to prepare the ground work for the July Conference. The outcome of this meeting was the draft of the Charter, some of whose provisions by indicating a radical departure from Ethiopian political practice served to raise OLF hopes of witnessing the beginning of the end of domination.

Thus far, the relationship between the TPLF and the OLF, an armed group claiming to represent the majority of the Oromo people, appeared amicable, especially in the face of a political order that had not accommodated diverse views like the one they believed in, e.g., that of self-determination. Once the old order was gone and the question of power had to be resolved, it was an open question of how these vanguard and secessionist fronts would behave towards each other and towards other organizations. Understandably, the draft Charter would reflect the ideological and political perspectives of the self-appointed authors and leaders of their respective ethno-nationalist organizations. Yet the essential point was whether this Charter would lead Ethiopia through a peaceful and democratic transitional period that would be acceptable to all stakeholders. Before discussing these issues, we examine the approach of the leading author, the TPLF, to the idea of convening a conference to establish a Transitional Government of Ethiopia (TGE).

As it stood as the major Front, the TPLF took the leading role in designing the political future of Ethiopia, simply because after it had played a leading military role in dislodging the *Dergue*, it found itself in a position to dictate terms. The Ethiopian people, having endured seventeen years of military dictatorship under the *Dergue* and seen its demise in May 1991, understandably hoped things would change for the better and were awaiting with great relief the political overtures of the victorious Fronts. Indeed, the fall of the *Dergue* was seen as the end of tyranny for good, but the general attitude towards the new powers-holders was cautious.

After the seizure of power by the TPLF/EPRDF, regarded as secessionist and with the looming picture of *de facto* secession of Eritrea under the EPLF, people began to raise a number of sensitive questions that could not be easily answered. The perceptions of many Ethiopians were juxtaposed against those of the new power holders, not only on the Eritrean secession issue but also in relation to its influence on other ethnic nationalities, on the surrender of all seaports, leaving Ethiopia land-locked, and on ethnic polarization that was taking a perilous dimension and by some seen as inviting violent confrontation. Widely and repeatedly raised points included the following issues: Is Eritrea, which was formerly considered a part of Ethiopia, going to secede without the people being given the option to decide? Who gave the TPLF leadership the mandate to conclude an agreement on behalf of Ethiopia? Is Ethiopia going to lose access to the sea and remain land-locked because of TPLF? Can a force that seized power by the 'barrel of the gun' willingly hand over power to the people? Will the new (insurgent) army return to its barracks or cling on to power like its predecessor and impose its will? Would the TPLF allow individual, collective and opposition parties democratic rights?

The relatively freer atmosphere created during the transition period allowed these views to be aired, and they were reaching those in power, e.g., through the newly emerging papers and public debates. By many in the leadership such concerns were not greeted as legitimate questions of concerned citizens, but instead treated as provocative remarks from 'remnants of the *Dergue* intent on causing public disorder' and from 'chauvinists' who were unhappy to see a Tigraian presence at the helm of power in Ethiopia.

Emerging from years of war in Tigrai, the TPLF leadership was in a dilemma as to how to construct a government in a country where it had not cultivated any kind of constituency. More perplexing still was the negative sentiment generated by some of EPRDF's unpopular positions. Although forging the EPRDF was, in a way, meant to create a pan-Ethiopian image for the ethno-nationalist TPLF, this recently improvised design was doomed to fail as it did not deliver. In fact, people began to label the partners in the formation of the EPRDF, the EPDM, as the 'Amharic mouthpiece' and the OPDO as the 'Oromigna mouthpiece' of the TPLF. Its dilemma was further exacerbated by the contradiction of its dictum of 'Grab the commanding heights', seen to mean 'Grab power by any means (see Chapter 8), and mounting pressure from Western powers and donor countries to follow the path of democracy. The then US Assistant Secretary of State for African Affairs, Herman Cohen had already warned the TPLF: '...no democracy, no cooperation' (in Leenco Lata 1999: 134) and '...advised the TPLF leaders should be held accountable on the basis of their declared principles [democratization in this case] and not merely on improvements registered over that of the *Dergue* era' (Ibid.: 22). By dislodging the *Dergue*, it was hoped they would provide the freedom the *Dergue* had denied the people. That was, in fact, the view of all the democracies that had been on their side during the struggle. The choices were clear but the situation was not so easy. As the TPLF had managed to negotiate between ethnicity and Stalinism, it appeared to choose a similar approach in a modified setting in governing the country. Moves towards democracy were announced and made, but central control of the TPLF-EPRDF was not to be relinquished. Support for an authoritarian-led transitional government was found in some Western circles, notably the US government, happy with the demise of the communist *Dergue*.[102] This approach was carefully designed not to embarrass the donor community, whose aid was crucial for the realization of the transitional enterprise discussed in London during the peace talks.

With aid from the West in the pipeline and over-confident regarding its military strength, the TPLF/EPRDF was now poised to dictate the terms for establishing a transitional government. Since free participation by the people in an open election would, in all probability, go against the TPLF and jeopardize the realization of its scheme, it was adamant not to let prominent, long-established opposition groups participate in the transition process. Even if we assume that the entire population of Tigrai would have been on the TPLF's side, the TPLF would have been a loser, for the constituency it claimed to represent was only about 6% of the Ethiopian population. This inherently weak position prompted the TPLF to seek other unconventional ways to secure the reins of government.

The TPLF was now looking for like-minded ethno-nationalists who could be loyal partners and would follow in the footsteps of the EPDM and the OPDO. From the beginning of June until the eve of the conference on 1 July 1991, invitations were extended to various 'ethnic organizations' or groups appearing to be such, but those groups expressing an 'Ethiopian' sentiment seemed less relevant. The justification for this was given by Meles Zenawi who said, 'People were already expressing themselves even at the early stage before the conference in terms of nationality: that is manifested in the way they organized themselves. There were so many nationality-based organizations. That is a representation of a certain sentiment' (in Vaughan 1994: 56). In a country of more than 80 different ethnic nationalities, where most of whom lived on the periphery of national politics, the TPLF's call attracted numerous candidates. Some of the ethnic group leaders were flown in from Mogadishu and Khartoum, while others were chosen from remote parts of Ethiopia. TPLF leaders went all out to attract ethnic organizations to their new political structure. Revealingly, Sibhat Nega, a TPLF CC member, conferred: 'We picked organizations from all over – two from here,

102 The TPLF thus won the blessing of Secretary Herman Cohen and the lobbyist Paul Henze of Rand Corporation, which opened the doors to US material support. Cf. Henze 1998.

two from there. One day Hayelom telephoned from Awassa to say that he had just come across another one....' (in Vaughan 1994: 38). Out of the 27 organizations invited to attend the conference, nineteen were ethnically based political organizations, five were national political organizations and the remaining three were civic or professional movements (for details, see Appendix 1). Later on the EPDM was transformed into an ethnic organization, the Amhara National Democratic Movement (ANDM) and five other ethnic organizations of Agew, Burji, Gedeo, Kaffa and Yem were included, raising the number of ethnic groups in the council to 25. This conglomeration of ethnic groups was designed not only to ratify the Charter drafted by the TPLF and the OLF but also to be the future power base for the TPLF leadership. No wonder then that suggestions from invitees to the conference and from scholars like Tecola Hagos[103] were ignored. Those suggestions included having representatives of administrative regions elected from *qebele* representatives; religious leaders from all religious groups; representatives of civil associations; representatives from long-existing movements; representatives from employees of the Ethiopian government employees; and representatives from associations or unions of employees of private enterprises.

Only with the alliance of the OLF and the advice of the EPLF could the TPLF design a charter to realize its plans for ruling the country. As Vaughan pointed out, 'According to OLF sources, the EPLF was heavily involved in the process which resulted in the draft document, and the three organizations spent some time hammering out the details' (ibid.: 35). It was clear that a charter drafted by ethno-nationalists, the TPLF and the OLF, with the secessionist EPLF as a compatible advisor, would not be conducive to the unity of the Ethiopian people – a unity which had created its own cross-current partly by the history of its evolution but largely because of the ineptitude of successive repressive governments.

The July Conference and the Transitional Charter[104]

In Africa Hall in the centre of Addis Ababa, the invited organizations assembled on 1 July 1991 to review the draft Charter prepared by the TPLF/ EPRDF and the OLF. The gathering was called the 'Peace and Democracy Transitional Conference of Ethiopia'. As the conference had been planned and organized by the TPLF/EPRDF, it reflected the objectives of its leaders.

103 See Tecola W. Hagos (1995), Appendix V, pp. 279-285.
104 This was a prearranged Charter made by the TPLF and OLF with the consent of the EPLF before July 1991. The remaining drama in the conference was more of a public exercise to legalize it.

The head of this organization, Meles Zenawi, had no challenger and became the conference chairman. There was no question about his chairmanship as the participants were his own supporters, loyal fronts or sympathetic organizations. Longstanding Ethiopian organizations like the EPRP and MEISON or the COEDF coalition that could pose a serious challenge to the ethnically charged objectives of the EPRDF had not been invited. The exclusion of such Ethiopian organizations undermined a possible mobilization of forces of unity and gave an easy ride to the ethnic fronts that espoused the secession of Eritrea. By keeping such political forces at bay, the EPRDF would remain in power with easily manageable forces. 'In this way, ethnic representation became wider, but less widely legitimized' (Pausewang, 2002: 29).

The USA was at the forefront in providing the necessary diplomatic backing for the Peace and Democracy Conference. Among those who sent observers were the UN, the OAU, the G7, the US, the USSR, Sudan, Kenya, Djibouti and Eritrea, the latter being represented by its future president Isayas Afeworki. Although the presence at the conference of members of the international community gave hope to democratic participation and a promising future for the conflict-ridden nation, the process was stage-managed to fit the ideological intentions of the EPRDF. By virtue of its military strength and organizational capability, it was able to set the agenda and determine the entire proceedings of the conference.

In the opening session, Meles Zenawi made his position clear by saying: 'We need ... a transitional government free of rumour and infighting' (EPRDF, July 1991). The statement may seem like normal advice for the participants from the outset but the context in which it was delivered signified growing opposition (referred to as 'rumour') to the ethnically charged conference and the dominance of ethnic organizations in it as opposed to pan-Ethiopian orientations. What was labelled as 'rumour' was the expressed fear among larger sections of the people that Ethiopia was to become an experimental field of governance based on ethno-linguistic structures, raising concomitant problems of definition and division. A heated argument came from the Ethiopian National Democratic Organization (ENDO) on the viability and implementation of the secession of ethnic groups in general, and that of Eritrea in particular. The discussion was aborted by the chairman before it went too far. As Vaughan (1994: 53) observed, 'The conference chairman's introduction to the document was direct: 'it is time to stop playing hide and seek; it is time that we called a state a state – out of conviction and because of the objective reality, not out of pressure' '. The pressure, however, was already at work – pressure coated with harsh words from the chairman and his associates in the conference hall, which in turn based its power on the military force outside the hall. On this very question, other EPRDF representatives responded in similarly strong terms: 'This is a cornerstone of the Charter. If ENDO has reservations on this point, it has reservations on the core of the Charter. Under these circumstances I cannot accept that ENDO accepts and participates in the adoption of the Charter' (ibid.: 51). From here on, conference participants had two choices: either to agree with the draft Charter as presented by the EPRDF or to withdraw from the conference. They chose to stick to the former choice, at least for the time being.

Deliberation about the draft Charter went quite smoothly although nominal disagreement emerged from a few individuals on issues like 'the establishment of an independent judiciary, and whether its jurisdiction would extend to the implementation of the Charter itself ...The EPRDF opposed suggestions that a 'body of lawyers' be appointed for this purpose' (Vaughan 1994: 50). From the start it was clear that the sole arbiters of the Charter were none other than the EPRDF's leaders. In this way, all twenty articles classified in five parts of the draft Charter were endorsed as the 'Transitional Period Charter of Ethiopia' (see Appendix 2) and became the 'supreme law of the land for the duration of the transitional period'. The Charter ratified the establishment of 'local and regional councils ... defined on the basis of nationality' (Article 13) and the right of Ethiopia's nations, nationalities and people to 'self-determination of independence' (Article 2), i.e. secession. On this basis, an ethnically structured government was formed. This formal recognition of ethnicity stretched to the level of forging an independent state, and was a new political structure that would definitely undermine the sense of pan-Ethiopian identity. In the regional and local elections that were conducted following the new ethnically based political arrangement, people were 'required to state their ethnic identity when they register to vote' (Tecola 1995: 275). Failure to comply would disqualify one from voting. By giving legal recognition to people with a single ethnic identity, the EPRDF proclamation left out people with dual or multiple ethnic identities, a large group of the population due to its long history of integration. In this case, a new type of authoritarian system with ethnicity as the cornerstone of state institutions and governance in the place of the former multi-ethnic institutions was established.[105] This constituted the fundamental provision of the Charter which was the interim Constitution on the basis of which the Transitional Government of Ethiopia was created.

Representatives of the 27 predominantly ethnic organizations formed a Council of Representatives (COR) from among themselves to act as a

---

105 As D. Turton noted (2006: 10), federalism in post-1991 Ethiopia emerged 'from the barrel of a gun' (and was then introduced from the centre by constitutional fiat).

legislative body ('Parliament'). This transitional parliament had 87 seats, 32 of which were taken by the TPLF-led EPRDF with the remaining 55 seats divided among the 23 non-EPRDF organizations associated to it. At the same time, a council of ministers as an executive branch was formed, with Meles Zenawi as the President of the Transitional Government of Ethiopia (TGE). Meles Zenawi then appointed a Prime Minister and a seventeen-member Council of Ministers. Key posts were given to his party members and the OLF.

As the only independent party, the OLF was the first to be disgruntled with the power sharing. 'As early as the summer of 1991 it became clear that TPLF and its EPRDF coalition did not intend to share power with all the other movements in the government coalition. The EPRDF member parties were given the local and regional administrative positions, and based their authority on the presence of TPLF troops' (Pausewang 2002: 30).

According to the Charter, which became effective on 22 July 1991, a new constitution would be drafted by a commission set up within the COR and be approved by the same COR. Regional and local elections were to be held within three months and a 'Constituent Assembly to be elected pursuant to the final draft of the Constitution' would be established. Because of clashes between the EPRDF and the OLF on a number of issues ranging from election procedures to security arrangements, the election was postponed several times until 21 June 1992, when it was held in acrimonious circumstances. There were major challenges from the people about the excessive control of power by the EPRDF and about its legitimacy. Amid much chaos, it was the EPRDF, which had more armed troops and cadres than the other parties that turned the election results in its favour. 'The struggle between the ruling party (EPRDF) and the opposition over the control of voter registration and candidate nomination led to the closure of bureaus (opposition offices), arrests of potential candidates and intimidation of sympathizers of opposition parties by the ruling party' (Kahsay Berhe 2005: 111). The National Election Commission (NEC) had been created by the EPRDF-led COR to run the election, so it was expected that it would be conducted in favour of the EPRDF. The Norwegian Observer Group reported that 'there were also several complaints about party-officials (of EPRDF coalition parties) carrying out the task of the Election Commissioner in the absence of a properly appointed Election Commissioner' (August 1992: 10). In its own statement, the German Observer Group also concluded that '...in most areas observed, essentially non-competitive, one-party elections were held... conditions were frequently maintained or created that prevented the opposition parties from equal participation' (26 June 1992). Beginning the July 1991 Conference and all the way to the June 1992 elections, it was clear the EPRDF had controlled and dominated the political landscape of the nation, keeping every critical opposition at bay.

Whose Charter and Constitution?

Close observation of the process by which the Charter was formulated and ratified and, more importantly, the essence of the provisions stipulated in it, clearly reflected the ideological and political thinking of its founders. There was no escape from this fact as the TPLF in the name of its umbrella organization, the EPRDF, had seized power and designed it to be so after toppling the military regime of the *Dergue*. With the blessing of the Western powers, happy to be rid of the *Dergue*, the EPRDF had the opportunity to fasten its grip on power. In the previous chapters we discussed how the TPLF used the double-edged ideology of ethno-nationalism on the one hand and Stalinism on the other to mobilize and control the people of Tigrai in war efforts that brought the political elites to power. The TPLF saw the dividends of this method of struggle and to remain in power it chose to pursue with that method in a modified setting. The old ideology was refashioned in the form of democratic centralism[106] and ethno-nationalism and was expounded as a revolutionary achievement that would release the Ethiopian ethnic nationalities and peoples from the ills that had haunted them for generations. In the preamble to the Charter, it was announced that the demise of the *Dergue* was followed by the beginning of 'a new chapter in Ethiopian history in which freedom, equal rights *and self-determination of all the peoples shall be the governing principle of political, economic and social life* and thereby … rescuing them from centuries of subjugation and backwardness' (emphasis added by the author). To rule the country *de jure,* the TPLF/ EPRDF had to transform the Charter into a Constitution (Articles 10-12) as its main transitional programme. Although it is beyond the scope of this study to discuss the 1994 Ethiopian Constitution, I nonetheless indulge in a brief review of its essential tenets to get a glimpse of the political system that was going to prevail in Ethiopia.

Based on the Charter, on 18 August 1992, the EPRDF-led Council of Representatives (COR) established a 29-member Constitution Drafting Commission (CDC) from the COR and elsewhere. The late *Ato* Kifle Wodajo, a high ranking civil servant and a close ally of Meles Zenawi, became the chairman of the CDC. A five-day symposium that lasted from 17-21 May 1993 was organized by a Kenya-based NGO called the Inter-Africa Group

---

106 Democratic centralism is Leninism's basic tenet of organizational rule found in all Communist parties with strict hierarchical obedience in the execution of decisions coming from above.

to reinforce CDC efforts. Many international donors, among them USAID, the Carter Centre, Oxfam US, the Ford Foundation, the UK and Germany, financed the work of the CDC. Several international scholars, constitutional experts and jurists were invited to share their ideas with the leaders of the TGE and the Commission. The majority of the participants were foreigners invited by the TPLF. Civic groups and the people at large for whom the constitution was intended to serve were not represented. Mesfin Araya (1993: 31) commented that 'despite the relevance of constitutional issues to the conditions of Ethiopian women, workers and peasants, the lack of their participation in the symposium is inexcusable'. A few of the scholars attempted to inject ideas into the making of a worthy constitution – a constitution that sets out the powers of a government and its various organs vis-à-vis the rights of its citizens, in other words, that defines power relations to bring about harmony and the development of civil society. Christopher Clapham highlighted the importance of considering the long history of the Ethiopian society and its intrinsic social values when putting together a constitution. Samuel Assefa explained the demerits of the right to secession as a constitutional provision. No matter how farsighted these suggestions might have been and as can be seen from the contents of the new constitution, they were discounted by the organizing Commission members who were already tuned to the ethno-nationalist directives of the EPRDF. Some other scholars and TPLF associates, however, were observed giving their approval to the ethnically charged experiment. For instance, Mohamed Salih (2001: 196) wrote: 'In effect, Ethiopia became the only country in Africa that gives ethnicity an explicit role in the democratization process'. Whether this was a democratic process or not, connotative events were in progress to make it explicit. In fact on another note, Mohamed Salih indicates how the process itself was tainted with pressures and manipulation: 'In 1993, SEPDU [an opposition political formation] split under pressure exerted upon it by the EPRDF because of its endorsement of the Ethiopian opposition Paris Conference, which supported the idea of removing the EPRDF government by force' (ibid.). Actually, the Paris Conference to which Mohamed Salih refers was a 'peace and reconciliation' undertaking and not a project of 'removing the EPRDF government by force'[107] (see the Declaration of the Paris Peace and Reconciliation in Ethiopia Conference, 4-6 March 1993).

In November 1993, the CDC published the draft constitution while the EPRDF/the TGE took responsibility for organizing a discussion forum to explain its content. The EPRDF declared that the constitution was prepared without commending 'any particular style of government or political

107 The Paris Conference of the Ethiopian opposition parties which was held from 4 to 6 March 1993, was strictly a 'Peace and Reconciliation' practical test which the EPRDF turned a blind eye to.

ideology' (Embassy of Ethiopia 1994: 1-2). However, the constitution envisaged by the EPRDF and its drafting Commission reflected its ideological and political persuasion, which already had its imprint on the Charter. In fact, close observation of the new constitution reveals that it was eclectically adopted from the constitutions of authoritarian regimes such as the former Soviet Union, East Germany, China and North Korea. The core stipulation of power relations, Article 8.1 of the EPRDF Constitution states that, 'All sovereign power resides in the nations, nationalities and peoples of Ethiopia'. This creed is in the style of Article 108 of the former Soviet Union, Article 66 of socialist Bulgaria, Article 87 of North Korea, Article 62 of Ethiopia under the *Dergue*, and Article 16 of the People's Republic of China which explicitly states that 'supreme power resides in the people's assembly which operates under the leadership of the communist party'. According to these articles, supreme power is invariably vested on an assembly of the 'people's representatives' that is controlled by one party which claims a majority vote by any means. Legislative, executive and judiciary power is thus amassed in the hands of the main party. To make the defined power relations strictly operative, 'democratic centralism' is used as a mechanism of hierarchical control. In its military structure as a rule and in its political dispensation as a matter of principle, the TPLF/EPRDF had effectively been employing democratic centralism and now saw no other mechanism to run the state machinery. In such a hierarchical power structure, the work of the three branches of state governance (legislative, judiciary and executive) are directed and controlled by the party which has the leverage to exercise sovereign power on behalf of the assembly of nations, nationalities and peoples of Ethiopia. In such vertical power relations, as one observer said, 'one can only speak of division of work and not division of power' (Negede Gobeze 2004: 105). This was evident in the fact that court rulings have been reversed a number of times by order of the EPRDF leadership. For instance, former Defence Minister Seye Abraha, who was arrested without due processes of law, after the split in the TPLF politburo in 2001, was set free by the High Court, but PM Meles Zenawi, the EPRDF leader who saw Seye Abraha probably as a political rival, overruled the court's verdict and ordered his incarceration for more than six years. The case of Aberra Yemaneab, a former leading member of Meison arrested in 1993 and who used to sign joint declarations with the current leaders of the EPRDF during the struggle against the *Dergue*, is not different from that of Seye Abraha.[108] The Prime Minister can pass any directives including that of going to war through the party structure to his party members who constitute the majority in the

---

108 Aberra Yemaneab still lingers in prison (2009). Many such cases can be cited; refer to annual reports of the Ethiopian Human Rights Council and/or Amnesty International.

parliament, and in accordance with democratic centralism he instituted, directives have to be enacted on. A state structure where a party boss can prevail over the law has been created. The leader of the party that claimed a majority of the seats in parliament eventually became the supreme arbiter of the nation's destiny, due to the party (EPRDF) that submitted power to its Central Committee and the CC to its politburo, and the politburo in turn to one person who amassed all state power in his own hands. This is the process by which monolithic government structures and authoritarian states are created. Tadesse and Young (2003: 401) noted 'In examining the role of Meles it can be seen that he has ... accumulated a disproportionate share of power in the Ethiopian state'. With the enforcement of its party-designed constitution, the EPRDF dictated the path along which Ethiopia trails. The Constitution poses the danger of fragmentation on the basis of ethnicity and is not sufficiently conducive to democracy and peace in the country. The proliferation of ethno-nationalist parties looks to set continue unabated. E.g., out of the 81 registered parties in August 2002, 73 were ethnic organizations.[109] Basic tenets of one minor force, like the political structure, the economic programme and the case of nations-nationalities, are imposed as the 'supreme law of the nation'. In addition, democratic avenues that could lead to a peaceful transformational process or to adaptation of the constitutional order seem closed off.[110]

When we summarize the above developments in the light of the history of the TPLF, we conclude that from the outset what the incumbency of the TPLF/EPRDF would bring with it was not entirely unpredictable. The movement began as an ethno-nationalist organization and later in 1985 within it forged a Stalinist leadership group, the MLLT, to provide ideological guidance during many years of armed struggle. Its power base was built up in Tigrai, although in the meantime it may be that 'Tigray is no longer politically united, and there has been a clear decline in support from the region, which was the backbone of the TPLF since 1975' (Tadesse and Young, 2003: 399). To extend its political territory to the rest of Ethiopia, it created the EPRDF with its junior partner the EPDM (eventually ANDM). Later on, other satellite ethnic organizations like the OPDO and the SEPDF (Southern Ethiopian Peoples' Democratic Front) were formed with the guidance of the TPLF, and joined the EPRDF. The whole idea of organizing, cajoling and sometimes forging ethnic organizations was to bring as many of them under the EPRDF's umbrella as possible and use them to reinforce the creation of the 'highest organ of state power' of the 'nations, nationalities

---

109 For a list of the registered ethnic and national organizations see APPENDIX - IV

110 For an interesting comparative discussion of the Ethiopian ethno-federal experience, see Turton, ed. 2006.

and peoples of Ethiopia', as stipulated in the Transitional Charter (1991) and finally in the federal Constitution (1995). This 'highest organ of state power' allows no division of power but only a 'division of work' controlled by one party. That is to say, the presence of the legislative, the judiciary or the executive branches in the EPRDF-run state of Ethiopia came to signify primarily a division of work instead of a division of power, as in democratic states. The Transitional Charter and subsequently the Constitution were crafted to define and reflect this power ideology. In this manner, 'as is the case with other political movements in Africa, the EPRDF has effectively merged with the state, therefore the crisis of the Front is in effect the crisis of the Ethiopian state' (ibid.). Such a power structure is the embodiment of authoritarian governance.

Chapter 12

The TPLF and African
Insurgent Movements: A
Comparative Perspective

Introduction

A comparison of the essential features of the TPLF with those of some other African insurgent movements from the same era can help to better understand the TPLF and explain the way it struggled successfully to realize its aims: the overthrow of the militarist *Dergue* and the establishment of a TPLF-led regime in Ethiopia. From the beginning, the TPLF had embraced Marxism as its guiding ideology and exercised strict centralism but at the same time made the most of ethnic-nationalism as a mobilizing ideology. Its approach to the masses and, in particular, the youth, which was exalted as the 'motor' or essential component of the Front was pragmatic and populist. This approach helped the TPLF-elite to create 'movement hegemony' and empower itself effectively manipulating the malleability of ethnic-nationalism. Most of the successful insurgent fronts in Africa seemed to have adopted a similar leftist ideological stance and had a highly centralized leadership which utilized ethnicity or nationalism with the attendant vague programs as means of drawing the people to the struggle. The ways in which these insurgent fronts operated, and especially their relations with the people with whom or in whose name they waged the struggle and their method of mobilization, especially of the youth that constituted the bulk of the fighting force, and finally how they appropriated power, were largely similar.

This section looks into various essential defining features of the TPLF and correlates them with those of others in Africa. For this purpose, ideology, leadership, youth mobilization and relations with society (civilians) will be considered to assess how these features relate to or differ from those of four other liberation movements of that era – the Front for the Liberation of Mozambique (FRELIMO), the National Resistance Army (NRA) of Uganda, the Sudan People's Liberation Movement (SPLM) and the Eritrean People's Liberation Front (EPLF). The selection of these fronts is based on the approximate time span they emerged, the resemblance of ideology – a mix of (ethno-) nationalism, regionalism and social revolutionary aims. Their conceptualizations of ethnicity depict similarities and differences, and show us much about the uses that their various political ideologies made of this fact.

The EPLF was geographically and ideologically close to and working with the TPLF against a common enemy; the SPLM was not far away in geographical terms but had no working relations with the TPLF. The NRA was further south from the SPLM area of operation but was a mass-based insurgency movement, in many aspects like the TPLF, emerging against state tyranny. FRELIMO, on the other hand, as a Southern African liberation movement was very far away from the operational area of the TPLF and primarily anti-colonial. Its armed struggle against Portuguese rule was also coming to the end when the TPLF was starting out, but it had a related socialist ideology and method of mobilization. In all these case the political elite of the fronts had the upper hand in defining and guiding the struggle, in swaying the population under their control, and finally in the disposition of power in their respective countries.

FRELIMO

The Front for the Liberation of Mozambique, FRELIMO, was formed in 1962 in Tanzania, where an African version of socialism was in the making. The University of Dar-es-Salaam played a major role here as intellectual centre. From 1964 until 1975, FRELIMO was engaged in an armed struggle that was popularly known as the 'People's War' for national independence from Portuguese colonialism. At the same time, it was carrying out a social revolution in the liberated areas, emulated from other revolutions that had waged people's wars. 'FRELIMO has undoubtedly drawn much inspiration not only from China but also from Tanzania's experiences', (Munslow 1974: 162) in carrying out revolutionary nationalism. Early FRELIMO combatants included Samora Machel, a leader during and after the liberation movement, who did his military training in both Tanzania and Algeria, where diplomatic activities also took place. The armed struggle went on for over ten years and resulted in the defeat of the Portuguese colonialists and the gaining of independence on 25 June 1975, 'but perhaps of great significance [was] the social revolution which ... ensued as a result of the war' (Ibid.: 139). Immediately after liberation, a reorganization of society along socialist lines took place, especially by the indoctrination of the youth and a nationalization of major sectors of the economy. In 1977, in line with what had been in progress politically, 'the Third Congress established FRELIMO as a 'Marxist-Leninist Vanguard Party' made up of the 'best revolutionary working people'. Its central role was to ensure that politics remained in command', (Hanlon 1984: 135).

The NRA

The National Resistance Army NRA in Uganda was formed in 1981 by forces under Museveni that were first known as the Popular Resistance Army (PRA). Museveni, who has ruled the country since his victory on 26 January 1986 until today (2009), was first influenced by the socialist teachings of Julius Nyerere, Eduardo Mondlane and Walter Rodney while he was a university student in Tanzania. Later he and his radical group visited FRELIMO-held territories in Mozambique, where they adopted the idea of an insurgent movement based on the masses and built up a power base from there. As Ngoga (1998: 94) noted, 'Museveni was clearly drawing on the doctrines of people's war that he had imbibed in the course of his training in Mozambique'. Although Museveni's political orientation appeared to be the most left-leaning of the era, he did not commit himself to the socialist ideology his contemporaries entertained. While almost all political groups focused on urban activities to pave their way to power, the NRA adjusted its struggle to evolve from the rural areas where the majority of the people lived. The NRA's struggle heavily depended on the cooperation of the people, who were systematically organized at grass-roots level. As Museveni (1997: 189) put it, 'Originally, we had secret committees of volunteers who banded together as support groups for the fighters, to mobilize food, recruits and intelligence information'. At the beginning of 1982, committees were elected in every village to take the place of the secret cells and were renamed 'Resistance Councils' (RCs). 'The RC system was built upon a pyramid-like structure', (ibid.) on which the government was built after the NRA's victory in 1986.

The SPLM

The SPLM had its roots in the Anya-Nya I, the first southern Sudanese rebel movement which started in 1955 and continued up to the signing of the Addis Ababa Agreement with the Khartoum government in 1972. It was a movement opposed to the imposition of Islam and Arab culture over the Christian and traditional religions of the south by the dominant northerners, as well as against the gross neglect of the South by the national government. Total independence on the one hand and effective regional autonomy on the other were seen as viable solutions to the problem, but these projected approaches were often sources of conflict among the southerners themselves and that kept the movement from making significant headway. In 1983, after a decade of uneasy truce, the conflict flared up again and a Southern political organization known as the Sudan People's Liberation Movement (SPLM) was created, with John Garang, from the largest Southern people, the Dinka, as its chairman. 'He advocated a united secular Sudan' (Human Rights Watch 1994: 20) and 'autonomous status to various regions within the context of a United Socialist Sudan, not a United Arab Sudan' (Scott 1985: 71) but he was opposed from two prongs: the Islamist northerners as well as the secessionist southerners (the Anya-Nya II). However, with support from the Marxist military regimes in Ethiopia and Libya, the then anti-Numeiri government, the SPLM emerged as a formidable military front that forced the government in Khartoum to eventually make concessions and ultimately a Comprehensive Peace Agreement (CPA) was signed in 2005.

The EPLF

The EPLF came into being in the early 1970s as a splinter group of the Muslim-dominated Eritrean Liberation Front (ELF) that had been created in 1961. The nationalist rhetoric and claims for independence from Ethiopia were similar in both cases; yet the EPLF tried to be more revolutionary than its predecessor, the ELF. The founders of the EPLF were left-leaning radical elements that made known their revolutionary positions in a manifesto entitled 'We and Our Objectives'. They also had a clandestine party called the Eritrean People's Socialist Party (Pool 2001: 91) and a programme that reflected its name. As Markakis (1990: 143) put it, 'The programme stipulated that the economy of independent Eritrea would be largely state-owned and centrally planned, land would be equally distributed, and the peasants would form associations to manage their affairs. Industry and foreign trade also would be nationalised.' The top leaders, among them Ramadan Mohammed Nur and Isayas Afeworki, were trained in China. The nature of their protracted war against Ethiopian regimes and the social revolution that they carried on in the Eritrean countryside resembled the

Maoist revolution. The EPLF, as it wiped out its long-time adversary the ELF with the cooperation of the TPLF, managed to defeat the Ethiopian *Dergue* regime in Eritrea and declared *de facto* independence in 1991.

Ideology

Nationalism and socialism of one form or another were the two ideologies that influenced and shaped all five fronts from the start of their struggles. In predominantly traditional societies where nationalism had not fully developed and socialism in its revolutionary form was considered an intrusive concept, the eclectic employment of the two ideologies was a new but expedient approach, although in new and unexpected forms. As van Walraven and Abbink (2003: 27-28) put it, 'The result is a bizarre combination of ideological components crafted in the course of struggle in which individuals find justification for their different agendas'. However this approach served the strategic goal of the fronts under discussion whose central purpose was to mobilize people with the hope of a better future and to utilize the mobilized mass force to overthrow oppressive regimes.

It was quite clear that the socialist-oriented radicalism that swept the world in the 1960s had an impressive impact on the theory of revolution of the leading, active elements of all the five fronts. As Colburn (1994: 28) put it 'The linkage between intellectual trends and revolutions is most apparent in the numerous revolutions that took place in the 1960s and 1970s. Not surprisingly, the successes of the Chinese, Vietnamese, Algerian and Cuban revolutions inspired intellectuals in other poor countries'. With some variation, all had embraced socialism as the just and egalitarian (also at times 'scientific') ideology that would liberate the whole population and bring social justice to the majority of the working class and peasantry of their countries, if not the whole world under the banner of 'proletarian internationalism'. In the context of the parallels drawn between the Chinese and Cuban revolutions on the one hand and the Ethiopian revolution on the other, Colburn noted that 'The most important similarity is the shared use of Marxism-Leninism to inform the choice of the revolutionary leadership' (ibid: 24). Only Museveni (1992: 282) was putting forward the rhetoric of a 'mixed economy' strategy. Of all the fronts under discussion, the TPLF was on the extreme left, forming the MLLT and poised to emulate socialist Albania. In his interview with R. Dowden of *The Independent* of 28 November 1989, TPLF leader Meles Zenawi declared that 'the Soviet Union and other Eastern bloc countries have never been truly socialist. The nearest any country comes to being socialist as far as we are concerned is Albania' (Dowden 1989: 19). Albania was governed by a socialist system of a Stalinist nature at the time and it appeared that Meles and his MLLT party were determined to take their ideological dream to great lengths. None of the other four fronts in the emerging EPRDF went that far but, in an ironic twist, it was again Meles Zenawi who, after seizing power in 1991, quickly seemed to shy away from Marxist ideology in the original form and embraced 'revolutionary democracy', the content of which is shrouded in controversy.

Since these fronts based their struggle on mass society and their traditional organizations for their survival and development, they found *nationalism* an indispensable ideological tool to mobilize and unite people from different class backgrounds. A class-based struggle alone was not seen to be effective and would have led to endless in-fighting. For all practical reasons then, the outlook of these fronts was a hybrid ideology of one or the other form of socialism and (ethno-)nationalism, geared to radical social change and revolutionary war. Even the reformist Museveni (1997: 28) had to declare that, 'By the time we left the university, quite a tradition of radical thinking had developed'.

In 1985 when the *TPLF* became ultra-left-wing by creating the MLLT and announced publicly that it had adopted Marxism (Stalinist variety) and Albanian socialism as its model (see Chapter 8), the other fronts then present in Ethiopia exhibited caution by playing down the revolutionary ideology for fear of inducing a clash of ideas within the front and with the predominantly traditional and agrarian societies in which they operated. The *NRA* in Uganda was at the other extreme, playing things more cautiously than the other fronts. Also they did not want to provoke the liberal West from who they sought material support and cooperation for their diplomatic campaigns to mobilize their own people in the diaspora.

At a secretly held congress with about 100 cadres at Merara, a place north of Asmara, in 1976, the *EPLF* formed a clandestine party, the Eritrean People's Socialist Party (EPSP). 'There, they committed the organization to a socialist political program for the long-term future and a national democratic agenda for the liberation of the country now' (Connell, 2001: 356). There was also a secret cadre school where 'classical texts of Marxism-Leninism, Stalin and Mao, translated into Tigrinya, were used' (Pool, 2001: 93). The existence of this Marxist party was unknown until a decision was reached to dissolve it in 1989, but one could easily observe from the programme and socio-political activities of the Front that Marxism was at work. Basically, the ideological alignment of the EPLF was similar to that of the TPLF, except that the latter made the formation of its MLLT public and considered the Soviet Union as a social imperialist power. Otherwise, the EPLF's National Democratic Programme represented 'reflections derived from the revolutionary upheaval that was taking place in Ethiopia at the time' (Markakis 1990: 143), and which was fed by Marxist-Leninist and Maoist thoughts.

Ideologically, *FRELIMO* was of a similar Marxist vein, but in its programme it emphasized the 'anti-colonial national liberation' (Dos Santos 1973: 35), and not without reason. 'Any attempt to clarify this programme further would have destroyed the unity of the leadership drawn from liberal democratic ... communist and tribalist persuasions' (Munslow 1974: 141). Failing to consider this problem and by creating the MLLT during the struggle, the TPLF alienated many people, who were forced to join other fronts, like the conservative EDU, or abandoned the struggle all together. Yet, towards the end of the anti-colonial war, FRELIMO expounded the slogan '*A Luta Continua*' (the struggle continues) to deal not only with the colonizers but also with their cronies whom they depicted as 'class enemies of the FRELIMO's revolution' (Vines 1996: 5). To continue the struggle at a socio-economic level, FRELIMO had to reform its approach and restructure the organization. 'At the Third Congress it was agreed to turn it from a mass movement into a 'vanguard party'. Although it was to be a Marxist-Leninist Party, theoretical knowledge or even basic literacy were not criteria for membership', (Hanlon 1984: 138). As in the TPLF and also the EPLF, loyalty to the revolutionary party was the crucial criterion of recruitment to the FRELIMO Marxist-Leninist Party. In this manner, like in the TPLF and the NRA, centralism and a command structure were put in place, leaving no room for opposition or other political forces – labelled 'counter-revolutionaries' or 'enemies of the revolution' – to operate. The so-called 'mass line' was also fading away, and was replaced by the elitist 'vanguard party' leadership. The NRA, however, was not using such Marxist terminology.

Like the TPLF, which started as a highly centralized movement that injected its ideology into its rank and file members and a limited sector of society, the *EPLF* was advancing in the same direction but discreetly, by creating *wahyo* (underground cells). In the NRA, such cells were called secret committees of volunteers. In FRELIMO, centralism did not follow a strict ideological formation as in the TPLF or the EPLF, at least not during the armed struggle. FRELIMO was in chaos in 1969 because 'the 'tendency' toward conservative, petty-bourgeois nationalism ran right through the movement and very far up the apparatus' (Saul 1973: 191). This was, however, corrected by adopting Marxist centralism, while the NRA was employing strict military and mass-line discipline. The SPLM, on the other hand, evolved through a series of factional debates in which each group allowed the participation of the community and traditional institutions in which it operated in a bid to gain support. In this process, negotiation, tolerance and compromise had a chance of gaining ground. This is not, however, to suggest that the impact of revolutionary Marxism as an ideology of liberation was non-existent in the SPLM. As Johnson (1998: 53-54) observed, 'Also in common with the TPLF/EPRDF and the EPLF, the SPLA has adopted Marxist language in its formulation of the 'nationalities' question as underlying the inequalities inherent in the Sudanese state' and it 'has been revolutionary in some of its language but not in its approach' (Ibid.: 71). Although the geographic location and the nature of the ethnic divide of northern and southern Sudan may have been factors to reckon with, the SPLM more seriously than the other four fronts believed in a negotiated settlement to the conflict with the Sudanese state and achieved considerable concessions. It did not succeed in annihilating its adversary, as we saw with the other fronts. Without indulging in Marxist rhetoric or 'vanguard party' formation like the three fronts, however, '[the] SPLM ... continued to emphasise socialism as being the only ideology which can unify a country of such sharp racial, religious and tribal diversities' (Scott 1985: 71). With regards to the content of the SPLM's socialism, John Garang explained:

> ... it cannot be determined mechanically and equated with Communism as Numeiri would like the Western World to believe. The concretisation and particularisation of socialism in the Sudan shall unfold as the armed struggle and as the socio-economic development programmes are implemented during and after the war and according to Sudanese local and objective conditions. (ibid.: 72).

In this case, a socialism that perhaps would permeate through the 'objective situation' of Sudanese society and bring self-determination in unison was envisaged as the guiding ideology of the SPLM.

The pledge of this socialist ideology concerning the aspirations of marginalized societies was especially attractive to the youth, who sought change, and particularly to the fronts that claimed to represent the people. It created motivation and gained wide acceptance during the struggle. Although they questioned its implementation, many people did not pose any challenge to the ideology as such, and in many instances gave their tacit endorsement without even attempting to comprehend its content. The severity of political repression, socio-economic exploitation and often humiliating inequalities of rank and status that these societies endured under different autocratic systems must have created a situation that allowed the people, living in predominantly peasant and traditional societies, to embrace such a revolutionary and radical ideology. Except for the more radical TPLF and its MLLT party within its own ranks,, the other fronts downplayed their Marxist rhetoric to gain access to or support from the West, which allowed them to carry on the struggle on the diplomatic front and mobilize their people in the diasporas. The NRA was unique in avoiding Marxist rhetoric but consistently relied on populist slogans like the 'mass line' and, as Kasfir (2005: 291) observed, 'the NRA's commitment to egalitarian, non-sectarian, non-coercive popular support came from its leaders' analysis of Ugandan society and their involvement with FRELIMO before the war began'. The radicalism seen in the TPLF, however, was partly indicative of the limited exposure and the lack of experience of the young TPLF leadership in international relations vis-à-vis the other fronts.

Although all five fronts upheld nationalism as a mobilizing and uniting factor, the nationalist struggle they were engaged in had variations. The nature of subjugation or repression that respective people felt and the modus operandi and attitude of the ruling forces would probably have a direct relationship with the variations we observe in the different fronts. Whereas the TPLF and the SPLM started as ethno-nationalist organizations and opted for the self-determination of their people within the would-be democratic nation-states of their respective countries, FRELIMO and the EPLF had defined their national struggle as an anti-colonial war of liberation and had a programme of national independence from the occupying regime. The NRA's nationalist movement was simply geared to overthrowing a national dictator.

Theoretically, there was the opportunity for the TPLF and the SPLM to coexist with the once-dominant ruling force in power if the latter allowed the people in question to determine their right to self-determination. And unlike the TPLF, the SPLM was attempting to resolve its conflict with the Islamist government along this line. But in the case of FRELIMO, the NRA and the EPLF, they felt they had to get rid of their occupiers (or oppressor in the case of the NRA) and run an independent state without the intrusion of the latter, although for tactical advantage both fronts were at times engaged in negotiations with their respective governments. In this case, the political education, propaganda and day-to-day agitation were based on the simple logic and general assumption that there was nothing to be negotiated with occupiers and once the colonialists were out and independence had been gained, all social and economic problems could be solved and the political rights and the dignity of the people would be respected. Yet, the process of realizing such aspirations was never seriously discussed during the struggle. If attempts were made by individuals or groups to initiate such discussions, the leadership of the respective fronts considered them as untimely topics that could distract the focus of the struggle against the enemy and were subject to punishment. The demands of the group dubbed *Menkae* by the EPLF in 1973 were 'inter alia, the election of a committee to supervise the actions of the leadership, the participation of all members in decision making ... and similar demands which the leaders denounced as anarchist' (Markakis 1994: 136). The revolutionary nationalists who raised such legitimate issues were in addition labelled 'class enemies' aiming to destroy the organization, and were thus to be subjected to punishment. David Pool (1998: 25) critically notes, 'The *manqa (menkae)* crisis was resolved through the execution of some of the dissident leaders and recantation through public self-criticism by others'. The TPLF too took such harsh measures in 1977 against certain individuals – dubbed *hanfeshti* – who had raised similar but less coherent discontent that challenged the leadership. Any form of challenge to the patrons of the unitary ideology was met with a deadly reaction. Since this ideology did not gain ground in the SPLM and even less so in the NRA, challenges that might have led to punishment by execution in those fronts were few in number.

Although this revolutionary ideology had the power to attract masses of people, among them the youth, the peasantry, workers and all unprivileged classes, in practice, it remained the best tool of the movements' leadership to centrally control and command the very people who sought liberation through it. The revolutionary leadership in almost all cases was from a small 'petty bourgeois' background, an intellectual group that was able to articulate Marxist and nationalist ideologies to mobilize and lead the social classes who could not produce leaders of their own. Whether the intellectuals were fighting their own battle for power or were working on behalf of the unprivileged classes for social justice is a subject that requires further analysis. The fact remains, however, that this ideologically inspired struggle was a new approach to seizing power. And more than the others, the TPLF, by creating the MLLT, made effective use of ideology to achieve its goal.

Leadership

Leadership in insurgent movements is often claimed or acquired in an unconventional fashion. Activists in student movements, unions or the army take the initiative to challenge an undemocratic state and turn out to be insurgent leaders as the readiness to bring change broadens. Assessing impatience and seeing people's tacit or open approval of their activities, the activists assume leadership of the ensuing movement. In most cases, such leaders, as Clapham (1988: 9) observed, 'were drawn from elite sections of society, as middle-level politicians, army officers or student radicals, and deliberately decided to pursue an insurgent route to power after alternatives were blocked'. In the process, the activists often proved to be qualified to be leaders. Often, a group of such individuals happen to be the founders of an inchoate insurgent movement and simply assume the leadership where there was none. Most of the movements created in this manner are then even identified with the leaders. 'In many cases, the leader and the movement are so closely associated that it is hard to conceive of one without the other' (ibid.). The NRA and its founder Museveni are a fine example of such a symbiosis: 'Yoweri Museveni, who led the NRA throughout the war, was the driving force behind the construction of the ideology' (Kasfir 2005: 275). The TPLF leadership was created through such a process in that the leaders were the same group of student activists who happened to become founders of the organization and leaders throughout the struggle and later. The same is true for the EPLF leaders except that they had spent some acrimonious years with the ELF before they formed their own rival front. Although the leaders in the NRA, FRELIMO and the SPLM had an intellectual and/or military background and showed a measured radicalism, the formation of the leadership of these movements was not qualitatively different from that of the TPLF or the EPLF.

In general, leaders who come to prominence in such unconventional circumstances stick indefinitely to the leadership position because they develop a sense of guardianship over the organization they created and usually fail to acknowledge or ignore the emergence of better-qualified and competent individuals suitable and poised to take over from them. Leadership in this process becomes the domain of those who came first and made effective use of ideology to control others. As Colburn (1994: 51) aptly remarked:

> The vanguard role usually played by committed socialists in inciting armed revolt not only made them the catalysts and linchpins of revolutionary coalitions, but it also left them well positioned to consolidate power in the aftermath of victory. Leaders of armed guerrilla organizations almost invariably have ended up heading the states that emerged subsequent to their victory. Because it is the guerrillas who ultimately defeat the government's forces and seize its institutions, the most viable resources through which political power can be exercised are at their disposal.

No wonder then that it becomes an uphill struggle and almost impossible to unseat such leaders. As has been widely observed in the past few years, it has become difficult to remove from power Meles Zenawi of the TPLF or Isayas Afeworki of the EPLF or Yoweri Museveni of the NRA – the so-called 'new breed' of African leaders of the 1990s. John Garang of the SPLM and Eduardo Mondale and Samora Machel of FRELIMO were removed, though unfortunately only in accidents or by assassination.

The TPLF leadership was relatively younger and less experienced than the leaderships of the other four fronts and one can observe more revolutionary radicalism, especially in the ideological rhetoric of the former. All the founding leaders of the TPLF (except the elderly Sihul who died in the early days of the struggle) were undergraduates at H.S.I. University in Addis Ababa, while the leaders of the other fronts had higher degrees in different fields and more past experience. Eduardo Mondale, FRELIMO's first president, and John Garang, the chairman of the SPLM, were well educated and highly qualified leaders with experience acquired in international politics. Ramadan Mohamed Nur and Isayas Afeworki, both top EPLF leaders, were Chinese-trained leaders and had extensive field experience which they acquired when they were with the ELF in the 1960s. Yoweri Museveni was a political-science student at the Dar es Salaam University in Tanzania and had contacts with the African liberation movements that were based there. He had also worked as Minister of Defence and Minister for Regional Cooperation before he went to the bush to wage an insurgent movement. On the other hand, the TPLF leaders and founders only had revolutionary theory at their disposal and the zeal to translate this into practice when they headed to the bush of Dedebit to launch their armed struggle. It would have been a difficult adventure had it not been for Sihul who guided them through the early days (see Chapter 3).

The early TPLF leaders had no outside contacts of any kind whereas FRELIMO had established itself in Tanzania and had links with China (Saul 1973) and to some degree with the Soviet Union. The SPLM had significant outside contacts and received support from Libya and Ethiopia (Scott 1983); the EPLF had longstanding contacts with Sudan, some Arab countries and China (Connell 2004; Pool 2001) and the NRA too received support from Libya in cash and arms (Museveni 1997: 141-42). When the TPLF started its armed struggle, the only contact it had was with the still relatively weak EPLF, and in an aberrant way with the ELF, with which it was more often than not in conflict as it intruded without permission into the operational zone of the TPLF. It was years later when its military force grew and began attacking *Dergue* units that the TPLF received recognition from the Sudanese government, which allowed it to open offices - that were camouflaged as humanitarian centres for fear of antagonizing the Ethiopian government.

Because of its limited exposure to the outside world and with no contacts to count on, the TPLF leadership was forced from the beginning to develop in theory and practice the sense of self-reliance it had gathered from Maoist literature. Its adherence to the idea of self-reliance, both as a matter of principle and expediency, resembled that of the NRA which emphatically claimed that 'the basic weapon of the struggle is the support of the people and their political consciousness' (Museveni 1997; Ngoga 1998; Kasfir 2005). As a result of a lack of practical experience, the TPLF leadership had also had to stick together to handle the numerous complex matters that arose in the guerrilla movement, thereby exercising collective leadership in almost every aspect of the struggle.

Since the start of the TPLF's struggle in 1975 and during the formation of the MLLT in 1985, the TPLF leadership was strictly collective and no one was singled out as its dominant figurehead of the Front. Decisions were reached collectively in a series of meetings, usually through consensus, and executed in the manner agreed upon. The inclusion of the formation of an independent Tigrai in the programme known as 'Manifesto 68' by the Meles-Sibhat group was a rearguard factional manoeuvre and an exception to the rule. It was corrected collectively in a matter of days after its emergence. In the other four fronts, dominant leaders emerged from the beginning: Eduardo Mondlane and then Samora Machel in FRELIMO, John Garang in the SPLM, Yoweri Museveni in the NRA and Isayas Afeworki in the EPLF. These leaders all prevailed as their respective fronts took off. After the formation of the MLLT within the TPLF, however, its ideologue and founder Meles Zenawi evolved as the dominant leader of both the TPLF and the MLLT. However, throughout the long period of struggle until the formation of the MLLT (1976-1985), the TPLF's collective leadership was so impregnable that it was not possible to even detect minor political differences in it. This entrenchment in turn led to a situation in which the leadership was feared and its policies and directives accepted without question. Except for the symbolic congresses that were convened and where policy matters were raised for endorsement, all important issues were settled at meetings of the leadership and then implemented. This was also the case with the EPLF. The NRA, FRELIMO and the SPLM, on the other hand, had allowed a level of participation by, for instance, traditional chiefs who had earned a degree of respect from their respective communities and encouraged partially open debate with the rank and file. This did influence the decision-making process, although, as in the TPLF and EPLF, it was the decisive say of the leadership that mattered in the final analysis.

Youth Mobilization

All the insurgent movements invariably and understandably required a young force to carry the burden of challenging government forces in the battle field. Although it might appear to be a demanding task, recruiting the youth to the insurgent movements under consideration was not a major problem. Due to the repressive nature of the often inept regimes, structural socio-economic problems, and the particular nature of global (Leftist) ideological ferment in the Cold War world, there was always a large number of youth, many of them unemployed, ready for a career in such movements by promises of meaningful activity and a better future. Orphaned and other marginal children facing a grim future were also drawn to the movements, although their roles varied. In most cases they stayed in the base areas and received education, including schooling, political and military training that prepared them to later join the fighting forces. In some cases also they were involved in combat. E.g., in the case of Uganda, 'Museveni was somewhat embarrassed by the many questions from reporters about his child soldiers, and tried to play down their role. 'We gave them guns because they asked for them. We don't use them as soldiers.' But in fact they did participate in the war' (Furley 1995: 37). As observed in movements such as Uganda's Lord's Resistance Army (Behrend 1998) or RENAMO (McIntyre, 2005), both of which had gone as far as abducting or kidnapping children, the recruiting of dissatisfied and unemployed youth had been going on for years. These recruitment methods were not reported in the case of the TPLF or the other four fronts being considered here, although subtle coercion when recruiting the youth was certainly used to some degree.

The TPLF was able to mobilize and continuously recruit youths throughout its armed struggle with no major difficulties (see Chapter 9). This was also the case, in general, with FRELIMO, the SPLM, the NRA and the EPLF. Although the process of recruiting a young fighting force into these Fronts had some differences, fundamentally they followed the same pattern. What made recruiting the youth so feasible is a subject that still requires further investigation. In his critical assessment of the situation of youth in Africa, Abbink (2005: 1) wrote:

> They are facing tremendous odds and do not seem to have the future in their own hands... They also are marginalized in national state policies and have a weak legal position. African youths are over-represented in armed rebel or insurgent movements of various kinds as well as in criminal activities, to which they are so easily recruited.[111]

---

111 Also because of sheer numbers, their availability, and their eagerness to take up an-

This objective situation, prevalent in most African countries, thus allows the mobilization of the youth for a struggle that ostensibly mitigates the severity of the situation they were in, and in fact such situations 'have led to the massive recruitment and involvement of youths in revolutionary or insurgent movements, starting in the 1970s' (ibid.: 12). Many armed movements, including those of the TPLF, FRELIMO, the SPLM, the NRA and the EPLF, evolved to become formidable forces by mobilizing youngsters that were caught in dire situations that would not easily disappear even after the end of the struggles. This implies that if new insurgent movements emerge, youths will be available for membership. We already have seen this in various parts of Africa and Asia, in the form of diverse social, political and also religious or criminal movements, with ideologies of mobilization and practices of violence different from those of the 1970s-80s.

Although the youth that voluntarily join an insurgent movement might be inspired by a host of factors, it has been widely documented that their recruitment to risky engagements, like guerrilla warfare, indeed requires methods and tactics of persuasion or coercion. Guerrilla life is a rough and dangerous venture and thus it requires some sort of propulsion to involve the youth. The TPLF and the other four fronts used persuasion and coercion as strategic methods of recruitment while they conditionally applied different tactical approaches. Persuasion was the most widely applicable pattern but coercion was applied when persuasion failed to yield the necessary number of recruits needed. But even when coercion was at work, it should not be overlooked that there has been and would always be some degree of consent as a latent impetus to draw the youth to be part of a momentum for change.

As suggested above, the TPLF by and large had no serious problems in drawing recruits to the Front and saw no need for coercion in flagrant ways, as was witnessed in other fronts. Often recruitment into the TPLF was 'ceremonial': with village communities organizing a farewell party in the name of those who were joining the Front. Such a farewell served as inducement for others to follow, on top of putting the burden of responsibility on those who had already started the process. These well-planned recruitment procedures, which gave the sense of voluntary recruitment, were common in the TPLF, but not in the other four fronts. This does not mean though that sophisticated ruses and pressure were not employed in the TPLF. For example, peer groups secretly organized for this purpose played songs at public gatherings that would haunt and intimidate those who might slip back.

---

ything that may relieve them of conditions of poverty, idleness or ennui, youth are easily recruited by political parties, armed groups or criminal networks (Ibid.: 2005: 3).

In this sense the TPLF was no different from the other fronts. 'FRELIMO did the same, sometimes using forced recruitment' (McIntyre 2005: 236). In southern Sudan, 'campaigns were undertaken by prominent SPLA/SPLM members going into the bush to recruit directly' (Scott 1985: 73) with a show of force. The EPLF too was using such methods of recruitment but in harsher ways. When the intensity of the war depleted its fighting forces and the flow of recruits started to dry up, the EPLF, with the consent of village councils, in some cases rounded up young men in the villages who had dodged recruitment. The recruits would be told that it was their 'national obligation' to join the front and fight the enemy.

Whereas the TPLF emphasized long-term promises of a rosy future under socialist development, coining the slogan '*Kalsina newihn meriren, aweta ny'gidine eyu*' (Our struggle is long and arduous but our victory is certain) and the EPLF agitated for a prosperous life after independence, FRELIMO and the SPLM, while not ignoring long-term pledges, were using promises of scholarships and a better life in the movement to appeal to the immediate needs of the youth. Once they had joined the movements, they found themselves caught up in the movement and faced with imposed rules of militaristic hierarchy, often referred to by the Fronts as 'democratic centralism', from which it was difficult if not impossible to withdraw. In the TPLF and the EPLF, resigning or quitting the Front once you were involved was not a real option. Attempts to leave were considered acts of betrayal and would lead to imprisonment, or even execution. In the SPLM and FRELIMO, on the other hand, the situation was relatively more relaxed. For instance, the young voluntary fighters in the SPLM could occasionally leave their barracks to spend time with their families (see Jok 2005), and young students would join FRELIMO on the understanding that they would receive a scholarship (in Munslow 1974). In other insurgent movements too there was always some kind of enticement to bring the youth to the front. Sawaba of Niger promised higher education abroad and access to job and social advancement (Van Walraven 2003), ZANU of Zimbabwe attracted peasant fighter by promising land and respect for traditional ancestors with the help of Shona spirit-mediums (Scarritt 1991) and the PAIGC in Guinea-Bissau pledge 'historical dignity' and better material life to win allegiance among the rural poor (Colburn 1994). However, these social relations between the Fronts and their young fighters lacked consistency.

With reference to the abject daily conditions the youth experienced and by employing methods of persuasion and coercion whenever applicable, the TPLF and the other four fronts under discussion were able to mobilize and recruit the youth to their war efforts. Yet what was achieved in concrete terms did perhaps not correspond to the sacrifices incurred or match the promises made. No matter how persuasive the call to engage in the struggle was, it became clear that the end of the war did not guarantee irreversible positive change for them. It is worth noting that 'While revolutions are often about young people challenging old orders, as regimes solidify and age, youth can once again develop the perception of being excluded and discontent foments' (McIntyre 2005: 240).

Relations with the Civilian Population

The TPLF and the other four fronts (like almost all insurgent movements for that matter) laid great emphasis, more often in theory than in practice, on the need to create solid and harmonious relationships with 'the masses', i.e. the ordinary, civilian population. The struggle they launched was in the name of the oppressed majority whose active participation in the movement, as a matter of principle and expediency, was taken for granted. We have seen above, in one of the TPLF songs, *Bahrina*, how a fish swimming in the sea was used as a symbol to represent the TPLF's positive standing with the masses. The EPLF named its radio station *Dimtsi Hafash* (Voice of the Masses). No wonder then that: 'All of the literature on insurgent warfare places an enormous emphasis on the relationship between the insurgents and the people among whom they operate' (Clapham 1998: 11). This fundamental approach to the relationship was best summarized by FRELIMO leader Samora Machel who said 'Our chief strength, the primary cause of all we do, is the people ... In solving our problems we should rely first on them, following a mass line' (in Munslow 1974: 144). 'We are educating our soldiers in practical and everyday examples that it is the people who matter in this exercise', (Museveni in Ngoga 1998: 99).

The idea of the 'mass line' was drawn from the doctrine of Mao Tse-Tung who led the Chinese Revolution based on this theory. Mass line is a theory that stands for the guided democratic participation of the people from below and believes in the power of mobilized people to bring about positive political and economic change. In theory, it appears as a negation of an elitist attitude of vanguardism. The notion of mass line puts full trust on the pro-active participation of mass society for the realization of social revolution and its envisaged outcome, such that, as Dos Santos emphasized, 'if the leadership starts to back-peddle or divert it will meet the resistance of the masses' (ibid.: 146). In all cases, the masses tended to believe in or adhere to this ideologically moulded theory, for they consistently saw, or had not other means of evaluating, the Front as a whole and the youth, in particular, incurring sacrifices ostensibly on their behalf.

From its inception, the TPLF, using such 'Maoist' ideas, appeared to give high regard to the mass line, though more in theory than in practice, and engaged carefully with the masses. Tampering with the traditional cultural values of the people it had a deep association with and that might cause alienation of the Front was considered anti-social and liable to disciplinary measures. As Abbink (2005: 19) put it, "Disciplining' is not only a matter of military leadership and internal cohesion but also of the strength of pre-existing values in the society from which a movement has emerged – religious leadership, gender relations, strength of the family, etc. – and of the way the insurgent movement has defined its relations with the civilian population'. Some aspects of the society's culture might not have aided the progress of the social revolution as it was envisaged, but that was tolerated in order to follow the mass line. 'Live the people's way' was a popular aphorism in the TPLF in the early days of the struggle and members were indeed trying to live it. This was partly true as far as the material livelihoods were concerned. It was acceptable and common for TPLF fighters to live the life of the ordinary poor peasant. Tuning to the aphoristic mass line, there were endeavours to uphold women's rights, protect individual or family property, respect religious and traditional values, abide by community norms and rules, and provide justice whenever and wherever required.

Hitherto marginalized masses thus felt recognized and respected, for this was a trend they had never seen before. The TPLF's relations with civilians were by and large harmonious, with the aim of the struggle being to attain the collective rights of the people to self-determination. The nationalist feature of the struggle was given prominence, which helped to strengthen the bond between the Front and the people. In this way, the TPLF earned the name *Widebna* (literally 'our own organization') and the regular fighters were referred to as *Dekina* (our kids). As the other fronts (FRELIMO, the SPLM, the NRA and the EPLF) followed the same ideological track in mobilizing their respective peoples, an apparently intimate relationship developed between the fronts and the people among whom they operated. That the people sincerely hoped for a better future after the struggle would, in itself, strengthen the bond between the fronts and their respective peoples.

The causes and conditions that led to the launch of the struggle were essentially the uniting factors between the insurgents and the people concerned, and the continuous repressive and military government measures intended to root out the insurgents reinforced the bond. As Clapham (1998: 14) put it, '…there is nothing that so readily cements a relationship of solidarity between insurgents and host populations as the experience of being bombed together'. In all five cases, atrocities committed by the respective reigning governments did little or nothing to contain the insurgent movements but increasingly helped keep alive the bond between the people and insurgents to the extent that sometimes all the people from a village in the NRA or TPLF-held territory would evacuate to the base area for shelter in the event of government army encroachment. Such displacement occurred in territories where the insurgents operated but to what extent such events strictly reflected the bond between the people and the respective Front is hard to establish unambiguously. The absence of freedom of expression in the fronts, however, made it difficult to openly discuss the exact nature of the relationship, and therefore '...the mythology of solidarity asserted by the insurgent leadership cannot be taken at face value' (ibid.: 15). There were moments when such mythology was put to the test. In 1985 when the TPLF leadership was confronted with the choice of focusing on the formation of the MLLT or tackling the worst famine in recent memory in Tigrai, the leadership chose to assemble all its able-bodied cadres in the base area in Worie for a month to enjoy festivities and discussions while thousands were starving.

The rhetoric and practice surrounding the mass line in general drew sympathy and material support for the fronts from mass society. By propagating the populist banner more intensively than the other four fronts, the TPLF may have managed to mobilize substantially more material and human resources for their war venture without having to resort to aggressive coercion. Yet the other fronts were not far behind the TPLF in this respect. For instance, it was largely because of the mass-line approach that all the five fronts were able to outwit rival movements in their respective territories. The TPLF swept away the *Teranafit*/EDU from Tigrai, the EPLF drove the ELF out of Eritrea, FRELIMO outshone RENAMO in almost every aspect of their struggle, the NRA defeated Dr Kayiira's Uganda Freedom Movement (UFM) politically, as Museveni (1997: 151) put it, 'without using any military means', and the SPLM stood out above the secessionist groups partly because of the populist mass line they propagated. Finally, they all got rid of regimes that were blamed for repressing and exploiting the masses, except for the SPLM that had to settle for negotiated concessions.

Conclusion

This book is written in an attempt to contribute to the historical study and explanation of an ethno-nationalist movement which emerged in 1975 rose to power in Ethiopia in 1991. It gave a critical, retrospective analysis of the political history of the Tigrai People's Liberation Front (TPLF), the *de facto* ruling party in today's Ethiopia under the name of the Ethiopian People's Revolutionary Democratic Front (EPRDF). The study began by explaining the political and social conditions under which the TPLF emerged, how the armed struggle started, and how the mobilization of the people took place. I also dealt with the background to the conflict between the various ethno-regional liberation fronts and other revolutionary groups and the military government that took power in the wake of the overthrow of the imperial government of Haile Selassie I in 1974. A core issue in the revolutionary turmoil of those days appeared to be the developments surrounding the issue of 'national self-determination' and how it was conceptualized at the various stages in the TPLF's struggle. The study went on to explain the nature of the TPLF's relationship with the various warring parties in Ethiopia as well as with the EPLF in Eritrea and the way in which the revolutionary elite of the TPLF leadership staged the 'vanguard of the revolution', namely via the Marxist-Leninist League of Tigrai (MLLT) as an important instrument to gain power and redefine the movement. It finally narrated how the TPLF captured power in 1991, and I then moved on to a comparative analysis of the TPLF and four other nationalist movements in Africa. It is on the basis of this analysis that a few concluding remarks will now be made.

The social and political conditions in Tigrai in the 1960s, and by extension, Ethiopia at large, from which the TPLF emerged, were characterized by rampant poverty, political repression, autocratic rule and ethno-regional and ethno-linguistic disparities. However, the interpretation of this situation that was politically ethnicized at one point and ideologically charged at another need to be revisited in order to engage the TPLF's current official historiography as well as several scholarly efforts made to this effect. Tigrai, like the rest of Ethiopia, experienced a grinding poverty that reduced the people to what Frantz Fanon once called 'the wretched of the earth'. In addition, political repression by the autocratic government of Emperor Haile Selassie suffocated political and economic change and generated deep unrest among the population, notably the emerging educated strata (students, teachers, civil servants). In the aftermath of the liberation of Ethiopia from Fascist Italian occupation in 1941 and in the light of high expectations of post-war restoration of order, there was a first rebellion in the greater part of Tigrai in 1942-43, the *Woyyane* rebellion. It was a precedent in the history of the country and created a regional consciousness and an 'example' of the sort that was carried over to the young generation. The founders of the TPLF had this consciousness as part of their background when they started to confront the military regime of the *Dergue*, although they developed different ideals. The rising tide of the Ethiopian student movement of the 1960s, that was Marxist through and through, also had a huge influence on the pioneers of the TPLF. As a result, theirs is a case that appears ideologically a fusion of Marxism and ethno-nationalism, emerging in a time of ideological upheaval on the national political scene. This was reflected at times of schism or critical moments in the history of the TPLF. The two major shades among the pioneers were, therefore, those who saw their movement as part of a national struggle by the Ethiopian people against autocracy and repression (represented by Sihul, Giday, Aregawi and, Teklu, among others), while the other shade resorted to a more 'parochial' orientation of ethno-regional exclusiveness (represented by Sibhat, Meles, Abbai and Seyoum).[112] By resorting to the elusive idea of self-determination, which included secession from Ethiopia and the formation of an independent Republic of Tigrai, essentially like that of the EPLF in Eritrea, the latter wing exploited the fluidity of ideas of ethnic identity and 'ethno-national self-determination' for its own ends. Since 'ethnic identity is often being used to construct differences that were not there before' (Abbink 1998: 60) or 'conveniently forget realities that have existed' (Roosens 1989: 161), ethnic exclusiveness was stretched to the extreme (as later reflected in the 1995 federal Constitution of Ethiopia, created under the aegis the same ethno-regionalist elite).

The historical irony is, however, that the parochial wing of the TPLF shifted its position once it had purged its rivals among the pioneers and claimed to be the champion of the pan-Ethiopian perspective, by forging the EPRDF. This was concluded around mid 1990, with the impending fall of Addis Ababa to the TPLF's final offensive. This shift of position reinforces the contention of this study that ethnicity serves as an ideology of mobilization or collectivises for political ends that may be resolved within or

112 From the beginning of the struggle, these political leaders were members of either the executive committee or the broader 'leading elements' group and who eventually rose to the executive level.

outside a given state, and that the elite, by claiming to represent the cause of the people but often running after their own power interests, play a decisive role in dictating the mobilization process. In the first place, envisaging the idea of Tigraian secession, an entity that constituted the historic core of the Ethiopian nation, was a questionable, if not delusive claim. In general, theoretically the grounds for secession from existing states are tenuous, and in constitutional theory recognition of an absolute right to secession is not common (see Buchanan 1997). The shift towards secession thinking by some in the TPLF was influenced by political events on the ground rather than by a change of ideology. The military government's victory over Somali forces in the 1977 war reverberated so quickly that its major protagonists in Eritrea resorted to a tactical retreat from the towns they had held since 1975. Pressure from the EPLF on the TPLF leadership to form a coalition with other fighting forces inside Ethiopia came at this time with a group calling itself the Ethiopian People's Democratic Movement (EPDM, a splinter group of the leftist urban guerrilla group EPRP) emerging on the scene in the Gondar region. Later in the 1980s, this EPDM formed a 'united front' with the TPLF in the shape of the EPRDF (Ethiopian People's Revolutionary Democratic Front). This was a case of an ideological shift towards pan-Ethiopianism by the TPLF sub-group (leadership) prompted by political expediency rather than conviction. It was made possible by the dual heritage of the Ethiopian student movement, which was inspired by both socialist thinking based on a national, class analysis and on ethnic/ethno-regional thinking, stimulated by the Eritrean question, seen as a national/colonial question. This basic ideological ambivalence continued in the TPLF leadership in the years that followed.

On the ground during the struggle, the political message used to mobilize the people of Tigrai was mainly that of ethno-nationalism. In the historical sense, ethno-nationalism poses a dilemma: is it only a convenient agenda or means of mobilizing people that did not have developed class and national identities, or can it be the basis for nation-wide political solutions to inequalities, etc. in federal or other form? Two factors are important here. On the one hand, there is often the oppression of a given community as a reality, with the ethnic exclusiveness of the dominant ethnic group(s) to rationalize that oppression. Ethnic exclusiveness may in such cases often be concealed, as Juteau (2004: 96) observed:

> When dominant groups reject ethnic labelling, even with the best of intentions in the name of equality, they are involuntarily hiding their own ethnicity from themselves. This allows them to define their organizations, their culture, their nation as non-ethnic, and to impose their ethnicity on to others, often under the guise of

universalism. Furthermore, this omission masks the very process through which majorities conceal their ethnicity.

Juteau's observation largely applies to the dominant Amhara ruling elite the TPLF was fighting to unseat, but it could be said that '[w]hat the Tigrayan elite has been trying since 1991 is a historical parallel of what the Amhara elite tried in the second half of the 19th century – the creation of Ethiopian unity [minus Eritrea] such that its own dominance is assured' (Merera 2002: 191). In the TPLF case, the guise of universalism is 'ethnic federalism' as opposed to a unitary state.

On the other hand, there is the question as to whether or not ethno-nationalism with self-determination in the form of ethnic-based federalism, seemingly pursued by the TPLF and the current Ethiopian government, is by its very nature and complexity a workable alternative.

As far as the first point is concerned, the big question was (and is) whether or not the form of the oppression that the people of Tigrai were experiencing was indeed only 'ethnically based' and exclusively against their language, culture, etc. and was exploiting Tigrai's 'resources'. Or was the rule and hegemony by a Shewan-Amhara-led elite (notably in imperial Ethiopia) the standard form of oppression that was found among the other non-Shewan-Amhara ethnic groups? It seems that Tigraians were not oppressed in the exclusive sense as the TPLF Manifesto of 1976 claimed. Its assertion that '...the Tigraians have been made to be the most hated, suspected and discriminated people in the empire, thereby making harmonious life absolutely intolerable' (TPLF Manifesto, February 1976 E.C. 20) was rather extreme. As always, the way the oppression was interpreted mattered a great deal, particularly in view of a search for alternatives. Because the Manifesto claimed that the oppression against the people of Tigrai was exclusive, it formulated the predicament in the form of what in Leninist discourse is called 'national oppression' (of a people or 'nationality'), and secession was then thought to be the solution. Despite this view, John Young, who conducted extensive research on the TPLF in the 1990s, believed that the '... establishment of the TPLF did not mark a retreat into ethnic parochialism' (1997: 32). This assertion misses the essential issue of the 'ethnic self-determination up to secession' on which the TPLF-led EPRDF political structure was constructed and was expanded beyond the Tigrai people into other ethnic regions' of Ethiopia. Also, Young contradicts himself when in a follow-up remark in the same work, he states that '[n]ationalism was critical to the success of the TPLF' (ibid.). Ethnic nationalism is, after all, the politics of distinctiveness and self-rule in a particular homeland in which case the internal 'we' must be distinguished from the external 'they' (see

Esman 1994), and it is also a suitable tool of mobilization to be manipulated by the left as well as the right, by the secessionist as well as by the 'unionist', by the religious extremist as well as the atheist, and so on. In fact, the oppression in Tigrai was no different from the oppression characterizing the masses of the other ethnic groups in Ethiopia. And the way both the imperial and military governments resorted to quelling the rebellions in the different parts of the country (Bale, Gojjam and Eritrea for instance) was of the same militaristic nature as the measures taken in Tigrai.

The TPLF leadership put forward ethno-nationalism with 'self-determination including and up to secession' as its principal goal mainly because it offered the best chance of building an effective fighting force that leads to power, which understandably is the elite's own goal. The self-determination agenda advanced to mobilize the masses of Tigrai was *not* largely adhered to by the people; on the basis of their historical experiences and achievements they even strongly believed that they were not only just Ethiopians but that they constituted the core of Ethiopia's ancient civilization. The disparity between the self-determination agenda and the inherent pan-Ethiopian aspirations of the masses was high. Tigraians generally, in their religious or cultural ceremonies, reflected their loyalty to the Ethiopian nation. But the largely peasant society of Tigrai appeared to have 'accepted' the self-determination enterprise, partly because they came to believe in the promises of socio-economic transformation programmes and in the liberation from state oppression, and partly for fear of reprisal or coercion of the TPLF if the mobilization process would be opposed.[113]

If the Tigraian masses had *not* bought the TPLF's self-determination agenda, what would that have made of the movement? Was it a social revolution, a people's movement or a movement in the service of the political elite? Let's begin with social revolution. A social revolution first of all constitutes a radical process that negates the *status quo ante*, characterized by a political overthrow of the *ancien régime* and its replacement with a popular power that follows thoroughly transformative political, social and economic programmes. After all, 'there have been revolutions as long as there have been systems against which to rebel' (Lipsky 1976: 494). For the TPLF movement to be dubbed social revolutionary requires the fulfilment of such conditions. Indeed, there were 'revolutionary' slogans and moves

---

113 A sign of this disparity of attitude was expressed in 2005 when in the parliamentary elections most of the residents of Addis Ababa of Tigraian origin (encouraged by the presence of international observers, diplomats and the media) voted for the opposition, denying the TPLF even a single parliamentary seat in the capital's council. One might speculate that in Tigrai many more people might have done the same had there been the chance of a free election.

on land reform, women's rights and participation of the people in self-administration. However as important as realizing change – much of which remained short of consummation - such measures were meant to induce and mobilize the people to primarily support the war rather than improve their lives or empower them.[114]

The second major element that could have made it a revolutionary power is the issue of democratic governance which needed the state's role to be that of regulating rather than dictating, as the military regime had earlier done. The TPLF's perception of governance already during its time in the struggle is the well-known Leninist concept of the vanguard. The theory of the vanguard allows no room for participation of the sector outside the ruling party, which has the role of monopolistic decision-maker for the masses, the civic movements and opposition organizations. After 1991, the space for the non-party political sector that had existed in Ethiopia was allowed mainly due to the complex heterogeneity of Ethiopian society, a lack of constituency outside Tigrai that necessitated tolerance, and the donor countries' pressure to open up. Without changing its role of dictating, the TPLF experimentally allowed space for media freedom, opposition parties, civic groups and local NGOs to participate in political life, while keeping a policy of ultimate authority towards them when it came to essential policy matters. But a competitive democratic system was not developed, as it would endanger the EPRDF's comprehensive programme for Ethiopia and their hard-won power and privilege. A substantial literature by both journalists and academics shows that the essentials of governance in Ethiopia since 1991 have not changed, and in fact have led to the imposition of dominant party rule across the country. Here one can see an almost seamless continuity with the pre-1991 period and the ideology and control practices of the TPLF/EPRDF then pursued in its route to power. Most freedoms were retracted

---

114 A given power cannot be labelled 'revolutionary' without comparing it to the nature of the power of the regime it overthrew. The anti-thesis to power under the *Dergue* military government that the TPLF overthrew should have been a broad-based, all-encompassing government and legislature in the first place. Instead, the TPLF seemed to resort to a double-edged policy, namely the exercise of power exclusively by the party but pretending that state power was open to contest. The litmus test came in the May 2005 elections, when the people of Ethiopia made a strong vote against the TPLF/EPRDF and favoured the opposition parties (Coalition for Unity and Democracy, the United Ethiopian Democratic Front, and the Oromo Federal Democratic Movement) to an unprecedented degree. For instance, all the 23 parliamentary seats for Addis Ababa, as well as the mayorship, were won by the opposition. Also in the countryside the vote for the opposition was huge, and a great shock to the EPRDF/TPLF. In the end the EPRDF was declared the winner, but the counting process was intransparent and suspicions remain that they may have lost in actual votes.

in the past decade, and political and economic control reasserted.[115] In all, the case can be made that the TPLF, far from being a mass revolutionary movement, actually turned into a parochial movement of a section of the Tigraian elite.

The claim to be 'revolutionary' has been reiterated in a much more elaborate fashion in the formula 'revolutionary democracy'. This concept is essential for an understanding of the TPLF and current politics of the government. It has been developed since ca. 1990 and its role came out clearly during and after the purge of a section of the TPLF's top leadership and, by extension, of the EPRDF leadership in 2001, (Paulos Milkias 2001; Tesfay Atsbaha and Kahsay Berhe 2001). Until then, the TPLF had played down its self-appointed revolutionary credentials and there was no more mention of Marxism-Leninism or indeed of the MLLT. During the leadership crisis of 2001 that emerged after a serious split over the war policy toward Eritrea and macro-economic policy, the TPLF opted to appear more 'revolutionary' than the 'nationalist' faction that was purged, partly because they were portrayed as a 'sell-out to US pressure'. In a 2001 document that became a government directive, the Front rejected liberal democracy as unfit for Ethiopia on a number of grounds and argued that the EPRDF had opted for what it calls 'revolutionary democracy'.[116] According to Meles Zenawi, because the TPLF/EPRDF is 'supported by the peasantry', it represents primarily their interests, and because Ethiopia is predominantly rural, the EPRDF therefore represents the interests of the majority of the population. It alleges that this aspect makes it democratic, while its 'radical' policies give it a revolutionary content; hence, the claim for 'revolutionary democracy'. This is the Leninist concept of 'the vanguard' turned inside out. But based on the widely accepted definition of revolution we saw above, it is hard to characterize the TPLF as revolutionary. In addition, for ideological reasons the TPLF is estranged from democracy as a system of representative and accountable government even with regard to the peasantry it claims as its constituency – because these have no independent say in matters.

As to the question of ethnicity and ethnic politics – that was the cornerstone of TPLF's political reforms after 1991, and which led to the institutionalization of an ethnic-based federal system, with regions and

---

115 Opposition parties were often intimidated by the government, NGOs and civic groups have been closed down or their activities curtailed, numerous journalists from the private media have been jailed, and thousands of refugees have fled to neighbouring countries.

116 See official documents of the EPRDF, 'The Development Lines of Revolutionary Democracy', Addis Ababa, 1992 E.C., and 'Fundamental Questions of Democracy in Ethiopia', Addis Ababa, 2001.

districts based roughly on ethno-linguistic lines. The discourse of rights and democracy is couched in terms of the 'nations, nationalities and peoples' of Ethiopia – to do justice to its diversity and to the claims of the various peoples. Democracy in this model is equated autonomy and (in principle) self-determination with secession as an option if groups are not happy in the federation. The model has been widely discussed[117] and it will not be pursued here except to relate it to the history of the TPLF and its ideologies as sketched in this thesis.

Ethiopia has a significant ethnic heterogeneity, with about 80 language groups. The TPLF had its social base only in Tigrai. As a 'mono-region' movement, controlling the whole of Ethiopia with its different groups and regions after the fall of the military regime carried great risks and challenges. There were a number of other opposition political groups claiming their stakes and it was necessary to bring about political stability as soon as possible. EPRDF forces were already met with opposition demonstrations after they entered the Addis Ababa on 28 May 1991 because their policies on a host of national issues were not seen to reflect nor be open to the concerns of people outside Tigrai. Scepticism towards the TPLF/EPRDF was widespread.

Once in power, the TPLF devised a political system based on ethnicity seen as the only suitable way to implement 'revolutionary democracy' and ensuring its rule. Refashioning Article 2-c of the 1991 Charter, it had Article 39 adopted in its 1995 Constitution: the right of nationalities and peoples to a self-determination, which also included the right to secede and form an independent state. Ethnic federalism on the basis of ethno-linguistic identity was the formula. But it was contested and carried risks. As Clapham (2004: 53) observed, 'This redefinition of Ethiopia along ethnic lines has created conflicts of its own, especially over demarcation of territories'. It was also noted that 'Most importantly, the Constitution has tried to reify, to freeze something which is by nature fluid and shifting: ethnic identity' (Abbink 1997: 172). It could be contended that the whole idea behind Article 39 was to set up a new mechanism of control (Clapham 2004; Melakou Tegegn 2004; Merera Gudina 2000). To this end, a number of 'ethno-national organizations' were set up such as the Oromo People's Democratic Organization (OPDO), the Southern People's(Peoples') Democratic Organization (SPDO)[118] and the Ethiopian People's Democratic Movement (EPDM), the TPLF's erstwhile partner in the formation of the EPRDF, which had to change its name to the Amhara National Democratic Movement (ANDM), suggesting that the

---

117 see also Alem Habtu. 2005. Multiethnic federalism in Ethiopia: A Study of Secession Clause in the Constitution. Publuis/Spring, pp. 313-335.

118 Later also known as Southern Ethiopian People's Democratic Front (SEPDF).

EPDM had never been independent in the first place and was adhering to the new ethnic politics of the TPLF. These were categorized as 'People's democratic organizations' (PDOs) which in many cases '...were led by ambitious individuals who had been based in Addis Ababa or even abroad, and had few evident links with their regions of origin' (Clapham 1995: 88). With the formation of PDOs in its orbit, the TPLF was able to extend its party and state structure[119] to all ethnic groups in the country.

Like the TPLF, these PDOs also had to have their own Marxist-Leninist vanguard core. These were established later on although the ANDM had earlier formed its own. The Marxist-Leninist nuclei are actually the elite core with actual power in the new regions. These nuclei have also formed a central fortress at the national level to lead the EPRDF, with the TPLF as dominant. What is seen in Ethiopia now is a cumbersome structure of governance where the party (EPRDF) and government structures overlap and sometimes clash. However, in the light of the former MLLT ideology, this is the best structure to guarantee control over society where they never had much constituency in the first place. The MLLT unofficial network takes major decisions and its sub-sections (the TPLF, OPDO, ANDM and other PDOs) are expected to follow suit and implement them without question. Officially though, TPLF politburo decisions are passed down to the EPRDF politburo, itself TPLF-dominated, for formal approval and then passed down to ministries, the non-independent court system and the PDOs in the regions for implementation (Aklilu 2000a; Aalen 2000a; Merera 2002: 150).

The ruling party's grand plan after 1991 was to proceed with forming Marxist-Leninist nuclei within the ruling parties in what it calls the 'backward regions' such as the Somali region, Afar, BeniShangul-Gumuz and Gambela and bring them into the party fold, paving the way for a grand coalition at EPRDF level.

We thus see that not unexpectedly the ideological and organizational structure of post-1991 Ethiopia has emerged quite directly out of the TPLF experience before its taking power. Its political ideology of rule, based on 'revolutionary democracy' and ethnic-based federalism is an updated adaptation of Leftist ideas and Marxist-Leninist models in the political

---

119 The TPLF/EPRDF has expanded its party/state structure to the other regions in the MLLT fashion. This structure stretches down from the *qebele* which was the lowest during the *Dergue* era and now divided into 3 or 4 *nu'us* (sub) *qebele*, then each *nu'us qebele* to 5 or 6 *gott'* or *kushet* and finally each *gott'* constituting 30 or 50 households called *mengistawi buden* or *m. gujile*. At each level there are three party/state represen-tatives assigned to work as administrators.

sphere, combined with a more liberalized economy, in which though the party and the state have a dominant role.[120]

Although clear data on the opinions of people are difficult to get, indications are that the TPLF approach to governance – both as to its authoritarianism and its ethnicization policy - is decreasing in popularity among the wider public. According to domestic and foreign observers, conflicts are frequent, ethnic group relations are tense, religious antagonisms grow, complaints about suppression of (political and human) rights and police and army over-reaction are a cause for concern,[121] and economic favouritism and corruption are lamented widely.

One of the TPLF's survival strategies has been to invoke the malleable material of ethnicity and ethnic nationalism. It claims that if the opposition takes over or wins power, the entire people of Tigrai will be doomed as a result of ethnic discrimination and hegemonism, if not worse. But this scenario is also a political ploy, more to stimulate the EPRDF's policies of language-based ethnic federalism than by a danger posed by the few countervailing forces[122] As a rule the difference between the political elite and the ordinary Tigrai people is made and people focus on common underlying problems that cross-cut the 'ethnic problems'.

As ethnic mobilization was the TPLF's means to seize power, it now appears that the ethnic polarization being created as a result is threatening the state power structure and national cohesion. There is widely spread mistrust against the government and among ethnic groups, many times irrational (political and economic) competition, and a new dynamics of 'we

120 The ruling party (and its affiliates), through private limited companies headed by party members, controls key sectors of the Ethiopia economy – banking, production, publishing, building, and import-export trade.

121 This was most evident in the wake of the controversial general elections of 2005, leading to a wave of arrests, street killings, and dismantling of opposition forces. This violence was criticized in the first report of a special Inquiry Commission, set up in 2006 by the government. Its report was unexpectedly critical, subsequently repressed and forcibly changed. As subsequent events have shown, indications are that even in the home region of Tigrai – where opposition parties had a very hard time to campaign in the 2005 and 2007 election campaigns or even to be tolerated –support for the TPLF is declining.

122 Only a few 'extremist' forces exist and have no adherence within Ethiopia. One is the Oakland-based 'Ethiopian Patriotic Front', which in its programme dated 7 May 1994, Section 2, Article 4/a, stated that 'anyone born into or related by marriage to the Tigraian ethnic group can not be a member'. People question whether members of this extremist group can be called Amhara patriots or Ethiopian patriots. The group's ideas have been condemned widely by all concerned Ethiopians and now-a-days it does not effectively function.

vs. them' conceptions. Collective consensus that was built for centuries as a people who shared common history, common political culture and economic process has been badly corroded. On the other hand, recent studies revealed that, perhaps sceptical towards, or dismayed with what ethnic politics has brought to them, more people are becoming defiant of ethnic categorizations that tend to overshadow notions of Ethiopian identity. New research almost a decade after the TPLF/EPRDF seized power was conducted where respondents from 14 ethnic groups were given 'the question and choice of whether they were primarily members of their specific ethnic group, Ethiopian, or neither of the two. It was found that 80% of the participants reported primarily 'being Ethiopian'. Only 17.5% opted for being primarily a member of their respective ethnic group and 2.5% preferred neither of the two' (Habtamu Wondimu 2001: 25). In his critical remarks on the Oromo nationalists whose position is not far removed from that of the TPLF, Merera Gudina (2002: 5) tends to corroborate the above findings when he wrote: 'The Southern Ethiopian ethnic groups and the multi-ethnic forces whose platform is to struggle for democracy and Ethiopian unity are not happy with the Oromo perspective either'. The realization of the pitfalls accompanying ethnic politics may, however, lead the nation eventually to forge a rational design where diversity becomes a more balanced building block of wider unity in a system that combines respect for the facts of diversity and the politico-economic needs for a workable unifying framework in a less ethnic federal form that would discourage political manipulation of ethnicity.

The research question of this thesis (Chapter 1) was about why, how and on what ethno-cultural and other basis the Tigraian nationalist movement emerged and prevailed, how it successfully *mobilized* a critical mass of people behind it, and what the role of the political elite vis-à-vis the masses was during and after the struggle. We highlighted the role played by ethnicity but in a peculiar combination with revolutionary socialist ideology that yielded both contradictions and elements of a strong though authoritarian power ideology.

It was hypothesized in a general sense that in an underdeveloped multi-ethnic society such as Ethiopia, where civil and political rights were traditionally not institutionalized, political-economic 'resource competition' was a regular feature, and collective claims are not recognized or adequately handled by the state administration, the tendency for ethnic resistance/conflicts to emerge is high. With power concentrated in the centre and in the hands of a privileged class, and basic resources being scarce and conflict-generating, the political elite of a dominant ethnic or regional group in its quest for power tends to manipulate ethnic antagonisms to remain in power, which in turn leads to forms of countervailing ethnic resistance.

The case study of the TPLF and its emergence and experience in government has borne out this hypothesis, and our account has also shown that the same mechanism may continue to operate under the new political regime based on the very notion of ethnic-based governance, showing deficiencies in the allocation of equity and rights.

In this thesis, the study of the rise and consolidation of an ethno-nationalist insurgent front turned government has no doubt shown that ethnic nationalism, is a forceful mobilizing ideology. In general it will remain so, also in comparable social conditions – as long as political repression, economic marginalization and social injustices are prevalent in a multi-ethnic and diverse society dominated by a political force that openly or tacitly claims to represent a certain ethnic group. Ethno-nationalism is forceful because it can be enacted as the embodiment of the material and social concerns of a given people. This situation makes ethnic mobilization inevitable and the imminence of confrontation real. On the basis of either primordial or instrumentalist views of ethnicity, the self-appointed political elite of an ethnic collectivity or group can draw this collectivity to become a force that can be mobilized for the realization of political, economic or military aims, as illustrated here with the TPLF. It can unseat an incumbent regime and achieve real or perceived advantages. We have seen this trajectory unequivocally in the case of the TPLF. But since the phenomena and agenda of ethnic nationalism are fluid, they can be easily manipulated by the elite in arbitrary and dubious ways. The political consequences for the people in whose name the struggles were fought can be a deception certainly when an institutionalized democracy is not realized that negotiates identities, rights and equitable economic development. In Ethiopia the future is still determined by the political elite which set the course of the ethnicized struggle. Ernest Gellner (1964: 169) has argued that nationalism 'invents nations where they do not exist', and over four decades after, TPLF/EPRDF's ethno-nationalist banner has paved the way for the emergence of 'ethnic nations' across the country and accentuated there 'rightful' differences. This had created a conundrum of choices and political dilemmas for the multi-ethnic society of Ethiopia. As much as the dominant elite of the TPLF/EPRDF utilized ethnicity to come this far and defend the present power structure, the marginalized elites may use similar tool to resist domination, fomenting ethnic conflicts in which civil liberties and human rights, the essential elements of building civil society, will be the casualties. Ethnic mobilization can only play a positive role only if it is based on establishing and institutionalizing civil liberties and human rights upon which diversities are accommodated and differences are mediated democratically.

This thesis has thus demonstrated that however real and justified ethnic grievances may be, and however understandable mobilization on an ethnic or ethno-regional basis can be, the consequent and often organized politicization – and thereby rigidification – of ethnic identity on a mass basis carries highly problematic aspects for a national political order. The 'ethnic model', especially when coupled to an authoritarian political system of governance, provides doubtful solutions to the issue of multi-ethnic identities and ethno-regional disparity of a country, and diverts institutional democratic options. This underlines the assumption of this thesis that ethnicity – by nature fluid and manipulable – is best handled with care, lest it takes on a life of its own and becomes the prime conflict-generating force in the social, political-economic and not the least psychological sense.

Bibliography

Note: as is customary, Ethiopian and Eritrean authors are cited on first name.

Aalen, L. 2000a. Ethiopia's paradox: constitutional devolution and centralized party rule. Paper presented at the 14ᵗʰ International Conference of Ethiopian Studies, November 2000, Addis Ababa.

_____. 2002b. *Ethnic Federalism in a Dominant Party State: the Ethiopian experience 1991-2000*. Bergen: Chr. Michelsen Institute.

_____. 2007. *Institutionalising the Politics of Ethnicity. Actors, Power and Mobilisation in Southern Ethiopia under Ethnic Federalism*. Oslo: University of Oslo (Ph.D. thesis).

Abbink, J. 1995. Transformations of violence in twentieth-century Ethiopia: cultural roots, political conjunctures, *Focaal. Tijdschrift voor Antropologie* 25: 57-77.

_____. 1997. Ethnicity and constitutionalism in contemporary Ethiopia. *Journal of African Law* 41(1): 159-174.

_____. 1998. New configurations of Ethiopian ethnicity: the challenge of the South. *Northeast African Studies* 5(1), N.S.: 59-81.

_____. 2003a. Badme and the Ethio-Eritrean border: the challenge of demarcation in the post-war period. *Africa* (Roma) 58(2): 219-231.

_____. 2003b. Ethiopia-Eritrea: proxy wars and prospects of peace in the Horn of Africa.
Journal of Contemporary African Studies 21(3): 407-426.

_____. 2005. Being young in Africa: the politics of despair and renewal. In J. Abbink & I. van Kessel, eds, *Vanguard or Vandals: Youth, Politics and Conflict in Africa*, pp. 1-34. Leiden - Boston: Brill.

_____. 2006. Discomfiture of democracy? The 2005 election crisis in Ethiopia and its aftermath. *African Affairs* 105 (419): 173-199.

_____. 2006. Ethnicity and conflict generation in Ethiopia: some problems and prospects of ethno-regional federalism. *Journal of Contemporary African Studies*, 24(2): 389-414.

_____. 2007. Mikael Sihul. In S. Uhlig, ed., *Encyclopaedia Aethiopica*, vol. 3: 962-964. Wiesbaden: Harrassowitz.

Aberra Jembere. 2000. *An Introduction to the Legal History of Ethiopia, 1434-1974.* Münster - Hamburg – London: Lit Verlag.

Addis Birhan. 1998. *Eritrea, a Problem Child of Ethiopia: Causes, Consequences and Strategic Implications of the Conflict.* N.p.: Marran Books.

Addis Hiwot. 1975. *Ethiopia: From Autocracy to Revolution,* Occasional Publication No.1, *Review of African Political Economy.* London.

Aklilu Abraham. 2000. *Towards a Political Resolution of Ethnic Conflicts in Ethiopia: The Case of Siltie Gurage Identity Question.* Research Report submitted to OSSREA, August 2000.

Alazar Tesfa-Michael. 1948. Eritrean heroes. *New Times and Ethiopia News,* 1-2.

Alemseged Abbay. 1997. The Trans-Mareb past in the present. *Journal of Modern African Studies* 35(2): 321-34.

_____. 2004. Diversity and state building in Ethiopia, in *African Affairs* 103(413): 593-614.

Alter, P. 1994 (2nd edition). *Nationalism.* London: Edward Arnold.

Andargatchew Assegid. 2000. *Beachir Yetekech Rejime Guzo: MEISON beItiopia Hizboch Tigil Wust'* (in Amharic). Addis Ababa: Central Printing Press.

Aregawi Berhe. 2000. Ethiopia: success story or state of chaos? In R. Munck and P.L. de Silva, eds, *Post-modern Insurgencies: Political Violence, Identity Formation and Peace-making in Comparative Perspective,* pp. 91-124. London and New York: Macmillan and St. Martin's Press.

_____. 2003. Revisiting resistance in Italian-occupied Ethiopia: the Patriots' movement (1936-1941) and the redefinition of post-war Ethiopia. In J. Abbink, *et al.,* eds, *Rethinking Resistance: Revolt and Violence in African History,* pp. 87-113, Leiden: Brill.

_____. 2004. The origin of the Tigray People's Liberation Front, *African Affairs* 103 (413): 569-592.

Arjomand, S. A. 1986. Iran's Islamic revolution in comparative perspective, *World Politics* 38: 383-414.

Bahru Zewde. 1991. *A History of Modern Ethiopia, 1855-1974.* London: James Currey.

Bairu Tafla. 1999. Review of Anthony d'Avery's *"Lord of the Sea: The History of a Red Sea Society from the Sixteenth to the Nineteenth Centuries."* *Eritrean Studies Review* 3(1): 181-187.

Balsvik, R.R. 1985. *Haile Selassie's Students: the Intellectual and Social Background to a Revolution, 1952-1977.* East Lansing: African Studies Center, Michigan State University.

Bauer, D.F. 1985. *Household and Society in Ethiopia. An Economic and Social Analysis of Tigray Social Principles and Household Organization* (second edition). East Lansing: Michigan State University, African Studies Center.

Behrend, H. 1998. War in northern Uganda: the Holy Sprit Movement of Alice Lakwena, Severino Lukoya and Joseph Kony (1986-97). In C. Clapham, ed., *African Guerrillas*, pp. 107-118. Oxford: James Currey.

Belai Giday. 1983 E.C. *YeItiopia Silitanie* (Ethiopian Civilization), Addis Ababa: Berhanena Selam Printing Press.

Bereket Habte-Selassie. 1980. *Conflict and Intervention in the Horn of Africa*. London: Monthly Review Press.

Buchanan, A. 1997. Theories of secession, *Philosophy and Public Affairs* 26(1): 31-61.

Budge, E.A. Wallis. 1970. *A History of Ethiopia, Nubia & Abyssinia: According to the Hieroglyphic Inscriptions of Egypt and Nubia, and the Ethiopian Chronicles.* Oosterhout, NL: Anthropological Publications (Reprint).

Bugajski, J. 1994. The fate of minorities in Eastern Europe. In L. Diamond and M.F. Plattner, eds. *Nationalism, Ethnic Conflict, and Democracy*, pp. 102-116. Baltimore and London: Johns Hopkins University Press.

Bullock, Alan, *et al.* 1988. *The Fontana Dictionary of Modern Thought*. London: Fontana Press.

Caetani, L., ed., 1911. *Annali dell'Islam*, vol. IV, 219, pp. 366-7. Milano-Roma: U. Hœpli - Fondazione Caetani della Reale Accademia dei Lincei.

Chua, A. 2004. *World on Fire: How Exporting Free Market Democracy Breeds Ethnic Hatred and Global Instability*. New York: Anchor Books.

Clapham, C. 1975. Centralization and local response in Southern Ethiopia, *African Affairs*, 74: 72-81.

_____. 1988. *Transformation and Continuity in Revolutionary Ethiopia*. Cambridge: Cambridge University Press.

_____. 1995. The Horn of Africa: a conflict zone. In O. Furley, ed., *Conflict in Africa*, pp. 72-91. London and New York: I.B. Tauris Publishers.

_____. 1998. Introduction: analysing African insurgencies. In C. Clapham, ed., *African Guerrillas*. Oxford: James Currey - Kampala: Fountain Publishers - Bloomington & Indianapolis: Indiana University Press.

_____. 2002. Rewriting Ethiopian history. *Annales d'Éthiopie* 18: 37-54.

_____. 2004. Ethiopia and the challenges of diversity. In *Africa Insight* 34(1): 50-55.

Colburn, F.D. 1994. *The Vogue of Revolution in Poor Countries*. Princeton NJ: Princeton University Press.

Comaroff, J. and J. Comaroff. 1992. *Ethnography and the Historical Imagination*, Boulder, Co. - San Francisco - Oxford: Westview Press

Connell, D. 2001. Inside the EPLF: the origin of the People's Party and its role in the liberation of Eritrea, *Review of African Political Economy* 28(89): 345-368.

Cornell, S. and D. Hartmann 1998. *Ethnicity and Race: Making Identities in a Changing World*. Thousand Oaks, CA: Pine Forge.

CSA, 1998. *The 1994 Population and Housing Census of Ethiopia. Results at the Country Level. Volume I: Statistical Report*. Addis Ababa: Central Statistical Authority.

Daniel Kindie. 2005. *The Five Dimensions of the Eritrean Conflict 1941 – 2004: Deciphering the Geo-Political Puzzle*. Prairieview, TX: Signature Book Printing.

Dawit Shifaw. 2005. *The Diary of Terror: Ethiopia 1974–1991*. Washington, DC.: Dawit Shifaw/BookSurge, LLC.

Dawit Wolde-Giorgis. 1989. *Red Tears: Class and Revolution in Ethiopia*. Trenton, NJ: Red Sea Press.

Dereje Feyissa. 2006. The experiences of Gambella Regional State. In D. Turton, ed., *Ethnic Federalism: The Ethiopian Experience in Comparative Perspective*, pp. 208-230. Oxford: James Currey.

De Waal, A. ed., 1991. *Evil Days: Thirty Years of War and Famine in Ethiopia*. New York: Human Rights Watch / Africa Watch.

Diamond, L. and M.F. Plattner, eds. 1994. *Nationalism, Ethnic Conflicts, and Democracy*. Baltimore - London: Johns Hopkins University Press.

Donham, D.L. 1999. *Marxist Modern: An Ethnographic History of the Ethiopian Revolution*. Berkeley - Los Angeles - London: University of California Press and Oxford: James Currey.

Doornbos, M. 1978. *Not all the King's Men: Inequality as a Political Instrument in Ankole, Uganda*. The Hague: Mouton Publishers.

_____. 1998. Linking the future to the past: ethnicity and pluralism. In Mohamed Salih, M.A. & J. Markakis, eds. 1998. *Ethnicity and the State in East Africa*, pp. 17-29. Uppsala: Nordiska Afrikainstitutet.

Dix, R. 1984. 'Why revolutions succeed and fail,' *Polity* 16 (Spring): 432-435.

Dos Santos, M. 1973. Interview with Joe Slovo, *African Communist*, no. 55, 4th Quarter, p. 35.

Eriksen, Thomas Hylland. 1993. *Ethnicity and Nationalism: Anthropological Perspectives*. London – Boulder, Co.: Pluto Press.

Erlich, H. 1981. Tigraian nationalism, British involvement and Haila-Selasse's emerging absolutism – northern Ethiopia, 1941-1943. *Asian and African Studies* 15(2): 191-227.

_____. 1996. *Ras Alula and the Scramble for Africa*. Lawrenceville, NJ.: The Red Sea Press.

Esman, M.J. 1994. *Ethnic Politics*. Ithaca, New York: Cornell University Press.

Fattovich, R. 2000. *Aksum and the Habashat: State and Ethnicity in Ancient Northern Ethiopia and Eritrea*. African Studies Centre Working Paper no. 228, Boston: Boston University.

Fanon, F. 1963. *The Wretched of the Earth.* New York: Grove Press, Inc.

Fentahun Tiruneh, 1990. *The Ethiopian Students: Their Struggle to Articulate the Ethiopian Revolution,* Chicago: N.p..

Foran, J., ed. 1997. *Theorizing Revolutions.* London - New York: Routledge.

Gabre-Selassie, Zewde. 1975. *Yohannes IV of Ethiopia: A Political Biography.* Oxford: Clarendon Press.

Gebre-Hiwet Baykedagn. 1912. *Emperor Menelik and Ethiopia.* Asmara: Swedish Mission.

Gebru Tareke. 1977. *Rural Protest in Ethiopia, 1941-1970: A Study of Three Rebellions.* Syracuse, NY: Syracuse University (Ph.D. Dissertation).

_____. 1991. *Ethiopia: Power and Protest, Peasant Revolts in the Twentieth Century.* Cambridge: Cambridge University Press.

_____. 2004. From Af Abet to Shire: the defeat and demise of Ethiopia's 'Red' Army 1988-89. *Journal of Modern African Studies* 42(2), pp. 239-281.

Gerima Tafere. 1956. *Gondare Begashaw,* Addis Ababa.

Gilkes, P. 1975. *The Dying Lion: Feudalism and Modernisation in Ethiopia.* London: Julian Friedman Publishers.

Gilkes, P. and M. Plaut. 1999. *War in the Horn: the Conflict between Eritrea and Ethiopia.* London: Royal Institute of International Affairs.

Goldstone, J.A. 1991. An analytical framework. In J.A. Goldstone, *et al.,* eds, *Revolutions of the Late Twentieth Century,* pp. 37-51. Boulder, Co. - San Francisco - Oxford: Westview Press.

Goldstone, J.A. *et al.,* eds. 1991. *Revolutions of the Late Twentieth Century.* Boulder, Co. - San Francisco - Oxford: Westview Press.

Goodwin, J. 1994. 'Old regimes and revolutions in the Second and Third Worlds: a comparative perspective,' *Social Science History* 18: 575-604.

Goulbourne, H. 1991. Conclusion: the future of democracy in Africa. In R. Cohen and H. Goulbourne, eds, *Democracy and Socialism in Africa.* Boulder, Co. - San Francisco - Oxford: Westview Press.

Gurr, T.R. and J.A. Goldstone. 1991. Comparisons and policy implications. In J.A. Goldstone, *et al.,* eds, *Revolutions of the Late Twentieth Century.* Boulder, Co. - San Francisco - Oxford: Westview Press.

Gurr, Ted R. 1970. *Why Men Rebel.* Princeton, NJ: Princeton University Press.

Habtamu Wondimu, in collaboration with B. Beit-Hallahmi and J. Abbink. 2001. *Psychological Modernity and Attitudes to Social Change in Ethiopian Young Adults: The Role of Ethnic Identity and Stereotypes,* NIRP Research for Policy Series 9. Amsterdam: Royal Tropical Institute - KIT Publishers.

Halliday, F. and M. Molyneux. 1981. *The Ethiopian Revolution.* London: Verso.

Hammond, J. 1999. *Fire from the Ashes: A Chronicle of the Revolution in Tigray, Ethiopia, 1975-1991.* Lawrenceville, NJ and Asmara: Red Sea Press.

_____. 1989. *Sweeter than Honey: Testimonies of Tigrayan Women.* Oxford: Third World First.

Hanlon, J. 1984. *Mozambique: The Revolution Under Fire*, London: Zed Books.

Harrison, G. 2002. *Issues in the Contemporary Politics of Sub-Saharan Africa: The Dynamics of Struggle and Resistance.* New York - Basingstoke: Palgrave-Macmillan.

Henze, Paul B., 1998. A political success story. *Journal of Democracy* 9(4) 40-54.

_____. 2000. *Layers of Time: A History of Ethiopia.* London: Hurst & Co.

Hess, R.L. 1963. Italy and Africa: colonial ambitions in the First World War. *Journal of African History* 4(1): 105-126.

Hizkias Assefa. 1996. Ethnic conflict in the Horn of Africa: myth and reality. In K. Rupesinghe and V.A. Tishkov (eds.), *Ethnicity and Power in Contemporary World*, Tokyo: UN University Press.

Hoare, Q. and G.N. Smith, eds. 1971. *Antonio Gramsci – 1929-35, Selections from the Prison Note Books.* London: Lawrence & Wishart; New York: International Publishers.

Horowitz, D.L. 1994. Democracy in divided societies. In L. Diamond and M.F. Plattner eds, *Nationalism, Ethnic Conflict, and Democracy*, pp. 36-56. Baltimore and London: Johns Hopkins University Press.

_____.1985. *Ethnic Groups in Conflict.* Berkeley - Los Angeles - and London: University of California Press.

Human Rights Watch. 1994. *Human Rights Watch/Africa*, vol. 6, no. 2. New York: HRW.

Huntington, S.P. 1968. *Political Order in Changing Societies.* New Haven - London: Yale University Press.

Ismagilova, R. 1994. Ethnicity, nationalism and self-determination. A paper presented at the XIIIth World Conference of Sociology, Bielefeld.

Johnson, D.H. 1998. The Sudan People's Liberation Army, in C. Clapham (ed.), *African Guerrillas.* Oxford: James Currey - Bloomington & Indianapolis: Indiana University Press - Kampala: Fountain Publishers.

Jok, J. Madut. 2005. War, changing ethics and the position of youth in South Sudan. In J. Abbink & I. van Kessel, eds, *Vanguard or Vandals: Youth, Politics and Conflict in Africa*, pp. 143-160. Leiden - Boston: Brill.

Juteau, D. 2004. 'Pures laines' Québécois: the concealed ethnicity of dominant majorities. In E.P. Kaufmann, ed., *Rethinking Ethnicity: Majority Groups and Dominant Minorities*, pp. 84-101. London - New York: Routledge.

Kahsay Berhe. 2005. *Ethiopia: Democratization and Unity - The Role of the Tigray People's Liberation Front.* Münster: MV-Verlag.

Kasfir, N. 2005. Guerrillas and civilian participation: National Resistance Army in Uganda, 1981-86, *Journal of Modern African Studies* 43(2): 271-296.

Kassahun Berhanu. 2000. *Returnees, Resettlement and Power Relations: The Making of a Political Constituency in Humera, Ethiopia*. Amsterdam: VU University Press.

Kaufmann, Ch. 1996. Possible and impossible solutions to ethnic civil wars, *International Security* 20(4): 136-175.

Kaufmann, E.P., ed. 2004. *Rethinking Ethnicity: Majority Groups and Dominant Minorities*. London - New York: Routledge.

Keane, J. 1995. Nations, nationalism and European citizens. In S. Periwal , *ed.*, *Notions of Nationalism*, Budapest: Central European University Press.

Kiflu Tadesse. 1993. *The Generation: The History of the Ethiopian People's Revolutionary Party* (Part I). Trenton, N.J.: The Red Sea Press.

Kly Y.N. , 2000. Preface, in: D. Kly & R. Falk, eds, *In Pursuit of the Right to Self-Determination. Collected Papers & Proceedings of the First International Conference on the Right to Self-Determination & the United Nations*, Gardena, Cal.: Clarity Press.

Kobishchanov, Y.M. 1979. *Axum*. University Park, Penn.: Pennsylvania State University Press.

Lal, B.B. 1995. Symbolic interaction theories. *American Behavioural Scientist* 38(3): 421-441.

Leenco Lata. 1999. *The Ethiopian State at the Crossroads: Decolonization and Democratization or Disintegration*. Lawrenceville, NJ and Asmara: Red Sea Press.

Lenin, V.I. 1971. *Critical Remarks on the National Question*. Moscow: Progress Publishers.

Lipsky, W. 1976. Comparative approach to the study of revolution: a historiographic essay. *Review of Politics* 38: 494-509.

Marcus, H.G. 1994. *A History of Ethiopia*. Berkeley - Los Angeles - London: University of California Press.

Markakis, J. 1990. *National and Class Conflict in the Horn of Africa*. London and Atlantic Highlands, NJ: Zed Books.

_____. 1996. The political challenge of ethnicity. In L. Gorgendiere, *et al.*

(eds.), *Ethnicity in Africa: Roots, Meanings and Implications*. Edinburgh: Edinburgh University, Centre of African Studies.

_____ & K. Fukui, eds. 1994. *Ethnicity and Conflict in the Horn of Africa*. London: James Currey and Athens, OH: Ohio University Press.

_____ & Nega Ayele. 1978. *Class and Revolution in Ethiopia*. Nottingham: Spokesman.

MacIntyre, A. 2005. *Invisible Stakeholders: Children and War in Africa.* Pretoria: Institute for Security Studies.

McAdams, D., *et al.* 2001. *Dynamics of Contention.* New York: The Free Press.

Medhane Tadesse. 1999. *The Eritrean-Ethiopian War: Retrospect and Prospect.* Addis Ababa: Mega Printing Enterprise.

Medhane Tadesse & J. Young. 2003. *TPLF: Reform or Decline,* in *Review of African Political Economy* 97: 389-403.

Melakou Tegegn. 2004. From social revolution to social regression: Ethiopia, 1974-2004. *Africa Insight* 34(1): 43-49.

Merera Gudina. 2000. The contradictory perspectives on Ethiopian politics and their implications for the country's quest for democracy. Paper presented to the 14th International Conference of Ethiopian Studies, November 2000, Addis Ababa.

_____. 2002. *Ethiopia: Competing Ethnic Nationalisms and the Quest for Democracy, 1960-2000.* (Ph.D. Dissertation), Maastricht: Shaker Publishing.

Mesfin Araya. 1988. *Eritrea 1941-52, the Failure of the Emergence of the Nation-State: Towards a Clarification of the Eritrean Question in Ethiopia* (Ph.D. Dissertation). New York: City University of New York.

_____. 1993. A review of the Addis Ababa May 1993 constitutional symposium, *Ethiopian Review* 3(9): 31-33.

Miller, N. and R. Aya, eds, 1971. *National Liberation: Revolution in the Third World.* New York: The Free Press.

Mohamed Salih, M.A. 2001. *African Democracies and African Politics.* London: Pluto Press.

Moshiri, F. 1991. Revolutionary conflict theory in an evolutionary perspective. In J.A. Goldstone, *et al.,* eds, *Revolutions of the Late Twentieth Century,* pp. 4-36. Boulder - San Francisco - Oxford: Westview Press.

Muller, J.Z. 2008. 'Us and them: the enduring power of ethnic nationalism', *Foreign Affairs,* March/April 2008, pp. 18-35.

Munslow, B. 1974. Leadership in the Front for the Liberation of Mozambique, Part I. In C.R. Hill and P. Warwick, eds, *Southern African Research in Progress,* Collected Papers 1, University of York.

Negede Gobeze. 2004. *Higge-Mengist, Mirchana Democracy Be'Ethiopia - Ketelant Wodia Eske Nege* (Amharic) (*Constitution, Election and Democracy in Ethiopia - Past and Future*). Washington, D.C.: ASEOP Publishers.

Nodia, Ghia. 1994. Nationalism and democracy. In L. Diamond and M.F. Plattner, eds, *Nationalism, Ethnic Conflict, and Democracy,* pp. 3-22. Baltimore - London: Johns Hopkins University Press.

Ottaway, M. and D. Ottaway. 1978. *Ethiopia: Empire in Revolution.* New York: Africana Publishing Co.

Patman, R.G. 1990. *The Soviet Union in the Horn of Africa: The Diplomacy of Intervention and Disengagement*. Cambridge: Cambridge University Press.

Paulos Milkias. 2001. The great purge and ideological paradox in contemporary Ethiopian politics, *Horn of Africa* 19 (1-4): 1-99.

Pausewang, S., *et al.*, eds. 2002. *Ethiopian since the Derg: a Decade of Democratic Pretension and Performance*. London - New York: Zed Books.

Perruchon, J. 1893. *Les Chroniques de Zar'a Ya'eqob et de Ba'eda Maryam rois d'Éthiopie de 1434 à 1478*. Paris: Émile Bouillon, Éditeur.

Pool, D. 1998. The Eritrean People's Liberation Front. In C. Clapham (ed.), *African Guerrillas*. Oxford: James Currey.

_____. 2001. *From Guerrillas to Government: The Eritrean Peoples Liberation Front*, Oxford: James Currey - Athens, OH: Ohio University Press.

Roosens, E. 1989. *Creating Ethnicity: The Process of Ethnogenesis*, London: Sage.

Rupesinghe, K. and V.A. Tashkov. 1996. *Ethnicity and Power in the Contemporary World*. Tokyo - New York - Paris: United Nations University Press.

Salole, G. 1979. Who are the Shoans? *Horn of Africa* 2(3): 20-29.

Salome Gabre-Egziabher. 1968. The Ethiopian Patriots 1936-1941, *Ethiopia Observer*, 12(2): 63-91

Sarkesian, S.C., ed., 1975. *Revolutionary Guerrilla Warfare*. Chicago: Precedent Publishing, Inc.

Saul, J.S. 1973. FRELIMO and the Mozambique revolution. In G. Arrighi & J.S. Saul (eds.), *Essays on the Political Economy of Africa*. New York and London: Monthly Review Press.

Scarritt, J.R. 1991. Zimbabwe: revolutionary violence resulting in reform. In J.A. Goldstone, T.R. Gurr & F. Moshiri, eds, 1991. *Revolutions of the Late Twentieth Century*. Boulder, Co.: Westview Press.

Schwab, P.. 1985. *Ethiopia: Politics, Economics and Society*. London: Frances Pinter.

Scott, Ph.. 1985. The Sudan Peoples' Liberation Movement (SPLM) and Liberation Army (SPLA), *Review of African Political Economy* 35: 69-82.

Seifu Abbawollo. 1960. *Yetarik Qeros* (in Amharic). Addis Ababa.

Sergew Habte-Selassie. 1972. *Ancient and Medieval Ethiopian History to 1270*. Addis Ababa: United Printers.

Shivji, I.G. 1991. The democracy debate in Africa: Tanzania, *Review of African Political Economy* 50: 79-91.

Skocpol, Th. 1994. *Social Revolutions in the Modern World*. Cambridge: Cambridge University Press.

Smith, A.D. 1976. *National Movements*. London: MacMillan Press.

Solomon Gashaw. 1993. Nationalism and ethnic conflict in Ethiopia. In C. Young, ed., *The Rising Tide of Cultural Pluralism: the Nation-State at Bay*, pp. 138-157. Madison: University of Wisconsin Press.

Stalin, J. 1942 (orig. 1913). *Marxism and the National Question*. New York.

_____. 1975. *Marxism and the National-Colonial Question*, San Francisco: Proletarian Publishers.

Stavenhagen, R. 1996. *Ethnic Conflicts and the Nation-State*. London - New York: Macmillan Press - St. Martin's Press.

Swain, J. 1996. *River of Time*. London: Minerva.

Taddesse Tamrat. 1972. *Church and State in Ethiopia, 1270-1527*. Oxford: Clarendon Press.

Tadesse Mecha. 1951. *Tikur Arbänya* (= Black Patriot, in Amharic). Asmara.

Tecola W. Hagos. 1995. *Democratization? Ethiopia (1991-1994): A Personal View*. Cambridge, Mass.: Khepera Publishers.

Tekeste Negash. 1996. *Eritrea and Ethiopia. The Federal Experience*. New Brunswick: Transaction Books - Uppsala: Nordiska Afrikainstitutet.

Tekeste Negash & K. Tronvoll. 2000. *Brothers at War: Making Sense of the Eritrean-Ethiopian War*. Oxford: James Currey – Athens, Oh.: Ohio University Press.

Teferra Haile-Selassie. 1997. *The Ethiopian Revolution 1974-1991: From A Monarchical Autocracy to A Military Oligarchy*. London - New York: Kegan Paul International.

Tesfatsion Medhanie. 1986. *Eritrea: the Dynamics of a National Question*. Amsterdam: B.R. Gruner.

_____. 1994. Eritrea and Neighbours in the 'New World Order': Geopolitics, Democracy and Islamic Fundamentalism. Münster - Hamburg: Lit Verlag.

_____. 2007. *Toward Confederation in the Horn of Africa. Focus on Ethiopia and Eritrea*. Frankfurt/M – London: IKO Verlag.

Teshale Tibebu. 1995. *The Making of Modern Ethiopia: 1896-1974*. Lawrenceville, NJ: Red Sea Press.

Trimingham, J.S. 1952. *Islam in Ethiopia*. Oxford: Oxford University Press.

Triulzi, A. 2006. The past as a contested terrain: commemorating new sites of memory in war-torn Ethiopia. In P. Kaarsholm, ed., *Violence, Political Culture & Development in Africa*, pp. 122-138. Oxford: James Currey.

Turton, D., ed. 2006. *Ethnic Federalism: The Ethiopian Experience in Comparative Perspective*. Oxford: James Currey – Athens, Oh.: Ohio University Press – Addis Ababa: Addis Ababa University Press.

Van Walraven, K. and J. Abbink. 2003. Rethinking resistance in African history: an introduction. In J. Abbink, M. de Bruijn and K. van Walraven, eds, *Rethinking Resistance: Revolt and Violence in African History*, pp. 1-40. Leiden and Boston: Brill.

Van Walraven, K. 2003. Sawaba's rebellion in Niger (1964-1965): narrative and meaning. In Abbink, J., De Bruijn, M. and K. van Walraven, eds, *Rethinking Resistance: Revolt and Violence in African History*, pp. 218-252. Leiden and Boston: Brill.

Vaughan, S. 1994. *The Addis Ababa Transitional Conference of July 1991: Its Origins, History and Significance*. Edinburgh: Edinburgh University, Centre of African Studies, Occasional Paper.

Vines, A. 1996. *RENAMO: From Terrorism to Democracy in Mozambique?* Amsterdam/London: Eduardo Mondlane Foundation/James Currey.

Walzer, M. 1965. *The Revolution of the Saints*. Cambridge, Mass.: Harvard University Press.

Wickham-Crowley, T. 1994. Elite, elite settlements and revolutionary movements in Latin America 1950-1980, *Social Science History* 18: 543-574.

Wolde-Selassie Asfaw. 1992. *The TPLF: From Guerrilla to Government*. London: Unpublished Manuscript.

Wylde, A.B. 1970. *Modern Abyssinia*. Westport, Conn.: Negro University Press (Reprint of the original 1901 edition).

Yohannes Petros. 1993. *Oromia National Awakening: A Brief Introduction*. London: Burqaa Publishing House.

Young, J. 1997. *Peasant Revolution in Ethiopia: The Tigray People's Liberation Front, 1975–1991*. Cambridge: Cambridge University Press.

Archival Materials, Brochures, Newspaper Publications

Abebe Haile-Selassie (Brig.-Gen.), in *Teraroch Yanketeket Tiwled*, Addis Ababa, Mega Publishers, 1989 E.C. (A Generation that Shocked Mountains, 1997).

Adulis, Official Organ of the EPLF, 1985, vol. 1, no. 8.

Aregawi Berhe, *Wetaderawi Strateji Bezimelket, Adi Mohamedai, Lekatit 1975*, ('Concerning our Military Strategy', Adi Mohamedai, February 1983).

_____, *Zetenawihe Hizbawi Kuinat, Gurure*, 1976, ('Protracted Peoples War', Gurure, 1984).

_____, *Kule-Medayawi Kuinat ab Tigray, Akmara, 1977*, ('Integrated War in Tigray', Akmara, 1985

_____, 'Origin and Development of the National Movement in Tigray: A Socio-Historical Analysis', MA Thesis 1993, ISS, The Hague.

ELF-R.C. 'History of the Ethio-Eritrean Conflict and Our Viewpoint on its Situation.' ELF Paper, 4th Annual Conference on Horn of Africa, City University of New York, May 27-28, 1989.

Embassy of Ethiopia: Report, London 1994: 1-2.

EMLF. *Ye-Itiopia Marxawi Leninawi Hayl Program, Ginbot 1981 E.C.* / Program of the Ethiopian Marxist-Leninist Force (EMLF), 1989.

EPLF. Department of Information, *Iske Meche T'orinet?* (Until When War?), Asmara: Merha Biher, 1981.

EPRDF News Bulletin, Statement by the Transitional Government Concerning Displaced Ethiopian Citizens from Eritrea, August 30, 1991

EPRDF, 'The Development Lines of Revolutionary Democracy', Addis Ababa, 1992 E.C. (2000).

EPRDF, 2001a. 'Fundamental Questions of Democracy in Ethiopia', Addis Ababa.

EPRDF, 2001b.'*Gimgema* Papers' (Papers of Appraisal/Evaluation), Addis Ababa.

Dowden, Richard. 'Tigrayans Home in on Ethiopia's Lifeline', Interview with Meles Zenawi, Prime Minister of Ethiopia, in *The Independent* (London), 28 November 1989.

German Observer Group, Statement on the District and Regional Elections in Ethiopia 1992, issued on June 26, 1992.

Giday Bahrishum, 1985 E.C. *Amora*, (memoir).

Giday Zeratsion, *Malelit Entittekilae –2: Firacha Netsegam Guuzo Nyeman, Sene 1979 E.C.,* (MLLT Exposed -2: Signalling Left Driving Right, June 1987)

Henze, Paul B., 1990. The Tigre People's Liberation Front: Conversations with Meles Zenawi, Washington DC, RAND Corporation, 18 April 1990.

Leenco Lata, The Making and Un-making of Ethiopia's Transitional Charter. Paper presented at the 37th Annual Meeting of the African Studies Association, Toronto, Canada, November 3-6, 1994, no.105

MLLT, 1985a. Minimum Program of the Marxist-Leninist League of Tigray, adopted in the founding Congress of the MLLT, July 1977(E.C.).

MLLT, 1985b. *Nai Marxe-Leninawi Lig Tigray Meseretawi-Higi* / *Hintsa, Hamle 1977(E.C. Tigrigna)* / the Constitution of MLLT, July 1985.

MLLT, 1985c. *Yehiwehat Kominist Hail Ye-10 Amet Guzo Gimgema, Hamle 1977* (Amharic) / Evaluation of ten years' performance of the TPLF communist force, July 1985.

MLLT, 1987a. *Nai Amet Propagand Andi Medebat ab Abalat Leaguen Serawiten, 1979 E.C. (Tigrigna)* / Yearly Propaganda main plan for League Members and Army, 1987.

MLLT, 1987b. *Tewedeb*. Ideological and Political Journal of MLLT, Meskerem 1, 1979 E.C. (September 1987), 1st Year, no.1.

Nharnet. 2005. From the Experiences of the Eritrea Liberation Army (ELA). Part VIII and Final. On: http://www.nharnet.com/Jan2005/ Nharnet Team_Jan13. htm

News from Ethiopia, 'Ethiopians Participate in Constitutional Discussion', Embassy of Ethiopia, Washington D.C., 26 January 1994, pp. 1-2.

Norwegian Observer Group, *Local and Regional Elections in Ethiopia 21 June 1992,* Norwegian Institute of Human Rights, Human Rights Report no. 1, August 1002.

Tekeste Agazi, 1983. *Agrarian Reform in Tigray: A case of Land Reform in the District of Adi-Nebried.* Occasional Papers on Tigray No. 1, Published by the Friends of Tigray in the UK.

Tesfay Atsbaha and Kahsay Berhe, *Two Groups of the TPLF and Two Issues of Ethiopia: Power Struggle and the MLLT from 1979 to 1985,* at http://www.tigrainet. ethioexpress.com//Articles/KahsayTesfay1.html.

The Constitution of the Federal Democratic Republic of Ethiopia, December 8, 1994, Addis Ababa, Ethiopia.

TPLF, *Ehapana Ye-Ethiopia Abyot,* April 1972 E.C.

TPLF, Manifesto of the Tigray People's Liberation Front, vol. 1, February 1976.

TPLF, *May Day,* vol. 1, no. 3, April 1978.

TPLF, *Woyeen,* Official Organ of the TPLF. August 1978.

TPLF, '*Temokero Zemechatatna',* (Tigrigna), Tiri 1974 E.C. / Experience of the Campaigns, January 1981.

TPLF, '*Meriet Mekelo ab Zoba Zana',* (Tigrigna), Meskerem 1977 E.C. / Land distribution in Zone Zana, September, 1984.

TPLF, '*Fitsametat-Woyyanena',* (Tigrigna), 1978 E.C. / Accomplishments of our Revolution, 1986.

TPLF, '*Biret hizbi Eritrea kulkul Afu Ayidefaen'* (Tigrigna), 1979 E.C. / Never will the gun of the Eritrean people hangdown, 1986.

TPLF, *People's Voice,* TPLF Foreign Relations Bureau, 1990.

TPLF, Tigray: *A Nation in Struggle.* TPLF Foreign Relations Bureau, 1979.

TPLF, '*Ye-Eritrea Hizb Tigil keyet Wediet'* (Amharic), 1979 E.C. / The Eritrean People's Struggle – from Where to Where, 1986.

TPLF, 'Ye-*Tigil Tiri'* bi-monthly journal of the TPLF Foreign Committee, vol. 1, no. 2, March 1977 E.C.

TPLF, 'Ye-*Tigil Tiri',* bi-monthly journal of the TPLF foreign committee, v-1, no.-1, September 1977 E.C.

TPLF, 'Ye-*Tigil Tiri',* bi-monthly journal of the TPLF foreign committee v-1, no.-3, May 1977 E.C.

Transitional Period Charter of Ethiopia, *Negarit Gazeta,* July 22, 1991.

Woyeen, TPLF Weekly, 17 Hidar 1990 E.C. (November 1997), vol. 22, no. 272.

Interviews

Abebe Hailu, former TPLF fighter, Washington, DC, USA, 7 August 2003.

Alemseged Gebre-Egziabiher, former member of the Parliament of Ethiopia, Los Angeles, USA, 18 August 2003.

Berhane Girmay (Lieutenant), former leader of Tigray People's Liberation Movement – *Teranafit* Committee, Atlanta, USA, 28 July 2003.

Berhe Hagos, former TPLF fighter, Ottawa, Canada, 27 August 2003.

Giday Zeratsion, founding member of the TNO and TPLF, Oslo, Norway, 16 March 2004.

Dima Nego, former CC member of Oromo Liberation Front and Information Minister under EPRDF, Silver Spring, MD., USA, 14 August 2003.

Fassika Bellete, CC member of the Ethiopian People's Revolutionary Party (EPRP), Washington DC, USA, 10 August 2003.

Gebremeskel Woldu, former TPLF fighter, Washington, DC, USA, 7 August 2003.

Kahsay Berhe, founding member of the TPLF, Münster, Germany. 27 March 2004.

Kefale Mammo, former President of the Ethiopian Free Press Journalists' Association, Amsterdam, the Netherlands, 30 March 2004.

Kibret Mekonnen, former editor of '*Aemiro*', Amsterdam, the Netherlands, 30 March 2004.

Mohammed Abrahim, CC Member of Afar Revolutionary Democratic United Front (ARDUF), Toronto, Canada, 25 August 2003.

Mekonnen Zellelow, former TPLF mass organizations officer, Washington DC. USA, 30 July 2003.

Meles Wolde Emmanuel, former leading member of the Sidama Liberation Movement, The Hague, Netherlands, 10 July 2004.

Tesfay Atsbaha, former TPLF military commander, Köln, Germany, 25 March 2004.

Yared Tibebu, former CC member of the Ethiopian People's Democratic Movement (EPDM), Washington, DC, USA. 08 August 2003.

APPENDIX – 1

PARTICIPANTS OF THE JULY 1-5, 1991 CONFERENCE

With number of seats allocated in the Council of Representatives of the Transitional Government of Ethiopia

1. Afar Liberation Front	3
2. Benishangul People's Liberation Movement	2
3. Gambella People's Liberation Movement	2
4. Gurage People's Democratic Organization	2
5. Hadiya National Democratic Organization	2
6. Harrari (Adere) National League	1
7. Horyal (Ogaden Liberation Front)	1
8. Islamic Front for the Liberation of Oromia	3
9. Issa and Gurgura Liberation Front	1
10. Kembata People's Congress	2
11. Oromo Abo Liberation Front	2
12. Oromo Liberation Front	12
13. Omotic People's Democratic Front	2
14. Oromo People's Democratic Organization*	10
15. Sidama Liberation Movement	2
16. Tigray People's Liberation Front	10
17. United Oromo People's Liberation Front	1
18. Western Somalia Liberation Front	3
19. Wolayta People's Democratic Front	2

20. Ethiopian Democratic Coalition	1
21. Ethiopian Democratic Union	1
22. Ethiopian National Democratic Organization	1
23. Ethiopian People's Democratic Movement*	10
24. Ethiopian Democratic Officers Revolutionary Movement*	2
24. Ethiopian Democratic Action Group	1
25. University/Higher Education Representative	1
26. Workers' Representatives	3

* Partners of the TPLF-led EPRDF

Ethnic organizations which had Council seats reserved:

• Agway People's Democratic Movement	1
• Burin People's Democratic Organization	1
• Geode People's Democratic Organization	1
• Kafa People's Democratic Union	2
• Yem National Movement	1

APPENDIX – 2

TRANSITIONAL PERIOD CHARTER OF ETHIOPIA

WHEREAS the overthrow of the military dictatorship that has ruled Ethiopia for seventeen years presents a historical moment, providing the peoples of Ethiopia with the opportunity to rebuild the country and restructure the state democratically;

WHEREAS the military dictatorship was, in essence, a continuation of the previous regimes and its demise marks the end of an era of subjugation and oppression thus starting a new chapter in Ethiopian history in which freedom, equal rights and self-determination of all the peoples shall be the governing principles of political, economic and social life and thereby contributing to the welfare of the Ethiopian Peoples and rescuing them from centuries of subjugation and backwardness;

WHEREAS peace and stability, as essential conditions of development, require the end of all hostilities, the healing of wounds caused by conflicts and the establishment and maintenance of good neighbourliness and co-operation;

WHEREAS for the fulfilment of the aforementioned conditions and for the reign of a just peace, the proclamation of a democratic order is a categorical imperative, and;

WHEREAS to this end, all institutions of repression installed by the previous regimes shall be dismantled a regional prejudices redressed and the rights and interest of the deprived citizens safeguarded by a democratic government elected by and accountable to the people;

WHEREAS from the Peace Loving and Democratic forces present in the Ethiopian society and having Varied Views, having met in a Conference convened from July 1-5 in Addis Ababa, have discussed and approved the Charter laying down the rules governing the Transitional Government as well as setting down the principles for the transitional period;

NOW, THEREFORE, it is hereby proclaimed as follows:

Part One

DEMOCRATIC RIGHTS

Article One

Based on the Universal Declaration of Human Rights of the United Nations, adopted and proclaimed by the General Assembly by resolution 217 A(III) of 10 Dec. 1948, individual human rights shall be respected fully, and without any limitation whatsoever. Particularly every individual shall have:

a) the freedom of conscience, expression, association and peaceable assembly;

b) The right to engage in unrestricted political activity and to organize political parties provided the exercise of such right does not infringe upon the rights of others.

Article Two

The right of nations, nationalities and peoples to self-determination is affirmed to this end. Each nation, nationality and people is guaranteed the right to:

a) Preserve its identity and have it respected, promote its culture and history and use and develop its language;

b) Administer its own defined territory and effectively participate in the central government on the basis of freedom and fair and proper representation;

c) Exercise its right to self-determination of independence, when the concerned, nation/nationality and people is convinced that above rights are denied, abridged or abrogated.

Part Two

PRINCIPLES GUIDING FOREIGN POLICY

The Transitional Government will conduct its foreign relation on the basis of the principles of respect for the sovereignty and equality of states and non-intervention and non-interference in internal affairs, as well as the promotion of mutual interests. Accordingly;

Article Three

The policy of destabilization and conflict promotion hitherto actively pursued by the previous regime with respect to the country's neighbours shall cease forthwith the issuance of this Charter.

Article Four

It shall abide by all mutual agreements that respect the sovereignty of Ethiopia and are not contrary to the interests of the people.

Article Five

Local governments shall have the right to establish direct contact with relief organizations with respect to relief work.

Part Three

STRUCTURE AND COMPOSITION OF THE TRANSITIONAL GOVERNMENT

Article Six

There shall be established a Transitional Government consisting of a Council of Representatives and a Council of Ministers.

Article Seven

The Council of Representatives shall be composed of representatives of national liberation movements, other political organizations and prominent individuals to make-up a total of no more that 87 members.

Article Eight

The Transitional Government shall exercise all legal and political responsibility for the governance of Ethiopia until it hands over power to a government popularly elected on the basis of a new constitution.

Article Nine

The Council of Representatives shall exercise legislative functions as follows and oversee the work of the Council of Ministers: a) draw-up it's rules of procedure, b) election of its Chairperson who shall also be the Head of State, and a Vice-Chairperson and Secretary, the Head of State shall appoint the Prime Minister, whose appointment shall be approved by the Council of Representatives. The Head of State, the

Prime Ministers, the Vice-Chairperson and Secretary of the Council of Representatives shall be from different nations/nationalities; c) approve the Prime Minister's nomination of the member of Council of Ministers, drawn-up on considerations of ascertaining a broad national representation, technical competence and unswerving adherence to the Charter; d) initiation and promulgation of proclamations and decrees pursuant to the Charter; e) adoption of national budget; f) provide for the administration of justice on the basis of the Charter; the Courts shall, in their work, be free from any governmental interference with respect to items provide for in Part One, Article One of the Charter; g) establish the Constitutional Commission; h) ratify international agreements; i) create committees for defence and security policy during the transitional period; j) provide the mechanism to ascertain the fair and impartial application of the mass media; k) issue just labour law that protect the rights and interests of the workers;

Part Four

TRANSITIONAL PROGRAMS

The following provisions for a transitional period have been adopted in order to lead the country towards full democracy.

A. POLITICAL

Article Ten

The Council of Representatives shall constitute the Constitutional Commission to draw up a draft constitution.

Article Eleven

Upon adoption of the draft constitution by the Council of Representatives, the Constitution shall be presented to the people for discussion.

The final draft shall be presented for adoption to the Constituent Assembly to be elected pursuant to the final draft of the Constitution.

Article Twelve

Election to a National Assembly shall be held on the basis of the provisions of the new Constitution.

The Transitional Government shall hand over power to the party or parties that gain a majority in the National Assembly.

The said national elections shall be held no later than two years after the establishment of the Transitional Government. Provided, however, that the period can be extended by the Council of Representatives for no more than six months.

Article Thirteen

There shall be a law establishing local and regional councils for local administrative purposes defined on the basis of nationality. Elections for such local and regional councils shall be held within three months of the establishment of the Transitional Government, wherever local conditions allow.

B. RELIEF AND REHABILITATION

The Transitional Government is unequivocally determined to ensure the delivery of relief assistance to areas ravaged by war and drought. In connection with this;

Article Fourteen

It shall give priority to the rehabilitation of those areas that have been severely affected by the war, prisoners of war, ex-prisoners of war as well as those sections of the population that have been forcibly uprooted by the previous regime's policy of villagization and resettlement.

The rehabilitation of those forcibly uprooted by the previous regime's policy of villagization and resettlement shall be done in accordance with their desire.

Article Fifteen

It shall take immediate steps to reconstruct or repair the infrastructure that has been destroyed or damaged by the war.

Article Sixteen

It shall give special consideration to hitherto neglected and forgotten areas.

Article Seventeen

It shall make special efforts to dispel ethnic mistrust and eradicate the ethnic hatred that have been fostered by the previous regimes.

Part Five

LEGALITY OF THE CHARTER

Article Eighteen

This Charter shall serve as the supreme law of the land for the duration of the transitional period. Any law or decision that is contrary to the Charter shall be null and void.

Article Nineteen

The Amharic and the English texts of this Charter have equal authenticity. Where disparity occurs between the two languages the Council of Representatives shall decide.

Article Twenty

This Charter shall be effective upon publication in the Negarit Gazetta.

Addis Ababa this 22nd day of July 1991

Meles Zenawi, Chairman of the Conference

APPENDIX – 3

Brief Profiles of the Founders and Leaders of the TPLF[123]

Gessesew Ayele (*Sihul*) See Chapter 3, par. 'The role of Sihul' (p. 71) for a whole section devoted to his profile.

Zeru Gesesse (*Agazi*) was born in Wukro, Kilte-Awlaelo. He was raised by his widowed mother who became a prison warder after her husband's death. Agazi was a second-year law-school student at Haile Silassie 1st University (H.S.I.U.) in Addis Ababa when he joined the Front. Before going to university, he lived in Asmara, Eritrea, with his aunt where he completed high school. He was influenced at a young age by the rebel Eritrean movements and at the university in Addis Ababa he was active in mobilizing Tigraians to fight for their right to self-determination. A year after the TPLF's struggle started, he was killed in the small town of Wukro-Marai by *Dergue* militias while on a mission.

Fantahun Zeratsion (*Ghiday*) was born to Eritrean parents and raised in Aksum and Shire-Enda Selassie, Tigrai. His father was, by Tigraian standards, a reasonably successful businessman who owned a hotel. After completing high school in Adwa and Meqele, Giday joined the Engineering Collage at H.S.I.U., where he was an activist in the Ethiopian Students' Movement. He was committed to the struggle of the TPLF and even 'borrowed' his father's rifle and took it to the bush thereby increasing the number of TPLF rifles at the start of activities to four. He served as the vice chairman of the TPLF from 1978 to 1985. During the formation of the MLLT, he was engaged in fierce debate with MLLT ideologue Meles Zenawi on the role of the rural bourgeoisie and the nature of the revolution. He was forced to resign from the organization and has lived in exile ever since.

Mulugeta Hagos (*Asfaha*) was born in Shire-Enda Selassie. His father was an employee of the Ethiopian Telecommunications Authority in Enda-Selassie. He went to high school in Meqele and was a fourth-year mathematics student in the Faculty of Education at H.S.I.U. when he became involved in the TPLF. He was active in the Tigraian

---

[123] The reader will hopefully forgive the author (as an ex-TPLF member) his sometimes somewhat personal reflections and remarks on some of these former colleagues and fellow combatants.

underground movements and, although not in very good health, worked hard in the early years of the struggle. He was not elected to the First Fighters' Congress but continued in the Front's foreign office, where he prepared important TPLF declarations and memorandums. Because he was critical of the establishment of the MLLT, he was harassed by the Meles faction and was forced to resign from the organization in 1988. He is still living in exile.

Ambaye Mesfin (*Seyoum*) was born in Adigrat where some of his family were well-to-do businessmen and others belonged to a section of the traditional 'feudal class' in Agame. He graduated from the Polytechnic Institute of Bahir Dar and later joined the Engineering College at H.S.I.U. He was initially a 'narrow nationalist' (i.e., pleading for the independence of Tigrai) and subsequently joined Sibhat's group to write the 1976 TPLF Manifesto, which clamoured for the secession of Tigrai. Since the start of the struggle, he has worked in the organization's foreign office and later became Ethiopia's Foreign Minister.

Amaha Tsehaye (*Abaye*) was born in Aksum and finished his high-school studies in Meqele. He was a second-year language student in the Faculty of Arts at H.S.I.U. when he was elected as an English editor for the university students' journal entitled 'Struggle'. He was also an activist in the Tigraian movement for self-determination. He was the head of the TPLF's political bureau from 1976 onwards but was always well known for 'blowing with the wind'. He was Meles Zenawi's political mentor until he was fired from this position. However, he still works with him in Addis Ababa.

Alemseged Mengesha (*Hailu*) was born in Abi-Adi, Tembien. He went to high school in Meqele and was a second-year student at the Arts Faculty at H.S.I.U. when he joined the Front. In the field, he was always deviating from the collective norms that governed the leadership at the time and so was not elected to the Front's leadership at the First Fighters' Congress in 1976. A year later, he abandoned the organization and since then has lived in the US.

Aregawi Berhe (*Berihu*) was born in Adwa and went to high-school there. His father was a district judge. He does not have any family ties with either Sibhat or Seyoum, as Tecola W. Hagos (1995: 7) erroneously claims.[124] He joined the Science Faculty at H.S.I.U., but after eighteen

124 In his book (1995), Tecola unfortunately started out with the misguided premise of characterizing the leaders of the TPLF as 'sons of feudal lords'. To justify his assumption, every leader, regardless of his class origins, had to be put in that basket. The theory of some intellectuals like Tecola (1995: 12), and also the *Dergue,* which states that the TPLF was created by sons of such Tigraian feudal warlords does not reflect reality.

months changed to political science at the Faculty of Arts and continued until the fourth year. Like any revolutionary of the day, he was an activist in the students' movement and later an organizer of the Tigraian youth who fought for self-determination within the Ethiopian polity. He served as the chairman of the TPLF from 1976 to 1979 and as head of the military committee until he was ousted by the Sibhat-Meles faction in 1986. Since 1988 he has lived in exile.

The following TPLF members were not among the founding members but were leading figures in subsequent stages of the struggle.

Mehari Tekle (*Mussie*) was born in Asmara, Eritrea, to Tigraian parents. His father was a quite successful businessman from Aksum. Mussie went to what was then called the Haile Selassie 1st High School in Asmara, and later joined the Building College at Haile Sellassie I University in Addis Ababa, where he continued until the fourth year. While there he was recruited by the EPLF and joined the Front in 1973, but his heart was set on the Tigraian struggle. When news of Tigraians initiating a struggle reached him, he immediately contacted the founders of the TPLF and, with the consent of the EPLF leadership, joined them from the start of their struggle. Because of his reliable track record and vital experience, he was elected as a member of the leadership. He was the Front's military commander when he died, fighting the EDU, in the Battle of Chiameskebet on 23 September 1977.

Woldesilassie Nega (*Sibhat*). A TPLF CC member since 1976 was born in a village called Adi-Abune near Adwa where his father was a *fitawrari* who owned substantial farmlands. Sibhat claims to be a descendant of a legendary warrior known locally as Wa'ero, who is said to have owned large tracts of land in the district of Adwa. In this sense he was filled with 'feudal sentiments', which earned him the nickname 'feudal intriguer'. He finished high-school in Meqele and studied agricultural economics at H.S.I.U. He joined the Front at Dedebit and was an ordinary member until he was elected to the leadership at the Fighters' Congress in 1976. He showed to be strongly ethno-nationalist, and organized like-minded individuals around himself and considers any 'Amhara' as his enemy.

Although organizationally ethno-nationalists, the fundamental consciousness of these TPLF leaders was shaped by the ideology of class struggle, which was the dominant view during that era. However, since ethno-nationalism is a fluid ideology, one could not deny the emergence of 'narrow nationalism' in the later years of the struggle, as Meles and Sibhat rose to power.

His relations with the other people in the Front are reputed to be clannish and nobody knows what tangible political or military contribution he had in the struggle; but, as Tecola W. Hagos (1995: 8) rightly put it, indeed he 'is the 'Exchequer' of the TPLF'.

Meles (original name **Legesse) Zenawi** was born in 1955 to a Tigraian father and an Eritrean mother in Adwa, Tigrai, where his father had 20-30 heads of cattle near the River Mereb. He went to the General Wingate Highschool in Addis Ababa, where he had close contact with various British teachers. He was a second-year pre-med student at H.S.I.U when he was recruited as a potential fighter in the TPLF. In Asmara in 1975, Meles slipped away from the first group that was bound for the EPLF base area for military training, but later joined the Front in Tigrai. Although he was assigned to the TPLF's political bureau as a subsidiary to Abbay Tsehaye, his political position at the time was never stable or consistent. During the second year of the struggle, Meles Zenawi together with Atsbaha Dagnew (*Shewit*), Raswork Kesela (*Atakelti*), Sahle Abraha (*Seye*), Tikue Woldu (*Awaalom*) were appointed by the CC to serve as deputy CC members. Meles Zenawi eventually became the MLLT/TPLF leader. Ideologically, he was very flexible, e.g., shifting from ethnic nationalism to socialist internationalism (in the MLLT) or from Maoist socialism to state-led capitalism (after 1991).

APPENDIX – 4

List of Ethnic and National Parties in 2002

No. Party	(Ethnic)	(National)
1 Afar National Democratic Party	*	
2 Agew People's Democratic Movement	*	
3 Alaba People's Democratic Unity	*	
4 All-Amhara People's Organization	*	
5 Amhara People's Democratic Movement	*	
6 Argoba Nationality Democratic Organization	*	
7 Argoba People's Democratic Movement	*	
8 Baherwork Mesmes Nationality Democratic Unity Organisation	*	
9 Baherwork Mesmes People's Democratic Organization	*	
10 Basketo People's Democratic Organization	*	
11 Bench-Maji People's Democratic Organization	*	
12 Benishangul-Gumuz People's Democratic Unity Front	*	
13 Burji People's Democratic Unity	*	
14 Council of Alternative Forces for Peace & Democracy in Ethiopia		*
15 Dawro People's Democratic Organization	*	
16 Denta, Debamo, Kitchenchla Democratic Organization	*	
17 Derashe People's Democratic Organization	*	
18 Donga People's Democratic Organization	*	
19 Ethiopian Berta People's Democratic Organization	*	
20 Ethiopian Democratic Party	*	
21 Ethiopian Democratic Unity Party		*
22 Ethiopian National Democratic Party		*
23 Ethiopian Peace and Democratic Party		*
24 Ethiopian People's Revolutionary Democratic Front		*
25 Ethiopia's Unity Democratic Organization		*
26 Endegegn People's Democratic Movement	*	
27 Gambella People's Democratic Union Party	*	
28 Gambella People's Democratic Congress	*	
29 Gambella People's Democratic Front	*	
30 Gamo Democratic Union	*	
31 Gamo-Gofa Zone Nationalities' Democratic Organization	*	

No. Party	(Ethnic)	(National)
32 Gedeo People's Democratic Organization	*	
33 Gideo People's Revolutionary Democratic Movement	*	
34 Gurage People's Democratic Front	*	
35 Gurage Zone Nationalities Democratic Movement	*	
36 Hadiya People's Democratic Organization	*	
37 Hadiya National Democratic Organization	*	
38 Harari People's Democratic Party	*	
39 Harari National League	*	
40 Joint Political Forum		*
41 Kafa People's Democratic Organization	*	
42 Kebena Nationality Democratic Organization	*	
43 Kembata, Alaba and Tembaro People's Democratic Org.	*	
44 Kembata People's Congress	*	
45 Konso People's Democratic Organization	*	
46 Konso People's Democratic Union	*	
47 Konta People's Revolutionary Democratic Organization	*	
48 Kore Nationality Unity Democratic Organization	*	
49 Mixed Nations, Nationality One-Ethiopia Democratic Party		*
50 Ogaden National Liberation Front	*	
51 Oida Nationality Democratic Organization	*	
52 Omo Peoples' Democratic Union	*	
53 Oromo Abbo Liberation Front	*	
54 Oromo Liberation National Party	*	
55 Oromo Liberation Unity Front	*	
56 Oromo National Congress	*	
57 Oromo People's Democratic Organization	*	
58 Selte Nationality Democratic Movement	*	
59 Selti Nationality Democratic Organization	*	
60 Selti People's Democratic Unity Party	*	
61 Sheka People's Democratic Movement	*	
62 Sheko & Mezenger People's Democratic Unity Organization	*	
63 Sidama Hadicho People's Democratic Organization	*	
64 Sidama People's Democratic Organization Unity	*	
65 Sidama Liberation Movement	*	
66 Sodo Gordena People's Democratic Organization	*	
67 Somalia Democratic Alliance Forces	*	
68 Somali People's Democratic Party	*	
69 Somali People's Liberation Front Party	*	

No. Party	(Ethnic)	(National)
70 Southern Ethiopia People's Democratic Coalition	*	
71 Southern Ethiopia People's Democratic Front	*	
72 Southern Omo People's Democratic Movement	*	
73 Tembaro People's Democratic Unity	*	
74 Tigray People's Liberation Front	*	
75 Tigri-Worji Nationality Democratic Unity Party	*	
76 Welayta People's Democratic Movement	*	
77 Western Somalia Democratic Party	*	
78 Yem Nationality Democratic Movement	*	
79 Yem People's Democratic Organization	*	
80 Zai People's Democratic Organization	*	
81 Zeyse People's Democratic Organization	*	

About the Author:

Aregawi Berhe was born on 8 July 1950 at Adwa, Ethiopia. He studied political science (as major) and sociology (as minor) at Haile Selassie I University, Addis Ababa, in 1971-1974. After the coming to power of the military government (*Dergue*) in 1974, he joined the TPLF as a founding member and combated the emerging military dictatorship. As a member of the TPLF leadership, he served the Front until 1986, when he was forced to go into exile. In 1991-1993 he enrolled in the Institute of Social Studies (ISS) in The Hague and graduated with an MA in Development Studies, specializing in the 'Politics of Alternative Development Strategies'. He lives in The Netherlands, and from 1994 to 2000, he worked as a research analyst for Disaster and Emergency Reference Centre (DERC) at the University of Delft. Between 2001 and 2008, he was an associate researcher at the African Studies Centre in Leiden University, working on his dissertation. Aside from his studies and profession, he is also involved, politically and as a writer, in ongoing efforts to advocate political reform and democratization in Ethiopia. He is a founding member of the TAND political party (Tigraian Alliance for National Democracy, active also in the Ethiopian diaspora) and member of the Ethiopian opposition coalition the United Ethiopian Democratic Front (UEDF), a "wing" of which has seats in the current Ethiopian parliament.

Index

Aaiga, 85, 121
Abadi Mesfin, 78
Abadi Zemo, 184
Abay (Abbay) Tsehaye, 40, 49, 100, 116, 118, 156, 159, 165, 166, 170, 173, 175, 178, 183, 263, 340, 342
Abdisa Ayana (Roba), 118
Abebe Haile-Selassie, B. General, 265
Abebe Tesema, 48, 49
Aberra Abebe, M/G, 262
Aberra Yemaneab, 279
Abi Zila Nikidmit (Great Leap Forward), 218
Abiy Adi, 106
Abraha (Ezana), King, 42
Abraha Hagos, 54, 128, 133
Abraha Manjus, 107
Abraha Wodi Sebaa, 82
Abraha, 62
Abune Tewoflos, 245
Abyot (Revolution), 171
Abyssinia, 197-199
Adal, 195, 197
Addis Ababa, 8, 38, 40-41, 47-50, 57, 63, 69, 71, 76, 83, 87, 117, 126, 157, 204, 221-222, 258, 261, 263-264, 266-269, 273, 294, 304, 307-311
Addis Agilachew, General, 260
Adi Awala, 69
Adi Daero (Adi-Daero), 76, 114
Adi Mohamedai, 56, 69, 327, 343
Adi Nebried, 69
Adiabo, 69, 107, 109, 111, 147
Adigrat, 85, 106, 121, 142-149, 233, 260, 340
Adi-Mohamedai, 56
Adulis, 42, 195-197, 217, 327
Adwa, 44-45, 78, 106, 114, 120-122, 1 35-136, 142-149, 163, 174, 199-203, 226, 339-342, 346
Aemero, 269
Af-Abet, 256-257, 261, 266
Afar, 15, 57, 89, 132, 195, 197, 201, 209, 311, 330-331, 343
Afelalayatna ab Giltsi Medrek Yekreb' (Let Our Differences be Public), 189, 218
Africa, 3, 10, 11, 15, 23, 38, 46, 92, 127, 132, 134, 144, 171, 174, 217, 255, 273, 277-278, 281-284, 296-297, 303, 317, 319-327
Agame, 73, 81, 84-85, 98, 118, 120-122, 158, 199, 226, 340

Agazi Gessesse, 40, 72, 87-88, 118, 339
Agew, 15, 42, 57, 163, 197, 273, 343
Agitprop, 85
Agordet, 257
Agriculture, 13, 51, 57, 88, 99, 139, 23, 247, 250
Ahferom, 71, 106-107
Ahmed ibn Ibrahim, (ahmed 'Gragn), 43
Akele Guzay, 198-202
Aklilu Habte-Wold, Prime Minister, 201
Akmara, 175-177, 235, 327
Aksum, 42-43, 77-79, 82, 114, 133, 138, 195-199, 244, 320, 339-341
Albania, Communists, 173, 217, 287
Alem Eshet, 56, 69
Alemayehu Gessesew (Dirar), 72, 74
Alemayehu Haile, Captain, 129
Alem-Bekagn, main prison, 267
Alem-Ketema, 265
Alemseged Gebre-Amlak, 175
Alemseged Gebre-Egziabi her, Ato, 50, 330
Alemseged Mengesha (Hailu), 340
Alemshet Tewolde, 95, 107, 248
Algeria, 30, 60, 65, 68, 136, 285
Alitena, 122, 208
Alula division, 265
Alula Gebru, 191
Amaha Desta, M/G, 62
Amaha Tsehaye (Abbay), 40, 340
Aman Michael Andom, General, 39, 128-129, 142
Amare Tesful, 46, 49, 80-83, 203
Ambay Tsion, Emperor, 198
Amentila, 139
American Embassy in Khartoum, 268
Amha Desta, 186
Amhara, 306, 312, 341, 343
Amhara Domination, 202
Amhara National Democratic Movement (ANDM), 268, 273, 310
Amharigna, 58
Amilcar Cabral, 31
Angola, 68
Anya-Nya, 286
Appraisal/Evaluation, 190, 328
Arab, 197, 202, 207, 286, 294
Aregash Adane, 153, 183, 237, 239
Aregawi Berhe, (Berihu), 4-20, 40
Armacheho, 107, 124

Army Logistics, 139
Asfaha Hagos, 179
Asfaw Wolde-Aregay, Ato, 50
Asgede, 4, 62, 66, 68, 137
Asgede Gebre-Selassie, 68
ASHA, 114
Asmara, 61, 62, 70, 146, 196, 198, 200, 221, 256-258, 263, 288, 321-328, 339-342
Assefa Abraha, Dr, 50
Assefa-Hailu Habtu, 71
assessments (gämgäm), 229, 252
Assimba, 118, 122, 208
Ataye, 265
Atnafu Abate, 126, 129
Atsbaha Dagnew (Shewit), 62, 191, 342
Atsbaha Hailemariam, 49
Atsbaha Hastire, 46
Aurora divisions, 264-265
Awaalom (Awalom) Woldu, 182-183, 342
Awgaro, 122
Axum obelisks, 78, 212, 196, 323
Aynalem Aregehegn, Ato, 50
Azeba, 120
Babylon [Mesopotamia], 42, 196
Bademe, 69-70, 110, 123
Bahabelom Mussie, 107
Baher Negash (sea region ruler), 198
Bahir Dar, 266, 340
Bahli-Tigrai, 48
Bahta Gebrehiwet, 48
Bahta, 48, 86
Baitos, Tabia Baito, Woreda baito, Zoba baito, 149, 230, 234, 237, 241, 245, 247-253
Bakla, 140
Balabats, 45
Bale, 4, 39, 52, 127, 131, 307
Barentu, 257
Barka, 145, 205-206, 208
Baryaw Paulos, Dejjach, 199
Battle of Adwa (1896), 44
BBC, 79
Bealu Girma, 146
Begemidir, 43
Bekele Berhane, Ato, 50
Belai Giday, 3, 196, 319
Belesa-Maihamato, 209
Belgium, 15
BeniShangul-Gumuz, 311, 343
Berhane Ayele (Fitewi), 57, 62, 66
Berhane Desta, 104
Berhane Eyasu (Iyasu), 49
Berhane Gebrekristos, 166
Berhane Girmay, Lieutenant, 104, 330
Berhanemeskel Redda, 71
Berhe Hagos, 83, 120, 330
Berhe Tewldebirhan, 205
Betena Holesha, 132
Birkuta, 67
Bizen, 197-198
Bizet, 122
Blata Admasu, 107-108

Bolsheviks, 7
Bourgeois Democracy, 190
British Royal Air Force (RAF), 45, 53
Bumbet, 109-110, 113
Burji, 273, 343

campaigns (zemecha), 79, 108, 129, 135, 140-149, 165, 177, 258
Carl von Clausewitz, 136
Carter Centre, 267, 278
CC of the MLLT/TPLF, 183
Central Committee, 98-99, 153, 165, 182, 205, 280
Che Guevara, 31, 52
Chiameskebet, 76, 107-108, 341
Chiefs, Balabats, 45
Chila, 134, 150
China, 30-31, 52, 60, 65, 70, 79, 136, 174, 225, 279, 284, 286, 294
Chinese revolutions, 299
civic organizations, 269
COEDF, 274
Cold War, 79, 103, 109, 266, 296
Commission to Organize Party of the Workers of Ethiopia (COPWE), 148
common front, 159, 165-167
Communist bloc, 144
Communist China, 79
communist core, 161-165, 179, 185
communist force, 161, 178, 181, 328
company (haili), 98, 106, 139, 145
Constitution Drafting Commission (CDC), 277-278
conventional warfare, 149, 214, 255
Corbetta, 45
Council of Representatives (COR), 275, 277
coup d'état, 171, 262
criticism and self-criticism (gimgema), 96
Cuba, 30-31, 60, 65, 68, 136
Cultural Department, 98-100

Dabat, 259
Danakil lowlands, 84
Dansha, 259
Debark, 259
Debra Libanos, 42
Debre Bizen (Debra Bizan), 197-198
Debre Damo, 246
Debre Zeit, 266
Debre-Tabor, 265
Dedebit, 38, 55-56, 62-63, 66-74, 77, 88, 118, 137, 139, 158, 204, 294, 341
Deima, 73, 83-87, 113, 139
deisaa (community ownership of land), 231-232, 334-335, 238
Dejena, 258
Deki-Amhare, 85, 88
Dekina (our kids), 300
Demissie Bulto, M/G, 262
Democracia, 54, 171
Democratic Movement for the Liberation of Eritrea (DMLE), 188

Dergue, 4-5, 11, 31, 34-35, 38-41, 49, 51, 54, 63, 76, 79-81, 85, 92-94, 101, 103- 106, 108-110, 112-113, 116, 117-118, 120-121, 124-135, 137-153, 163-167, 172-173, 175-177, 181, 185, 186, 189, 208-209, 211-222, 225-228, 233-234, 236, 240-241, 245, 249, 255-272, 277, 279, 283, 287, 294, 304, 308, 311
Dessie. 246, 260-264
Desta Bezabih, 48-49
Desta Tesfay, 83
departments of political work (04), 88
dictatorship of the proletariat, 175, 185, 206
Dimtsi Bihere Tigrai (Voice of the Tigrai Nation), 50
Dimtsi Hafash (Voice of the Masses), EPLF Radio, 217, 299
Dimtsi Woyyane (Voice of Revolution), 219
Dinka, 267, 286
Dirfo, 72
Djibouti, 274
Dogali, 135-136, 200
Domino effect, 16, 21-22
Dos Santos, 289, 299, 320

East German technicians, 144
East Germany, 215, 279
Eastern Bloc, 214, 216, 287
Economy. 05, 28, 131, 139, 173, 222, 235, 247, 285-287, 311-312, 318-319, 324-325
Edaga-Arbi, 164
EDU, *See* Ethiopian Democratic Union
Eduardo Mondlane, 285, 295, 327
Education, 012, 50, 88, 96-102, 139, 198, 243, 250, 291, 296, 298, 332, 339
Egypt, (Egyptians), 43, 202, 207, 319
Election Commissioner, 276
ELF, *see* Eritrean People's Liberation Front
ELF-SAGIM progressive, 188
Empiricism, 179, 192
Enda-Selassie, (Indasilase), 55, 62, 66, 76, 78, 260, 339
Engels, 178
Enticho, 121, 145, 147
Enver Hoxha, 173, 217
EPDM, *See* Ethiopian People's Democratic Movement
EPLF, *See* Eritrean Liberation Front
EPRDF, *See* Ethiopian People's Revolutionary Democratic Front
EPRP, *See* Ethiopian People's Revolutionary Party
EPRP CC 4th Plenum, 121,124
Era of Princes, 4, 43, 199
erfe-meske, 114
Eritrea, 4, 9, 11, 22-23, 39, 42-43, 46-47, 52, 55, 60, 63, 70, 71-72, 74, 76, 79 -80, 83, 85, 88, 93, 103, 108, 117, 122-123, 127-130, 136, 141. 146, 150, 152-153, 159, 164, 183, 185, 189, 193-216, 218-223, 255, 259, 261, 266, 270, 274, 284, 286-288, 301, 303, 305-308, 317-321, 324-329

Eritrean Democratic Movement (EDM), 210
Eritrean Liberation Front (ELF), 11, 20, 46-47, 55, 60-61, 70, 80-84, 103-122, 130, 145, 188, 194, 201-223, 286, 293, 301, 327
Eritrean Liberation Front Central-Command (ELF-CC) or Sagem, 210, 220
Eritrean People's Liberation Front (EPLF), 9, 11, 47, 60-62, 70-74, 77, 80, 83, 108, 117, 120, 128, 130, 137, 142, 143-146, 161, 188-189, 199, 201, 203-222, 226, 240, 255-260, 265-270, 273, 284, 286-301, 303-305, 319, 327-328, 341-342
Eritrean People's Socialist Party (EPSP), 286, 288
Etek (Get Armed). 50
Ethiopia Tikdem, Ethiopia First, 39-40, 92-93, 128, 133, 141-142
Ethiopian Constitution, 23, 162, 217, 234, 277, 310
Ethiopian Democratic Officers' Revolutionary Movement (EDORM), 263
Ethiopian Democratic Union (EDU), 11, 51, 63, 85, 94, 96, 100-114, 122-123, 140-147, 180, 205-214, 225-240, 289, 301, 341
Ethiopian Democratic Union Party (EDUP), 266
Ethiopian Marxist Leninist Force (EMLF), 187
Ethiopian National Democratic Organization (ENDO), 274
Ethiopian National Liberation Front (ENLF), 131
Ethiopian Orthodox Church, 198, 244-246
Ethiopian People's Democratic Movement (EPDM), (now ANDM), 5, 153, 163, 165, 167, 178, 180, 187-189, 221, 263-264, 268, 271-273, 280, 305, 310
Ethiopian People's Revolutionary Democratic Front (EPRDF), 4, 5, 6, 8, 49, 170, 187, 190-191, 217, 221, 234, 256, 263-264, 266-281, 288, 290, 303-306, 308-314, 328, 330, 332
Ethiopian People's Revolutionary Party (EPRP), 11, 49, 54, 60, 63, 71, 74, 80, 83, 84, 85, 100, 102, 108, 117 124, 141, 147, 153, 157-159, 161, 171, 186-187, 204, 206-209,211-214,225 230, 233, 235, 241, 263, 266, 274, 305, 330, 186, 188, 339, 341, 342
Ethiopian Proletarian Organizations Unity' (EPOU), 190
Ethiopian Revolution, 47, 58, 71, 165, 167, 263, 287, 320-321, 326
Ethiopian Workers' Party, 266
ethnic based federalism, 306, 311
Ethnic entrepreneurs, 8, 17, 23, 156
Ethnic federalism, 6, 306, 310, 312, 317, 320, 326
Ethnic mobilization, 3, 24, 37, 130, 256, 312, 314
Ethnic nationalism, 18, 20, 126, 131, 158, 283, 306, 312, 324, 342
Ethno-nationalism, 5, 9-10, 17-18, 34-35, 42, 46, 277, 304-305, 307, 314, 341
ethno-nationalist, 4-26, 34, 42, 50-53, 83, 91-94, 130-133, 161, 170, 193, 211, 263 -264, 270, 280, 291, 303, 314, 341
Ewostatewos of Geraälta, Evangelists, 198
Ezze (commands), 256-257

famine, 44, 47, 49, 53, 94, 134, 144, 170, 176-178, 180, 183-184, 219, 222, 301, 320
Fanta Belay, Major General, 257, 262
Fantahun Zeratsion (Giday), 40, 339
Fascist Italian, 304
Fassika Bellete, 119, 121, 330
Federal Constitution, ratified on 8 December 1995, 191, 280, 304
federal system, 309
Federation, 19-20, 142, 201, 310
Fersmai, 164
Fetha Nagast (Law of the Kings), 198
Fighters' Congress, 86, 98, 165-166, 204, 340-341
Filipos, the founder of the Debre Bizen monastery, 198
firdi baito (tribunal), 248
first congress, 73, 174
Fitewi, 62-63
Flemish, 15
Frantz Fanon, 303
Front for the Liberation of Mozambique (FRELIMO), 284-285, 289, 291, 293-300

Gabaz, administrator of the church, 233,245
Gambela, 311
Gämgams, evaluation procedures, 229
Ge'ez, 39, 42, 196
Ge'ez civilization, 42
Gebrehiwet Baykedagne, 45
Gebrehiwet Kahsay, 185,191
Gebre-Hiwet Meshesha, Dejazmach, 136
Gebre-Kidan Asfaha, 51, 60, 79, 83, 203
Gebrekidan Desta, 49
Gebremeskel Abbay, 48
Gebre-Meskel Hailu, 46
Gebremeskel Kahsay, 107-108
Gebremichael, 76
Gebrezghi, Bashai, 199
Gebru Asrat , 153, 183
Gebru Bezabih, 81
Gedeo, 273, 344
Gemmahlo, 208
General logistics, 011, 139
Gerhu-Sernay, 145
German Democratic Republic, GDR, 262
German ML party, 178
German Observer Group, 276, 328
German Radio (Deutsche Welle), 79
Germany, 75, 109, 215, 277, 279, 330
Gessesew Ayele (Sihul), 46, 105, 339
Getachew Maru, 117
Getahune Sisay, 118
Giday Zeratsion, 1, 4, 40, 110, 117, 118, 153, 162, 182, 184-185, 235
Giday Bahrishum, 104, 107, 328
Giday Gebrewahid, 49, 54
Gimgema, 96, 181, 190, 328
Girmay Jabir, 61, 72
Girmay Lemma, (Girmay Bahli), 87, 100
Glasnost, 192
Gojjam, 4, 39, 52, 108, 127, 142, 199, 266, 307

Goldsmiths, 234
Gondar, 43, 56, 108, 124, 142, 148-149, 164, 188, 197, 199, 245, 260, 264, 305
Great Britain, 43, 108
Greece, 42
Greek into Geez, 196
guerrilla [Maoist] stratagem, life, 265
guerrilla units (kirbit), 79, 89, 95, 137
guerrilla warfare, 31-32, 38, 65-73, 85, 88, 111, 115, 136, 145, 218, 297, 325
Guguftu, 265
Guinea-Bissau, 60, 65, 136, 298
Gulgula, 104
Gulti, 231-233, 244-245
Gundagunde, 83
Gurae, 44, 135-136
Gurage, 15, 318, 331, 344

Habesha, 198
Hadgu, 140
Hagere Selam, 179
Hagos Alemayehu, Ato, 48
Hagos Atsbaha, Ato, 50, 123
Hagos Desta, 104
Haile Abbay, 117
Haile Giorgis, 262
Haile Mariam Redda, Blata, 46
Haile Portsudan, 61, 106-107
Haile Selassie I University (H.S.I.U), 48, 172, 203, 346
Haile Selassie I, Emperor, 4, 44-50, 126-129, 171-178, 201-204, 232, 265, 303-304, 326-327, 341, 346
Haile Sobia, 82
Haile-Giorgis Habte-Mariam, M/G, 262
Haile-Giorgis, General, 262
Hailekiros Aseged, 83
Haile-Mariam Reda, 46
haili (company) formation, 106
Haili (force), 88, 99, 106, 139
Hailu Gebre-Michael, M/G, 262
Hailu Kebede, General, 260
Hailu Mengesha, 62, 78, 113
Hailu Tewolde Medhin, Dejjach, 199
Hakfen Military School, 140
Halefom, 140
Halewa woyyane (security of the revolution), 06, 101, 103
Hamassien, 197-199, 201
med Idris Awate, 46, 55, 201
Harar, 39, 140
Harar military academy, 140
Harare, 267
Hawelti Aksum, 82
Hawzien, 134, 150, 259
Hayelom Araya, 259
Health department, 03, 98, 139
Herman Cohen, 267, 271-272
Hiluf, 75
himsho (a fifth of what was produced on the land), 233

Hinfishfish, chaos, 75-76, 113, 116
Hintalo, 45
Hired labour, 234
Hirmi, 72, 77, 137, 159
Ho Chi Min, 52
Humera, 104, 106-107, 109, 149, 260
Hutus, 15
Hybrid ideology, 288

Idaga-Aarbi, 249
India, 42, 47
Instrumentalists, 13
Integrated War in Tigrai' (Kule-Medayawi Kuinat ab Tigrai), 153
International Covenant on civil and Political Rights (1966), 19
Iranian prophet Mani, 196
Irish National question, 52
Isayas Afeworki, 71, 274, 286, 293-295
Italian colony of Eritrea, 47
Italian invasion, 44, 56
Italy, 43, 201-202, 322
Itbarek Gebre-Egziabiher Dr, 50
Itioppia Tikdem ('Ethiopia First'), 128
Ittek (Get Armed), 100
Iyassu Baga, 61
Iyoas, King, 56

Jibo Zemecha, devour like a hyena, 144
Jimma, 267
Jimmy Carter, President, 267
John Garang, 286,290,294-295
John Swain, 108
Julius Nyerere, 285

Kaffa, 273
Kafta terrains, 149
Kahsay Abraha, Captain, 104
Kahsay Berhe (Misgina), 1, 4, 62, 75, 162, 174, 181-182, 184, 187, 276, 309, 322, 329, 330
Kahsay Dori, gerazmach, 81
Kahsay Mircha, Emperor Yohannes (1872-1889), 43-44, 136, 200
Kaie, which means 'revolt', 132
Kalai Woyyane ('second Woyyane'), 7, 87
Kalenjin, 15
Karen, 22
Kassa Hailu, Emperor Tewodros, 43-44, 199
Kayiira, Dr, 301
Kebede Bizuneh, 128
Kebede Gashe, General, 257
Kebre Nagast (Glory of Kings), 198
Kelakil, 72, 159
Kenya, 15, 267, 274, 277
Kenya-based NGO called the Inter-Africa Group, 277
Keren, 256-257, 266
Khalifa Umar al-Khattab, 197
Khartoum, 108, 111, 221, 259, 266, 268, 272, 286
Kidane Asayehgn, 50
Kifle Wodajo, 277

kifli hizbi, 101-103, 229-230, 242, 249, 251
Kikuyu, 15
Kimer-Dingay, 265
Kingdom of Ifat and Adal, 195, 197
kingdom of Rome, 42, 196
kingdom of the Axumites, 42, 196
kingdom of the Chinese, 42, 196
Kirbit, 99, 112, 137
Kiya Tigrai, 80
Kodere, 248
Kohaito, 196
Kokeb, 48, 72
Kokeb Wodi-Aala, 61
Korean War, 129
Kotsalo, 114
Kuadere, 97
Kumlachew Dejenie, 186,262
Kumlachew Dejenie, General, 186,262
Kunama, 23, 57, 195, 201
Kurds, 22
Kutir, calendar, Awde-Awarih, 42, 196

Land reform, 58, 131-132, 141, 172, 207, 228, 230, 233, 235-236, 238, 308, 329
Land Rover, 45, 78
Land to the tiller, 59, 104, 112, 141, 172, 233
Lasta, 197
Leenco Lata, 169-171, 323, 328
Leftist-Marxist, 7
legacy of Aksum, 198
Legesse (Meles) Zenawi, 62, 342
Legesse Asfaw, Sergeant, 150, 259
Lemi, 265
Lenin, 7, 178, 190, 323
Liberal Democracy, 191, 309
Libya, 202, 286, 294
Lindsey Tyler Dr, 108
London conference, 267

Maebel divisions, 264
MAGEBT in Tigrigna, 51, 157
Mahari Tekle (Mussie), 204
Mahber Gesgesti Bihere Tigrai (MAGEBT), 51
Mahber Politica, 51, 79-80
Mahber Politica Tegaru, 79
Mahil-Meda, 265
Mai Kuhli, 67, 69
Maichew, 45, 135, 149
Malaya, 31
Malays, Chinese, and Indians in Malaysia), 15
Manifesto 68, 5, 8, 157-163, 181, 213, 295
manqa (menkae), 292
manual workers, 234
Mao Tse-Tung, 31, 47, 115, 136, 173, 299
March 8 School, 239
Marcus, 3, 195, 231, 323
Maria Theresa thalers, 199
Mariam-Tsion, Holy Church of Aksum, 244
Markakis, 3, 15, 39-43, 57, 109, 128, 286, 289, 292, 320, 323
Marrihentte (leadership), 87-88

Marsa Teklai, 257
Marta (Kahsa) Tesfai, 61
Marwa, 118, 212
Marx, 175, 178
Marxist Leninist League of Tigrai (MLLT), 5, 10-
    11, 100, 114, 153, 156-159, 161, 163-164,
    167, 169, 170-171, 173, 175-192, 218-221,
    236, 263, 268, 280, 287, 288-289, 291-292,
    295, 301, 303, 309, 311, 339, 240, 242
Marxist-Leninist, 5, 8, 10, 98, 153, 169, 176, 178-
    179, 185, 190-192, 218, 285, 289, 303, 311,
    328
mass association, 230, 239
Massawa, 196, 199-200, 257, 265
Matara, 196
Matias Meshona, 132
May-Day divisions, 167, 264
Mebrahitu Aradom, 107
Mecha Tulama development association, 131
Medebai, 79
Meftuh, 75
Mehari Tekle (Mussie), 133, 341
MEISON, 131, 171, 274, 279, 318
Mekdela divisions, 264
Mekkit (Challenge) Ezze, 257
Mekonnen Wossenu, 132
Mekonnen Zelelow, 123
Melake Baher (emissary to the sea), 198
Melake Tekle, 80
Melay (Meley), 62
Meles Bezabih, 235
Meles Tekele, 49
Memhir Haddis, 184
Menelik II, Emperor, 44, 136
Mengesha Seyoum, Ras, 47-48, 50, 55, 58, 103,
    205
Mengesha, Ras, 50, 51, 55, 104, 105, 107
Mengestu Haile Mariam, 5, 10, 39, 45-47, 126, 178,
    203, 244, 257, 261-262, 266, 268
Mengistu Gemechu, Captain, 262
Mengistu Haile Mariam, Colonel, 5, 10, 39, 47, 126,
    178, 257, 261, 268
Menkae, 61, 292
Mentebteb, 107
Meqele, 41, 45, 47, 53, 69, 76, 83, 139, 147, 149,
    190, 246, 258, 260, 339-341
Meragna, 265
Merara, 288
Merchants, 96, 234
Mereb Melash, 199
Mereb River, 77, 123, 194, 210
Merid Negussie, M/G, 262
Merid Niguse, General, 186
Merieto, 122
Merih Baeta (leading elements), 169-174
Mesfin, Mekonnen Merid, 200
Meskel (the 'Finding of the True Cross'), 107
Metema (Metemma), 104, 109, 1355
Michael, 39, 62, 129, 199, 262, 318
MiGs and MI-24 helicopter gunships, 148

Mikael Sihul, Ras, 56, 199, 317
military committee, 38, 88, 98-99, 152, 341
militia (Woyenti), 99, 112
Ministry of Defence, 262
Misiwwa, 199
Mitiku Asheber, 48-49
Mitnekar, Refresher courses, 140
MLLT congress, Conference, CC, Constitution,
    153, 161, 176-177, 183-185
Moges Wolde-Michael, Captain, 129
Moguee, 208
Mohamed Kiduwi, 205
Mount Alajie, 89
Movement hegemony, 226, 283
Mozambique, 30-31, 284-285, 322, 324-325, 327
Mr. Kafka, 178
Mt Atarit, 259
Mt Dembelailay, 259
Mt Qoyetsa, 259
Mulu Tesfay, 46
Mulugeta Hagos (Asfaha), 40, 339
Museveni, 285, 287-288, 293-296, 299, 301
Mussie, 46, 61-62, 71-73, 75-83, 87-88, 106-107,
    117, 133, 137-138, 160, 204, 206, 258, 341
Mussie Kidane, 46, 81-83

Na'ib, 199
Nadew (Demolish) Ezze, 256-257
Nairobi, 267
Nakfa, 145-146, 215, 256
National Democratic Revolution (NDR), 128-129,
    170
National Democratic Revolution Program (NDR),
    128-129, 170
National Election Commission (NEC), 276
National Resistance Army (NRA) of Uganda, 284-
    285
Nebelbal, counter-guerrilla forces, 106, 144
Nefas-Mewcha, 265
neftegna (warrior, gun bearer), 231
Nega Tegegn, General, 103
New Democracy, 173-174
NGOs, 267, 277, 308-309
Nharnet Team, 209
Niguse Taye (Kelebet), 62
Nikah (Be Conscious), 100
Nimeiri government, 111
Norwegian Observer Group, 276

OAU, 274
Obelisks, 42, 196, 197
Ogaden National Liberation Front (ONLF), 23, 213
OLF, 23, 132, 213, 221, 255, 267, 269, 270, 273,
    276
Organizational Congress, 98, 116, 140, 165-166
organizing commission, 178-179, 278
Oromia, xi, 327, 331
Oromo, 5-6,15, 39, 43, 128, 131-132, 221, 270, 313
Oromo Liberation Front (OLF), 23
Oromo People's Democratic Organization (OPDO),
    5, 187, 221, 263, 268, 310

Tigrigna, MAGEBT in 51, 157
Tigraian University Students Association (TUSA), 40, 49
Tigrai-Tigrigni (Pan-Tigrinya), 198
Tigray Liberation Front (TLF), 11, 49, 51, 60, 63, 70, 74, 79-85, 88, 94, 114, 158, 161-162, 203-206, 209, 211-214, 225, 227
Tigrigna, 41, 57, 81, 103, 113, 157, 201
Tikue Woldu (Awealom), 62
Tokonda, 196
TPLF, CC, Congresses, communist force, communist Core, politburo, 98, 99
Training department, 02, 98-99
Transitional Charter, 191, 270, 280-281, 328
Transitional Government of Ethiopia (TGE), 270, 276, 278
Transitional Period Charter of Ethiopia, 275, 329, 333
Tsadkan Gebretensai, 183
Tsegay Gebremedhin (Debteraw), 118
Tsegay Tesfay (Kokab), 75, 88
Tsegaye Hailu, Ato, 50
Tsehaitu Gebreselasie / Wz, 50, 69
Tsehaytu Fekadu, known as 'Mother', 69
Tselemti, 177
Tselimoye, 56, 67
TUSA, 40, 49-51
Tutsi, 14-15

Uganda Freedom Movement (UFM), 301
UN, 19, 274, 322, 328
Union of Tigraians in North America (UTNA), 176
united front, 121, 152, 157-160, 165-167, 180, 215, 305, 330
United Kingdom, 200
University of Dar-es-Salaam, 284
USA, 48, 50, 274, 330
USAID, 277
USSR, 144, 274

vanguard party, 10, 98, 157, 185, 190, 285, 289-290
vanguard party hegemony, 185
vanguardism, 299
Vietnam, Vietnamese revolutions, 30, 60, 65, 68, 136, 171

Waku Guto, 131
Wallelign Mekonnen, 49, 52
Walloon, 15
Weri-Elu, 265
Western Somalia Liberation Front (WSLF), 130, 331
Wetaderawi Baito (Military Council), 116
Widak, 77
Widebna (our own organization), 253, 300
Wodi Ala, 72
Wolde Michael, Ras, 129, 199
Wolde Selassie, Ras, 199
Woldeab Woldemariam, 201
Wolde-Emmanuel Dubale, 132

Wolde-Selassie Girmay, 121
Wolde-Selassie Nega, Sibhat, 69
Wolkait, 69, 106-107, 123-124, 208, 219, 258
Wollega, 266
Wollo, 43, 49, 56, 108, 124, 134, 142, 148, 164, 188, 200, 258, 260-261, 264-265
Wombedé, wonbedé, bandits, 142
Women Fighters Association (WFA), 239
woreda (district), 102, 229, 251
woreda assembly, 250
woreda baito, 234, 250-251
woreda court, 251
woreda mass associations, 250
woreda people's assemblies, baitos, 237, 245, 252
Worie River, 148
Worku Zewdie, M/G, 262
Woyeen, TPLF party magazine, 57, 100, 151, 157, 159, 265, 329
Woyenti (militia), 99, 112, 137, 251
Woyyane rebellion, 304

Yared Tibebu (Jebesa), 5, 167, 330
Ye Sefiw-Hizb Deemts (Voice of the Masses), 171
Yechla, 134
Yeha, 42, 196
Yekuno Amlak, Emperor, 43, 197
Yem, 273, 332, 345
Yemane Gebre-Meskel, 83
Yemane Kidane (Jamaica), 72, 82, 206
Yifat, 195
Yikuno Amlak, Emperor, 198
Yishaq, Emperor, 198
Yodit, queen, 42, 197
Yohannes, 43-44, 51, 60, 62, 79-83, 114, 131, 136, 200, 203, 205, 267, 321, 327
Yohannes Andebirhan, 205
Yohannes Gebre-Medhin (Walta), 62, 136
Yohannes IV, Emperor, 43-44, 82, 200, 321, 327
Yohannes Teklehaimanot, 51, 79-83, 114, 203
youth associations, 242
Yoweri Museveni, 293-295

Zagir, 145
Zagwe dynasty, 43, 197
Zegebla, 81-82
Zeila, 42
zemecha (campaigns), 258
Zemene Mesafint (Era of Princes), 4, 43, 199
Zenawi Tekola, Ato, 50
Zendo (python), contingent, 147
Zer'a Ya'eqob, Emperor, 198
Zerona (Tsorona), 134
Zeru Gessese (Agazi), 40
Zetenawihe Hizbawi Kuinat, 152, 327
Zimam Gebre-Hiwet, Woizero, 56
Zimam Gebre-hiwet, Woizero, 56
Zimbabwe, 268-269, 298, 325
Zoba (zonal) Baito, 114, 250-251, 329
Zula (Eritrea), 196

CPSIA information can be obtained
at www.ICGtesting.com
Printed in the USA
BVHW081958220121
598424BV00009B/917